D0214922

Music and Religious Identity in
Counter-Reformation Augsburg, 1580–1630

To Lisa

Music and Religious Identity in Counter-Reformation Augsburg, 1580–1630

ALEXANDER J. FISHER

ASHGATE

Published by
Ashgate Publishing Limited
Gower House, Croft Road
Aldershot, Hants
GU11 3HR
England

Ashgate Publishing Company
Suite 420
101 Cherry Street
Burlington, VT 05401–4405
USA

Ashgate website: http://www.ashgate.com

British Library Cataloguing in Publication Data
Fisher, Alexander J.
  Music and religious identity in Counter-Reformation
  Augsburg, 1580–1630. – (St Andrews studies in Reformation history)
  1. Music – Germany – Augsburg – Religious aspects – Christianity 2. Music –
  Germany – Augsburg – History – 16th century 3. Music – Germany – Augsburg –
  History – 17th century. 4. Counter-Reformation – Germany – Augsburg
  5. Identity (Psychology) – Germany – Augsburg – Religious aspects –
  Christianity 6. Augsburg (Germany) – Church history – 16th century
  7. Augsburg (Germany) – Church history – 17th century 8. Augsburg (Germany) –
  History – 16th century 9. Augsburg (Germany) – History – 17th century
  10. Augsburg (Germany) – Religious life and customs
  I. Title
  781.7'1'00943375'09032

Library of Congress Cataloging-in-Publication Data
Fisher, Alexander J.
  Music and religious identity in counter-reformation Augsburg, 1580–1630/Alexander J. Fisher.
    p. cm. – (St Andrews studies in Reformation history)
  Includes bibliographical references and indexes (alk. paper).
  1. Church music – Germany – Augsburg – 16th century 2. Church music – Germany –
  Augsburg – 17th century. 3. Counter-Reformation – Germany – Augsburg.
  4. Music – Religious aspects – Christianity. I. Title. II. Series.
  ML3129.F57 2003
  781.71'00943'37509031–dc22   2003057864

ISBN 0 7546 3875 8

Contents

St Andrews Studies in Reformation History

The Bible in the Renaissance
Essays on Biblical Commentary and Translation
in the Fifteenth and Sixteenth Centuries
edited by Richard Griffiths

The Sixteenth-Century French Religious Book
edited by Andrew Pettegree, Paul Nelles and Philip Conner

Music as Propaganda in the German Reformation
Rebecca Wagner Oettinger

Christianity and Community in the West
Essays for John Bossy
edited by Simon Ditchfield

John Foxe and his World
edited by Christopher Highley and John N. King

Obedient Heretics
Mennonite Identities in Lutheran Hamburg
and Altona During the Confessional Age
Michael D. Driedger

Reformation, Politics and Polemics
The Growth of Protestantism in East Anglian Market Towns, 1500–1610
John Craig

Usury, Interest and the Reformation
Eric Kerridge

Confessional Identity in East-Central Europe
edited by Maria Crăciun, Ovidiu Ghitta and Graeme Murdock

Hatred in Print
Catholic Propaganda and Protestant Identity
During the French Wars of Religion
Luc Racaut

The Correspondence of Reginald Pole:
Volume 1. A Calendar, 1518–1546: Beginnings to Legate of Viterbo
Thomas F. Mayer

Self-Defence and Religious Strife in Early Modern Europe
England and Germany, 1530–1680
Robert von Friedeburg

William Cecil and Episcopacy, 1559–1577
Brett Usher

William of Orange and the Revolt of the Netherlands, 1572–84
K.W. Swart, edited by R.P. Fagle, M.E.H.N. Mout and H.F.K. van Nierop,
translated by J.C. Grayson

A Dialogue on the Law of Kingship among the Scots
A Critical Edition and Translation of George Buchanan's De Iure Regni
apud Scotos Dialogus
Roger A. Mason and Martin S. Smith

Women, Sex and Marriage in Early Modern Venice
Daniela Hacke

Figures

Tables

Music Examples

Acknowledgements

Much of the material in the present study originated as a doctoral dissertation for the Department of Music at Harvard University, and could not have been written without the support and encouragement of colleagues, friends and family. Financial support from the German Academic Exchange Service and the Graduate School of Arts and Sciences at Harvard University enabled an extended trip to Germany in 1998–99, during which I completed much of the relevant research. A Packard Fellowship in the Humanities from Harvard University in 1999–2000 allowed me to complete the major part of the writing in a timely fashion. I am indebted to Christoph Wolff, Lewis Lockwood and Thomas Kelly for their detailed and cogent comments on the dissertation, and I am also grateful for the advice and support of others among the current and former Harvard faculty, including Robert Kendrick, Kay Kaufman Shelemay, Reinhold Brinkmann, Carol Babiracki and Richard Wolf.

The diverse nature of the sources used in this research required the kind assistance of various libraries and their staffs, for which I am most grateful. I would especially like to thank the staff of the Eda Kuhn Loeb Music Library at Harvard University, including Virginia Danielson, Sarah Adams and Douglas Freundlich, for their assistance in obtaining microfilms and for tolerating my ubiquitous presence in the Isham Memorial Library. I would also like to thank the staffs of several European libraries whose resources were vital for my research, including the State and City Library of Augsburg, the Augsburg City Archives, the Episcopal Archives of the Diocese of Augsburg, the Bavarian State Archives in Augsburg and Munich, the Bavarian State Library in Munich, the Episcopal Central Archive in Regensburg, the Berlin State Library and the British Library. Among the library staff and archivists who made my research possible I would like especially to thank Wolfgang Mayer, Georg Feuerer, Raymund Dittrich and Alois Senser.

When I arrived in Augsburg to begin my research on this project I was gratified to find an international network of fellow scholars who helped me to unravel the mysteries of these archives and provided me with many fruitful ideas that continue to animate my work. Mitchell Hammond, Duane Corpis, Allyson Creasman, Hans-Jörg Künast, Helmut Zäh, Beth Plummer, Benedikt Mauer and B. Ann Tlusty were among those whose friendship and support ensured a happy as well as a productive time in Augsburg. During my stay I benefited greatly from the scholarly advice of Professors Franz Krautwurst, Marianne Danckwardt and Theodor Wohnhaas, without which this work would be much poorer.

Having compiled literally hundreds of pages of research during my time abroad, I was greatly appreciative of the advice of numerous scholars who helped me to refine my material and develop a coherent narrative. Robert Kendrick, in particular, lent his expertise and sympathetic ear at every stage of the project. Many others read and commented upon drafts and abstracts of this material, including David Crook, Rebecca Wagner Oettinger, Susan Lewis, Craig Monson, John O'Malley, Jane Bernstein and Susan Jackson. More recently I have benefited greatly from the comments of Andrew Pettegree, editor of the series in which this book appears; I am also thankful for the careful copy-editing of Bonnie Blackburn and for Leofranc Holford-Strevens's assistance with the Latin translations. The writing process itself can often be an isolating one, but friends and colleagues were supportive at every stage. In particular I would like to thank Charles McGuire, Jen-yen Chen, Edward Gollin, Andrew Talle, Brian Hart, Jennifer Baker-Kotiliane, Jessica Sternfeld and David Lieberman for their friendship and advice during the whirlwind of graduate school and beyond.

Finally, I owe a great debt to my wife, Lisa Slouffman, who turned my attention to Augsburg in the first place and proved to be the most thorough and perceptive of my readers. Our discussions of earlier drafts of this material led to welcome changes in the overall shape of the study, and it has also benefited from her judicious editing skills. I feel very fortunate to have enjoyed both her intellectual expertise and loving support throughout the duration of this project.

Abbreviations

ABA	Archiv des Bistums Augsburg
BHSM	Bayerisches Hauptstaatsarchiv München
BSA	Bayerisches Staatsarchiv Augsburg
D-As	Staats- und Stadtbibliothek Augsburg
D-Mbs	Bayerische Staatsbibliothek München
DR	Domrezessionalien, 1555–1640 (BSA: Hochstift Augsburg/Neuburger Abgabe, Akten 5501–5556)
D-Rp	Bischöfliche Zentralbibliothek Regensburg, Proske'sche Musiksammlung
HCA	'Historia collegii Augustani', Bibliothèque cantonale, Fribourg, L95
JVAB	*Jahrbuch des Vereins für Augsburger Bistumsgeschichte*
MGG	*Die Musik in Geschichte und Gegenwart*, ed. Friedrich Blume, 17 vols (Kassel: Bärenreiter, 1949–86)
MGG²	*Die Musik in Geschichte und Gegenwart*, 2nd edn, ed. Ludwig Finscher (Kassel: Bärenreiter, 1994–)
New Grove II	*The New Grove Dictionary of Music and Musicians*, 2nd edn, ed. Stanley Sadie and John Tyrrell (London: Macmillan, 2001)
RISM	Répertoire international des sources musicales
StAA	Stadtarchiv Augsburg
EWA	Evangelisches Wesensarchiv
KWA	Katholisches Wesensarchiv

CHAPTER ONE

Music and Religious Identity in a Divided City

At the end of August 1584, when the city council of Augsburg received two written denunciations of a weaver who had been singing anti-Catholic songs in the streets, the memory of religious strife was still fresh. Tensions between the city's Protestant majority and the confessionally divided council had nearly boiled over the previous June, when the city exiled the popular preacher Georg Müller for inciting popular resistance to Pope Gregory XIII's introduction of the new Gregorian calendar. Gregory's motives were probably pragmatic, but the move angered German Protestants who saw in the new calendar a unilateral expression of Catholic hegemony. Responding to the news that Müller was to be expelled, crowds of Protestants had flooded Augsburg's streets on the fourth of June and confronted city soldiers in front of the Rathaus. A city bailiff was wounded by musket fire from the crowd, although cooler heads among the city's secular and religious leadership prevailed at the last minute and avoided a larger conflagration. Meanwhile, Müller was safely spirited out of Augsburg by sympathizers.

Jonas Losch, a weaver who supplemented his income by writing songs and performing them at local weddings, had been among the armed Protestant crowd that day. About two weeks before the uprising one of the city *Bürgermeister* had confiscated from him a handful of songs that may have had inflammatory content, including one about the Pope; fearing his arrest, Losch fled Augsburg once the unrest had subsided. He spent time in the Protestant towns of Stuttgart and Ulm before returning to Augsburg some time before the end of August, when the authorities received the two aforementioned denunciations. On the night of Sunday the 26th of August, Losch allegedly created a scene in the streets, loudly cursing and shouting epithets against the Jesuits and the Pope; one of the denunciations further stated that he had been singing anti-Catholic songs in front of the Jesuit college and had broken several windows there. Promptly arrested by the authorities, Losch was imprisoned and interrogated three times in the next two weeks. Although he stood accused of several types of subversive behaviour (including singing, writing inflammatory songs, breaking windows and posting anti-Catholic placards), the interrogators expressed especial interest in his songwriting activity. The transcripts of these interrogations suggest that a visiting apprentice from Ulm had given Losch a forbidden song about the recent uprising. He brought the apprentice into his house and copied the song, changing some of the words in the process. Furthermore, he copied the song in such a way that it could be sung to both a benign secular tune and a Protestant chorale, *Lobt Gott, ihr frommen Christen*, a militant song decrying Catholic opposition to Luther's teachings. Before his arrest Losch showed his creation to at least two other individuals, but no copy of the actual song survived, since he claimed to have ripped up the only extant copy in his prison cell.[1] Nevertheless, his contrafactum was only one of a number of songs criticizing the city council and Catholic authorities in the wake of the so-called *Kalenderstreit*.

Far from being an isolated incident, the Losch case symbolizes a much broader development that would have crucial consequences for both music and religion in this biconfessional city. The *Kalenderstreit* was the first watershed event in the rise of a 'confessional' consciousness among the city's residents, a gradual and uneven process by which distinctly Catholic and Protestant cultures and mentalities began to emerge in the broader populace. The unrest could not have taken place without the growing presence of a militant Catholicism on the part of prominent secular officials and churchmen, a phenomenon encouraged by the religious propaganda of the Jesuits, who had been granted a permanent residence in the city four years previously. The period between the Jesuits' arrival and the Imperial promulgation in 1629 of the Edict of Restitution – a wartime decree that officially marginalized Protestantism in the city – was outwardly peaceful, but there is much evidence to suggest that the cultural boundaries between Augsburg's religious communities were hardening. Augsburg, the largest of the 'free' Imperial cities to house substantial Catholic and Protestant populations within its walls, was gradually becoming a microcosm of the religious struggles that would threaten to tear the Empire apart.

The growing divide between Catholicism and Protestantism deeply implicated Augsburg's musical culture, which was reaching its apex in the decades leading up to the devastation of the Thirty Years War (1580–1630). Although the musical repertory of the Lutheran church and school of St Anna, under the direction of Adam Gumpelzhaimer (1559–1625), betrayed little in the way of confessional politics, common Protestants like Jonas Losch continued to cultivate and disseminate a propagandistic song repertory that expressed resistance against a perceived Catholic hegemony. One target of their ire was the Jesuits,

---

[1] This case will be discussed in detail below in Ch. 2.

who had settled in the city in 1580 and embarked on a campaign of education and conversion. They and the confraternities that with their encouragement blossomed by the turn of the seventeenth century created new opportunities for Catholic sacred music, heard in devotional services, pilgrimages to local shrines, and processions that wound their way through Protestant neighbourhoods. The Jesuits' main sponsors were members of the Fugger banking dynasty. That family was nearly without rival in late sixteenth-century Europe with respect to music patronage; apart from their massive collections of music and instruments they received numerous dedications from the most famous composers of the day, and directly patronized local musicians like Hans Leo Hassler (1564–1612), Gregor Aichinger (1564–1628) and Christian Erbach (c.1570–1635).[2] More important from a religious standpoint, however, was their fervent embrace of Counter-Reformation Catholicism. Catholic composers like Aichinger and Erbach, encouraged by their Fugger patrons as well as the availability of new contexts for Catholic devotional music, responded with numerous settings of texts emphasizing devotional symbols like the Virgin Mary and the Eucharist, music that would typify the subjective intensity of Counter-Reformation spirituality and draw stylistically on the Italian models that would transform German Baroque music in subsequent decades. At the same time, liturgical music within church walls was reshaped by the bishops' embrace of the Roman Rite, the adoption of elaborate polychoral repertories, and the expansion of paraliturgical services like the Forty Hour Prayer. The *Kalenderstreit* and the ruin of the Thirty Years War marked the respective beginning and end of a period during which sacred music in Augsburg flourished, yet reflected the gradually increasing cultural divide between Protestantism and Catholicism. To understand this process, however, it is necessary to recall the political, religious and musical contexts that made it possible.

Augsburg in the Reformation and Counter-Reformation

From the early 1520s, the Lutheran Reformation found enthusiastic support in the free Imperial city of Augsburg, one of the largest cities of

---

[2] Among the composers who dedicated music to the Fugger family were Andrea and Giovanni Gabrieli, Orlando di Lasso, Orazio Vecchi, Philippe de Monte and Jacob Regnart; for a list of music dedicated to the Fugger, see Franz Krautwurst, 'Die Fugger und die Musik', in Eikelmann, ed., *Die Fugger und die Musik*, pp. 47–48. An overview of the family's musical interests and activities may be found in Alexander J. Fisher, 'Fugger', in *MGG²*, Personenteil, vol. 7, pp. 246–52.

Key:
1. St Georg (Catholic, with adjoining Protestant church)
2. St Stephan (Catholic)
3. Cathedral of Our Lady (Catholic)
4. Jesuit church and school of St Salvator
5. Heilig Kreuz (Catholic, with adjoining Protestant church)
6. Rathaus
7. St Moritz (Catholic)
8. St Anna (Protestant)
9. Barfüßerkirche (Protestant)
10. SS Ulrich and Afra (Benedictine church and cloister, with adjoining Protestant church)

1.1 Map of Augsburg, with major churches, c.1600. Adapted from Matthäus Seutter, 'Neu verfertigt accurater Grund Riß der ... Statt Augspurg', c.1740–60. D-As, Graphiken 31/38

the Empire (see Figure 1.1).[3] Taken as a whole, the diocese of Augsburg, including this city but also a broad swath of land extending to the north, south and south-west, followed a typical pattern in that the more literate and educated urban 'middle' classes embraced the new teachings, while the rural countryside remained relatively untouched.[4] Inside city walls, the Carmelite cloister of St Anna became a bastion of Lutheranism after the prior, Johannes Frosch, befriended Luther and began to preach the Reformation there from 1525. Protestant sentiment spread quickly among the city's large middle classes, although fragmentation among followers of Luther, Zwingli and Caspar Schwenkfeld would prevent a complete consolidation of power and allow a small Catholic minority to survive.[5] The disruptions of the Reformation not only obscured Catholic cultural footprints, but also brought a temporary end to the flowering of art and music during the reign of Emperor Maximilian I (r. 1493–1519), who had often visited the city with his court chapel; in the first two decades of the sixteenth century the talents of Heinrich Isaac, Ludwig

---

[3] 'Imperial' cities such as Augsburg, Nuremberg and Strasbourg were directly subject to the Empire and not to the territorial states that surrounded them (nearby Munich, by contrast, was the seat of the Bavarian state). Populated by relatively large proportions of literate and semi-literate tradesmen, most Imperial cities embraced the Reformation quickly in the 1520s and 1530s. This was true of Augsburg, but political and religious circumstances allowed a substantial Catholic minority to survive. The total population of the city around 1600 was around 40 000–50 000; for slightly contrasting estimates see Paul Warmbrunn, in *Zwei Konfessionen in einer Stadt: Das Zusammenleben von Katholiken und Protestanten in den paritätischen Reichsstädten Augsburg, Biberach, Ravensburg und Dinkelsbühl von 1548 bis 1648* (Wiesbaden: Franz Steiner, 1983), p. 135, and Claus-Peter Clasen, 'Arm und Reich in Augsburg vor dem Dreißigjährigen Krieg', in Günther Gottlieb et al., eds, *Geschichte der Stadt Augsburg: 2000 Jahre von der Römerzeit bis zur Gegenwart* (Stuttgart: Konrad Theiss Verlag, 1985), pp. 312–13.

[4] In Augsburg, patrician families like the Fuggers remained largely Catholic, setting the stage for their support of the Counter-Reformation later in the century. As for the rural territory of the diocese, much of it was administered by the Hochstift, the secular arm of the bishop headed by the Augsburg Cathedral chapter. This direct episcopal oversight helped to ensure that Protestantism did not spread beyond city walls, especially in the era of Bishop Otto Truchseß von Waldburg (r. 1543–73), who vigorously enforced confessional conformity in border areas of the diocese. See Wolfgang Wüst, *Das Fürstbistum Augsburg: Ein geistlicher Staat im Heiligen Römischen Reich Deutscher Nation* (Augsburg: Sankt Ulrich Verlag, 1997), pp. 114–16. A similar pattern prevailed in Bavaria, where rural areas remained religiously conservative; see Philip M. Soergel, *Wondrous in His Saints: Counter-Reformation Propaganda in Bavaria* (Berkeley: University of California Press, 1993), pp. 19–20. R. Po-Chia Hsia, in *Social Discipline in the Reformation, Central Europe 1550–1750* (London and New York: Routledge, 1989), pp. 114–15, has noted that even in the Catholic revival of the early seventeenth century, Catholic children in Augsburg remained less likely than Protestant children to receive primary education.

[5] Despite this, the Protestant council would force the Catholic clergy into exile between 1537 and 1547, and again for several months in 1552.

Senfl, Paul Hofhaimer and others had helped to enrich Augsburg's musical life.[6]

Maximilian's successor Charles V (r. 1519–1556) did not often come to the city despite his continued dependence on financial credits from the Fugger house, and the religious struggles tended to dampen Augsburg's reputation as a cosmopolitan, international cultural centre.[7] In 1531, however, the Protestant *Gymnasium* at St Anna was founded and became a focus for Protestant musical activity. From 1535 singing instruction was offered to students, who subsequently earned money for their upkeep by regular singing of chorales and sacred songs in front of the homes of well-to-do citizens. By 1560 some 80 students, divided into several choirs, were involved in these outdoor performances, which supplemented the regular polyphonic music heard on Sundays and feast days at St Anna.[8] If extant music inventories copied in the early seventeenth century may serve as a guide (see p. 81), the repertory of the St Anna cantorate was highly eclectic, embracing both traditional and modern music from both sides of the confessional divide. The cantor during the institution's greatest flourishing, Adam Gumpelzhaimer (cantor from 1581 to 1625), was a composer with international tastes and seems to have been little interested in confessional politics.

Events in the Empire at mid-century fundamentally altered the course of Augsburg's political history. Charles V's victory over a Protestant army at Mühlberg in 1547 led to the introduction of the Augsburg Interim in 1548 and the curtailing of Protestant rights in Imperial cities like Augsburg. Patricians of mixed confession from leading families – including the Fuggers, Welsers, Rehlingers and Peutingers – supplanted the Protestant guilds in the city council, and began to preside over a

---

[6] See Adolf Layer, ed., *Musik und Musiker der Fuggerzeit* (Augsburg, 1959), pp. 3–4, and Franz Krautwurst, 'Musik der Blütezeit', in Gottlieb et al., eds, *Geschichte der Stadt Augsburg*, pp. 386–87. Maximilian's financial dependence on the Fugger family (and particularly on Jakob 'the Rich' (1459–1525)) helps to explain his frequent presence in Augsburg. On the financial relationship between the Habsburg emperors and the Fugger, see Franz Karg, 'Die Fugger im 16. und 17. Jahrhundert', in Eikelmann, ed., *Die Fugger und die Musik*, pp. 99–101.

[7] On this point see Adolf Layer, 'Augsburger Musikkultur der Renaissance', in Wegele, ed., *Musik in der Reichsstadt Augsburg*, pp. 58–60.

[8] On the street-singing by the St Anna cantorate, see Otto Mayr's introduction to Adam Gumpelzhaimer, *Ausgewählte Werke*, vol. 19, Jahrgang 10/2 of *Denkmäler der Tonkunst in Bayern* (Leipzig: Breitkopf & Härtel, 1909), pp. 10–21, and Louise Cuyler, 'Musical Activity in Augsburg and its Annakirche, ca. 1470–1630', in Johannes Riedel, ed., *Cantors at the Crossroads: Essays on Church Music in Honor of Walter E. Buszin* (St Louis, Mo.: Concordia Publishing House, 1967), p. 42. After the Peace of Augsburg (1555) choirboys from the cathedral also participated in street-singing, but lack of corresponding documentation makes it difficult to generalize about numbers or repertory.

population that was, at best, 20 per cent Catholic.[9] The Peace of
Augsburg in 1555 formalized this 'biconfessional' arrangement, which
persisted until the political upheavals of the Thirty Years War.[10] The
patrician control of the city and its guarantee of religious freedom to the
Catholic minority created the basis for Catholic renewal in the late
sixteenth and early seventeenth centuries. The first musical manifestation
of this renewal came in 1561, when the cathedral chapter established a
permanent cantorate with a *Kapellmeister* charged with the direction
and composition of polyphonic music. Archival documents and
choirbooks from the cathedral and the Benedictine church and cloister of
SS Ulrich and Afra suggest a gradual increase in the scope and quality of
Catholic church music in Augsburg, culminating in the performance of
Venetian-style polychoral repertories at both institutions by the early
seventeenth century. Musical life in Augsburg's Catholic churches was
further enhanced by the cultivation of paraliturgical devotional services
(such as the Forty Hour Prayer) and by the controlled permission of
congregational singing in the vernacular.

   Catholic music in Augsburg, however, responded more vigorously to
the creation or revival of performance contexts outside of the church
liturgy, such as processions, pilgrimages and the devotions of
confraternities; in other words, public expressions of faith that
characterized the militant spirit of the Counter-Reformation. Much of
the impetus for this can be attributed to the influence of the Jesuits, who
obtained a permanent residence in the city in 1582 with the financial

---

[9] The figure is given by Étienne François in *Die unsichtbare Grenze: Protestanten und
Katholiken in Augsburg 1648–1806* (Sigmaringen: Jan Thorbecke Verlag, 1991), p. 45.
Local and regional political circumstances forced the city oligarchy, which was divided
roughly evenly between Protestant and Catholic councillors, to take a neutral stand in
religious politics. Although Protestants were a majority of the population and other
Protestant strongholds, like Ulm and Nuremberg, were not far removed, the city was
surrounded by Catholic territories, including the Habsburg County of Burgau to the west
and the powerful Duchy of Bavaria to the east, not to mention the more fragmented
territories of the bishop (the *Hochstift*) on all sides. Augsburg's rather precarious position
on the boundaries between German Protestantism and Catholicism contributed to its loss
of political stature in the Empire by the late sixteenth century; as Bernd Roeck argues in
*Eine Stadt im Krieg und Frieden: Studien zur Geschichte der Reichsstadt Augsburg
zwischen Kalenderstreit und Parität* (Göttingen: Vandenhoeck & Ruprecht, 1989), pp.
201–2, the city was forced to take a largely defensive position, favoring the religious *status
quo*.

[10] After the war the Peace of Westphalia led to the offical observance of parity between
the two confessions at all levels of city government. The nature and development of
'biconfessionality' in Augsburg has been explored in depth by Warmbrunn, who identified
Augsburg along with the other Swabian cities of Biberach, Ravensburg and Dinkelsbühl as
the only places where city governments with significant Catholic representation ruled over
Protestant majorities; see Warmbrunn, *Zwei Konfessionen in einer Stadt*, pp. 11–14.

assistance of the Fugger family. The Jesuits had been active in the diocese of Augsburg since the 1550s, when Bishop Otto Truchseß von Waldburg (r. 1543–73) sought the assistance of Petrus Canisius, the so-called 'Second Apostle of Germany', and installed him as cathedral preacher in Augsburg between 1559 and 1566.[11] Despite his short tenure in Augsburg (a consequence of friction with the landed nobility of the cathedral chapter), Canisius encouraged numerous conversions to Catholicism, especially among the patrician class.[12] The Jesuits intensified their missionary work in Augsburg after taking up residence at St Salvator, where they established a church and school offering a free, humanistic education to Catholic and Protestant students alike (the Protestants of St Anna immediately responded by founding a college of their own).[13] In addition to their public sermons and propaganda, the

---

[11] For an account of Petrus Canisius's activities in Augsburg during this period, see Rummel, 'Die Augsburger Diözesansynoden: Historischer Überblick', *JVAB*, 20 (1986), pp. 49–61. The 'First Apostle' of Germany was considered to be the martyr and Archbishop of Mainz St Boniface (*c*.672–754). Otto Truchseß von Waldburg himself was a staunch partisan of the Counter-Reformation, and called two diocesan synods during his reign. The synod of 1548 represented an attempt to consolidate the Catholic position in the diocese in the wake of the Interim; the decrees were also aimed at curbing clerical 'abuses', reasserting older statutes. Otto called a second diocesan synod in 1567, which was the first attempt to promulgate the Tridentine decrees in the German-speaking territories of the Empire. The synod was hampered from the start by the absence of the cathedral chapter, which refused to attend. Although numerous resolutions for reform were passed, later implementation was effectively prevented by resistance from the entrenched, corporate interests of collegiate chapters and older cloisters. On both synods, see Rummel, 'Die Augsburger Diözesansynoden', pp. 29–36. The synodal decrees of 1567 included directives for church music; see below, Ch. 4.

[12] Around 1561, for example, Canisius influenced Sibylla von Eberstein and Ursula von Lichtenstein, the wives of Marcus and Georg Fugger respectively, to convert to Catholicism. Both women became active supporters of Canisius and of the Jesuit presence in Augsburg. See Peter Rummel, 'Petrus Canisius und Otto Kardinal Truchseß von Waldburg', in Oswald and Rummel, eds, *Petrus Canisius – Reformer der Kirche*, pp. 54–55. The links between Canisius and the Fugger family may also be seen in a well-publicized exorcism that Canisius performed on a Fugger maidservant at the Marian shrine of Altötting in 1570; see Soergel, *Wondrous in His Saints*, pp. 119–26. Unlike the Capuchins (who arrived in Augsburg with support from Bishop Heinrich V in 1600), the Jesuits placed great emphasis on the conversion of highly placed figures; Hsia provides a partial list of these in *Social Discipline in the Reformation*, pp. 44–45.

[13] A part of the Jesuits' success rested on the fact that they did not make the *Gymnasium* a centre for Catholic propaganda, and thus were able to attract a wider variety of students; see Josef Bellot, 'Humanismus – Bildungswesen – Buchdruck und Verlagsgeschichte', in Gottlieb et al., eds, *Geschichte der Stadt Augsburg*, pp. 351–52. This should not take away from their broader mission in the city, however; Otto Krammer has described the relationship between Jesuit education and the Counter-Reformation in *Bildungswesen und Gegenreformation: Die Hohen Schulen der Jesuiten im katholischen Teil Deutschlands vom 16. bis zum 18. Jahrhundert* (Würzburg: Gesellschaft für deutsche

Jesuits agitated for the prohibition of confessionally mixed marriages, demanded that Catholic patricians release their Protestant servants and carried out spectacular exorcisms.[14] Their activities were buttressed by a rising tide of propagandistic literature, including simple vernacular songs, produced at the nearby Jesuit universities of Dillingen and Ingolstadt.[15]

By the end of the century the militant Catholic ideology espoused by the Jesuits, certain patrician families – especially the wealthy Fugger clan – and the diocesan bishops (especially the zealous Heinrich V von Knöringen (r. 1598–1646), one of the strongest partisans of the Counter-Reformation in the empire and a former student at the Jesuit university in Dillingen) had attracted a wider swath of Augsburg's Catholic populace. A consequence of this was an explosion in the number of Catholic confraternities for lay men and women, groups that often adopted a militant stance against Protestantism and demanded of their members regular participation in devotional services, processions and pilgrimages.[16] An example of this antagonistic attitude may be seen in a

Studentengeschichte; Archivverein der Markomannia, 1988); on the founding of the Jesuit college in Augsburg, see pp. 121–22. The nineteenth-century Jesuit Placidus Braun chronicled the arrival and activities of the Augsburg Jesuits in his *Geschichte des Kollegiums der Jesuiten in Augsburg* (Munich: Jakob Giel, 1822). He described in great detail the contributions of the Fugger family and other patricians to the building and decoration of St Salvator; see esp. pp. 35–38. In sum the Fugger contributed some 96 000 florins to the Jesuits in the sixteenth century.

[14] Warmbrunn (*Zwei Konfessionen in einer Stadt*, p. 136) has argued that the Jesuits and the founding of new religious orders in Augsburg contributed to a gradual increase of the Catholic proportion of the population from approximately one-fifth in the 1580s to about 27 per cent in 1618. The extant manuscript chronicle of the college, the 'Historia Collegii Augustani' (hereafter *HCA*; Bibliothèque cantonale, Fribourg, L95; my thanks to Dr Helmut Zäh of the Staats- und Stadtbibliothek Augsburg, who generously provided me with a partial photocopy), attributed largely to Matthäus Rader, is peppered with references to Protestant conversions, although these are difficult to corroborate. Other religious orders, perhaps having less of a missionary emphasis, were introduced into Augsburg during this period, including the Franciscans, who arrived with Fugger family support in 1609, and the discalced Carmelites, who arrived in 1629. See Herbert Immenkötter, 'Kirche zwischen Reformation und Parität', in Gottlieb et al., eds, *Geschichte der Stadt Augsburg*, p. 405.

[15] Hsia notes that the Jesuits sought to take over the theology and philosophy faculties in Catholic universities, leaving the fields of law and medicine to laymen. When they failed to take control of universities, they often established *Gymnasia* to train future generations of Catholic scholars (see *Social Discipline in the Reformation*, pp. 119–20). On the Jesuits and the university in Dillingen in particular, see Herbert Immenkötter and Wolfgang Wüst, 'Augsburg: Freie Reichsstadt und Hochstift', in Anton Schindling and Walter Ziegler, eds, *Die Territorien des Reichs im Zeitalter der Reformation und Konfessionalisierung* (Münster: Aschendorff, 1993), vol. 5, pp. 24–26.

[16] An extant manuscript housed at the Staats- und Stadtbibliothek Augsburg entitled 'De initijs ac progressu omnium Fraternitatum, quæ in alma hac vrbe Augustana fuerunt

letter from one of the co-founders of the Corpus Christi Confraternity, the Capuchin preacher Ludwig Sax, to Bishop Heinrich V von Knöringen in January 1604:

> Since I perceive that these people are moved more by actions than by words, I have thought for a long time how to proceed, so that these poor, deceived persons can be helped; lately I have thought, with the advice of the most prominent men of this worthy Imperial city, to establish a brotherhood of the holy body of Christ, as has been customary in Italy, France, and also in Prague, Munich and Switzerland, so that that holy, most worthy Sacrament, and Christ present in the same, may be carried around with all solemnity in processions and to the sick, [actions] which would be a public protestation of our belief and would confound our adversaries or move them to piety.[17]

By venerating the sacrament as the authentic body of Christ, the confraternity embraced a highly controversial religious symbol, and Sax's comments demonstrate that from the outset the group was engaged not only in devotion, but also in propaganda.[18] With the support of

---

diversis temporibus erectæ à Christi fidelibus, narratio MDCXVII' [On the founding and growth of all brotherhoods that have been established in Augsburg at various times by Christ's faithful; D-As: 2° Aug 346], dated 1617 and once belonging to the library of the church of Heilig Kreuz, records the establishment of no fewer than 14 confraternities between 1574 and 1603, including many specifically for lay tradesmen, such as a weavers' confraternity at the church of St Georg (1596) and a soldiers' confraternity at the church of St Moritz (1603). Some of these confraternities may have been formed in response to Protestant boycotts of Catholic tradesmen. For example, in 1597 the Jesuits proposed the founding of a Marian congregation for Catholic bakers, since Protestants were refusing to patronize them; see Peter Rummel, 'Zur 400-Jahr-Feier der St. Annabruderschaft in Augsburg', *JVAB*, **32** (1998), p. 61. In other cases, the manuscript 'De initijs' notes that these brotherhoods were re-establishing themselves after decades of Protestant opposition; the weavers' confraternity, for example, 'which had formerly held its divine offices at St Ulrich and St Georg, but was interrupted in the time of the heretics, returned and was revived at St Georg this year and flourishes with great praise' (fol. 36r). One should not, however, take these (overdrawn?) assertions as a sign of widespread confessional conflict in the city. Although certain segments of the Protestant population (tradesmen in particular) may not have patronized Catholic shops, confessional relations for the most part remained peaceful.

[17] Letter of 14 January 1604, in ABA: BO 2480, no. 1.

[18] Although this brotherhood certainly owed its existence partly to the general upswing in sacramental devotion seen throughout late medieval Europe in which older grave cults were partially supplanted by visual and imagistic forms of piety (see Soergel, *Wondrous in His Saints*, p. 23), the Counter-Reformation gave new impetus to the worship of the Host as the 'real presence' of Christ's body, an act that would have openly offended the sensibilities of Protestant communities. The late sixteenth century saw a rising tide of apologetic literature in support of Eucharistic devotion and pilgrimage destinations; key figures were authors like Johann Nass, Johann Rabus and Johann Sartorius, who defended the miraculous properties of the Eucharist, holding it up as a symbol of Catholic triumph over Satanic deception (ibid., pp. 91–95). For the founders of the Corpus Christi

Bishop Heinrich V, Sax, along with Marcus Fugger, founded this group with only ten members, but within a few years the membership had grown to several hundred, including nobility and clergy as well as common laypersons, men as well as women.[19] Among its members was Gregor Aichinger, the most prolific Catholic composer in the city; in 1606 he dedicated to the leadership and members of the brotherhood a collection of liturgical and processional music for the feast of Corpus Christi, the *Solennia augustissimi Corporis Christi*, which may well have been performed in the group's devotional services or processions (see Chapter 4).

In the years around 1600 Catholics from a broad cross-section of society were beginning to assert their own religious identity through public, visually oriented displays of their faith that were intended, in part, to make an impression on Protestant bystanders.[20] In the mid-1590s Catholic processions that originally were restricted to the northern, ecclesiastical quarter of the city began to wind their way

---

brotherhood in Augsburg, the foundation of a sacramental confraternity in this biconfessional city would have simultaneously bolstered a distinctive Catholic identity for its members while widening the cultural divide between Catholics and Protestants.

[19] By 1607 the membership had grown so rapidly that a vote was held to elect eight persons to serve as a governing board. Those elected to these posts on 5 January 1607 received a combined total of 315 votes from the members, which may be taken to represent the minimum number of members in the confraternity at this time; see 'Kurtze beschreibung, wie die andächtige bruederschafft des allerheiligsten Fronleichnambs *Jesu Christi*', ABA: BO 2480, no. 2, fols. 8v–9r. It is unclear whether or not women members would have participated in this vote, but it is clear that they joined the group in significant numbers. The 'Kurtze beschreibung' and other sources often specify that the brotherhood's processions and devotions were attended by men and women [*Manns- vnd Weibspersonen*]; women were forbidden only from participating in the Good Friday procession, which was held at nighttime ('Kurtze beschreibung', fol. 10r). A satellite of the Corpus Christi brotherhood founded in nearby Oberhausen in 1606 counted 28 men and 35 women among its founding members; see 'Kurtze beschreibung', fol. 7r. The confraternity established numerous branches in neighbouring towns in the early seventeenth century, including Utzwingen, Rain, Dillingen, Oberhausen, Haunstetten, Mindelheim, Thierhaupten, Zumarshausen and Lechhausen, and very likely elsewhere: see ABA: BO 2480, no. 2, fols. 6v–7r; no. 3; and no. 7; also, in 'De initijs ac progressu omnium Fraternitatum', D-As, 2° Aug 346, fols. 23r–24r, 27r, 29v and 30r.

[20] Public display of faith, as many historians of the period have noted, was a central feature of Counter-Reformation Catholicism. Robert Scribner saw processions and pilgrimages in honour of the Eucharist, for example, as a 'materialist conception of the workings of the sacred' that had deep roots in the medieval tradition (see *Popular Culture and Popular Movements in Reformation Germany* (London and Ronceverte: Hambledon Press, 1987), pp. 14–15). For Ernst Walter Zeeden, the Catholic ideal of public display was closely linked with a theology of a *lived faith* in which belief embraced works as well as faith; charity, asceticism, processions and pilgrimages all embodied this emphasis on the tangibility of belief, particularly in mixed confessional areas where the stakes were the highest; see Zeeden, 'Aspekte der katholischen Frömmigkeit in Deutschland im 16.

through Protestant neighbourhoods. Processions on Good Friday and Corpus Christi achieved their greatest extent by the middle of the next decade, involving hundreds of participants carrying banners, crucifixes and images, acting out bloody representations of Christ's Passion, and singing litanies and songs of the Virgin, the Eucharist and the saints. Around the same time Catholics began to organize large-scale pilgrimages to the 'Holy Mountain' of Andechs, a popular Eucharistic shrine in Bavaria. Simple litanies and devotional songs helped to pace the pilgrims along their route, while professionally performed polyphonic motets entertained them at the various churches that served as intermediate way stations. Although the precise proportion of Augsburg's Catholics who participated in public devotions, pilgrimages and processions is unclear, these spectacles would have required the voluntary participation of significant numbers.[21]

This expansion of Catholic devotional contexts helped to bring about a dramatic shift in the nature of Catholic polyphonic music after 1600. While composers active in Augsburg earlier in the sixteenth century like Jacobus de Kerle and Johannes de Cleve concentrated on liturgical music or on ceremonial motets to honour particular patrons, Catholic composers after 1600, including Bernhard Klingenstein, Gregor Aichinger, Christian Erbach and Philipp Zindelin, developed a new repertory of mostly Latin devotional polyphony in honour of the Virgin, the Passion

---

Jahrhundert', in *Konfessionsbildung: Studien zur Reformation, Gegenreformation und katholischen Reform* (Stuttgart: Klett-Cotta, 1985), pp. 326–27. Catholicism as spectacle reached its greatest heights, perhaps, in Counter-Reformation Bavaria, where the ducal court directly promoted processions and pilgrimages in honour of the Virgin Mary and the Eucharist. Nowhere else was a concrete and sensual relationship to sacred objects and images cultivated so deliberately; as Philip Soergel has written, the presence of Christ in the Eucharist, for example, 'could only be felt and witnessed by those who watched humbly as God embodied himself in the wafer and guided the course of history by means of his miraculous intervention' (*Wondrous in His Saints*, pp. 97–98).

[21] The extent to which such events were expressions of popular feeling on the one hand, or official propaganda on the other, remains hotly contested, particularly in the literature concerning pilgrimage. Victor and Edith Turner's idea of *communitas* in pilgrimage, developed in *Image and Pilgrimage in Christian Culture: Anthropological Perspectives* (New York: Columbia University Press, 1978) and suggesting a communally felt and cathartic experience, has been challenged by more recent historians, especially in John Eade and Michael J. Sallnow, eds, *Contesting the Sacred: The Anthropology of Christian Pilgrimage* (London and New York: Routledge, 1991), and Ian Reader and Tony Walter, eds, *Pilgrimage in Popular Culture* (London: Macmillan, 1993). Although pilgrimages were indeed organized by Catholic elites, their success did depend on large-scale voluntary cooperation. As Soergel has argued in the case of Bavaria (*Wondrous in His Saints*, p. 102), Catholic propaganda succeeded in no small part because the Catholic emphasis on miracles, quasi-magical rituals and the intercessory power of the Virgin Mary and the saints appealed to the traditional belief systems of many people, especially in rural areas.

of Christ and the Eucharist. Much of this music, drawing upon fashionable and easily performable styles derived from the Italian canzonetta, villanella and vocal concerto, was well suited to musical amateurs in Augsburg and in other Catholic German cities.[22] Though sharing much in common stylistically with contemporary Protestant composers, Catholic composers responded to the new Counter-Reformation spirit with texts and imagery particular to Catholic devotional practices. Composers were further encouraged in this direction by the religious interests of their patrons, notably members of the Fugger family and local and regional clergy who promoted the Counter-Reformation in the city and in the diocese. The production of Catholic devotional polyphony was also facilitated by the rise of regional printing presses (in Augsburg, Dillingen, Ingolstadt, Munich and elsewhere) that devoted themselves partly or wholly to Catholic literature and music. Many of these presses enjoyed the direct patronage of the clergy or the Jesuit order.

The services of confraternities, processions and pilgrimages also provided ample opportunity for monophonic music, ranging from liturgical chant sung by church choirs, to German and Latin litanies performed in a call-and-response manner by the clergy and the people, to simple vernacular songs sung by the populace. Like contemporary polyphony by Aichinger and his colleagues, the topical association of this music with Marian, Eucharistic and saintly devotion ensured its contribution to the formation of a specifically Catholic identity among performers and listeners. Instrumental music, too, participated in this process: the yearly Corpus Christi processions, for example, employed groups of trumpeters and military drummers to accompany the Eucharist around the city, lending the exaltation of the host a distinctly militaristic atmosphere.[23] Given the mixture of professional musicians, patricians,

---

[22] The city of Augsburg, lying on a major trade route leading from Venice over the Brenner Pass, was particularly well positioned for the importation of newer Italian musical styles, especially given the musical interests of the Fugger family. On the economic importance of Augsburg for north–south trade, see Hermann Kellenbenz, 'Wirtschaftsleben der Blütezeit', in Gottlieb et al., eds, *Geschichte der Stadt Augsburg*, pp. 270–73. Apart from the large music libraries of the Fugger, local booksellers also offered large quantities of Italian musical prints. Richard Schaal, in *Die Kataloge des Augsburger Musikalien-Händlers Kaspar Flurschütz, 1613–1628* (Wilhelmshaven: Heinrichshofen, 1974), has described the heavy proportion of Italian music for sale in Kaspar Flurschütz's shop in the early seventeenth century. On Flurschütz and other bookdealers in Augsburg, see also Theodor Wohnhaas, 'Der Augsburger Musikdruck von den Anfängen bis zum Ende des Dreißigjährigen Krieges', in Gier and Janota, eds, *Augsburger Buchdruck und Verlagswesen*, pp. 319–21.

[23] If Marian devotion was at the centre of the Bavarian state cult, the cult of the Eucharist seems to have been of greater significance to Augsburg Catholics, expressed

clerics and laypersons in these contexts, it is only to be expected that they performed music ranging widely from complex polyphony to simple songs. If dissimilar in style, this music would have shared a common emphasis on controversial devotional themes.

As mentioned above, the polyphonic music cultivated by the Protestant cantorate of St Anna was eclectic and ecumenical. The Protestant musical reaction against the increasing Catholic assertiveness took place instead at the level of popular culture, as poorer men and women created, circulated and sang monophonic songs criticizing the Pope, the Jesuits and Catholic elements within the city council. The first main focus for this musical resistance had come with the *Kalenderstreit* in 1584, as commoners like Jonas Losch defied the council through the singing and dissemination of propagandistic songs. In the wake of the conflict printed and manuscript songs about the event – generally contrafacta of traditional tunes – began to filter into the city from the outside, and others were created or copied within city walls despite public ordinances banning the ownership, distribution or performance of religiously inflammatory music. Protestant weavers, a large and semi-literate class of economically disadvantaged tradesmen, often combined well-known tunes from psalms, chorales or secular songs with new texts attacking Catholicism and the city government, and distributed or sold them throughout the city. Although songs were but one form of public discourse regulated by the city authorities, they were an effective vehicle for the transmission of forbidden texts: singing in public places like taverns or street corners attracted attention, and the simple melodies helped illiterate persons to memorize the words. Extant transcripts of criminal interrogations (discussed in Chapter 2) shed light on this aspect of popular culture, and demonstrate that although the city council could not hope to stamp out the singing of illicit music, it did seek to control the circulation of these songs in printed or manuscript copies, using or threatening judicial torture to discover the origins of the music while imposing stiff penalties on transgressors.

Surveillance of Protestant singing was stepped up in the wake of the Edict of Restitution in 1629, an imperial mandate that demanded the

---

through the rise of the Corpus Christi Confraternity, the Andechs pilgrimage, elaborate Corpus Christi processions and the veneration of the so-called *Wunderbares Gut*, an allegedly miraculous host housed at the local church of Heilig Kreuz. The militant character of Corpus Christi processions symbolizes the divisiveness of the Eucharist as a confessional symbol. As Soergel notes (*Wondrous in His Saints*, p. 180) with respect to Eucharistic tracts in Counter-Reformation Bavaria, 'the purpose of pilgrimages to Deggendorf and Passau, among other sites, was ... to memorialize a crucifixional torture and victory and to celebrate Catholicism's prowess in repulsing onslaughts against its truths'.

return of all Catholic properties that had been occupied by Protestants since 1552 (see Chapter 8). The city council refused to implement the Edict, and as a result the emperor and bishop took religious authority into their own hands, dismissing Protestant preachers and city councillors, taking over Protestant churches, and banning all Protestant religious observances.[24] Naturally, the rich polyphonic repertory previously cultivated at St Anna ceased to be heard, but the city council also banned the singing of all Protestant music, whether in public or private. If city councillors had always striven to prevent the singing and dissemination of inflammatory religious songs (such as those concerning the 'injustices' of the new calendar and Georg Müller's exile in 1584), they moved decisively during the period of the Edict to stamp out German psalms and chorales, which local Protestants continued to sing in defiance of the new Catholic regime. All music that did not fall under the category of 'Latin songs with Catholic texts' was proscribed, and the city hired informers to report any private gatherings for German songs and prayers. If song had helped to shape Protestant identity in the previous period of mixed confessional government, it also became an open act of disobedience in the era of the Edict.

The next decade was a demographic and cultural disaster for the city. In April 1632 Swedish armies under Gustavus Adolphus took control of Augsburg without a fight; the Catholic clergy, excepting only the Benedictines of SS Ulrich and Afra, fled to the south and east.[25] The Catholic city council was deposed and replaced with a Lutheran one, and local Catholics found themselves in the same position as the city's Protestants previously. The Protestant defeat at the Battle of Nördlingen in September 1634 led to the arrival of a Habsburg/Bavarian army, which surrounded Augsburg and demanded the surrender of the Swedish garrison. The latter refused, and the winter of 1634–35 saw a terrible siege accompanied by severe famine and plague. The Catholic army proved victorious in March, reinstating the terms of the Edict of Restitution; however, the earlier persecutions of the Protestants largely ended as the mostly Bavarian city administrators allowed them limited freedom of worship.[26] Peace prevailed until another siege by French and Swedish forces in 1646, followed by three years of plague. The Peace of

---

[24] For an overview of Augsburg's turbulent political history in this period, see Immenkötter, 'Kirche zwischen Reformation und Parität', pp. 408–11.

[25] All Catholics who refused to swear an oath of fealty to the Swedish crown were expelled in May 1633; only the Benedictines of SS Ulrich and Afra professed their loyalty. See ibid., pp. 409–10.

[26] The Protestant community was allowed to form a committee, under the former *Stadtpfleger* Johann David Herwart, which represented Protestant interests and served as a counterweight to the Catholic city council. See ibid., pp. 410–11.

Westphalia in 1648 provided the basis for a gradual recovery – now with official parity between the confessions at all levels of city government – but the demographic damage had been done. By the mid-1630s the population of the city had been reduced by two-thirds, and organized cultural life was largely decimated. Arguably, Augsburg never again reached the level of musical sophistication it had before the war.[27]

Music and Confession: Notes on Methodology and Historiography

The flourishing of sacred music in Augsburg and the city's position as a proving ground for confessional relations raises the question of how music reflected and contributed to the growing cultural divide between Catholicism and Protestantism. Broadly speaking, the term 'confessionalization' (*Konfessionalisierung*) describes the rise and consolidation of the main confessional churches (Lutheran, Calvinist and Catholic) and asserts the importance of religion in early modern statecraft; but it also refers to the formation of confessional identity among the common people.[28] Ernst Walter Zeeden, one of the first to study the relationship of confession and identity, wrote that the rise of these distinct churches 'took place as a process that involved not only the church, but also sympathetically the areas of the political and the cultural, and above all the public and the private'.[29] At issue is how, and when, the people of early modern Europe began to see themselves not

---

[27] The percentage of Catholics among the city's population continued to increase during the war, as well; Warmbrunn estimated that by the war's end Catholics accounted for fully one-third of the population. See *Zwei Konfessionen in einer Stadt*, pp. 136–37.

[28] Some of the foundational literature on European confessionalization includes Wolfgang Reinhard's 'Gegenreformation als Modernisierung?', *Archiv für Reformationsgeschichte*, 68 (1977), pp. 284–301; 'Konfession und Konfessionalisierung in Europa', in *idem*, ed., *Bekenntnis und Geschichte: Die Confessio Augustana im historischen Zusammenhang* (Munich: Verlag Ernst Vögel, 1981), pp. 165–89, and 'Zwang zur Konfessionalisierung? Prolegomena zu einer Theorie des konfessionellen Zeitalters', *Zeitschrift für historische Forschung*, 10 (1983), pp. 257–77. Some more recent discussions of the thesis may be found in Reinhard, 'Was ist katholische Konfessionalisierung?' and Heinz Schilling, 'Die Konfessionalisierung von Kirche, Staat und Gesellschaft – Profil, Leistung, Defizite und Perspektiven eines geschichtswissenschaftlichen Paradigmas', both in Reinhard and Schilling, eds, *Die katholische Konfessionalisierung*, pp. 1–49 and 419–52 respectively; see also Schilling's 'Die Konfessionalisierung im Reich: Religiöser und gesellschaftlicher Wandel in Deutschland zwischen 1555 und 1620', *Historische Zeitschrift*, 246 (1988), pp. 1–45.

[29] Ernst Walter Zeeden, 'Grundlagen und Wege der Konfessionsbildung in Deutschland im Zeitalter der Glaubenskämpfe', *Historische Zeitschrift*, 185 (1958), p. 17. This article served as the foundation for his later studies, including *Die Entstehung der Konfessionen: Grundlagen und Formen der Konfessionsbildung im Zeitalter der Glaubenskämpfe*

simply as Christians, but rather as Catholics, Lutherans or Calvinists.[30] Music's dual role as a vehicle both for religious expression and for propaganda (a function seen clearly, for example, in the history of the Lutheran chorale) ensured that it would play a significant role in this process of identity formation.

Music's contribution to confessionalization, however, was hardly straightforward or unambiguous. To what extent was 'confessional' music, in Augsburg as elsewhere, a spontaneous, collective expression of religious values, or a form of indoctrination imposed from above? Confessionalization was closely linked with the evolution of social discipline: early modern states, working in concert with the confessional churches, expanded their control over public and private behaviour and encouraged the creation of an obedient society and, ultimately, the basis for modern, capitalist culture.[31] How quickly individuals assimilated this social discipline is a crucial question – at least one study has argued that on a local level, confessionalization was largely a failure.[32] With respect to Augsburg's musical culture, the answer is complex: there is little doubt that church leaders on both sides of the confessional divide actively sought to indoctrinate the population with correct forms of dogma, yet the initiative of individual Protestant singers like Jonas Losch and the explosion in the quantity of Catholic non-liturgical, devotional music after 1600 hints at a burgeoning popular interest in specifically confessional forms of musical expression.

It is vital to realize that all of the major confessional churches, not the Protestant churches alone, tried to enforce religious conformity and

---

(Munich: R. Oldenbourg, 1965), *Das Zeitalter der Glaubenskämpfe, 1555–1648* (Munich: Deutscher Taschenbuch Verlag, 1973) and *Konfessionsbildung: Studien zur Reformation, Gegenreformation und katholischen Reform* (Stuttgart: Klett-Cotta, 1985).

[30] 'Christianity' was such a complex and contradictory phenomenon by the late sixteenth century that it could no longer serve as a coherent system. The resulting confessional fragmentation, Wolfgang Reinhard argues, went hand in hand with the political differentiation of territories and national states. See 'Konfession und Konfessionalisierung in Europa', pp. 176–77.

[31] On the phenomenon of social discipline, see Gerhard Oestreich's influential essay 'Strukturprobleme des europäischen Absolutismus', in his *Geist und Gestalt des frühmodernen Staates* (Berlin: Duncker und Humblot, 1969), pp. 179–97. The confessionalization thesis advanced by Schilling and Reinhard was, in part, intended as a corrective to Oestreich, who did not concern himself with religion; see Reinhard, 'Was ist katholische Konfessionalisierung?', p. 421. Among other recent scholars, R. Po-Chia Hsia has continued to emphasize the centrality of social discipline to confessionalization; see especially his *Social Discipline in the Reformation*.

[32] See Marc Forster, *The Counter-Reformation in the Villages: Religion and Reform in the Bishopric of Speyer, 1560–1720* (Ithaca, NY: Cornell University Press, 1992); see also his article 'The Thirty Years' War and the Failure of Catholicization', in Luebke, ed., *The Counter-Reformation: The Essential Readings*, pp. 163–97.

obedience to authority; thus early modern Catholicism, traditionally seen as backward and opposed to 'progress' in the modernist sense, takes its rightful place as a full participant in the creation of modern societies and nation-states.[33] The union of Counter-Reformation ideology and the apparatus of state power may be seen most dramatically in neighbouring Bavaria, where the efforts of dukes Albrecht V, Wilhelm V, and Maximilian I, as well as the Jesuits, culminated in a 'total Catholic state' that aimed at complete confessional homogeneity.[34] Augsburg's biconfessional status made such a goal impossible, but local Catholic elites – notably the patrician families, the bishops and the religious orders – pursued the Catholic cause with similar zeal. The heavy representation of Catholic families in the city council and the threat of the Bavarian military (which would flex its muscles in 1607 by occupying and forcibly re-Catholicizing the nearby Imperial city of Donauwörth) ensured that Augsburg's minority Catholic community enjoyed more status and support than normally would have been the case for a German Imperial city of the sixteenth century. As later chapters will make clear, the Catholic minority took the initiative in promoting public activities and cultural objects (including music and visual images) that dramatized the boundaries between the two communities. Protestant residents were certainly aware that they were not proportionally represented in the city's governing bodies, and this awareness contributed to the near-violence of the *Kalenderstreit*, a watershed moment in the crystallization of confessional identities among the city's population. However, on balance Catholic activities – including the missionary work of the Jesuits, the formation of confraternities, the cultivation of spectacular public processions and the composition and dissemination of Marian and Eucharistic music – contributed more heavily to confessionalization, musical and otherwise.

The central role of Catholicism in the confessionalization process (in Augsburg as elsewhere) raises the question of the relationship between music and the idea of 'Counter-Reformation'.[35] Traditionally scholars

---

[33] This contrasts with the common assertion, popularly articulated in studies such as Max Weber's *The Protestant Ethic and the Spirit of Capitalism* (first pub. as *Die protestantische Ethik und der 'Geist' des Kapitalismus* (Tübingen, Leipzig: J.C.B. Mohr (P. Siebeck), 1904)) and R.H. Tawney's *Religion and the Rise of Capitalism* (London: J. Murray, 1926), that the rise of the modern capitalist system depended heavily on specifically Protestant value systems.

[34] On this point see Reinhard, 'Konfession und Konfessionalisierung in Europa', pp. 184–86.

[35] The term 'Counter-Reformation' itself has been the object of vigorous debate among religious historians, at least since Hubert Jedin proposed that 'Counter-Reformation' (representing the reaction against Protestantism) and 'Catholic Reform' (representing *internal* efforts of reform by the Church) were in fact two sides of the same coin; see his

have focused on the deliberations of the Council of Trent and their consequences for the composition of sacred polyphony, seeing Giovanni Pierluigi da Palestrina, above all, as a paragon of post-Tridentine Catholic style.[36] Recent work, however, has questioned the centrality of Trent for an understanding of Catholic music; most of the Council's discussions on music, for example, were never enshrined as canons, save the (deliberately) vague mandate that music avoid 'lascivious or impure' elements.[37] Enforcement of this mandate, significantly, was left entirely to local dioceses. There is little evidence, in fact, for a unified style of 'Tridentine' music: clarity of text declamation, often cited as a hallmark, was in fact a concern widely shared across confessional boundaries and

---

Katholische Reformation oder Gegenreformation? Ein Versuch zur Klärung der Begriffe nebst einer Jubiläumsbetrachtung über das Trienter Konzil (Luzern: Verlag Josef Stocker, 1946), esp. pp. 7–38. At stake for Jedin and his followers was the issue of continuity: to what extent were the Tridentine reforms outgrowths of late medieval efforts, and to what extent were they merely reactions to Protestant success? More recent scholars have questioned the centrality of the Council of Trent, and institutional reform in general, to the Catholic renewal. H. Outram Evennett, for example, proposed that the essence of the Counter-Reformation lay in a new kind of *spirituality*, embodied by Ignatius of Loyola's *Spiritual Exercises* and involving a transition from medieval mysticism to disciplined meditation, worldly activism and a revival of the sacraments; see his essay 'Counter-Reformation Spirituality', in his *The Spirit of the Counter-Reformation*, ed. John Bossy (Notre Dame, Ind.: University of Notre Dame Press, 1970), pp. 23–42. More recently, John O'Malley has criticized what he sees as Jedin's overemphasis on institutional reform. He has proposed the more embracing term 'Early Modern Catholicism', which 'implicitly includes Catholic Reform, Counter-Reformation, and even Catholic Restoration as indispensable categories of analysis, while surrendering the attempt to draw too firm a line of demarcation among them'; see O'Malley, 'Was Ignatius Loyola a Church Reformer? How to Look at Early Modern Catholicism', *Catholic Historical Review*, 77 (1991), p. 193. The present study uses the term 'Counter-Reformation', recognizing the distinctly reactive character of Catholic culture against Augsburg's Protestant majority; at the same time, the debates on terminology have lessened the risk of seeing the Counter-Reformation merely as derivative of a Protestant model. 'Counter-Reformation' in this study should be understood as an era in the history of Catholicism in Augsburg, embracing aspects not only of 'Catholic reform', but also of 'Catholic renewal'.

[36] For examples, see Gustave Reese, *Music in the Renaissance* (rev. edn, New York: Norton, 1959), pp. 448–81 (which includes a brief detour into the music of Jacobus de Kerle and the oratorical *lauda*; see pp. 451–55); Allan W. Atlas, *Renaissance Music: Music in Western Europe, 1400–1600* (New York: Norton, 1998), pp. 580–605; and Leeman L. Perkins, *Music in the Age of the Renaissance* (New York: Norton, 1999), pp. 873–97. Although the myth of Palestrina's role in 'saving' church polyphony before the Council has been thoroughly debunked, this has not affected the historiographical tradition of seeing Palestrina and the Council of Trent as inextricably linked. On the other hand, Lewis Lockwood has suggested the figure of Vincenzo Ruffo as a much more direct and dramatic example of Tridentine church music; see *The Counter-Reformation and the Masses of Vincenzo Ruffo* (Vienna: Universal Edition, 1970).

[37] See Craig Monson's important article 'The Council of Trent Revisited', *Journal of the American Musicological Society*, 55 (2002), pp. 1–37.

one that arose as much from humanist as from churchly circles. Compositional styles were shared across the different confessions, and new stylistic directions, whether influenced by Rome, Venice or elsewhere, were driven more by changes in taste than confessional politics. Finally, despite the Council's injunctions secular models continued to serve as a basis for polyphonic composition; note, for example, the Magnificats based on secular models by Orlando di Lasso, who worked for a court closely identified with the Counter-Reformation.[38]

There was, in fact, no single musical style associated with the Counter-Reformation.[39] Catholic music in the early modern era was diverse in style and function, and often took its cue from secular as well as sacred models: the influence of the madrigal, villanella, canzonetta and opera was rarely absent in church music, especially by the seventeenth century. With respect to Germany, especially, a fuller understanding of this diversity of Catholic music has been obscured by a historiographical tradition that has emphasized the 'progressive' nature of Lutheran church music, echoing a broader, traditional identification of Protestantism with modernity. This phenomenon deserves separate treatment and so will not be discussed in detail here, but it is worth emphasizing that the received narratives of German music history were first developed in an era of intense German nationalism, one that looked to the Reformation as a spiritual foundation.[40] This may help to explain

---

[38] On this repertory see especially David Crook, *Orlando di Lasso's Imitation Magnificats for Counter-Reformation Munich* (Princeton: Princeton University Press, 1994).

[39] Marianne Danckwardt has argued that the lack of a unified musical response to Trent was a consequence of music's inherent inability to make specific dogmatic statements, as well as the tension between the motivation to restore a 'lost' past of Gregorian chant while seeking to regulate a contemporary practice of composition in the present. See her 'Konfessionelle Musik?', in Reinhard and Schilling, eds, *Die katholische Konfessionalisierung*, pp. 371–83.

[40] David M. Luebke (*The Counter-Reformation: The Essential Readings*, p. 6), succinctly described this development as follows: 'Liberal nationalists described German identity through stories about the historical development of high culture and state power that bound the fate of Protestantism with national destiny – narratives that also associated papal power with political disunity and cultural backwardness.' For a recent and thorough study of the influence of confession on German historical writing, see Helmut Walser Smith, *German Nationalism and Religious Conflict: Culture, Ideology, Politics 1870–1914* (Princeton: Princeton University Press, 1995). In the field of musicology, not surprisingly, the Protestant Reformation came to be seen as a locus for progressive tendencies in the (sacred) music of the sixteenth to eighteenth centuries, although Heinz von Loesch has recently argued against the origins of the modern 'work concept' in the circle of Luther, Melanchthon, and Bugenhagen; see *Das Werkbegriff in der protestantischen Musiktheorie des 16. und 17. Jahrhunderts: Ein Mißverständnis* (Hildesheim and New York: Olms, 2001).

the chronic lack of German Catholic music in modern editions, especially Latin-texted works that celebrate the Virgin Mary, the Eucharist or the saints in the subjective, emotive language characteristic of Italian Baroque spirituality.

If there was no single identifiable Catholic polyphonic style, a different picture emerges by considering other aspects that are essential to an understanding of musical culture: monophonic music (including both chant and popular song), the imagery and texts chosen by composers, and the contexts for which sacred music was intended.[41] The truism that there was no one 'Counter-Reformation style' should not obscure the existence of a musical culture that in many ways was informed by the spirit of the Catholic reform and renewal. Understanding this musical culture requires asking questions that go beyond the issue of polyphonic technique: what were the religious motivations and needs of musical institutions and patrons? What performance contexts would have demanded 'Catholic' music? What role was played by individual composers' religious beliefs and experiences? What was the nature of sacred music, not only within the confines of the church, but also in more popular contexts like processions and pilgrimages? What was the relationship between polyphonic and monophonic repertories? And what influence might the performance of this music have had on local confessional relations?

These are questions that the present study will address, but it should be emphasized that the answers will be as complex and multivalent as the religious history of Augsburg itself. The cultural division in Augsburg between the two faiths was real and growing, but it should obscure neither the commonalities between Protestant and Catholic music, nor the more general lack of overt religious tension in the city at large. The formation of confessional identities, though encouraged by religious elites on both sides, proceeded very unevenly. Many commoners only had vague notions of the doctrinal differences between Protestantism and Catholicism to begin with, and syncretism, though discouraged by the authorities, was common.[42] In the daily lives of most Augsburgers,

---

[41] Zeeden has emphasized the potential of popular song, and 'unliterary' sources in general, for an understanding of confessional relations in the sixteenth century; see 'Aspekte der katholischen Frömmigkeit', pp. 333–37.

[42] Roeck cites the case of a goldsmith, David Altenstetter, who was arrested by the city in 1598 under suspicion of being a Schwenkfeldian. The subsequent interrogation demonstrates that Altenstetter's religious beliefs embraced elements of both Catholic and Protestant doctrines. The city council, anxious to prevent the spread of potentially 'threatening' beliefs outside the sphere of the approved churches, insisted that he choose either Lutheranism or Catholicism; he opted for the former. Always conscious of the need to prevent the rise of religious tensions, the council took the public dissemination of religious ideas very seriously. See Roeck, *Eine Stadt im Krieg und Frieden*, pp. 117–19.

who had regularly to cross confessional boundaries to carry out the basic functions of trade and government, toleration was the norm. This was true among musicians as well: the eclectic contents of Adam Gumpelzhaimer's choirbooks for the Protestant church of St Anna, for example, suggest that he enjoyed close relations with the Catholic composers Gregor Aichinger and Christian Erbach. Furthermore, the devoutly Catholic Octavian II Fugger employed Hans Leo Hassler, a Protestant from Nuremberg, as his personal chamber organist.[43] Although they composed their sacred music for different performers and audiences, Protestant and Catholic composers shared a common stylistic language influenced greatly by contemporary Italian music. Inspired by the widespread availability of Italian music locally (a consequence of Augsburg's favorable position on north-south trade routes) as well as by their own travels to Italy (Aichinger and Hassler in the early 1580s), these musicians embraced the fashionable idioms of the canzonetta, villanella, madrigal, and the vocal concerto. Their music not specifically intended for the liturgy is characterized by simplicity and ease of execution, favoring homophonic, declamatory textures which would have suited the abilities of musical amateurs in the city's middle and upper classes. Although the texts of these pieces often suggest that composers targeted their music to one side of the confessional divide or the other, it is difficult to make this assessment based on style alone.

More important to this study, perhaps, are archival sources that provide a richer sense of the contexts for sacred music in early modern Augsburg. Few documents, as might be expected, concern themselves explicitly with identifiable works by specific composers. Rather, they provide valuable information about other aspects of musical life: the organization of church ensembles, payments for musical performances, descriptions and itineraries of processions and pilgrimages involving music, official interrogations of singers who ran afoul of the law, and many other areas. From these sources as well as surviving music in print and manuscript, this study attempts to piece together a picture, admittedly incomplete, of Augsburg's religious and musical landscape in the decades immediately preceding the privations of the Thirty Years War. This picture necessarily embraces both polyphony and monophony, ranging from the polyphonic masses sung by professional church choirs to popular songs sung in taverns by poor craftsmen. This approach requires a serious assessment not only of musical style, but also of texts

---

[43] In addition to several collections of secular music, Hassler obliged his patron with a collection of Latin motets for the principal feasts of the church year (*Cantiones sacrae de festis praecipuis totius anni 4. 5. 6. 7. 8. et plurium vocum* (Augsburg: Valentin Schönig, 1591; RISM A/I, H2323)) as well as a set of Masses (*Missae quaternis, V. VI. et VIII. vocibus* (Nuremberg: Paul Kauffmann, 1599; RISM A/I, H2327)).

and performance practices; in other words, all of the aspects that constitute music as a cultural practice.[44]

The perspective of religion is, of course, only one of many possible approaches to the music history of Augsburg in this period. Augsburg was also a vital centre for secular music, housing many talented lutenists (Jean-Baptiste Besard, Melchior Neusiedler, Hans Kaspar Kärgel) who were patronized by music-loving patrician families such as the Fugger and the Hainhofer.[45] The Fugger themselves were active as performers; musical training, especially on the lute, was considered essential to the upbringing of young males in the family.[46] The city likewise enjoyed the long-standing services of several *Stadtpfeifer*, instrumentalists who were engaged for city functions, secular entertainments and sometimes for church functions. A group of *Meistersinger* remained active into the seventeenth century, as well. The nature of surviving sources and the demands of the present subject preclude a detailed consideration of these areas, which otherwise demonstrate the richness of musical culture in one of the grandest cities of the Holy Roman Empire. This study cannot possibly do justice to all of the facets of Augsburg's musical history during this time, but it will demonstrate that the rising tide of confessionalization had crucial consequences for Augsburg's musical culture.

---

[44] The study of 'popular' culture alongside the more traditional objects of musicological study – the development of specific polyphonic genres and the biographies and works of individual composers – is a necessary condition for a broader understanding of the relationship of music and religion. It is also unavoidable given the commonalities between 'popular' and 'elite' music and the difficulty of assigning specific musical contexts exclusively to one or another social group. As Roger Chartier has noted, 'when, on the one hand, the concept of popular culture obliterates the bases shared by the whole of society and when, on the other, it masks the plurality of cleavages that differentiate cultural practices, it cannot be held as pertinent to a comprehension of the forms and the materials that characterize the cultural universe of societies in the modern period' (from *The Cultural Uses of Print in Early Modern France*, trans. Lydia G. Cochrane (Princeton: Princeton University Press, 1987), p. 5).

[45] Layer, *Musik und Musiker der Fuggerzeit*, pp. 6–7, and Krautwurst, 'Die Fugger und die Musik', p. 45. A recent overview of secular music cultivated in Fugger celebrations may be found in Dana Koutná-Karg, 'Feste und Feiern der Fugger im 16. Jahrhundert', in Eikelmann, ed., *Die Fugger und die Musik*, pp. 89–98.

[46] Anton Fugger (1493–1560), for example, insisted that his two youngest sons should augment their studies in France and Italy with 'zu gepürender zeit musica, als singen, tantzen, fechten und dergleichen ehrlich kurzweil, jedoch ausserhalb lautenschlagen lernen und ieben'. Quoted in Krautwurst, 'Die Fugger und die Musik', pp. 41–42.

CHAPTER TWO

Protestant Song and Criminality

In the decades before the Thirty Years War, confessional differences in Augsburg became externalized in new ways, especially through the public assertiveness of the Catholic minority and Protestant resentment of a government they believed to be biased in favour of the Catholic party. The authorities were successful in preventing confessional tensions from boiling over after the violence of the *Kalenderstreit* in 1584, but they were able to do so only by controlling – or attempting to control – public discourse, including the dissemination and performance of popular religious songs sung in taverns, public streets and private homes. During and after the Protestant protests against the introduction of the Gregorian calendar in 1584, song became a medium of popular dissent against the council's decision not only to adopt the new calendar, but also to expel Georg Müller, superintendent of St Anna and one of the instigators of the unrest, from the city.[1] In response, the city council banned the singing or distribution of songs supporting the preacher and vigorously prosecuted violators.

In succeeding decades the council tried to suppress religiously inflammatory songs that would endanger the religious peace. When this peace ended and a fully Catholic city council took control of Augsburg in early 1629, it banned the singing of Lutheran chorales and psalms altogether in public and private contexts, using mandates, espionage and criminal prosecutions to eradicate this potent expression of Protestant identity. They failed to do so, although their efforts are understandable in the light of the fact that public religious expression among Catholics and Protestants alike had assumed a highly polemical cast by the early seventeenth century. As the pastoral activities of the Jesuits and the increasing number and ostentation of Catholic processions sharpened the display of Catholic identity in Augsburg's public sphere, the religious song of the city's Protestant majority in streets, taverns and private homes became an object of intense scrutiny. Whether or not local Protestants intended their songs to have political significance (they certainly did, at least, during the period of Catholic Restitution),

---

[1] As superintendent Müller was the leader of Augsburg's Protestant preachers, a 'first among equals' who answered to the city council's church administrators (the *Kirchenpfleger*).

Augsburg's city fathers believed these songs to contribute to the potential for religious unrest.

We are able to trace the council's attempts to suppress such song largely thanks to an unparalleled collection of criminal interrogation records, the so-called *Urgichtensammlung*, which is housed today at the Stadtarchiv Augsburg.[2] These documents, which provide details of criminal proceedings beginning in the late fifteenth century and extending at least into the late eighteenth century, have come to the attention of historians only in recent decades, and have yet to be fully examined. In the early modern era, the city council conducted interrogations perhaps twice per week, questioning a handful of suspects on any given day. Normally two councillors, both patricians, conducted the trials. Each fascicle, which normally contains all of the documents pertaining to a single case, includes a small slip of paper on which are written a series of questions for the interrogator, the so-called *Fragstück*. The main body of the fascicle contains the answers of the suspect, written in the third person by a scribe, and following the precise order of questions seen on the *Fragstück* (for reproductions of these documents, see Figures 2.2 and 2.3 below).[3] Other kinds of evidence, such as letters of intercession, testimony of witnesses and actual evidence taken from the person of the suspect, are frequently inserted into the fascicle.

As studies of early modern law and justice have revealed, the primary goal of such interrogations was to extract a confession, without which a conviction, under the precepts of Roman-canon law, was impossible.[4]

---

[2] StAA, Strafamt, Urgichtensammlung.

[3] Since the questions were fixed before the interrogation began, the substance of the suspect's testimony did not ordinarily affect the course of the interview. For example, if a suspect provided all of the relevant details of a case at the beginning of the interrogation, subsequent questions were frequently redundant, forcing the suspect either to restate his or her story, or to refer the interrogators back to his or her original statement. If the suspect provided new information that the interrogators desired to follow up, another interview was arranged.

[4] See, for example, John H. Langbein, *Torture and the Law of Proof: Europe and England in the Ancien Régime* (Chicago: University of Chicago Press, 1977), pp. 4–5, and Richard van Dülmen, *Theatre of Horror: Crime and Punishment in Early Modern Germany* (Cambridge: Polity Press; Cambridge, Mass.: Blackwell, 1990), p. 13. A suspect who withstood all torture without confessing his or her crime had to be pronounced innocent and released. Under this system, circumstantial evidence, the so-called *indicia*, could only represent a 'half-proof' that a crime had been committed, in other words, no more than 'probable cause'. Unless two eyewitnesses also testified to the crime, a conviction was impossible without a voluntary confession by the defendant. The entire judicial apparatus was designed, according to the Roman-canon law rules of evidence, to extract a confession from a suspect and simultaneously to establish the details of the crime, which, according to the Imperial *Constitutio Criminalis Carolina* of 1532, 'no innocent person can know'.

A secondary goal was to establish the details of the crime; the individual motivations of the accused, no matter how interesting to the modern observer, were entirely beside the point. In the Augsburg *Urgichten*, the questions to be asked of the suspect were carefully designed in advance, and proceeded logically according to the assumption that the suspect was guilty of the charge. After preliminary questions establishing name, age, origin and occupation, the suspect would be asked whether he or she had committed the crime in question. The final question in almost every interrogation demanded to know how the suspect believed that he or she could have committed the crime and escape punishment, to which the defendant often replied by asking for mercy [*bitt vmb gnad*].

To extract a confession, the interrogators often turned to torture, or the threat of torture.[5] If the first interview was unsatisfactory, the interrogators displayed the instruments of torture during the second interview (the suspect would be 'ernstlich bedroht', or 'gravely threatened'), and actually used them during the third (what was known as a 'peinlich verhör', or 'questioning with pain'); generally the *Urgicht* notes instances where suspects were tortured. The most common form of torture was hoisting the victim by his or her arms, which had been tied behind the back, on a device known as the strappado, inevitably resulting in dislocation of the shoulders. If necessary, weights were attached to increase the pain. Any confession extracted under judicial torture later had to be repeated voluntarily by the accused; otherwise torture would be applied again. Regardless of whether the suspect was convicted or acquitted, he or she was obligated to sign an 'oath of truce' (*Urphed*), which foreswore any retribution against the city.

The range of crimes that would merit such an investigation was wide, extending from cases of public disorder, drunkenness and rudeness, to cases of assault and murder. Although in many cases there is ample reason to doubt the veracity of suspects' testimony (especially that obtained under torture), the *Urgichten* are nevertheless fascinating documents of social history, and they provide unparalleled insight into the trafficking in religious song at lower levels of society. Four surviving cases, three related to the *Kalenderstreit* and a fourth to the disruptions of the Edict of Restitution (1629), shed light on various aspects of

---

[5] This is known as *judicial* torture, a fundamental element of the Roman-canon-law system of proof. It is to be carefully distinguished from the physical afflictions of punishment. See Langbein, *Torture and the Law of Proof*, p. 3. The touch of the executioner, who carried out the torture, was considered to be an act of ritual pollution that often resulted in the banishment of the individual from his or her social circle. See Kathy Stuart, *Defiled Trades and Social Outcasts: Honor and Ritual Pollution in Early Modern Germany* (Cambridge and New York: Cambridge University Press, 1999), pp. 140–41.

religious song.[6] In the first case from April 1585, the weaver Abraham Schädlin turned himself into the authorities, hoping for lenient treatment. The previous year he had written a song about the *Kalenderstreit* that seems to have circulated widely in the city; the surviving song, which takes as its musical model an already propagandistic Protestant chorale, affords a view into the creative process. Schädlin's song makes another appearance in the second case, mentioned at the beginning of Chapter 1, which took place in the aftermath of the violence of June 1584: a Protestant weaver was arrested for copying, distributing and singing songs attacking the actions of the city government and the Catholic authorities in general. In the third case, from 1588, a nurse in a city hospital was charged with giving copies of an illicit song about the *Kalenderstreit* to a patient, whom she expected to learn the song and sing it. The fourth case took place in 1630, a year and a half after an entirely Catholic city government had taken control of the city: here a Protestant weaver and his wife were arrested for the ownership and suspected distribution of anti-Catholic songs. In the conclusion of this chapter I will discuss the general significance of these cases and their relationship to the rise of confessional identity and the role of music within it. These three proceedings, along with other relevant cases and archival documents, shed unusual light on the production, circulation, performance and criminalization of Protestant song in Counter-Reformation Augsburg.

'Wo es Gott nit mit Augspurg helt': The Case of Abraham Schädlin (1585)

The unrest of the *Kalenderstreit* and the banishment of Georg Müller in June 1584 doubtless incited many local Protestants to sing songs against the Catholic establishment and the city government, which they felt to be biased in favour of Augsburg's Catholic minority. Müller himself encouraged his former flock to sing in order to console themselves: two years after his expulsion, he wrote a public *Send und Trostbrieff* to his former congregations, admonishing them not to lose hope in the face of their repression by the city council:

> In the meantime you should assemble yourselves together at arranged times with your children and domestics, consult your

---

[6] A discussion of the cases against Abraham Schädlin and Jonas Losch, as well as others, may be found in Alexander J. Fisher, 'Song, Confession, and Criminality: Trial Records as Sources for Popular Musical Culture in Early Modern Europe', *Journal of Musicology*, **18** (2001), pp. 616–57.

> collections of sermons and other pure books, [let] the word [of God] live richly among you, and let your prayers and singing of psalms [*das Gebett vn[d] die schöne Psalmen gesäng*] sound out in consolation.[7]

In the summer of 1584, shortly after the uproar surrounding Müller's expulsion from Augsburg, a weaver by the name of Abraham Schädlin wrote and distributed a song critical of the city government's actions.[8] Fearing arrest, he soon fled to nearby Ulm, not returning until almost a year later. Perhaps hoping for lenience, he turned himself in to the Augsburg authorities in the first week of April 1585, and faced an interrogation on 5 April:[9]

> Abraham Schädlin, in prison, shall be questioned.
> 1. What is his name, and where is he from?
>   His name is Abraham Schädlin, and comes from Augsburg.
> 2. How does he support himself?
>   He is a weaver, and can also write.
> 3. Did he not flee the city, and why?
>   Yes, he fled to Ulm on account of a song he wrote concerning Doctor Müller. But he did not distribute it. Rather, he wished to dedicate it to Daniel Weiss's wife, but another named Georg Braun found it on [Schädlin's] person and asked him if he could have it so he could show it to his wife. Then Braun copied it and distributed it, so that everyone knew that [Schädlin] had [written] it. He was warned about this and fled to Ulm until things improved and he would have less worry, because he wrote this song about the council's action, [a song] in which everything that had transpired was included. He did indeed make this song and showed it to others, but he only found out later that he had done wrong.

---

[7] D-As, 4° Aug 735, *Kalenderstreit* I and II: *Send vnd Trostbrieff/ Georg: Müllers/ Doctorn vnnd Professorn zu Wittemberg/ an seine liebe Landtsleut vnd Pfarrkinder/ die Euangelische Burgerschafft in Augspurg/ vber jrem betrübten Zustande/ da jhnen jhre liebe Seelsorger vnd Prediger abgeschafft/ vnnd alle zumal auff einen Tag zur Statt außgetriben worden* (Wittenberg: Matthäus Welack, 1586), fol. 7r.

[8] It is possible, but unlikely, that Schädlin was identical with Abraham Schädlin (1556–1626), a pedagogue, author and *Meistersinger* who wrote textbooks and several religious plays, and who converted to Catholicism in 1588 (a 1606 dialogue, entitled *Urteylsprecher*, involves the conversion of a Lutheran; see *Augsburger Stadtlexikon*, s.v. 'Schädlin, Abraham' (Augsburg: Perlach, 1998), p. 776). The documents for the present case give no indication of Schädlin's age, so it is impossible to discount the possibility that the two men may have been the same person.

[9] From StAA, Kalenderstreit-Criminalia, 1583–89. For the reader's convenience, I have interpolated suspects' answers into the questions of the *Fragstück*. A transcription of the trial may be found in the Appendix, no. 1.

4. Where did he stay in the meantime, and who helped him?

He stayed in Ulm at the Red Lion Tavern and made money by writing. He was also in Nördlingen for two weeks.

5. It is known that he has written many shameful songs and poems; he should describe all of them.

He wrote the 'Peasant's Lament' [*Bauern Klag*] and nothing else, apart from the song noted above.

6. Did he not also write a song about Doctor Müller and the city council?

He wrote the above-mentioned song with 49 stanzas, in which the entire affair with Doctor Müller is given as it was told to him.

7. Who ordered him to do it?

Nobody.

8. Why did he unjustly and hatefully attack the city authorities in [the song]?

He simply repeated what everyone else was saying.

9. What did he intend by this deed?

He intended nothing by it.

10. What other shameful writings has he made and posted?

He has made nothing else, and begs for mercy.

One day later the authorities granted Schädlin his freedom in recognizance of his honesty. The *Strafbuch* for 6 April reads:

Done Saturday, 6 April 1585. Abraham Schädlin, a weaver and citizen of this city, wrote a song during the recent uprising harshly attacking the authorities without justification. Thus he was imprisoned; but today, in the light of the fact that he turned himself in for punishment, he was released after signing a general oath;[10] from this time forward, and under pain of bodily punishment, he shall neither write nor sing any writing, song or poem against the authorities or any other person. Nor shall he copy or distribute such writings of others. Rather, should he be aware of such things on the part of others, he should tell the *Stadtpfleger* immediately and hand the writings over. He shall also avoid any gathering in which the government is criticized and be obedient to the authorities; if he sees or hears anything against them, he shall immediately make this known.[11]

No copy of Schädlin's song was laid into the fascicle for this case, but the weaver's admission of the subject matter and exact length allows us to identify his song with one version of a printed contrafactum that

---

[10] The sworn *Urphed*, an oath not to seek retribution against the city for any perceived wrongs, always preceded the release of a prisoner.

[11] StAA, Strafamt, Strafbücher 1581–87, fol. 155v.

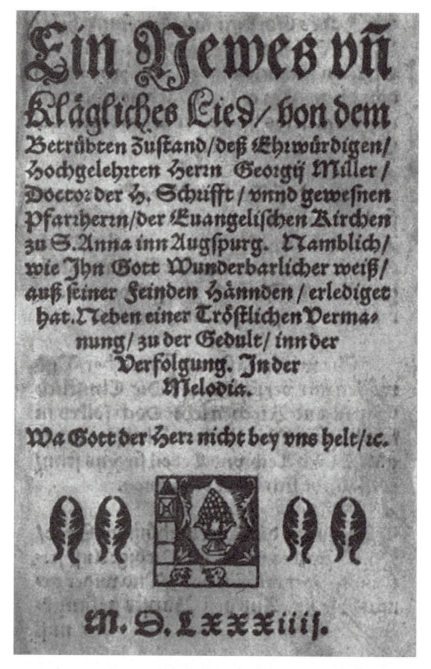

2.1   Title page of *Wo es Gott nit mit Augspurg helt*, a contrafactum by
Abraham Schädlin (1584). D-As, 4° Aug 735, Kalenderstreit I and II, no. 3

survives in a number of copies in the Staats- und Stadtbibliothek Augsburg. The survival of *Wo es Gott nit mit Augspurg helt*, a political contrafactum of the Lutheran psalm tune *Wo Gott der Herr nicht bei uns hält*, offers an opportunity to examine the creative process in detail. Two versions of this *klägliches Lied* survive: one of 32 stanzas and one of 49 stanzas (the title page of the latter appears in Figure 2.1).[12] It is possible that Schädlin merely copied his version from a pre-existing song, but given that he admitted to 'writing' (*machen*) rather than merely 'copying' the song (*abschreiben*), it is likely that the weaver was responsible for the original content.[13] Since most sixteenth-century Protestants would have known the psalm *Wo Gott der Herr* well, the interrelationship of the original psalm, the translation, and the new text of 1584 may be analysed as an intertextual complex. This is not a new method for the analysis of contrafacta; Rebecca Wagner Oettinger has recently shown the continued relevance of musical models in new propagandistic contrafacta during the Reformation, while Bernd Roeck pointed to one example of such contrafacture in Augsburg during the period of the Catholic Restitution.[14] The consideration of a new text along with the music and text of its model is especially fruitful in the case of Schädlin's *Wo es Gott nit mit Augspurg helt*, which derived some of its subversive power from the close meaningful relationship among all these levels.

The narrative of the original psalm, *Nisi quia Dominus erat* (124, 123 Vulg.), is one of persecution by enemies, symbolized by a raging flood and a hungry beast; God's salvation of the soul is likened to a bird that has escaped from its cage:

---

[12] D-As, 4° Aug 735, *Kalenderstreit* I and II, no. 3.

[13] 'Doch hab er diß Lied gemacht, allein vff anderer leuth anzaig[en].' From interrogation of Abraham Schädlin, 5 April 1585. The verb *abschreiben* is indeed commonly encountered in other cases and indicates copying as opposed to composition. *Machen* is a generic verb referring to the creation of a song, but in most cases it refers to the writing of a contrafactum rather than the composition of a new melody. Given that the spread of song texts, provocative or otherwise, was facilitated by the reuse of popular existing melodies, musical 'composition' as such is rarely a factor.

[14] See Rebecca Wagner Oettinger, *Music as Propaganda in the German Reformation* (Aldershot: Ashgate, 2001), pp. 89–136, and Roeck, *Eine Stadt im Krieg und Frieden*, pp. 669–71. The song cited by Roeck, a politically relevant text set to the psalm tune *An Wasserflüssen Babylon*, was disseminated and sung in response to the Catholic city council established by Emperor Ferdinand II's Edict of Restitution in 1629. The Edict was a direct consequence of Catholic military success during the previous decade and mandated the re-Catholicization of all ecclesiastical properties taken over by Protestants since 1552. In Augsburg the city council banned all Protestant observances and took measures to stifle song and speech critical of its actions. Chapter 8 of the present study offers an overview of the turbulent political and musical circumstances of this period.

1. Nisi quia Dominus erat in nobis	If it had not been the Lord who was with us,
dicat nunc Israhel	now let Israel say:
2. nisi quia Dominus erat in nobis	If it had not been the Lord who was with us,
cum exsurgerent in nos homines	when men rose up against us:
3. forte vivos degluttissent nos	Then they had swallowed us up quick,
cum irasceretur furor eorum in nos	when their wrath was kindled against us:
4. forsitan aqua absorbuisset nos	Then the waters had overwhelmed us,
5. torrentem pertransivit anima nostra	the stream had gone over our soul:
forsitan pertransisset anima nostra	Then the proud waters
aquam intolerabilem	had gone over our soul.
6. benedictus Dominus qui non dedit nos	Blessed be the Lord, who hath not given us
in captionem dentibus eorum	as a prey to their teeth.
7. anima nostra sicut passer erepta est	Our soul is escaped as a bird out of the snare
de laqueo venantium; laqueus contritus est	of the fowlers: the snare is broken,
et nos liberati sumus	and we are escaped.
8. adiutorium nostrum in nomine Domini	Our help is in the name of the Lord,
qui fecit caelum et terram.	who made heaven and earth.

The early years of the Reformation saw at least two German versions of Psalm 124. Martin Luther's translation, *Wär' Gott nicht mit uns diese Zeit*, was set by Johann Walter and appeared in the early *Geystliche gesangk Buchleyn* of 1524. The song consists of three stanzas that follow the content of the original psalm closely. Although his version is longer than the original, Luther faithfully reproduces the imagery of the flood, the ravenous beast, and the caged bird; at no time, however, does he directly implicate the incipient confessional divide, which is understandable in the light of his early reluctance towards confessional schism:

1. Wer Gott nit mit vns dise zyt,	1. Were God not with us in this time,
so sol Israel sagen:	Thus may Israel say:
Wer Gott nit mit vns dise zyt,	Were God not with us in this time,
wir hettend müßt verzagen.	We would lose all hope.
Die so ein kleines huflin sind,	These who are such a small number,
veracht von so vil menschen kind,	Despised by so many children of men,
die an vns setzen alle.	Who set themselves all against us.

2. Vff vns ist so zornig ir sin,

wo Gott das hett zůgeben:
Verschlunden hettend sy vns hin,
mit gantzem lyb vnd läben.
Wir wärn als die ein flůt
  ersoufft,
vnd über die groß wasser loufft,
vnnd mit gewalt verschwemmet.

3. Gott lob vnnd danck der nit
  zůgab,
das ir schlund vns möcht
  fangen:
Wie ein vogel des stricks kumpt
  ab,
ist vnser seel entgangen.
Strick ist entzwey vnnd wir sind
  frey,
des Herren namen stand vnns
  bey,
des Gotts himmels vnd erden.

2. Their thoughts are so angry
  against us,
Where God would allow it:
They would swallow us whole,
With entire body and life.
We would be as those drowned
  in a flood,
The great waters flowing over us,
And scattered with force.

3. Thanks and praise to God,
  who will not allow
Their jaws to seize us:

Like a bird from its cage,

Our soul flies away.
The cage is broken and we are
  free,
Let the name of the Lord be
  with us,
That of God's heaven and
  earth.[15]

Another German translation of Psalm 124, the eight-stanza version of Justus Jonas shown in Example 2.1, had gained greater currency by the late sixteenth century. Jonas, a contemporary of Luther's at the University of Wittenberg, used the same rhyme scheme and metre of Luther's version but sharpened the portrait of injustice suffered at the hands of enemies. Although he does not name the Catholic church directly in his translation, the implication of confessional strife is clearer. For example, the first line of stanza 4, 'Sie stellen uns wie Ketzern nach', uses the term *Ketzer* favoured by German Catholics as a label for Protestants in the early modern period. The next stanza also contains a reference to the unnamed enemies' 'falsche Lehr', or 'false teachings', an allusion to doctrinal conflict. In the first few decades of the Reformation a number of melodies were attached to Jonas's text, but by the end of the sixteenth century that shown in Example 2.1 appeared most commonly in songbooks and broadsides.[16] The first five stanzas run as follows:

---

[15] From *Nüw gsangbüchle von vil schönen Psalmen vnd geistlichen liedern/ durch ettliche diener der kirchen zů Costentz vn[d] anderstwo mercklichen gemeert/ gebessert vnd in gschickte ordnung zesamen gstellt/ zů übung vnnd bruch jrer ouch anderer Christlichen kirchen* (Zurich: Christoffel Froschouer, 1540), my translation.

[16] Text: Philipp Wackernagel, *Das deutsche Kirchenlied von der ältesten Zeit bis zum Anfang des 17. Jahrhunderts* (Leipzig: B.G. Teubner, 1864–77; repr. Hildesheim: Olms, 1964), vol. 3, p. 42 (no. 62); music: Ambrosius Lobwasser, ed., *Psalmen Dauids In Teutsche Reymen verständtlich vnd deutlich gebracht* (Düsseldorf: Bey Bernhardt Buyß, 1612), pp. 606–7.

Example 2.1   A common melody for Justus Jonas's translation of Psalm 124,
Wo Gott der Herr nicht bei uns hält

1. Wo Gott der herr nicht bey
   vns helt,
   wen vnser feynde tobenn,
   Vnnd er vnnser sach nicht zu felt
   ym hymel hoch dort oben,
   Wo er Israhel schutz nicht yst

   vnd selber bricht der feynde list,

   so ysts mit vns verloren.

2. Was menschen krafft vnnd
   witz anfeht,
   soll vnns billich nicht schrecken:
   Er sytzet an der hochten stet,
   der wirt yhrn radt aufdecken:
   Wen sies auffs klugest greyffen
   an,
   so geht doch Got eyn ander ban,
   es steht yn seynen henden.

3. Sie wueten fast vnd faren her,

   als wolten sie vns fressen.
   Zu wurgen steht al yhr beger,
   gots ist bey yhn vergessen.
   Wie meeres wellen eynher
   schlahn,
   nach leib vnnd leben sye vns
   stahn,
   des wirt sych got erbarmen.

4. Sie stellen vns wie ketzern
   nach,
   zu vnserm blut sy trachten,
   Noch rhumen sye sych Christen
   hoch

Were God the Lord not with us,

when our enemies rage,
and if he were not on our side
in heaven high above,
Were he not the defender of
Israel
and did not himself break our
enemies' cunning,
then all would be lost with us.

The force and cunning of men
against us
should rightly not terrify us:
He sits in the highest place,
he will uncover their treachery:
if they most cleverly attack,

God will find another way,
it is in his hands.

3. They rage harshly and come
at us,
as if they wished to swallow us.
They wish only to slay us,
God is forgotten among them.
Like the ocean's waves coming
up,
they wish to take life and limb,

God will have mercy.

They take us to be heretics,

they clamour for our blood,
yet they take themselves for
Christians,

dy Gott alleyn gros achten:	who alone revere God greatly:
Ach got, der theure name deyn	O God, your precious name
mus yhrer schalckheyt deckel seyn!	must put an end to their evil ways!
du wirst eyn mal auffwachen.	One day you will rise up.
5. Auffsperren sy den rachen weyt	Vengefully they open wide their jaws,
vnd wöllen vns verschlingen:	and wish to devour us:
Lob vnd danck sey got allezeyt,	praise and thanks be to God always,
es wird yhn nicht gelingen,	that they shall not succeed,
Er wird yr strick zureyssen gar	he will rend their cage completely
vnd störtzen yre falsche lar,	and overthrow their false teachings,
sie werden Got nicht weren.	they shall not resist God.

Jonas's propagandistic version of Psalm 124 served as the immediate model for Abraham Schädlin's *Wo es Gott nit mit Augspurg helt* in 1584, four stanzas of which are given here:[17]

1. Wo es Gott nit mit Augspurg helt,	Were God not with Augsburg,
Weil jhre Feinde toben:	because its enemies rage;
Vnnd der Christen sach nit zustelt,	and did he not take the Christian side,
Jm Himel hoch dort oben.	in heaven high above.
Wa er der Warheit schutz nit ist,	Were he not the defender of truth,
Vnnd selbs bricht der Veruolger list,	himself breaking the persecuters' cunning,
SO ists mit vns verlohren.	then all would be lost with us.
2. Was deß Teuffels Werckhzeug anfacht,	How the tool of the devil attacks us,
Soll vns billich nicht schröckhen:	should rightly not terrify us:
Vil falsch anschläg hat er erdacht,	he has imagined many evil plots,
Doch thut sie Gott erdecken.	but God will uncover them.
Da sie es weißlich greiffen an,	Even if they attack,
Dan[n]och gieng Gott ein andre ban,	God will find another way,
Es ist in seinen Händen.	it is in his hands.
18. Man stelt im als als ein kezer nach,	They take him to be a heretic,
nach seinem blut sie trachten,	they clamour for his blood,
Die sich güt Christen rümbten hoch,	yet they take themselves for Christians,

---

[17] D-As, 4° Aug 735, no. 3. The shorter 32-stanza version may be found as no. 2 under this shelf mark.

und Gott allein groß achten,	who alone revere God greatly:
Der Kalender in schlectem schein,	The deception of the calendar
müst irer Schalckheit deckel sein,	must be the end of their evil ways,
aber Gott thet auffwachen.	but God shall rise up.
29. Als man zahlt fünffzehen hundert jar,	As one counts, fifteen hundred,
vier und achzig genennt,	four and eighty years,
an S. Urbans tag das ist war,	on St Urban's day,[18] it is true,
hat der fried sich getrennt,	the peace left us,
und auffrür gnumen uberhandt,	and unrest took the upper hand,
in der Statt Augspurg weit erkand,	in the city of Augsburg, as is known;
Herr Gott dein fried uns sende.	Lord God, send us your peace.

Like the vast majority of contemporary printed songs, exemplars of this contrafactum lack a notated melody, simply identifying the tune (*Thon*) on the title page (see Figure 2.1). To aid memorization, Schädlin was careful to preserve the iambic metre and rhyme scheme, ABABCCB, of the original song. The first several stanzas of the contrafactum, furthermore, are closest to the model in terms of

---

[18] Protestants in Augsburg who refused to accept the new Gregorian calendar reckoned the date of the uprising as St Urban's Day, 25 May, ten days before the Gregorian date of 4 June. Schädlin's choice of St Urban's Day, then, is itself loaded with significance. Leofranc Holford-Strevens, who kindly brought my attention to this fact, has also noted, in *The Oxford Companion to the Year* (Oxford: Oxford University Press, 1999), p. 221 (citing Wilhelm Uhl, *Unser Kalender in seiner Entwicklung von den ältesten Anfängen bis heute* (Paderborn: Ferdinand Schöningh, 1893), p. 101), the existence of a 'Bawrenklag Vber des Röm. Bapsts Gregorii XIII newen Calender', a poem which in one stanza criticizes the Pope for moving St Urban's Day ten days earlier:

Hettest doch nur in seiner massen,	If only you had let St Urban's Day
St Urbans tag vns bleiben lassen.	remain as it was before,
Da wir Bawren vns trancken voll,	so that we peasants could drink our fill,
So gefiel vns dein Kolender wol.	then your calendar would please us well.
Aber du hast den auch entzogen,	But you have taken [that day] away as well,
Vnd mit dem Weinwachß vns betrogen.	and cheated us out of our wine harvest.

Holford-Strevens writes that fair weather on St Urban's Day was thought a harbinger of a good wine harvest, thus explaining the reference to viticulture. Abraham Schädlin, in fact, may have been the author of this text as well: beyond the reference to St Urban's Day common to both the 'Bawrenklag' and *Wo es Gott nit mit Augspurg helt*, Schädlin himself admitted in his interrogation to writing a 'Bauern Klag'!

content. The impersonal victims in the original psalm's first stanza are replaced by the city of Augsburg, and the changes in lines three and five make the link between Christianity and truth (*Warheit*), which is subjected to persecution. Already in the first stanza, then, the conflict is a doctrinal one. The second stanza of the contrafactum is also related to that in *Wo Gott der Herr*, but the connection is more subtle, replacing the 'force and cunning of men' with the stronger 'tool of the Devil'. Further correspondences exist between the two texts in later stanzas as well, notably stanza 16 of the contrafactum, which identifies Dr Müller as the 'kezer' for whose blood the Catholics thirst. In these alterations Schädlin draws upon the already antagonistic vocabulary of Jonas's original text, extends it, and links it to the events surrounding Müller's expulsion. The weaver, however, freely invented some of the new material: the contrafactum includes a number of later stanzas that draw parallels between the city council's behaviour and the tyranny of the anti-Christian Roman emperors. It is likely that the Augsburg city magistrates, who governed a free Imperial city of the Holy Roman Empire, would have taken this offence to heart.

Schädlin's new text of 1584 was not solely responsible for the symbolic power of *Wo es Gott nit mit Augspurg helt*. The offensiveness of the song to the Augsburg city authorities may also partially be explained by the strong political orientation of Justus Jonas's popular original, whose melody and words would have been known to most contemporary Protestants. The first stanzas of the original song and the contrafact text are so closely related that one must assume that Schädlin deliberately sought to link the two songs in the audience's mind, thus reinforcing the political message while providing a ready memory aid. From the standpoint of the city government, which made the preservation of religious peace its primary goal, the highly inflammatory text combined with the propagandistic quality of the original tune made the song a threatening symbol of confessional strife. To Protestant singers, *Wo es Gott nit mit Augspurg helt* represented an opportunity to express their confessional identity and resistance by linking religious and political imagery.

'Ein schmachlied vom Babst vnd Jesuitern': The Augsburg *Kalenderstreit* and the Case of Jonas Losch (1584)

Abraham Schädlin's *Wo es Gott nit mit Augspurg* had been circulating in Augsburg for some time when the weaver Jonas Losch was arrested for copying, circulating and singing songs critical of the authorities and the Jesuits.[19] Losch, who supplemented his income by singing at weddings, appeared before two patrician interrogators (Christoph Rehlinger the Younger and Leonhard Widenmann) and submitted a writing sample (presumably to compare against the manuscript songs found in his possession), and was asked where he had been during the recent uprising. A reproduction of the first pages of the *Fragstück* and the weaver's responses, respectively, appear in Figures 2.2 and 2.3.[20]

The interrogators believed that Losch had not been active in his trade as of late, but the weaver assured them that he had been supplementing his income by writing songs and singing at weddings:

> Jonas Losch answered the questions of the attached *Fragstück* as follows, under grave threat [of torture].
>
> 1. What is his name, and where is he from?
>
> His name is Jonas Losch and he is a citizen [of Augsburg].
>
> 2. What is his profession, by which he supports himself?
>
> He is a weaver and supports himself by this trade, but he also sings songs at weddings between the dancing and supper, and makes extra money from this. When asked if he could write, he said he could, and was asked to write [a sample] which has been included here.[21]
>
> 3. Since he has not been working for some time, he should state where he has been receiving money with which to support himself.
>
> He answers that he has been working diligently, and that he has supplemented his [income] by singing at weddings, where he begins after five o'clock and continues until supper.

For the interrogators the most pressing matter in this first interview was Losch's participation in the June uprising and his subsequent flight from the city. The day after the unrest Losch claimed to have witnessed an altercation between, one must assume, a Protestant named 'Michael' and a Catholic on the Barfüsser bridge, who had called the former a 'spinner of Doctor Müller's' [*ein Redlefüerer des Doctor Müllers*]. This 'Michael' had reported the incident to the authorities, and evidently Losch had been summoned as a witness. However, two weeks before the uprising one of the city Bürgermeister had confiscated some of Losch's songs, and the weaver feared that their contents would put him in jeopardy if he appeared before the authorities.

---

[19] StAA, Kalenderstreit-Criminalia, 3 September 1584, Jonas Losch. Transcription in the Appendix, no. 2a. This *Urgicht* originally belonged to the general collection of interrogations, but has been removed to a special collection concerning the *Kalenderstreit*. I am indebted to B. Ann Tlusty for introducing me to this collection of *Criminalia*.

[20] A transcription of excerpts from the case may be found in the Appendix, no. 2.

[21] Unfortunately this writing sample has not been preserved in the fascicle.

2.2 *Fragstück* from interrogation of Jonas Losch, 3 September 1584. StAA, Kalenderstreit-Criminalia, 3 September 1584

2.3 First page of *Urgicht* from interrogation of Jonas Losch, 3 September 1584.
StAA, Kalenderstreit-Criminalia, 3 September 1584

> Because he now feared that he was in danger, not only because of
> these statements, but also because Christoph Ilsung, while he held
> the office of Bürgermeister, confiscated several songs from him
> about 14 days before the uprising (among which he wrote six with
> his own hand, and the others were printed; and among these six
> [handwritten songs] he made five himself, but the sixth was copied
> from a print), he departed, and stayed in Stuttgart for one day and
> for three weeks in Ulm, where he practised his trade at Samuel
> Faulhaber's [shop]. He returned from Ulm only after his wife told
> him that things had settled down.

Before turning to the actual contents of Losch's songs, the interrogators
questioned him about the events of the previous Sunday, when several
witnesses had reported him cursing and singing anti-Jesuit songs in the
streets. Losch would deny singing the song or breaking windows at the
Jesuit college, but he did admit to having been provoked into anger by
an altercation with one of his neighbours. As for his songs, the record
makes it clear that a number of them contained religiously inflammatory
sentiments. For the first time, furthermore, Losch implicated Abraham
Schädlin as a songwriter.

> 11. It is known that he has long been making many shameful and
> insulting songs; he should describe all of them.
>
> > He has made up to 30 songs for dancing and singing, five of
> > which are now in the hands of Herr Ilsung (including one
> > about the Pope); he wrote the others into a book, which is
> > now in his house, lying on a shelf over a bag in his chamber,
> > but these are nothing but love songs, and not insulting.
>
> 12. When did he write the insulting songs about the weaving
> masters of Ulm, and about the cook, and why?[22]
>
> > He did not write that song, but Abraham Schädlin wrote the
> > song about the cook; who wrote the other he does not know;
> > a ring-maker in Ulm, who lives in the Frauengasse not far
> > from the Nusshart tavern, gave it to him.
>
> 13. Where did he get the song about the Pope and the Jesuits, which
> has been found in his books, and did he not make it himself?
>
> > He made this song himself; he took it from a popular print he
> > bought from Aaron,[23] the bookseller under the Gieger, and
> > turned it into a song. Herr Ilsung now has this song.

The authorities believed this to have been the song that Losch sang in the
darkened streets, but Losch denied this, admitting only that he had sung

---

[22] Neither of these songs has been preserved in the fascicle, so their contents remain
unknown. As Rebecca Wagner Oettinger has pointed out in a personal communication, the
term 'cook' often designated the concubines that Catholic priests were sometimes accused
of keeping.

[23] Probably Aaron Stier, who would be implicated by Losch's friend Deisenhoffer, and
whose wife Barbara would later be arrested for selling illicit songs and images (see note 55
below).

a different song (which he failed to identify) in public some nine months previously. Further contradicting his denouncers, Losch also denied breaking any windows at the Jesuit college. Finally, the interrogators turned to another song of much more recent import concerning the uprising and the persecution of Georg Müller.

> 16. He should state where he made the song about the recent uprising and Doctor Müller against the authorities, or else the executioner shall bring it out of him.
>
> > Last Sunday an apprentice from Memmingen named Michael Karg came to him and brought him a printed song, which he copied, writing at the top, 'I, Jonas Losch, made this song'. But he did nothing more than add a little bit to it, and change a few stanzas; in particular he wrote the entire last stanza himself. He does not know where Karg went thereafter; he thinks he went to Ulm. There is a preacher in Ulm named Herr Peter who also wrote a song about the uprising, which he had heard sung there.
>
> 17. Who helped him in this?
>
> > The above-mentioned Karg lent him the printed song, which he changed and improved as stated above.

Losch's testimony here is significant, for it points to one of the means by which illicit songs may have circulated in the city. Given the strict censorship of propagandistic songs and literature in Augsburg itself, it is not surprising that other Protestant towns in the region like Memmingen and Ulm were sources for this kind of material, which in turn could be smuggled into Augsburg by individuals like Michael Karg. Ulm is of special importance since Georg Müller made it his residence in exile; this and other criminal proceedings suggest that Ulm may have been the most active centre for the production of songs and literature concerning the *Kalenderstreit*. The fact that the interrogators only threatened Losch explicitly with torture if he refused to discuss one of these songs suggests that the authorities may have been especially concerned with this mode of discourse.

A more explicit connection between Losch's copied song and the town of Ulm would emerge two days later, when councillors Leonhard Widenmann and Hieronymus Rem subjected him to another round of questioning, this time under torture. Having drawn the weaver up on the strappado, the councillors asked him again about his song. He repeated much of his earlier testimony but added some details of interest.

> Jonas Losch shall be questioned under pain of torture, and the truth shall be brought out of him with all seriousness.
>
> 1. One finds from his first interrogation that he has not been willing to tell the truth; therefore it is decreed that a truthful confession be

brought out of him by the executioner. He should act accordingly and save himself from further pain.

After statement of the first [point in the *Fragstück*]:[24]

2. When and where did he make the song about Doctor Müller and the authorities, and why did he do it, or who compelled him to do it?

> On the second question, he states that on Sunday a week ago an apprentice from the Memmingen area named Michael Karg approached him at the Perlach [tower], and told him that he had a fine song about Doctor Müller and the uprising, and asked him if he also had it. Since he [Losch] did not own it, he led Karg into his house, and copied the printed song there, changing some of the words as he went and adding the last stanza of his own composition. Since the song had no melody [indicated], he copied it in such a way that it could be sung to the tune of *Ich stund an einem Morgen, heimlich an einem Ort*. But the song he copied and altered was not against the authorities, and he did it out of lack of understanding and did not think that it would cause any problems. Furthermore, he understood from the above-mentioned Karg that the printed song had been made in Ulm, and that a month ago [Karg] had heard another song about the uprising and Doctor Müller sung in the public square, and this song was made by a preacher there named Herr Peter. He also states that no one asked him to copy and alter the song, rather he did it for himself. After this [testimony] he was shown another written song about Doctor Müller and the uprising to the tune of *Wo Gott der Herr nicht bei uns hält*, and asked who made it. He answers that Abraham Schädlin, a weaver who also fled the city, made this song.

Thus Losch confirmed that the model for his song was composed in Ulm, and he identified the tune to which it was to be sung: *Ich stund an einem Morgen, heimlich an einem Ort*, a popular secular *Tageslied*. Perhaps the authorities were more troubled, however, by the song *Wo es Gott nit mit Augspurg helt*, for they seem to have hoped that Losch could provide them with the name of its author. Losch having implicated Abraham Schädlin, the scribe took the trouble to write on the back of Losch's *Urgicht*, 'Abraham Schedl, weaver from Augsburg, made the insulting song against the authorities concerning Doctor Müller.' Asked whether anyone else in Augsburg created songs of writings similar to his, Losch implicated Schädlin yet again: 'Abraham Schädlin also makes songs, but he does not know what kind.'

Schädlin certainly would have been arrested at this point had he been

---

[24] 'Nach fürhaltung des ersten', a formula indicating the first statement required no response from the suspect.

in the city, but it is likely that he was still in Ulm at this time. One of Losch's friends, a fellow weaver by the name of Leonhard Deisenhoffer, was not so lucky. As his interview continued, Losch claimed to have torn up the only copy of his song in his jail cell (which explains why no copy of the song survives), but not before having shown it first to Deisenhoffer. This information seems to have prompted the interrogators to draw up a new list of questions, for the *Fragstück* states that 'Jonas Losch soll ferner befragt werd[en] [Jonas Losch shall be questioned further].' Losch admitted in this new round of questioning that he had stayed briefly with Deisenhoffer after having returned from his self-imposed exile in Ulm. The authorities then questioned Losch more sharply about his friend, whom they alleged to have called publicly for the defenestration of the Catholics in Augsburg's city council. Losch denied any knowledge of this and again denied having sung anti-Jesuit songs on the darkened streets. Still dissatisfied with his answers, the councillors had the weaver hauled up on the strappado again, evidently demanding that he tell the 'truth' about his song and about his friend Deisenhoffer:

> After much speaking [to him] and warning, since he was unwilling to admit anything further, he was hauled up without weights,[25] and as he hung on the machine he said that Deisenhoffer had said to him, about four days after the uprising, that those who had dealt with Doctor Müller should themselves be hung from the windows of the Rathaus; further, he copied and gave the song that he had altered and torn up to the painter Lutz, and this Lutz lives by the Brüelprug.[26] After he had been hanging on the machine for a long time, but wished to reveal nothing further, he was let down, and after his statements were read back to him and he confirmed them, he [signed] a confession so that he could be released. Because of this, and since he appeared to be in very bad [condition], and also because the executioner recommended against further torture, he was spared further torture for the present. He begs for mercy by God's will.

Although Losch confessed under torture to hearing Deisenhoffer's seditious statements and to giving a copy of his song to someone else, the painter Lutz, a conviction was technically impossible unless he confessed again *without* torture after a suitable period of time. Another document in the fascicle, dated 6 September, appears to be such a confession:

---

[25] 'Nachdem er nun vber vilfeltig zu sprech[en] vnd vermanen weiter nichts bekhennen wöllen, ist er erstlich mit leeren scheiben aufgezog[en].' Suspects were initially hauled up on the strappado without attached weights ('mit leeren scheiben') but these could be added if he or she continued to resist.

[26] A bridge in the eastern, mostly Protestant quarter of the city.

I wish to state to Your Lordships that it happened that eight days ago an apprentice named Michael Karg approached me at the Perlach and asked me whether I had the song about Doctor Müller and the uprising. I said that I did not, and he said that he did, so he came with me into my house, and I copied it, changing some of the words but adding nothing against the authorities. And I gave it to my godfather Lutz in secret, and he promised me to keep quiet about it, but before this I let Leonhard Deisenhoffer read it. He asked me who made it. I said to him that I made it, and the evil Satan suggested to me that he would make me shame the authorities. But [I swear] as long as God lives that I never had it in my mind to [sing] songs on the streets against the Jesuits, break windows in their church, post or pick up any placards, or do anything else against the authorities. Concerning the other song about the uprising, about which I was questioned and was shown to me, it was indeed Abraham Schädlin who made it here, and it was printed in Ulm and brought back here. Concerning the statement of Leonhard Deisenhoffer, after the uprising he said to me that on that Monday they should have seized those who dealt with Doctor Müller and thrown them [from the windows] of the Rathaus. I know nothing further about him. Therefore I ask you, by Jesus's will, for mercy and charity, that by almighty God I can return to help my poor wife.

Promising to avoid any such activities again, Losch concludes with the assurance that 'I can swear a proper oath that I did not believe this wicked poetry [boß dichten] as much as was supposed of me, God have mercy on me.' Losch essentially confirmed what he had confessed under torture, but insisted on his lack of malice, attributing his actions to the wiles of Satan and to his own ignorance.

It is striking that after two interrogations, extended torture, and a written confession, the authorities still demanded to know more about the song Losch copied and distributed. On 10 September they subjected Losch to a third round of questioning, but without torture:

Jonas Losch, in prison, shall be questioned further.

1. Since he has recently confessed that he altered some words in the song about Doctor Müller and the authorities, and wrote the last stanza entirely himself, [we] wish to know how these words and the last stanza sound.

> On hearing this question he says that he doesn't remember [them] by heart. He only copied them twice; otherwise he would gladly tell.

2. Is not this song, which has been shown to him,[27] the same as the one he received from Michael Karg? Who wrote or it made it?

---

[27] 'Ob nit eben diß Lied, so Ime fürgehalten werden soll' may indicate that the authorities confiscated a copy of the song from Lutz and confronted Losch with it during the interrogation; however, fürhaltung in this case may simply mean that the authorities described it to Losch.

He did not make the whole thing, but altered some of it, and added the last stanza himself. Furthermore, he made the 25th stanza about Doctor Müller's wife.[28]

3. He should clearly and specifically state whatever he made, or altered, in this song.

He added only the two above-mentioned stanzas, and otherwise changed nothing else within.

4. Since this song has a different melody than the one he recently stated, did he not make the entire song himself?

He meant that he had indicated the tune *Ich stund an einem Morgen* at the beginning, and added to this: 'as well as *Lobt Gott, ihr frommen Christen*'. Michael Karg gave this printed song to him originally, and he copied and altered it as stated above.

5. For whom did he copy it, or [to whom] did he give it?

He copied it twice; one [copy] he tore up in prison, and the other he gave to Lutz, which is the same as that described to him.

By God's will he begs for mercy, stating that for the rest of his life he will avoid such things.

Losch's admission that his song could be sung to the tune of *Lobt Gott, ihr frommen Christen* is significant, for this song, unlike the benign *Ich stund an einem Morgen* (a secular *Tageslied*), was a propagandistic song decrying Catholic opposition to Luther's teachings (see Example 2.2), the first five stanzas of which are:

Example 2.2   *Lobt Gott, ihr frommen Christen*

Lobt got, ir frum-men cri - sten, freüt euch und iu - bi - liertt,
Mit da - vid dem psal-mi - sten, der vor der arch ho - fürt:
Die harp-fen hört man klin - gen in teü - scher na - ci - on, dar - umb vil cri - sten
trin - gen zum e - wan - ge - li - on.

---

[28] Georg Müller's wife had died in childbirth and came to be seen as a martyr for the Protestant cause in Augsburg.

1. Lobt got, ir frummen cristen,	Praise God, you pious Christians,
freüt euch und iubiliertt	be glad and rejoice,
Mit david dem psalmisten,	with David the psalmist,
der vor der arch hofürt:	who showed reverence to the Ark:
Die harpfen hört man klingen	The sound of the harp is heard
in teüscher nacion,	in the German nation,
darumb vil cristen tringen	and many Christians
zum ewangelion.	flock to the Gospel.
2. Vor miternacht ist kume[n]	Before midnight came
ain ewangelisch man,	a man of the Gospel,
Die gscrifft hat er für genumen,	he heard the Holy Scripture,
dar mit gezanget an,	and began to say
Das vil der frumen cristen	that many pious Christians
falschlich verfüret seint	have been treacherously deceived
durch falsch ler der sophisten	through the false teachings of the Sophists
und ire wechßel kindt.	and their changelings.
3. Die yetzund grymig schreyen,	Now they shriek bitterly
wanß auff der kantzel stand,	when they stand at the pulpit,
'Mord yber de ketzereyen!'	'Death to the heretics!'
der glaub wil vnnder gann!	The faith will perish!
Des gweichten wassers kraffte	No one will honour the power
will nyemandt achten mer,	of the holy water any longer,
dar zů der briesterschaffte	and no one will show respect or honour
důt man kain zucht noch err!	to the priesthood!
4. 'Wer glaubt auß lutterß lere	'He who believes in Luther's teaching
ist ewiglich verdampt!'	shall be damned forever!'
Des gleichen un[d] anderß mere	For this reason and others
schreyen sy unverschampt,	they shriek without shame,
Dar mit vill cristen treiben	so that many Christians flee
vom ewangelion,	from the Gospel,
die bey dem scoto bleiben	those that remain with [John Duns] Scotus
und seiner opinion.	and his opinion.
5. Ir gsalbten und ir bschoren,	You anointed and bare-headed ones,
lost ab von solchem tandt!	away with such prattle!
Das recht habt yr verloren,	You have lost your claim,
seint gewarnet und vermant:	so be warned and reminded:
Got wil yetz an eüch straffen	God will now punish you
den mord un[d] grossen neyd	with the same murder and great hatred
den ir mit seinen schaffen	that you have visited on his flock
habt triben ain lange zeyt.	for a long time.

It is noteworthy that Losch divulged the tune to the authorities only after having been tortured once, for he may have feared further time on the strappado if did not come clean about the chorale tune.

Losch was sent back to prison, but on the same day the councillors Hieronymus Rem and Leonhard Widenmann interrogated his friend Leonhard Deisenhoffer 'under grave threat of torture'. At this point in the affair the interrogators turned away from Losch's song and began to investigate other aspects of the case, including the allegation that Losch and Deisenhoffer had been posting writings ('Zedell') or placards critical of the authorities. Seeking to determine the source of these writings, the city arrested and interrogated Leonhard's brother Hans as well as Ulrich Müller, a watchman on the Perlach tower. Before being asked about the placards, however, Leonhard Deisenhoffer admitted one other revealing detail about song dissemination:

> 4. It is known that he [Deisenhoffer] has made many shameful songs and writings, and that he keeps them in his house; he should tell us about all of them.
>
>> He has not composed a song in his life, nor has he copied any, since he hardly knows how to write at all, as the enclosed writing [sample] makes clear;[29] he has no songs other than the four which Jonas Losch gave him last St Bartholomew's Day, in return for which he gave him [Losch] a spool [of thread] in a glass. One [song] was against Doctor Müller, another was against those who had produced the aforementioned song, and was composed by Jonas Losch;[30] the third song was about Christ and the Pope, which Losch also made; and the fourth was about Nass, but he doesn't know who composed it.[31] He understood from Losch that he did not compose this song, and that these four songs were only written [and not printed]. Otherwise he [Deisenhoffer] has several printed songs, of which only one is about Doctor Müller and the uprising, which he bought from Aaron Stier; he does not know, however, who composed it.

Since Deisenhoffer could read but not write, he gave Losch a spool of thread ('Haspel'), perhaps useful for weaving, in exchange for four

---

[29] Deisenhoffer's nearly illegible writing sample is included in the fascicle.

[30] 'vnnd sei das ein lied wider D. Müller, das ander wider den jenig[en] so erstermelt lied außgeen lassen, vnd hab solch ander lied der Jonas Losch gemacht ...'. The testimony is confusing but implies that songs both for and against Müller were circulating in the city. Catholics may have disseminated songs critical of Müller, but there may also have been many Protestants who abhorred the civil unrest that he allegedly encouraged.

[31] The name 'Naßen' may refer to the Bavarian preacher Johann Nass (1534–90), a zealous promoter of the cult of the Eucharist who was based at the Jesuit University at Ingolstadt and was supported by Duke Albrecht V. On Nass, see Soergel, *Wondrous in His Saints*, pp. 91–95.

manuscript songs, some of which indeed concerned the affair with Georg Müller. As for the printed song about the uprising that Deisenhoffer admitted to owning, it is curious that he would have been able to purchase it from Aaron Stier, a local bookdealer, for the latter might have expected a harsh punishment for selling such materials within city walls. Although I have not found any criminal proceedings against Stier himself, his wife Barbara would be arrested two years later along with another woman and man for openly selling printed pictures of and songs about Georg Müller (see note 55 below). She would admit to the councillors that she had sold up to 50 copies of a printed song about the preacher, copies which her husband had imported from the Protestant towns of Tübingen and Ulm. In at least a limited fashion, then, local booksellers did aid in the propagation of illicit songs.

In the end, Losch and Deisenhoffer spent another month in prison before being released (20 October) on the condition that they would refrain from any such activities ever again, and report any other offenders to the authorities. These brief prison terms were remarkably light punishment, especially given the recent memory of the *Kalenderstreit* and the openly seditious nature of their statements and songs.[32] However, Losch, Deisenhoffer, and indeed Abraham Schädlin belonged to the large and restive community of Protestant weavers, a group that was suffering from slackening demand for their products and rising inflation, and was increasingly wont to hold Catholic elements in the city government responsible for their woes. The near violence of the *Kalenderstreit* fresh in their minds, the authorities may have feared a new revolt if they meted out harsher punishments such as the pillory or exile. Not surprisingly, the social standing of the convict could have been crucial in assigning an appropriate punishment.

The Case of Anna Borst and Sabina Preiss (1588)

In subsequent years songs about Doctor Müller and the *Kalenderstreit* continued to be of concern to the city council, which in January 1588 arrested two women for singing and distributing such a song in a local hospital. Anna Borst was a 60-year-old widow who worked as a nurse [*Stubenmutter*] there, while Sabina Preiss was a patient, about 24 years old. Both were interrogated on 13 January, along with Sabina's father Leonhard, who had attempted to prevent his daughter's

---

[32] Compare this, however, with the more extreme sentences brought down against Anna Borst and Sabina and Leonhard Preiss (see below), who would not have enjoyed a social network as coherent and collectively powerful as that of the weavers.

arrest.[33] According to Sabina Preiss's testimony (obtained under 'grave threat' of torture), she had been in the hospital for about a year suffering from pain in her limbs. Within a month of her arrival there, Borst had asked her if she could read, and she responded that she could read printed materials, but 'only a little'. Borst's son Hans, a weaver, owned a printed song about Doctor Müller, and the nurse gave it to Preiss, asking her to learn it 'by heart' [außwendig] and read (or perhaps sing) it back to her. After eight or nine weeks Preiss returned the song, having been unable to learn it, 'since there were some very hard words in it'; besides, she had also been ill. Dissatisfied, Borst returned the song to her son.

On the Eve of St Martin's Day (11 November) Anna Borst's son Hans was in hospital with a friend, and they began to discuss the old and new calendars [vom alt[en] vnd neuen Calender zustudiern]. Preiss, who was within earshot, asked them to cease their conversation and sing a song instead:

> Then the nurse said to her son, 'sing the song about Doctor Müller for us'. So her son did, and it happened just so. From this singing she [Preiss] realized that it was the same song that she once had seen in the possession of her brother. Thus she went to him and asked to have it ... and she received it one week before Christmas. She didn't show it to others, or give it to anyone else, but kept it with her at all times.

Preiss admitted that she later sang the song herself in the hospital; the Ziechvatter, an official there, confiscated it. Questioned about the origins of the song, Preiss claimed that she did not know where her brother obtained it. She also denied knowing that such songs were forbidden in the city, or that others had been punished previously for similar offences.

On the same day, the nurse Anna Borst was brought before the judges. She confirmed some of Preiss's story, but deviated from it in other respects. She admitted that she allowed Preiss to sing the song about Doctor Müller, claiming that she would not have allowed it had she known it was forbidden; besides, the Ziechvatter himself had not objected to it (this contradicts Preiss's Urgicht, which states that he confiscated the song). Confronted with the accusation that her own son Hans had sung the song himself in the hospital, Borst insisted that Preiss, along with two other female patients, had put him up to it:

> Her son did not sing this song on his own account; rather Sabina Preiss and two old women, called Appel Schützin and Fridlin, kept

---

[33] StAA, Strafamt, Urgichten, 13 January 1588, Anna Borst [Müller], Sabina Preiss and Leonhard Preiss. Transcriptions in the Appendix, nos 3a and b.

on asking him to sing it, which he did not want to do. There were 21 patients there, and they all gladly listened, but she does not know any of the words herself since she has a poor memory. Truthfully, she must say that this song would have been neither sung nor spoken of had Sabina Preiss not been there. She started it all, she who was once a seamstress in Doctor Müller's house. Otherwise they had never sung very much in their room, for they are all old women who care little for song, since they have their own aches and pains to deal with. But Sabina Preiss came to them, and sang a song once in a while, being still a young person. This time she sang a song called the 'Fool's Vespers', and was punished for it, and told to sing the 'Dorothee' instead.[34] Then she began to sing the song about Doctor Müller, and said that she got it in her brother's house, and her brother was a weaver.

Borst, then, did not admit to giving Preiss the song in the first place months before. Having concluded their interrogation, the judges then brought Sabina Preiss back into the chamber and told her to recount her version of the story in the nurse's presence. Borst then admitted to having given the song to Preiss originally, but claimed that the patient had asked for it:

> Then Borst admits that she first brought the song to Preiss, but Preiss wanted it. Preiss answers that had Borst not spoken of the song herself, then she would not have known that her son had such a song. Moreover, she [Preiss] did not know which song she was talking about, so she asked her whether she meant to sing *Wir müssen alle sterben*. She [Borst] said, 'No, it is about Doctor Müller, and how he was exiled.' That would not be so bad, so she said that yes, she should bring it to her.

Concerning the events of St Martin's Eve, Borst finally admitted that Sabina Preiss was *not* the instigator of the singing, but rather she herself had told her son to sing the song about Doctor Müller. She did so, however, only at the urging of one of the other elderly patients, who 'wished to hear the song once more before her death'. Although (according to Borst) Preiss did not ask Hans Borst to sing, she and another patient promised to pay the boy a half-Batzen and a mug of beer for doing so, even though the boy did not want to sing.

What was this song? Luckily, the exemplar confiscated from Sabina Preiss is preserved along with the *Urgicht* for her father, Leonhard. The octavo print is entitled *Augspurgische Calender Zeittung. Kurtze Historische erzölung deß Calender streits/ vnd darauß entstandenen*

---

[34] Neither the so-called 'Närrisch vesper' nor the 'Dorothee' seem to appear in Franz Magnus Böhme's *Altdeutsches Liederbuch: Volkslieder der Deutschen nach Wort und Weise aus dem 12. bis zum 17. Jahrhundert.* (Leipzig: Breitkopf & Härtel, 1877; repr. Hildesheim: Georg Olms, 1966).

Entpörung zu Augspurg 25. Maij/ 1584 [Augsburg calendar news: brief historical account of the calendar-struggle and the consequent unrest in Augsburg, 25 May 1584].[35] Meant to be sung to the popular tune *Herzog Ernst*, the song decries the city council's actions four years previously. The melody with two stanzas appears in Example 2.3:[36]

Example 2.3   *Ewiger Gott im Höchsten Thron*, contrafactum of *Herzog Ernst*

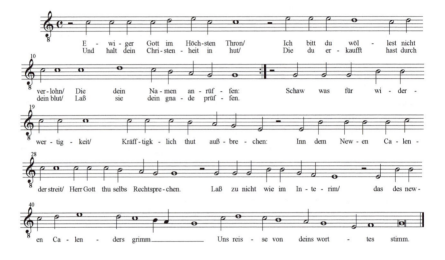

1. Ewiger Gott im Höchsten Thron/
Jch bitt du wöllest nicht verlohn/
Die dein Namen anrüffen:
Vn[d] halt dein Christenheit in hůt/
Die du erkaufft hast durch dein blůt/
Laß sie dein gnade prüffen.
Schaw was für widerwertigkeit/
Kräfftigklich thůt außbrechen:
Jnn dem Newen Calender streit/
Herr Gott thů selbs Recht sprechen.
Laß nicht zu wie im Jnterim/
das deß newen Calenders grim[m]/
Vns reisse von deins worttes Stim[m].

Eternal God in the highest throne,
I ask that you not abandon those that call your name:
and protect Christendom which you have purchased with your blood,
let them see your mercy.
See what resistance breaks out strongly
in the new calendar-struggle,
Lord God, speak your truth.

Do not allow, as in the Interim, that the evil of the new calendar
rips us from the voice of your Word.

---

[35] The date of 25 May instead of 4 June reflects the Protestant adherence to the Julian calendar, which was ten days behind the new Gregorian calendar.

[36] Melody from Böhme's *Altdeutsches Liederbuch*, pp. 19–21, no. 4.

2. Als er zu Augspurg auch einkam/	When it arrived in Augsburg
Der Raht alda jn gleichs annam/	The council accepted it immediately,
Die Protestirendt schare:	The Protestant masses
Die wolt hn gar annemen nicht/	Did not wish to accept it at all,
Nach dem Alten jhr Zeit noch richt/	They still kept to the old time,
Das New verwarffens gare.	and rejected the new.
Das macht vil Zwitracht inn der Statt/	That caused much discord in the city,
Vnrhů vnnd schweres Fechten:	Unrest and rough fighting:
Die Gmein zuwider war dem Raht/	The people were against the council,
Vnd griffen beyd zum Rechten.	And both claimed their rightness.
Das Cammergricht den Außspruch thet/	The [Imperial] court declared
Der Raht das Recht gewon[n]en het/	That the council had won the right,
Drauff folget gar ein scharff Decret.	And there followed a harsh decree.
...	...

Unsurprisingly, the print gives no publication information, as Preiss mentioned during her interrogation. On the back of the print is inscribed 'Sabina Preiss, a patient in the hospital, sang this song in the hospital on 8 June 1585, and the nurse heard this and allowed it.'[37] Since Preiss had only been in the hospital for a year, the date must be erroneous.

The punishments meted out to Anna Borst and Sabina and Leonhard Preiss on 16 January were harsh.[38] Sabina Preiss was immediately exiled from the city 'for having sung a forbidden song about Doctor Müller', and was not allowed to re-enter until 18 May 1589. Her father, having resisted the arrest of his daughter, was also exiled. He attempted to re-enter Augsburg within the next few weeks, but was caught and expelled again on 4 February. Anna Borst, despite her advanced age, received the harshest punishment for giving Preiss a forbidden song about the preacher, telling her to learn it, and then allowing the patient to sing it in the hospital. For her crime Borst too was exiled, and not allowed to return until 5 August 1589, over a year and a half later. Significantly, her son, who had sung in the hospital, was not punished at all. These punishments suggest that the council feared the consequences of singing such songs in the hospital, which was meant to remain a

---

[37] 'Sabina Preisin Spitalerin hab diß lied den 8. Juno anno 85 Im Spital gesung[en] vnd die stuben Muetter In der Newen stuben hat zugehördt vnd Irs verwirdt haben soll.'

[38] StAA, Strafbücher, 1588–96, fol. 2v, 16 January 1588.

confessionally neutral institution. Furthermore, these cases point to the fact that while actual singing was difficult for the authorities to control, they turned aggressively against the dissemination of illicit songs and punished offenders severely.

'Die Zeit die Ist So Trawrigkleich': The Case of Martin Haller (1630)

A few decades later, Protestant resistance against the Augsburg city council would take on a new urgency. On 3 March 1629 Emperor Ferdinand II promulgated the Edict of Restitution, returning to the Catholic Church all properties lost to the Protestants since the previous century and, with few exceptions, banning the observance of Protestant services in the city. When the 14 Protestant pastors refused to comply, they were summarily dismissed by the city council. In the course of the year the now entirely Catholic city council not only took control of such Protestant bastions as St Anna and the Barfüsserkirche, but also strictly forbade private prayer meetings, the preaching of Protestant doctrine and the singing of Protestant psalms and chorales.

It was under this regime that a 53-year-old weaver by the name of Martin Haller was arrested in October 1630 for owning a number of illicit songs. Marcus May, one of the city *Burgermeister*, had reported that Haller not only had behaved offensively during a Catholic baptism in the Johanneskirche, and had failed to give his own children a Catholic baptism, but also was in the possession of a forbidden song against the Catholic church and the Empire.[39] Questioned about the song, Haller refused to give the interrogators the information they wanted:[40]

> 7. Who composed the insulting song found on him, in which it is cried out that the Roman Emperor is a tyrant who should fall on his own sword, that His Princely Grace the Bishop of Augsburg is godless, and that the clergy are the bishop's knaves and a nest of vipers? From whom did he obtain it? And to whom else has he communicated it?
>
>> After much and long questioning and gentle warnings, he explains that he would rather suffer the punishment himself than implicate others and put them in danger. When asked from where he obtained this insulting song, and who composed it, he said that a woman gave it to him, and that he did not compose it himself. He asks that the charges not be pressed further, and that he and others be spared. He protests also that he communicated the song to no one.

---

[39] This testimony is entered at the top of Haller's first *Urgicht*, StAA, Strafamt, Urgichten, 21 October 1630, Martin Haller.

[40] Transcription in the Appendix, no. 4a.

Haller further claimed that he had no intention of attacking the authorities, but rather was following his own conscience. Two songs, in fact, were found in his possession, both of which have been laid into Haller's *Urgicht*. The first is simply titled 'Ein Lied A[nno] 1630' and, based on the prosody of the text, is clearly a contrafact of the chorale *Der Tag der ist so freudenreich*. The first page is reproduced in Figure 2.4.

2.4   First page of manuscript contrafactum, *Die Zeit die ist so Trawrigkleich*, laid into *Urgicht* for Martin Haller. StAA, Strafamt, Urgichten, 21 October 1630

In this song we find some of the attacks on the emperor, bishop, clergy, and local authorities mentioned above. The first few stanzas read as follows:

1. Die Zeit die Ist So
   Trawrigkleich, allen
   Creatura[m] [sic],
   weil in dem Remischen reich,
   Ist überall auffrürisch,
   weil der Keißer ein Eÿd hatt
   geschworen.
   Sein Keißerthumb solt sein
   verlohren:
   Oder er wolt aus Rotten,
   Die Augspurgerisch
   Confession,
   O gott wach auff thue vnß
   beÿstehn,
   Thue des Thÿranne Spotten.

The time is so troubled in all
   creation,

For in the Roman Empire,
There is unrest everywhere,
For the emperor has sworn an
   oath.
He shall either lose his empire,

Or he will destroy
The Augsburg Confession.

O God, rise up and stand by us,

Put down this tyrannical
   mockery.

2. Dÿses Kindelein herr Jesu
   Christ,
   Zue Bethelhem geboren
   der von dem Stamen Juda ist

   kann dem Keißr sein Zorn,

   bald brech[en] durch sein
   starckhe hand,
   das er noch neues mit spott vnd
   schand,
   an sein schwert selber fallen,
   wann er das Maß der Sünden
   sehen
   Erfillet So gibt Gott iedem denn
   lohn,
   wie dann gottloßen allen.

This child, Lord Jesus Christ,

Born in Bethlehem,
Who comes from the tree of
   Judah,
Can soon break the emperor's
   wrath
With his strong hand,

So that he again, with disgrace
   and shame,
Shall fall upon his own sword,
When he sees the amount of his
   sin.
So shall God give each his due,

As to all the godless.

3. O Sonna du gerechtigkeit
   wie tunckhel thuet scheinen,
   Jetzs in dem Remischen Reich,
   mit singen kann Manns
   wewainen,
   den Jumer So in vnßrer Statt,
   der teÿffel an gerichtet hat,
   Durch die beschornen bueben,

   Gott ietzt selber angericht,
   Laß das gottloßen otter gezicht,

   Selbes fallen in die gruben.

O Sun, you righteousness,
How darkly you shine
Now in the Roman Empire.
With singing one can lament

The distress that the Devil
Has caused in our city
Through the bald-headed
   knaves.
God shall now act himself;
Let the godless face of the
   snake
Fall into the grave.

4. Die herren in Augspurger Statt,	The lords in the city of Augsburg
der Euangelischen Scharen,	Over the Protestant masses:
Er füren gar ein schweres manthat,	They carry out a harsh mandate
des Keÿserts Kom[m]ÿsarÿ	Of the emperor's commisar,
des gleiche die Bischoff gottloß,	And of the godless bishop.
aufs Rathauß müessen kohm[m]en,	To the city hall must they come,
die Reinen hirten Jung vnd alt,	The pure flocks, young and old,
wardt der gmeinen mit List vnd gwalt	And God's word is taken away
dz wort Gottes genomen.	From the people with deceit and force.

Haller was not the first to sing a political contrafactum of *Der Tag der ist so freudenreich*: nearly thirty years earlier the weaver Hans Daniel had been arrested and punished for singing the song in a tavern, with a text referring to the contemporary political situation as well as the *Kalenderstreit*.[41] By simply changing one word, the first line of the psalm text offered a clear opportunity to both singers to mount an ironic critique. Haller's second song, written directly after the first, was to be sung to the tune of *Zwey Ding thue ich begehren* and is devotional rather than explicitly political in content. Also included in the fascicle is a tongue-in-cheek 'confession of faith' in which, among other things, Protestants forced to worship according to Catholic mores were to profess that they 'believe in the Virgin Mary, and that she is to be prayed to more highly than the Son of God'.[42]

One day after Haller's first interrogation, his wife Regina wrote to the council asking for his release, claiming that her husband has 'not been well in the head', a defence that Haller would use in later questioning. Further, 'in highest truth he neither wrote nor composed the songs found in his possession, but rather they were given to him. He put them on his books and gave them little thought.'[43] The council certainly was

---

[41] StAA, Strafamt, Urgichten, 7 and 11 January 1602, Hans Daniel. See also StAA, Strafbücher 1596–1605, fol. 160r. Roeck comments on this case at length in *Eine Stadt im Krieg und Frieden*, pp. 180–82. Haller may well have obtained this song from Christoph Glatz, another Protestant who was arrested during this period for the ownership of illicit songs (see Ch. 8 below); the handwriting of Haller's song matches that of a song preserved in Glatz's *Urgicht*, as noted by Roeck in *Eine Stadt im Krieg und Frieden*, p. 668. For other early sixteenth-century contrafacta of this song, see Oettinger, *Music as Propaganda in the German Reformation*, p. 257.

[42] 'Wir glauben an die hailige Jungfrau Maria das sie höher vnd mehr anzuebetten seÿ als der Son Gottes.'

[43] 'Er hieuor ein mal nit recht im kopff gewesen.... So hat Er in höchster Warheit die bei Ime gefundene lieder, selbsten weder erdicht noch gemachet, sondern sÿ sein Ime

unsatisfied with Haller's refusal to identify any accomplices and brought him back for another round of questioning on 25 October. This time he was slightly more forthcoming, but still refused to implicate specific individuals:[44]

> Martin Haller shall be questioned further under grave threat [of torture].
>
> 1. Since in the previous *Urgicht* he did not wish to tell the truth about where he obtained the song along with the rhymed confession [of faith], he should now [tell us], or he may expect different [treatment], for he will not be released until he has confessed the truth.
>
>> After much thorough and serious persuasion that he should willingly tell [us] the desired information, he is not explaining anything; rather he continues to insist that he not be pressed any further, since he wishes to bring danger or difficulty to no one.
>
> 2. Since he has said that he received the song from a woman, one wishes to know who that woman was. And when did she give it to him?
>
>> After his first response, he says that he no longer remembers when he received the song from the woman. However, he confesses that a friend of his wife by the name of Magenbuch, the wife of Wohlkhember, came to his house on a Sunday evening about a quarter-year ago, and brought the song with her. He indeed read it, but was shocked by it, and placed it in his book without thinking about it any further. He did not give it to anyone, even less did he intend that it should find its way to other places, or be found in another form.
>
> 3. Since he knows doubtless who made the song, he should tell us who it was. Otherwise he will be assumed to have been the author, until he names another with good reason.
>
>> He does not know the author of the song himself, and also does not know who made it, but perhaps his wife knows. He begs greatly that she be spared, if at all possible.
>
> 4. Did he, or another, write the song which was found in his possession? Has he given it to others to read or made copies of it? And has he not sung it many times in his workshop and in the taverns?
>
>> He claims no knowledge of this, and his innocence. He protests that, after he read the song and put it away, no one else read it, much less did he give it to anyone to read, or sing it in any place.
>
> ...

---

anderwerts zugestellt worden. Der hats auch auf seine Büecher hinauf geleget, vnd derselben sich nie vil geachtet.'

[44] Transcription in the Appendix, no. 4b.

6. Does he not have more of the same kind of shameful writings? Where are they to be found? And from whom did he receive them?

> He says no, and continues to maintain his innocence. He begs tearfully to be shown mercy, and that he not be forced to name the [other] persons more directly. He asks that he be forgiven, since his fearful heart kept him from knowing what he should say, and so that he will not have to cause any unnecessary troubles for those closest to him. And also because in his understanding he was unable to recognize how improper the [writings] were, and since he did not give the song or the confession to anyone, nor did he keep them with any evil intentions. He also wishes to make it clear that he may not in any case have always been of sound mind, and therefore he asks that much more vigorously for merciful release.

In the following several days Haller's wife sent two letters of intercession on his behalf, claiming in one of them that the songs were left behind in their home by their two sons, who were serving at the time as soldiers in the Imperial army.[45] This testimony, however, did not influence the third interrogation of Haller which took place on 4 November. The council demanded to know how many other songs Barbara Magenbuch brought into his house; Haller insisted that he did not know, paid no attention to them, and could not even remember how they sound.

By the end of October the authorities had located and arrested Barbara Magenbuch, whom they interrogated on the 31st.[46] She freely admitted having given the song *Die Zeit die Ist So Trawrigkleich* to Haller, but also confessed that she had also brought two other songs to him, namely the notorious *Wo es Gott nit mit Augspurg helt*, known as 'Doctor Müller's Song', and *Ach Gott, mein Seel ist sehr betriebt*. Since neither of these songs is preserved in her *Urgicht*, we do not know the precise content of the latter. Claiming that she obtained them from her son, who was a soldier in the Imperial army, she insisted that she had brought them to Haller before any official ban on such materials had been promulgated. Magenbuch, who was 49 years old and had six children, was released from prison one week later. In his interrogation of 4 November, however, Haller continued to beg for mercy, insisting that

---

[45] 'Wann dann Gnedig, gebürttendt vnd groß gl: herrn, es mit Ime erzelte waare beschaffenheit hat, die beÿ Ime gefundene lieder Ime auch in Baaß vnbegert zu hauß gebracht, welche auf beschehene zu red stellung berichtet, dz selbige Ire beede Sön, welche sich newlich vnder der Röm: Kaÿ: Maÿt ~: Kriegsvolckh vnderhallten: hinderlassen, Sÿ auch darauf leben vnd sterben vnd Ir allso wol vnd wehe geschehen lassen können, dz Sÿ nit wisse, wahrer Sÿ sollche gehabt haben.' From letter from Regina Haller and a neighbour to the city council, 26 October 1630, included with the case documents.

[46] StAA, Strafamt, Urgichten, 31 October 1630, Barbara Magenbuech. Transcription in the Appendix, no. 4d.

he had not shown the songs to anyone. Despite this the council decided three days later to place him in the pillory, rebuke him publicly, and expel him from the city. Despite numerous intercessions from friends and family, Haller was not allowed to re-enter Augsburg until 4 May 1632, after the entry of the Swedish armies and the demise of the Catholic city government. Remarkably, the judges never found that Haller actually sang any of these songs in public. It was his ownership of the songs, the suspicion that he had copied and disseminated them, and his refusal to name possible accomplices that brought down the sentence of exile.

Summary and Conclusions

One of the most valuable aspects of the *Urgichten* is the opportunity to reconstruct compelling narratives involving the actions and motivations of specific individuals, narratives that may have greater implications for the study of musical culture. These interrogations shed welcome light on the production, circulation, performance and legal consequences of religious song in an early modern city. They often provide vital information on the ages and social backgrounds of the accused, allowing the scholar to place the individual within a wider network of social relations. Physical evidence included with the documents, especially printed and manuscript songs, may also prove useful. Furthermore, these records paint a vivid picture of the consequences of criminal behaviour, ranging from imprisonment, to judicial torture, to conviction and punishment.

As with any historical document, however, one must approach these sources with caution.[47] Indeed, transcripts of suspects' testimony bring us closer to the elusive 'voice of the people', but this testimony, of course, is mediated by notaries, who may or may not faithfully record the answers. The notary may misunderstand the suspect's dialect, omit testimony, or embellish. It is significant in this regard that testimony is always recorded in the *third* person, not in the first person. The

---

[47] Trial records are one of six 'mediators' of popular culture identified by Peter Burke in *Popular Culture in Early Modern Europe* (rev. repr. Aldershot: Scolar Press; Brookfield, Vt.: Ashgate, 1994), pp. 68–77; all these mediators, which include learned writers, sermons, broadsides and chapbooks, oral traditions, trial records and evidence from riots and rebellions, pose different challenges to the historian of popular culture. In the case of trial records, Burke argues that confessions may not have been spontaneous, but compelled; furthermore, difficulties in translating the dialect of the defendant may bring difficulties. By taking seriously the role of these mediators in distorting our view, one may 'obliquely', rather than directly, arrive at conclusions about the nature of popular culture. On 'oblique' approaches to popular culture, see ibid., pp. 77–87.

Urgichten do provide a glimpse into the social behaviour of singing and song dissemination, but the details of individual cases are always open to question. The threat or application of judicial torture was no guarantee of accurate testimony, even if the process was intended to extract a true and voluntary confession. Finally, these sources tell us much about the concerns of city authorities, who sought at all costs to preserve the religious peace. However, their concerns are not necessarily the same as those of the modern historian. The goal of an interrogation was to establish the details of a crime and to extract a voluntary confession; the individual motivations of the accused, no matter how significant to us, were entirely of secondary importance, and often emerge only as a by-product of the trial process. Given these difficulties, it is vital not to examine these trials in isolation, but rather to search for common themes that emerge from a consideration of many cases, and affect our understanding of production, circulation, performance and the social consequences of singing.

The notion of a 'composer' of popular vernacular song, too, is fraught with difficulties. Certainly there were those who composed melodies, but the vast majority of songs seem to have employed pre-existing tunes, ranging from secular songs to German psalms and Lutheran chorale melodies. Contrafacture, the composition of a new text to be wedded to a well-known tune, was the primary mode of production and, as Oettinger has argued, is indispensable for an understanding of the musical and social significance of song in this era.[48]

The cases against Jonas Losch and Martin Haller both illustrate the process by which a printed song was reworked into a more politically relevant version in manuscript. The creativity involved in transforming one song into another shows that the authors of these contrafacta were not simply illiterate members of the underclass, even if their work circulated among the common people.[49] The surviving evidence suggests that weavers, who collectively formed the largest group of tradesmen in Augsburg, were most likely to be the authors and consumers of such songs. The textile industry, employing thousands of mostly Protestant weaving masters and apprentices, experienced a severe decline in the late

---

[48] See Oettinger, *Music as Propaganda in the German Reformation*, esp. ch. 4. The verb 'to compose', or *komponieren*, indeed turns up in several *Urgichten*, but it always seems to refer to the author of a contrafact text, and not to a composer of melody. A much more common verb associated with contrafacture is *machen*, 'to make'. The creator of the contrafact was often identified as *Author* (author) or *Dichter* (poet), but never as *Komponist* (composer).

[49] Several decades earlier, the repertory of Protestant songs attacking the Interim of 1548 was also largely produced by the educated classes, and later 'soaked through all layers of society' (ibid., p. 144).

sixteenth century as demand slackened. Rapidly rising bread prices also hurt the weavers' overall economic situation.[50] By the time of the *Kalenderstreit* a large, economically disadvantaged class of Protestant weavers held Catholic patricians responsible for its loss of prosperity, and formed a ready audience for polemical songs against the government and Catholic institutions. If the events of 1584 and the increasing assertiveness of the Catholic minority promoted the formation of confessional identity among Augsburg's population at large, financial difficulties accelerated this process among the weavers, who saw Catholicism as a scapegoat for their problems and resorted to resistance, musical and otherwise. Both Jonas Losch and Martin Haller very likely belonged to this disgruntled group, and they used their skills in reading and writing to produce and disseminate a repertory of polemical songs. Others less educated than Jonas Losch, for example, likely saw him as a source for new songs, and in at least one instance a weaver who could read, but not write, bartered with Losch to obtain some of them.

The selection of a tune was a vital stage in the creative process, and authors of contrafacta were often careful to choose a melody that was simple to sing, well known and had symbolic import of its own.[51] Singers of and listeners to 'Doctor Müller's Song', for example, could not fail to recognize the popular melody of *Wo Gott der Herr nicht bei uns hält*, and it is not unlikely that they would have remembered the original text, which decried Catholic resistance to Lutheran 'truths'. Although Losch did not admit it in his first interrogation, he eventually said that he intended his own song to be sung to the tune of *Lobt Gott ihr frommen Christen*, a well-known song with an even more virulent text. In another case to be discussed in Chapter 8, a fisherman by the name of Christoph Glatz was arrested in 1630 for owning an anti-Restitution song meant to be sung to the psalm tune *An Wasserflüssen Babylon*, whose text explicitly treats the theme of exile ('We sat on the shores of Babylon and wept at the memory of Zion').[52] Here the authorities could not have missed Glatz's link between the sorrows of the Hebrews and those of Augsburg's Protestant clergy, which had been dismissed by the city council when the Edict was promulgated the previous year. The song *Die Zeit die Ist So Trawrigkleich* found in Haller's possession, though, takes

---

[50] The fact that weavers tended to be concentrated together in poorer areas of the city, and especially in the northern *Frauenvorstadt* and eastern *Jakobervorstadt* quarters, may have added to the tensions. On the geographical distribution of weavers in Augsburg, see Clasen, 'Arm und Reich in Augsburg', pp. 320–21.

[51] On simplicity as a criterion for the choice of a model, see Oettinger, *Music as Propaganda in the German Reformation*, pp. 93 f.

[52] StAA, Strafamt, Urgichten, 7 March 1630, Christoph Glatz. Bernd Roeck has discussed the symbolism of Glatz's choice in *Eine Stadt im Krieg und Frieden*, pp. 669–71.

a different tack, ironically joining a bitter denunciation of the city government with one of the most traditional Christmas songs in the popular repertory.

For the Augsburg city council, the circulation of illicit songs was equally, if not more, troubling than their performance.[53] Even if singers were prosecuted on occasion, the authorities could hardly expect to stamp out the singing of banned music on public streets, in taverns and in private homes, especially given the popularity of these songs. The authorities hoped, perhaps, to regulate the trafficking of this music more easily than cracking down on singers themselves. One surviving ordinance from 1618 banning the printing or sale of *Pasquille*, including songs, poems and other kinds of writings, points to the authorities' concern:

> As the honourable council in previous years has forbidden printers, booksellers and others ... to print, distribute, publish (openly or in secret) or sell any shameful, frivolous, or insulting books, songs, writings, newsletters, indulgences, paintings and engravings in any language, and particularly those against the Emperor, secular princes, estates and lords, or special persons; thus has this honourable council, not without misgivings, seen and recognized for some time not only that this ban has not been observed, but also that many hateful, blasphemous and insulting placards, poems, shameful writings (mostly in verse), newsletters and images destructive of the peace have been brought into the city, publicly sold, read and sung. ... Therefore all printers, booksellers, illustrators, engravers, sellers of images and songs, writers of newsletters, citizens and foreigners are again ordered from this point forward not to print, import, publish, sell (openly or in secret) or introduce any of the same ... books, writings, tracts, poems, songs, newsletters, paintings, placards or engravings, regardless of religion, and particularly those in which the true author, printer, place of publication and year are not given.[54]

Singing, then, was not treated differently than other modes of public discourse, including the delivery of speeches and the display and

---

[53] For a recent detailed study of the mechanisms and social consequences of censorship in Augsburg, see Allyson F. Creasman, 'Policing the Word: The Control of Print and Public Expression in Early Modern Augsburg, 1520–1648' (Ph.D. diss., University of Virginia, 2002). Creasman argues for a broader definition of censorship that embraces media and modes of communication beyond books and print, traditionally considered to be the principal targets of official bans. With respect to song the Augsburg city council did indeed concentrate its efforts on the elimination of written or printed copies, but this only reflects the difficulty of controlling performance, which remained the most effective and widespread means of transmission.

[54] 'Verbott der *Pasquill*', from 'Statuta civitatis Augustae', vol. 4, pp. 21–23, no. 8, 27 November 1618. D-As, 2° Aug 324, No. 4.

dissemination of poems, images, placards or pamphlets. In fact, certain criminal cases involve several of these media at once: Jonas Losch, for example, was convicted not only of copying forbidden songs but also of posting placards attacking the authorities. The distinction between a 'song' and a 'poem' was not always clear, since song texts were invariably in verse and could be spoken as easily as sung. On the other hand, the sources suggest that song may have been of special concern to the city council, since popular melodies with originally confessional texts like *Wo Gott der Herr nicht bei uns hält, Lobt Gott, ihr frommen* or *An Wasserflüssen Babylon* had strong political symbolism of their own and, together with the new text, could form a potent expression of resistance.

In determining the source of these materials city officials sometimes suspected local printers, who could deliberately omit or falsify publication information on illicit songs. In June 1586 two printers, Hans Schultes and Josias Wörli, were accused of printing a 'song of the preachers' exile' whose title page contained the seal of the city of Nuremberg, even though the authorities were sure that the song had been printed locally.[55] Although Schultes admitted to having carved and printed a woodblock image of Müller, he strongly denied any involvement in printing the song. Wörli, for his part, was accused not only of printing this song but also the infamous *Wo es Gott nit mit Augspurg helt*, which had circulated widely in the direct aftermath of the *Kalenderstreit* (see above).[56] Both Schultes and Wörli were acquitted of

---

[55] StAA, Kalenderstreit-Criminalia, 13 June 1586 (Schultes) and 25 June 1586 (Wörli). Two days before Schultes' interview the authorities interrogated three individuals, a male bookseller and two female accomplices, who were suspected of selling images, poems, and songs about Georg Müller in the city. Although they variously claimed that the songs were printed in Nuremburg, Ulm or Tübingen, they said that Schultes had carved the woodblock image of Müller that they had been selling (see StAA, Kalenderstreit-Criminalia, 11 June 1586, Anton Schneider, Margaret Helbling [Schrötin] and Barbara Zollinger [Stierin]). From the testimony of others it appears that the 'lied von der abschaffung der predicanten' was in fact the old song *Von hertzen thü ichs klagen*, composed by Ulrich Holtzmann and published in 1551, decrying the expulsion of several Protestant preachers from Augsburg during the period of the Interim. With Müller's expulsion in 1584, this event from 30 years earlier would have taken on renewed significance. See Oettinger's detailed discussion of this song in *Music as Propaganda in the German Reformation*, pp. 168–70 and 362–67.

[56] When asked who printed the latter song, Wörli confirmed Jonas Losch's earlier testimony: 'He says no, and testifies to this on his very soul. But it is said that the song about the calendar was made by Abraham Schedle, but he [Wörli] has never seen it himself. It is said that the song was printed in Ulm.' The arrest of Wörli on suspicion of printing Protestant propaganda is ironic, since Wörli's known prints are Catholic in orientation (including the songsheets of Johann Haym for the Trinity Confraternity); from 1591 the printer was active at the cloister print shop of the Benedictine abbey of Thierhaupten. See Layer, *Musik und Musiker der Fuggerzeit*, p. 55.

having printed either of these two inflammatory songs, but city ordinances and the nature of the council's questions make it clear that either would have been punished had he been convicted of printing them.[57]

Although selling these songs, in established bookshops or elsewhere, could result in arrest and punishment, it seems that many were undeterred. The three individuals who implicated the printer Hans Schultes in the above case had been arrested themselves for selling images, poems and songs about Georg Müller.[58] They all admitted their awareness of the ban on materials relating to Georg Müller, but cited their own 'ignorance' (Unbedacht) as an excuse; the male bookseller, Anton Schneider, protested further that he was only seeking 'to earn a few pennies'. Margaret Schrott, one of the two women questioned in the case, claimed that 'many people came to her, and since others were selling [the song about Doctor Müller], they wanted to know why she was not also selling it. They asked why some should be allowed to sell it, while others are not.' It is possible that the three had been involved in such distribution networks for some time; Barbara Stier's husband, the bookseller Aaron Stier, had already been implicated in the case against Leonhard Deisenhoffer (see above), who claimed to have purchased 'a song about Doctor Müller and the unrest' from him. It is perhaps more likely that songs of this kind circulated in more informal channels than bookshops, however. Other cases suggest that economic need compelled some local residents to sell songs door to door, or out of their homes.[59]

---

[57] In 1625 two printers, David Frank and Matthaeus Langenwalter, were in fact convicted of printing forbidden poems, songs and pamphlets, having placed deliberately false publication information on them. They were kept in prison for about two weeks. StAA, Strafbücher, 1615–32, p. 471 (13 February 1625).

[58] StAA, Kalenderstreit-Criminalia, 11 June 1586, Anton Schneider, Margaret Helbling [Schrötin] and Barbara Zollinger [Stierin].

[59] In November 1586, for example, one Regina Hurter was arrested for selling prayers and songs about Doctor Müller door to door. She claimed to have five children, and was pregnant with another; she had also been receiving public assistance for about three years. In her testimony she claimed that her husband had purchased the materials in nearby Ulm from a preacher identified only as 'Herr Peter', and brought them back to Augsburg to be sold. Note that in the case against Jonas Losch, the weaver had also identified a 'Herr Peter' from Ulm who was making songs concerning the Kalenderstreit. Losch and Hurter may have been referring to the preacher Peter Huber, who served as superintendent in Ulm from 1594 onward and was active into the second decade of the seventeenth century. This man and others in nearby Protestant towns may have understood that Augsburg's Protestant community was a ripe market for such music, and used poor Augsburgers like Regina Hurter's husband to spread their wares in the city. On Huber, see D.F. Fritz, Ulmische Kirchengeschichte vom Interim bis zum dreißigjährigen Krieg (1548–1612) (Stuttgart: Chr. Scheufele, [1934]), pp. 216, 293. For the case documents concerning Regina Hurter [Braun], see StAA, Kalenderstreit-Criminalia, 19 November 1586.

Not surprisingly, once illicit songs made their way into the city, the sharing of songs between friends was a primary means of transmission. Jonas Losch obtained the printed model for his contrafactum from a friend of his, Michael Karg, who in turn had bought the song in Ulm. Once he copied the song, Losch then showed it to at least two people, his fellow-weaver Leonhard Deisenhoffer and his godfather, Lutz. It is easily conceivable that people shared this music on public streets, in private homes and in taverns. In March 1630, for example, a local tavern called 'Bey der Gretha' would be the scene of a wager between several men concerning a song protesting the Edict of Restitution, set to the tune of the Lutheran psalm 'An Wasserflüssen Babylon' (this case will be discussed in detail in Chapter 8).

More complicated arrangements such as bartering were possible, however. Since Jonas Losch's friend Deisenhoffer could read but could not write himself, he gave Losch a spool of thread in exchange for four songs in manuscript. These cases illustrate a number of ways in which this music could circulate among people with different levels of education. At the top of this system were literate persons like Jonas Losch, who had the ability to copy old songs and create new ones. Those only able to read could purchase or barter for them, while entirely illiterate persons could learn these songs simply by listening (see below). The tendency of most contrafacta to have a well-known chorale or psalm as their melody ensured their easy memorization.

Performance, of course, was perhaps the most effective means of circulation, since those unable to read or write could learn songs through their singing in public and private circumstances. Robert Scribner has argued that reading aloud was in fact the more usual form of reading in the sixteenth century; thus gatherings in private homes, workshops and inns served as forums for the transmission of potentially unorthodox ideas, whether through prose, poetry or song.[60] The *Urgichten* point to several arenas for the performance of song, including public streets, weddings, taverns and private homes. More important than the locations of singing, however, are the singers' motivations: what led them to sing songs that, in many cases, they knew to be offensive to the city

---

[60] On the continuing importance of oral culture as a mediator of print culture, see Scribner, *Popular Culture and Popular Movements in Reformation Germany*, pp. 49–69. Roger Chartier has cautioned, however, against too radical a distinction between the spheres of individual (silent) and collective reading. Reading aloud remained a popular pastime in elite social circles, while printed matter often found a place in humbler circumstances, 'where it imbued modest objects (which were not by any means always books) with the memory of an important event in the owner's life, recalled strong emotions, and served as a sign of personal identity'. See *The Cultural Uses of Print in Early Modern France*, p. 347.

authorities and banned under city ordinances? Here the *Urgichten* themselves may be less useful, for the singers and owners of songs rarely admitted knowledge of their provocative content. Threatened with judicial torture, most suspects claimed 'lack of understanding' [*Unverstand*], drunkenness or unfamiliarity with the law; those who admitted the inflammatory nature of the songs in their possession often insisted that they did not show their songs to anyone else, but rather kept them to themselves. While it is likely that some of these people did not realize the gravity of what they were doing, the cases taken together suggest certain patterns of performance, patterns that in turn point to the role of song in shaping Protestant identity in a confessional age.

When and where would such songs be performed? Although it would be impossible to define all of the potential settings for performance, at least a few cases suggest that polemical songs against the Catholics were not simply to be consumed in private, but were also used as weapons in public religious controversies. Jonas Losch was accused not simply of singing 'an offensive song about the Pope and the Jesuits' on the street, but also at nighttime, when the daily tumult would have subsided and a larger number of people would have been able to hear Losch through their windows. Losch was also accused simultaneously of breaking a window in one of the Jesuits' buildings, implying that he may have sung his song in close proximity to their college. If these allegations were true, then his performance would have constituted an explicit defiance of the leading local symbols of Roman Catholicism.[61] In another case from 1601 the city accused the weaver Jakob Hötsch of committing a similar act: he sang at least two songs loudly in public, apparently in response to a Jesuit student who was mocking his singing of psalms.[62] Both cases

---

[61] Losch was not directly convicted of this crime, so the truthfulness of the accusation must remain in doubt.

[62] StAA, Strafamt, Urgichten, 27 August 1601, Jakob Hötsch. Hötsch claimed that he had been provoked by a Jesuit student named Ludwig Zimmermann. Questioned on this himself, Zimmermann responded that 'he and Zindelin and Hertfelder often made music in polyphony and monophony [*figuraliter vnd choraliter*] in a certain house, and when they heard Hötsch singing, they laughed, but it was not meant for Hötsch [alone]; only once did he sing *Gegruesset seistu Maria Zart*'. 'Zindelin' here may well refer to Philipp Zindelin, the cornettist and music-teacher attached to the cathedral (see Ch. 4). This was not the first time that Hötsch had been involved in a musical altercation: during his interrogation he claimed that five years previously a Catholic had mocked him for singing psalms in his workshop. A few months after Hötsch's trial a Protestant mason and part-time musician falsely accused a Catholic of making fun of Protestant psalm-singing in the Barfüßerkirche. The mason, who had previously quarrelled with the Catholic, probably hoped that the council would severely punish the Catholic for attacking a practice held dear by many Protestants. However, the mason's ruse was discovered and he was punished for making false charges. StAA, Strafamt, Urgichten, 12 December 1601, Hans Wirth.

suggest the significant role of singing in the formation of confessional identity, and its occasional usefulness in public confrontations.

Rash acts like the public singing by Losch and Hötsch, however, were probably uncommon given the strict official ban on open confessional strife. There were numerous more intimate spaces in which songs against the Catholics and the city government were learned and performed. Jakob Hötsch, for example, admitted to having sung polemical songs in his workplace, and the authorities believed the weaver Martin Haller to have sung his songs in his shop and in local taverns (see above). Taverns, indeed, may have been common meeting places for disgruntled Protestants who, emboldened by drink, sang songs attacking the Catholics and the city government. Another weaver, Hans Daniel, was arrested in January 1602 for singing at least two such songs in a local tavern.[63] One attacked the Dominican Order, while the other was the contrafactum *Die Zeit die Ist So Trawrigkleich*, a copy of which was found 28 years later in the possession of Martin Haller. Daniel, when asked why he sang these songs, could only respond that he did it 'auß vnbedacht[en] muet', or, roughly, 'without thinking'. In this case the judges seem to have sensed no conspiracy; 'since he has greatly asked for mercy', the sentence reads, 'the honourable council has decided on this day [one week after his initial arrest] to release him, having sternly warned him to refrain from this in the future'.[64]

It must be re-emphasized that the idiosyncrasies of the early modern judicial process itself raise significant questions about the reliability of testimony, no matter how compelling. The fact that some suspects answered the judges under torture, or the threat of torture, raises serious questions about their claims concerning their motivations, which they may have shaped to present themselves in the best light. There is reason to doubt, for example, Christoph Glatz's plea that he made his song against the Catholics and the authorities as a 'song of lament with which to console himself' [*ein traur oder klaglied wölle machen, sich damit zu trössten*], given that he did admit to having wagered over the song in a tavern.[65] Other suspects, like Jakob Hötsch, blamed intoxication for their crimes; Martin Haller went further, claiming not to have been of sound mind [*nit allerdings* sanæ mentis *sein möchte*], which does not explain his insistence on not revealing the names of any others who may have provided him with forbidden songs or received such materials from him. As in other cases, the defendant's claims do not always square with

---

[63] StAA, Strafamt, Urgichten, 7 January 1602, Hans Daniel. Bernd Roeck has discussed this case in *Eine Stadt im Krieg und Frieden*, pp. 180–82.

[64] StAA, Strafbücher, 1596–1605, fol. 160r, 15 January 1602.

[65] From StAA, Strafamt, Urgichten, 11 March 1630, Christoph Glatz (with *Urgicht* from 7 March 1630).

the circumstantial evidence, complicating any effort to discover the truthfulness of the testimony.

The threat or application of judicial torture creates new problems, even if it was considered an essential element in uncovering the 'truth' according to the rules of Roman-canon law. Torture was generally not a haphazard or vindictive exercise, but rather a fully integrated and systematized component of the judicial process, and was only to be applied if guilt seemed likely and the defendant remained incalcitrant. The application of torture sometimes extracted the desired confession from the defendant (and seems to have done so in the case of Jonas Losch), but a suspect who withstood torture without confessing had to be declared innocent by the court and released. In 1601 Jakob Hötsch was threatened with torture if he did not reveal the author of a forbidden song in his possession. Hötsch insisted that he did not know who the author was, nor was he the author himself; 'he wishes to state that he will gladly suffer anything [*well darüber gern alles aussteen*], for [the events] happened in just the way he explained above. He was then released.'[66]

If the authorities managed to extract a 'voluntary' confession from a defendant, then they would consider an appropriate punishment. In many of the cases concerning forbidden song, the jail time served by the defendant was considered a sufficient punishment in and of itself. Jonas Losch, for example, remained imprisoned for about a month and a half, while Jakob Hötsch was released after only a few days.[67] These relatively light punishments are difficult to square with some of the harsher penalties dealt to others for similar crimes, such as the exile of Sabina Preiss for over a year, or the exile of Anna Borst for more than a year and a half, despite her advanced age of 60.[68] For his part Martin Haller was banished for almost two years, not being reallowed to return until the Protestant Swedish army had taken control of the city. The differing punishments meted out by the city council may have involved a degree of political calculation. Both Jonas Losch and Jakob Hötsch were weavers, and the city council may have chosen to show them mercy so as not to overly antagonize the large and troubled community of which they were a part. For his part, Hötsch did not lack support from the community: a plea for intercession is included with his case, signed by no fewer than 23 persons. Anna Borst and Sabina and Leonhard Preiss, perhaps, could not expect the same degree of public outrage at their

---

[66] From StAA, Strafamt, Urgichten, 31 August 1601, Jakob Hötsch (included with his *Urgicht* for 27 August 1601).
[67] StAA, Strafbücher, 1596–1605, fol. 149r–v, 1 September 1601.
[68] StAA, Strafbücher, 1588–96, fol. 2v, 16 January 1588.

capture and punishment, and the city resolved to make an example of them.

After the promulgation of the Edict of Restitution in 1629, Catholic officials, backed ultimately by Bavarian military power, were naturally less interested in preserving the rights and privileges of Augsburg's Protestant population, and thus may have moved more decisively against offenders like Martin Haller. The last chapter of this book will return to this final period before the onslaught of the Thirty Years War finally reached Augsburg's gates, a period in which Catholic authorities took even more severe measures against Protestant song despite the resistance of individual singers and larger groups. By contrast, the previous decades beginning with the *Kalenderstreit* in 1584 saw a gradual and uneven crystallization of confessional identity on the part of Augsburg's citizenry, one which found its musical outlet in the processions, pilgrimages and public devotions of Catholics and in the polemical religious contrafacta of Protestant tradesmen.

CHAPTER THREE

Musical Life and Lutheranism at St Anna

If Protestant tradesmen and commoners sought to resist the perceived hegemony of Catholic institutions through the medium of music, the same cannot be said about the leading Protestant musical institution in Augsburg, the cantorate of the church and school of St Anna.[1] Led for over 40 years by the composer, pedagogue and theorist Adam Gumpelzhaimer (1559–1625), the cantorate displayed an ambivalent relationship to contemporary confessional politics, neither participating in activities likely to cause religious friction nor restricting itself to an explicitly 'Protestant' musical repertory. The music library of St Anna, described in detail below, was indeed remarkable in its scope, variety and ecumenism. This relative neutrality in confessional affairs, which contrasts markedly with the musical culture supported by Catholic institutions in Augsburg, can be attributed to at least three factors: the intimate relationship and financial dependence of St Anna on the biconfessional city bureaucracy; the consolidation of an unbroken and conservative tradition of Protestant sacred music (unlike the music of Catholic institutions, which had to be invented anew after the Peace of Augsburg); and Gumpelzhaimer's own educational background in Catholic institutions.

Converted from a Carmelite monastery in 1525 by the former prior Johannes Frosch, a zealous partisan of Luther, St Anna became the institutional centre of the Reformation, that swept through the city in the late 1520s and 1530s.[2] Its Gymnasium, founded in 1531, was the

---

[1] Studies of musical repertories at St Anna include Otto Mayr, 'Adam Gumpelzhaimer: Ein Beitrag zur Musikgeschichte der Stadt Augsburg im 16. und 17. Jahrhundert' (Phil. Diss., Munich, 1908) and his edition of Adam Gumpelzhaimer, *Ausgewählte Werke*; also Richard Schaal, *Das Inventar der Kantorei Sankt Anna in Augsburg: Ein Beitrag zur protestantischen Musikpflege im 16. und beginnenden 17. Jahrhundert* (Kassel: Internationale Vereinigung der Musikbibliotheken, Internationale Gesellschaft für Musikwissenschaft, 1965); and Richard Charteris, *Adam Gumpelzhaimer's Little-Known Score Books in Berlin and Kraków* (Neuhausen: Hänssler-Verlag; American Institute of Musicology, 1996).

[2] Frosch sheltered the fugitive Luther in 1518 and followed his mentor to Wittenberg, where he received his doctorate in theology before returning to Augsburg. In 1531, as Zwinglian elements took over Augsburg's city government, Frosch was relieved of his duties and spent the last years of his life at St Sebald's church in Nuremberg. Although he

first of its kind in Swabia, and from an early stage included singing in its curriculum. Responding in part to the popularity of the new Jesuit College at St Salvator, which offered a rigorous education to poor students at no cost, a number of Protestant citizens helped to endow a similar *Kollegium* at St Anna in 1582, initially admitting 30 students.[3] At this time the city engaged Adam Gumpelzhaimer, a native of Trostberg in Bavaria and a former student at the church school of SS Ulrich and Afra, as preceptor and cantor, charging him with responsibility for music at St Anna as well as the basic education of the youngest class of boys. During the 45 years of his tenure Gumpelzhaimer raised the musical standards of St Anna to an unprecedented level through his musical pedagogy, compositions and cultivation of one of the richest school music libraries in Germany.

In the light of Gumpelzhaimer's position at the heart of Protestant culture in Augsburg, his lifelong connections with Catholics and Catholic institutions inside and outside of the city is striking, and provides evidence that he had little interest in contemporary confessional frictions.[4] The Protestant branch of his family may have fled their traditional base in the Bavarian Catholic town of Wasserburg am Inn to settle in Trostberg in the mid-sixteenth century,[5] but he was educated almost entirely under the auspices of Catholic institutions. As a boy he studied music with Jodocus Entzenmüller at the Benedictine school of SS Ulrich and Afra in Augsburg, and may have travelled to Munich around 1570 to perform in the ducal chapel's choir under the direction of Orlando di Lasso.[6] Shortly after his appointment at St Anna in 1582 Gumpelzhaimer matriculated at the Jesuit-controlled university in

---

composed some music (some of which appeared in the *Form und Ordnung Gaystlicher Gesang vnd Psalmen, auch etlich Hymnus, welche Gott dem Herren zu lob gesungen werden* of 1529), Frosch is not identical with the author of the music treatise *Rerum Musicarum Opusculum rarum ac insigne*, published in Strasbourg in 1535. See G. Franz, 'Johannes Frosch, Theologe und Musiker in einer Person?', *Die Musikforschung*, **28** (1975), pp. 71–75.

[3] See Mayr, 'Adam Gumpelzhaimer', pp. 8–9.

[4] Karl Batz has also made this point with reference to Gumpelzhaimer's attendance at the University of Ingolstadt, a Jesuit-run institution. See Batz, 'Universität und Musik', in Hofmann, ed., *Musik in Ingolstadt*, pp. 116–17.

[5] Mayr, in Gumpelzhaimer, *Ausgewählte Werke*, pp. 9–10. This edition, and Mayr's dissertation, 'Adam Gumpelzhaimer', remain the most substantial secondary sources for Gumpelzhaimer's life and works.

[6] On Gumpelzhaimer, Entzenmüller, and SS Ulrich and Afra, see esp. Mayr, 'Adam Gumpelzhaimer', pp. 3–4, and Gumpelzhaimer, *Ausgewählte Werke*, pp. 10–11. Adolf Sandberger, in *Beiträge zur Geschichte der bayerischen Hofkapelle unter Orlando di Lasso. Drittes Buch: Dokumente. Erster Theil* (Leipzig: Breitkopf & Härtel, 1895), pp. 47 and 52, inferred Gumpelzhaimer's presence in Lasso's choir from two entries in the chapel's account books: '1570. Den 20 Oktober ainem Priester von AugsPurg wegen etlicher Cantorey

nearby Ingolstadt in order to obtain his *Magister* degree. His activities and the extent of his associations at Ingolstadt are unknown, but Otto Mayr pointed to a possible connection there with certain members of the Fugger family.[7] Upon returning to Augsburg, Gumpelzhaimer almost certainly became acquainted with the local Catholic composers Christian Erbach, Gregor Aichinger and Philipp Zindelin, many of whose works would be copied into the St Anna choirbooks.[8]

Among Gumpelzhaimer's responsibilities was the administration of the school's *Kurrendengesang*, the regular singing before the homes of well-to-do citizens as a means of supplementing students' income. Trained choirs singing figural music (and perhaps, polychoral repertories), as well as younger groups of boys singing psalms, chorales and simple songs (the so-called *Psalmrotten*) sang in the streets on Friday mornings and on Sundays after the sermon. The specific repertory performed is not clear, but there is some evidence to suggest that the city council regarded the practice with some suspicion; we have already seen the council's intense interest in controlling the public performance of religious song by individuals. The authorities may have been concerned by the rapid expansion of street-singing in the mid-sixteenth century: the practice had begun with a modest number of students from St Anna in 1535, but by 1560 some 80 students were taking part, and they were joined by Catholic student choirs from the cathedral and from St Moritz.[9]

The establishment of Catholic and Protestant *Kollegia* – offering a free education to local students – at St Salvator and St Anna in the early

---

Khnaben ver Ehrung 12 fl.' (the 'Priester' is probably Johannes Dreer, the choir director at the abbey and noted copyist of Lasso's works); the other entry reads: '1571. Dem KaPelmeister zur Abuertigung aines Canntorey Knaben von AugsPurg 6 fl.'

[7] Gumpelzhaimer's name appears directly below those of Constantine, Troianus and Matthias Fugger in the matriculation register; see Mayr, in Gumpelzhaimer, *Ausgewählte Werke*, p. 21. There is no evidence to support the possibility, suggested ibid., p. 11, that Gumpelzhaimer studied in Italy with financial assistance from the Fugger family.

[8] See Charteris, *Adam Gumpelzhaimer's Little-Known Score Books*. The appearance of a number of *unica* by Erbach (see, for example, *Sepelierunt Stephanum*, *Peccantem me quotidie*, *Dic nobis Maria quid vidisti*, *Immolatus est Christus*, *O Jesu rein ich druck der Pein* and the canzona *La Paglia* in the Berlin manuscript (Mus. Ms. 40028)) suggests a particularly close relationship between the two composers.

[9] At that time the city council insisted that Catholic choirs *not* sing in Latin, a practice to which they had been accustomed; see below. After this time only choirs from St Anna, St Ulrich (the Protestant church attached to Ulrich and Afra), St Moritz and the cathedral were permitted to sing on Saturdays and Sundays. See Mayr, in Gumpelzhaimer, *Ausgewählte Werke*, p. 13. On the numbers of students involved in St Anna's street choir, see Alfons Singer, 'Leben und Werke des Augsburger Domkapellmeisters Bernhardus Klingenstein 1545–1645' (Inaug. Diss., Munich, 1921), pp. 44–45, and Mayr, in Gumpelzhaimer, *Ausgewählte Werke*, p. 13.

1580s may have been the pretext for the city council's banning of street-singing altogether as unnecessary for the students' upkeep. A concerted effort by Gumpelzhaimer, together with the faculty of St Anna, helped to reinstate the practice at that institution in 1596,[10] but in turn the choirs were expected to abide by city ordinances banning religiously inflammatory songs. The city council, recommending on 17 August 1596 that street-singing be reinstated, stipulated that 'the students shall refrain entirely from songs that are forbidden or otherwise incite trouble'.[11] A report in the following year by the city's school administrators suggests one reason why the council felt the need to be so explicit: unapproved groups of foreign students were also singing for money (and thus depriving the St Anna cantorate of part of its income); these youths 'behave immodestly, with insulting, mocking words, and [comport themselves] unpleasantly towards reputable, notable citizens and residents'.[12] Thus after 1596 the St Anna street choirs were obligated to police themselves carefully: their repertory, along with their dress and general behaviour, were strictly regulated by the school's staff, which in turn reported directly to city officials.[13]

Inside the walls of St Anna, Gumpelzhaimer's own musical activities reflected his preoccupation with music pedagogy and the daily execution of his duties, which may have been sufficiently onerous to prevent him from composing and publishing as much as he would have

---

[10] The negotiations between St Anna and the city magistrates are discussed by Mayr, in Gumpelzhaimer, *Ausgewählte Werke*, pp. 15–17. Original documentation, including supplications by Gumpelzhaimer and Georg Henisch, as well as the recommendation by the *Unterschulherren* that street singing be reinstated, may be found in StAA, EWA 1042.

[11] 'den vnnd[er]schuellherren Ist Ir begeren, des vmbsingens zue vnnderhaltung der Cantarey bey S. Anna, bewilligt, die Schueller sollen sie aber verbotten auch sonnsten zue widerwillen anraitzennden gesanngen, genntzlich endthalten, *Decretum in Senatu Secretiori .17. Augustj. 1596.*' Laid in with a supplication (1596) by Adam Gumpelzhaimer to the *Schulherren* (1596), StAA, EWA 1042.

[12] 'Dieweil aber solche vnbekhandte frembdling E: G: Hrt: vnnd Gsten: gemainer Stat Schuelen vnnd deren *præceptorib[us]* mit der *disciplin* nit vnderworffen, vil münder das sich dieselbigen beÿ Ihne[n] erzaigt, oder der Euangelischen Kürchen ordenlichen vnnd erlaubten *Musicanten* einuerleibt, sondern vnseren alten Schuel Ordnung strackhs entgegen, mit Iren Seÿtten wöhren Erntzig herrumber Singen, vnnd sich vnbeschaidenlichen mit Spöttischen, hönischen worten vnnd ganntz vnuernüeglich gegen ansehenlichen Namhafften burgern vnnd Innwonnern erzaigt vnnd verhalten, darneben sie auch vnderstanden, Etliche von vnseren *præfecto Musicæ* bestelte vnnd angenomne *Musicanten* an sich zulockhen vnnd zuuerfuhren, darauß aber anders nichts dann ein muettwillige vermessenheit vnnd vnleidenliche *Confusion* der *Musica* eruolgen mueß'; StAA, EWA 1042 (27 February 1597). It is not clear, however, that these groups were using religious insults.

[13] For details on the respective obligations of the *praefectus musicorum* and the singers themselves, see Mayr, in Gumpelzhaimer, *Ausgewählte Werke*, pp. 15–17.

liked.[14] At least two of his publications are entirely pedagogical: the well-known *Compendium musicae* of 1591 and the *Contrapunctus quatuor & quinque vocum* of 1595.[15] His popular *Compendium*, based on Heinrich Faber's *Compendiolum musicae* of 1548 and its German translation (1572) by Christoph Rid, presents a comprehensive course in basic musical instruction and includes numerous (mostly conservative) examples by Lasso, Josquin, Jakob Reiner, Hans Leo Hassler, Fernando de Las Infantas and Gumpelzhaimer himself. The *Compendium* (stressing the simple counterpoint of the *bicinium*)[16] and the *Contrapunctus* together stress the pedagogical value of writing musical canons. Given the practical aims of these collections it is not surprising that the pieces composed and selected by Gumpelzhaimer do not suggest a specific confessional orientation.

Pedagogy was indeed one of several appropriate contexts for Gumpelzhaimer's output of strophic, canzonetta- or villanella-inspired compositions. His collection of *Neüe Teütsche Geistliche Lieder* [New German Sacred Songs] of 1591, scored for three voices, was the first of these collections. In the dedication to this volume, directed to the four *Schulherren* appointed by the city council to oversee the schools, Gumpelzhaimer wrote that these works were not only valuable in that their sacred texts reminded the educated of spiritual things, but they would also have 'the same use among youth, in addition to [their] recreation'.[17] Though scored for Cantus, Altus, and Bassus, the high clef

---

[14] See Mayr, 'Adam Gumpelzhaimer', p. 31 and Gumpelzhaimer, *Ausgewählte Werke*, p. 28. Karl Pittroff suggested that this may partly explain the richness of St Anna's music library, for the cantor would have had to rely on purchased or copied music; see 'Aus vier Jahrhunderten evangelischer Kirchenmusik in Augsburg', *Zeitschrift für evangelische Kirchenmusik*, 9 (1931), p. 120. The demands of teaching together with mounting economic difficulties led Gumpelzhaimer to ask the city council for salary raises in 1599 and 1606.

[15] *Compendium Musicae, pro illius Artis Tironibus. A. M. Heinrico Fabro Latine conscriptum, & a M. Christophoro Rid in vernaculum Sermonem conversum, nunc Praeceptis & Exemplis auctum* (Augsburg: Valentin Schönig, 1591; RISM A/I, G5116; twelve further editions of this popular manual appeared between 1595 and 1681); and *Contrapunctus quatuor & quinque Vocum* (Augsburg: Valentin Schönig, 1595; RISM A/I, G5137, with one later edition in 1625).

[16] Gumpelzhaimer in fact attached a set of *bicinia* (mostly by Orlando di Lasso and himself) to the second edition of the *Compendium* in 1595, the *Bicinia sacra in Usum Juventutis scholasticæ collecta* (Augsburg: Valentin Schönig). The genre of the *bicinium* was held to be of particular value in the Protestant Latin schools of the sixteenth century, where it served as a vehicle for instruction in counterpoint. See Bruce A. Bellingham, 'The Bicinium in the Lutheran Latin Schools during the Reformation Period' (Ph.D. diss., University of Toronto, 1971).

[17] 'Dan[n] dise löbliche Kunst die Music neben dem/ dz sie die Leüt auffmundert/ vn[d] frölich macht/ auch disen trefflichen nutzen hat/ das sie bei dem Text/ so mehrers teils vnd

combination of G$_2$, G$_2$, and C$_3$ suggests the book's usefulness for the training of choirboys (the possibility, however, of downward transposition into the indicated ranges should not be discounted). Furthermore, the texts and given occasions for the 27 pieces in this volume suggest not only liturgical usage, but also the daily routines of schoolboys. Gumpelzhaimer identifies several of the pieces as appropriate for given feasts of the church year: *Gott Vatter vns sein Son fürstelt* for the First Sunday of Advent, *Auff dein zukunfft Herr Jesu Christ* for the Second Sunday of Advent, *Herr Jesu dein Barmhertzigkeit* for the Third Sunday of Trinity, and so forth. He labels many other pieces, however, as appropriate for routine daily observances, such as *Wenn vns die sorg will krencken, O Gott vn[d] Herr, dein ist die ehr* and *Herr Gott zu dir, Mit gantzer gier* for grace at table, or *Die nacht ist kummen* for the evening benediction. Still other pieces are given no particular context, including many German translations of psalms or biblical phrases. Gumpelzhaimer sets a mixture of psalms, chorales, and biblical paraphrases, some in both German and Latin; confessionally inflammatory texts like *Erhalt uns Herr bei deinem Wort* and *Wo Gott der Herr nicht bei uns hält* are conspicuous by their absence.

Although the high percentage of chorale texts and psalm translations identifies this book and other similar volumes by Gumpelzhaimer as a Protestant collection, there is little attempt to embrace the kinds of divisive confessional symbols embodied in the Marian and Eucharistic polyphony of Augsburg's Catholic composers. A case in point is Gumpelzhaimer's setting of Psalm 124, *Nisi quia erat Dominus* (see Ex. 3.1). The psalm's most popular German paraphrase was that of Justus Jonas, *Wo Gott der Herr nicht bei uns hält*, a highly inflammatory text that served as the model for Abraham Schädlin's *Wo es Gott nit mit Augspurg helt* (see Chapter 2). In his version, however, Gumpelzhaimer avoids Jonas's well-known polemic and sets a different translation in which the enemies of Christendom – an idea that, indeed, is derived from the original Latin psalm – are defined more abstractly. The piece, written in the stylish and accessible idiom of the Italian villanella, has the following text:

billich auß heiliger Schrifft genommen wirdt/ vnd hoher vn[d] Göttlicher sachen erin[n]ert. Daher vns auch der Apostel zugemelter übung Geistlicher Gsang nit nur einmal vermanet: Vnd ein alter Lerer saget/ das die Music benem[m]e den vnmůt/ wellicher die gemüter verdunckle/ vnnd von betrachtung hoher sachen abhalte. Solche[n] vnd dergleichen nutze[n] auch bei der Jugent/ neben der belustigung/ zuschaffen: Hab ich dise schöne Geistliche Text/ nach verrichtung meiner obligenden dienst/ zu meiner zeit/ mit dreien Stim[m]en/ nach art der Welschen Villanellen/ gesetzt vnd zusammen getragen/'. From dedication to Gumpelzhaimer, *Neüe Teütsche Geistliche Lieder, mit dreien Stimmen, nach art der Welschen Villanellen, welche nit allein lieblich zusingen, sondern auch auff allerlei Instrumenten zugebrauchen* (Augsburg: Valentin Schönig, 1591; RISM A/I, G5129).

Example 3.1   Gumpelzhaimer, *Von gferlikeit der Christenheit*, from *Neüe Teütsche Geistliche Lieder*, vol. 1 (1591)

Von gferlikeit der Christenheit/	Of the danger to Christendom
hört man noch täglich klagen/	One hears daily laments,
Nach grosser not/ mord/ bra[n]d vn[d] tod/	Of great need, murder, fire and death.
die Christen billich sagen/	The Christians rightly say,
Wann Gott der Herr/ nicht bei vns wer/	If the Lord God were not with us,
Vnd hillf vns vber winden/	And helped us to prevail,
Kein Mensch auff Erd/ blib für gferd/	No man on earth would be safe,
Kein Christ wer mer zufinden.	No Christian would again be found.
Fürwar nun kan/ Ein Christenman/	Indeed a Christian man
Von seinen Feinden sagen/	May say of his enemies,
Wann Gott der Herr/ Nicht bei vns wer/	If the Lord God were not with us,
Wir hetten müst verzagen/	We would have to lose all hope,
Dann sich die Feind/ All auffgeleint/	Then the infuriated enemy
Sie theten grausam streiten/	Would evilly attack;
Die Christen schar/ Wolten sie gar/	With their violence they hope
Mit jrem gwalt außreütten.	To destroy the Christian flock.

This translation of Psalm 124 appears neither in Wackernagel's chorale text compendium nor in Zahn's collection of melodies, possibly pointing to its composition by Gumpelzhaimer or one of his colleagues at St Anna. In fact, Gumpelzhaimer consistently rejected the more popular translations of the Psalms in this first book of sacred villanellas, such as *Erhör mich wann ich rufe zu dir* for Psalm 4, or *Wohl dem, dem die Übertretungen vergeben sind* for Psalm 32 (although in neither of these two cases can the usual translation be considered inflammatory). With the exception of two traditional chorale motets (*Vom Himmel hoch da komm ich her* and *Gelobet seist du Jesu Christ*) in the second book of his *Wirtzgärtlins* in 1619, Gumpelzhaimer avoided cantus-firmus technique, thus refraining from any suggestion of the original melodies. It is impossible to say whether he did this on artistic or on religious grounds, but the overall profile of these pieces suggests little interest in overt confessional symbolism on the composer's part.

Similarly, little evidence of explicit confessionalism can be found in a series of small collections of vernacular sacred lieder brought out by Gumpelzhaimer between 1617 and 1620. The *Zehen Geistliche Lieder mit 4. Stimmen, Jungen Singknaben zu gut auff etliche Fest gericht* [Ten Sacred Songs for Four Voices, Arranged for Young Choirboys for Several Feasts] of 1617, for example, provides a set of simple polyphonic settings of traditional chorale melodies for the use of choirboys on major feast days.[18] Another collection of five songs, *Fünff geistliche Lieder zu 4. Stimmen*, appeared in the same year and provided a similar repertory for the feasts of the Ascension, Trinity and St Michael Archangel.[19] Although the feast of St Michael continued to be observed in the Protestant church, Catholics had by this time seized upon the saint as a symbol of the Catholic Church triumphant. This did not deter Gumpelzhaimer, however, from including one song for the feast with the macaronic Latin and German text *Creare te purissimos / Gott du hast bstelt die Engel rein*.[20] Other small books of Gumpelzhaimer's songs for Christmas and Lent, published around this time, are traditional in textual orientation and were probably intended for pedagogical or private use.[21]

Gumpelzhaimer's most substantial musical compositions are found in his two books of motets, *Sacrorum Concentuum ... Liber primus* and *Liber secundus*, published in Augsburg in 1601 and 1614 respectively.[22]

---

[18] Augsburg: Johann Ulrich Schönig, 1617; RISM A/I, G5144. Gumpelzhaimer provides settings of *Als der gütige Gott/ Vollenden wolt sein Wort* for Annunciation; *Lob sei dem Allmächtigen GOTT* and *A solis ortus cardine*, and *Puer natus in Bethlehem* for Christmas; *Helfft mir Gotts gütte preisen* for the New Year; *O GOTT laß mich nit sincken* for times of 'fear and need' [*Jn Angst vnd Nötten*]; *Wenn wir in[n] höchsten nöten sein* for times of plague; *Herr JESV Christ war Mensch vnd GOTT* for one's deathbed; *Ihr lieben Christen freund euch nun* for the Day of Judgment; and *Sei Lob/ ehr/ preis vnd Herrligkeit* for the Holy Trinity.

[19] Augsburg: Johann Ulrich Schönig, 1617; RISM A/I, G5145.

[20] In the Augsburg diocese, Bishop Heinrich V had mandated special observance of the feast of St Michael in 1605, 'memores hunc Principem Caelestis militiae, Praefectumque a Deo Ecclesiae militanti & propugnatorem fortissimum Imperio Romano concessum'. See 'Bischofl. Erlass wegen feÿer der feste Maria Geburt und St. Michael in sämtlichen Kirchen', StAA, KWA B10[11]. The new Jesuit church in Munich was consecrated in the name of St Michael in 1597, and the symbolism of the archangel as a Catholic champion was stressed in the interior and external decoration, as well as in the elaborate Jesuit play *Der Triumph des hl. Michael* on the occasion of the church's consecration. See Paul Mai, 'Die Michaelsverehrung an der Schwelle zur Neuzeit', in *idem*, ed., *Sankt Michael in Bayern*, pp. 31–35. On the symbolism of St Michael in Peter Paul Rubens's canvases for Duke Wolfgang Wilhelm of nearby Pfalz-Neuburg in the early seventeenth century, see also Franz Josef Merkl, 'Kunst und Konfessionalisierung – das Herzogtum Pfalz-Neuburg 1542–1650', *JVAB*, **32** (1998), pp. 188–211.

[21] See his *Zwey Geistliche Lieder, zu vier Stimmen, von dem H. Leiden und Auferstehung unsers Herren und Heilands Jesu Christi* (Augsburg: Johann Ulrich Schönig, 1617; RISM A/I, G5146), *Zwai Schöne Weihenächt Lieder* (Augsburg: Johann Ulrich Schönig, 1618; RISM A/I, G5147) and *Christliches Weihenacht Gesang Zu Ein und Außgang eines Fried und Freudenreichen Neuen Jahrs* (Augsburg: David Frank, 1620; RISM A/I, G5148).

[22] *Sacrorum Concentuum octonis Vocibus modulandorum ... Liber Primus* (Augsburg: Valentin Schönig, 1601; RISM A/I, G5139); and *Sacrorum Concentuum octonis Vocibus modulandorum cum duplici Basso ad Organorum Usum ... Liber Secundus* (Augsburg: Valentin Schönig, 1614; RISM A/I, G5143). As the title implies, the second volume was provided with a continuo part, but it is entirely of a *basso seguente* nature and has little

The dedications to these two volumes reflect Gumpelzhaimer's close ties with and financial dependence upon the city administration: the first volume is dedicated to eight Protestant members of the city council, while the second is dedicated to the seven members of the *Geheimer Rat*, the topmost city authority.[23] Not surprisingly, the contents of these two volumes – consisting of Venetian-inspired works for double choir – have a confessionally neutral character, befitting Gumpelzhaimer's position as an employee of a biconfessional city administration. All of the 28 pieces in the first volume set Latin texts, including 15 psalms; the remainder include Gregorian texts for Holy Week and Easter (the antiphon *Vespere autem sabathi venit Maria Magdalena* for Vespers on Holy Saturday, and the responsory *Maria Magdalena et altera Maria* for Easter), as well as a responsory for the feast of St Michael (*Venit Michael Archangelus*). Likewise, the majority of the 24 works in the second volume are settings of Latin texts, including nine psalms, three biblical verses, and several Gregorian antiphons; in addition we find Greek versions of the Pater Noster and *Ave gratia plena*, a passage from Luke recording the Annunciation of the Virgin Mary, as well as three German-language settings: Psalm 71 (*Auff dich mein Gott vnd Herr allein*), Psalm 124 (*Von gfärligkeit der Christenheit*) and the Lutheran chorale *Was mein Gott will das gschech allzeyt*. In short, Gumpelzhaimer provided a collection of mostly Latin music that was unlikely to raise any eyebrows, outfitted with fashionable Venetian-style settings for double choir, and attractive to Protestant and Catholic choirs alike. The same cannot be said for the contemporary compositions of Catholic composers like Aichinger and Erbach, who tended to turn in this period towards settings of Marian or Eucharistic devotional texts.

Confessional Ecumenism in the Music Library of St Anna

As the next chapter outlines, the surviving records of music acquisitions by the Augsburg Cathedral chapter in the late sixteenth and early

---

independence. Many of these pieces were taken into the anthologies of Erhard Bodenschatz, although without attribution; see Werner Braun, 'Kompositionen von Adam Gumpelzhaimer im Florilegium Portense', *Die Musikforschung*, 33 (1980), pp. 132–35.

[23] The dedicatees of vol. 1 are Johann Georg and Daniel Österreicher, Johann Staininger, Markus Hopfer, Martin Zobel, Johann Philipp Scheler, Philipp Zeller and Melchior Erhart (see Mayr, in Gumpelzhaimer, *Ausgewählte Werke*, p. 26). Members of the Österreicher, Hopfer, Staininger and Scheler families in particular joined the entirely Protestant city council after the Swedish takeover of Augsburg in 1632; see Roeck, *Eine Stadt im Krieg und Frieden*, p. 715 n. Despite their confessional orientation, none of these councillors was notable for confessional polemics. Both of the *Stadtpfleger* honoured in the dedication to Gumpelzhaimer's second book, Marcus Welser and Johann Jakob Rembold, were Catholics, while the remaining dedicatees were a confessionally mixed group.

seventeenth centuries point to a strong preference for sacred music by Catholic composers or from Catholic territories. St Anna most certainly did not provide a Protestant parallel. The music library contained not only numerous prints by Catholic composers, but also a significant amount of secular music, including many collections of Italian canzonettas and madrigals. Of course, not all this music was intended to be sung during church services; much of it, in fact, may have been intended for music pedagogy or for the choir's street-singing; nor does its purchase by the cantorate prove that it was routinely performed. However, the sheer diversity and quality of the music present at St Anna suggests, at least, that confessional purity was not a criterion for the music's purchase. A surviving inventory of the music books at St Anna in 1620, with additions in 1625 and later years, demonstrates this ecumenism clearly.[24]

The inventory contains references to over 90 collections of music, including single-composer prints and anthologies, in both manuscript and printed form. It is alphabetically organized, and does not suggest a distinction according to the nature of the texts, or even according to the division of sacred from secular. Apart from printed and manuscript anthologies, the composers most often mentioned in the inventory are Michael Praetorius (nine entries), Orlando di Lasso (six entries), Hans Leo Hassler (five entries), and Gumpelzhaimer himself (four entries). Gumpelzhaimer's Augsburg colleague Christian Erbach, however, is only represented by one volume (his *Modorum sacrorum … Liber secundus* of 1604), while Gregor Aichinger and Philipp Zindelin are entirely absent. Other Catholic composers and works with Marian texts, however, are liberally represented. For example, the 'Cant[iones] sacrae' by Orlando di Lasso identified close to the beginning of the inventory is in fact a collection of Magnificats by Orlando and his son Ferdinand.[25] Although polyphonic Magnificats certainly held a place in the Protestant liturgy, Marian litanies like the 'Litania 7 deipare Virg.' identified in the inventory certainly did not.[26] Other Catholic-oriented music in the inventory includes Erbach's aforementioned *Modorum sacrorum … Liber secundus*, consisting of Proper settings designed explicitly for the Roman liturgy (see Chapter 4); Konrad Hagius's polyphonic settings of the Ulenberg Psalter, intended as a Catholic response to 'falsified' Lutheran psalm translations; Ferdinand di Lasso's *Apparatus musicus* of

---

[24] A complete transcription of the inventory appears in Hans Michael Schletterer, *Katalog der in der Kreis- und Stadt-Bibliothek, dem Staedtischen Archive und der Bibliothek des historischen Vereins zu Augsburg befindlichen Musikwerke* (Berlin: T. Trautwein'sche kgl. Hof- Buch- und Musikalienhandlung, 1878), pp. 11–16.

[25] *Liber primus Cantiones sacrae Magnificat vocant*, for five and six voices (Munich, 1601; RISM B/I, 1602¹).

[26] The composer of this Marian litany is unknown.

1622, containing mostly Marian antiphons, Magnificats and litanies; and so forth. Also appearing in the inventory is the *Quarante et neuf Psalmes à David* (Lyon, 1559) of Michel Ferrier, a collection of three-voice settings of Marot's French translations of the Psalms. Its presence here is remarkable, since this type of music became associated with the Calvinist observances that were banned under Augsburg's constitution.[27] The *Chansons spirituelles* of Didier Lupi (1548), also listed in the inventory, originate in the same tradition. Although sacred music is well represented, we also find numerous volumes of secular madrigals, canzonettas, instrumental dance music and wedding songs.

This ecumenical trend also appears in two extant manuscript score books belonging to Gumpelzhaimer described by Richard Charteris.[28] Unsurprisingly, music by local musicians is well represented among the 58 named composers; among the 266 works (many of them unica), the most frequently encountered names are Christian Erbach, Hans Leo Hassler and Gumpelzhaimer's colleague Wilhelm Lichtlein; the best-represented foreign names are Giovanni Gabrieli, Ruggiero Giovanelli and Philippe de Monte. The score books include numerous contemporary Italian composers, however, such as Felice Anerio, Giovanni Animuccia, Marenzio, Tiburtio Massiano, Claudio Merulo, Orazio Vecchi, and Lodovico Viadana, attesting to the cosmopolitan outlook of the cantorate. Gumpelzhaimer does not shy away from Marian or Catholic-oriented texts in his choices: we find, for example, a *Beata es Maria* by Paolo Animuccia, a *Duodecim Stellae Corona Mariae* by Orazio Vecchi, a set of Italian *madrigali spirituali* by Amante Franzoni and Rore's ten madrigal settings of Petrarch's *Vergine bella*. The 37 prints recently identified by Jane Bernstein as having belonged to the St Anna music library are also a diverse lot.[29] In addition to many motet collections issued by Susato in the early sixteenth century and by the Berg & Neuber firm in Nuremberg in the 1550s, this group contains

---

[27] Stetten gives the following ordinance, from June 1566: 'Den *18. Junii* wurde denen Buchführern ernstlich verboten, einige Calvinische, Zwinglische oder Schwenckfeldische Bücher zu verkauffen.' See Stetten, *Geschichte der Heil. Röm. Reichs Freyen Stadt Augspurg* (Frankfurt am Main and Leipzig: In der Merz- und Mayerischen Buch-Handlung, 1743), vol. 1, p. 573. In the wake of the Interim and the Peace of Augsburg, the city government allowed Lutheranism and Catholicism as the only 'approved' faiths, while other religious sects were seen as threats to religious stability.

[28] See Charteris, *Adam Gumpelzhaimer's Little-Known Score Books*. The manuscripts in question are located at the Staatsbibliothek zu Berlin, Preußischer Kulturbesitz, Mus. ms. 40028, and the Biblioteka Jagiellońska of Kraków, Mus. ms. 40027.

[29] Bernstein, 'Buyers and Collections of Music Publications: Two Sixteenth-Century Music Libraries Recovered', in Jessie Ann Owens and Anthony M. Cummings, eds, *Music in Renaissance Cities and Courts: Studies in Honor of Lewis Lockwood* (Warren, Mich.: Harmonie Park Press, 1997), pp. 21–33.

Palestrina's 1589 hymn cycle (*Hymni totius Anni*) for the Roman liturgy, the *Sacrarum Modulationum ... Motecta ... octonis Vocibus* (1598) by Palestrina's successor at St Peter's, Ruggiero Giovanelli (a composer whose music is also heavily represented in the score books mentioned above) and Viadana's *Opera omnia sacrorum Concentuum* of 1620, suggesting that thoroughbass practice had arrived at St Anna before the dispersal of this library during the Thirty Years War. In sum, the extant inventories, score books and prints originating from St Anna collectively demonstrate no strong confessional orientation in the cantorate's repertory.

Of course, this may all have changed in 1630, when the Catholics assumed control of St Anna in the wake of the Edict of Restitution (for more on this era see Chapter 8). An anonymous chronicle reports that 'on 7 February [1630] the Papists, through the consecrating bishop and several Fuggers, consecrated the choir of St Anna and thereafter arranged for some music'.[30] By the October of the following year the Jesuits would also take control of the Gymnasium.[31] The venerable tradition of street-singing, furthermore, was considered sufficiently threatening to be banned outright on 27 April 1630.[32] An order to the city bailiff during this period makes clear that only Catholic choirs were to be allowed:

> Furthermore ... although the city guards and patrols have been ordered to disperse persons begging and singing in front of houses at night, except for the Catholic choirs at the usual times and on feast days, it would be useful if the city bailiff's men, when they are on streets outside of their normal rounds or on their own business, also remove [them] appropriately from the streets; they should lock the stubborn ones up for an hour or two in the poor house.[33]

---

[30] 'Adj 7. Feb. haben die Papisten durch den Weichbischoff sampt ettlichen Fuggern dz Chor bej St: Anna geweÿhet, darauf ein *Music* gehaltten.' From 'Gründtliche Beschreibung Dessen was sich von A:° 1629. biß A°~1648. Jn Gaist: vnd Welttlichen Händlen Zwischen beeden *Religionen* Inn Augsburg begeben vnd zugetragen. Durch Eine Wahrhaffte, vnd der sachen selbst erfahrne Persohn aufgezaichnet', fol. 2v. StAA, Reichsstadt Chroniken, p. 28.

[31] 'Vigesimo tertio octobris cantatum est insigni celebritate, in Templo S. Annæ officium diuinum, more Societatis suo instaurationem litterarum, die Sp[iritu] Sancto:'; *HCA*, vol. 2, p. 58.

[32] A Protestant chronicle records the event as follows: 'Adj 27 Aprill hat man inn der Eÿl den Euangel: Schuelherrn vnd *studenten* daß singen vor den häusern abgeschafft am vormittag vnd Nachmittag hat man die Werckhleuth vnd andern werckleuthen, an der herrn Arbeitt seind gewesst, ins baw ambt erfordert, vnd ihnen vorgehalten, sollen inn die Päbstische Kürchen gehen, aber sie haben sich deß gewaigert, vnd nit gewilliget'; from 'Gründtliche Beschreibung Dessen was sich von A:° 1629. biß A°~1648. Jn Gaist: vnd Welttlichen Händlen Zwischen beeden *Religionen* Inn Augsburg begeben vnd zugetragen. Durch Eine Wahrhaffte, vnd der sachen selbst erfahrne Persohn aufgezaichnet', StAA, Reichsstadt Chroniken 28, fol. 3v.

[33] From 'Instruction. für ~ Herrn Hanß Voten vom berg ~ Reichs Statvot, sich inn der,

Also in that year, the organ, which had been built decades earlier by the Fugger family in their own chapel in St Anna, was removed and transferred to St Moritz.[34] We lack further details about the music cultivated at St Anna during the Restitution, but we must assume that city ordinances banning the performance of all sacred music except that with Latin, Catholic texts were observed.

It would be a mistake to draw firm conclusions about Gumpelzhaimer's religious attitude on the basis of his published compositions and extant inventories alone. He was hardly an independent actor: engaged as a teacher by St Anna and paid directly by the city council, he was obliged not only to fulfil his duties as a cantor and as a pedagogue, but also not to endanger the religious peace maintained by the city authorities. He was a public figure in a way that Aichinger and Erbach were not, ultimately responsible for music-making – ranging from the performance of church music to the activities of street choirs – in the most prominent Protestant institution of the city. The dedications to his printed works point to his dependence upon the good will of the city council and his colleagues. Working mostly in the decades after the *Kalenderstreit*, Gumpelzhaimer found himself a part of an institution that, for the most part, avoided taking an active role in promoting confessional tensions. Although his religious position itself is impossible to fathom, the nature of his music and the contents of his diverse and ecumenical music library are entirely consistent with the generally moderate position taken by his superiors. While the St Anna music library contained an astonishing variety of music regardless of the confessional orientation of the composer or the text, Gumpelzhaimer himself strove to create a repertory that was useful in various contexts, stylistically fashionable and religiously unprovocative. Though open to new musical influences, he continued and strengthened a stable musical tradition in Augsburg that had been in place for many decades. His Catholic counterparts, on the other hand, were compelled to forge a new musical tradition, one that went hand in hand with the Catholic revival of the late sixteenth century and participated actively in the definition of confessional boundaries. Protestant music may also have been defined by this process, but largely in spite of itself.

---

von dem Kaÿser: herren *Com[m]issarien* vnd *Executoren*, Ihme aufgetragner mit *execution* nach gelegenheit haben zuegebrauchen', D-As, 2° Cod. Aug. 123, 'Singularia Augustana', no. 25, fols. 2v–3r.

[34] See StAA, KWA B8[16]; and Cuyler, 'Musical Activity in Augsburg and its Annakirche', p. 43.

CHAPTER FOUR

The Counter-Reformation and the Catholic Liturgy in Augsburg

In contrast to the studied ecumenism of musical life at the Protestant bastion of St Anna, confessional politics left a more distinct impression on the liturgical music of Augsburg's Catholic institutions, including the cathedral, the Benedictine monastery and church of SS Ulrich and Afra and the Jesuit church and college of St Salvator. This is unsurprising given the fact that the Counter-Reformation was promulgated chiefly by the church hierarchy and secular Catholic rulers, even if persons on every level of society felt its effects.[1] Although there is scattered evidence for musical activity at Augsburg's other Catholic churches (including St Moritz and Heilig Kreuz), the surviving musical and archival evidence is too thin to allow a detailed description of musical life there, much less allow conclusions concerning the influence of the Catholic renewal. On the other hand, a substantial amount of music and archival data survives that gives some insight into musical practice at the three institutions mentioned above. The surviving works of composers active at the cathedral and at SS Ulrich and Afra like Bernhard Klingenstein, Gregor Aichinger and Christian Erbach are supplemented by such materials as the extant minutes of the cathedral chapter's meetings, manuscript liturgical books and chronicles describing ceremonial occasions. The extent of these composers' relationships with St Salvator is less clear, but a number of surviving manuscript records and chronicles from the Jesuit college shed some light on its liturgical music as well.

In the late sixteenth and early seventeenth centuries, liturgical music in Augsburg's Catholic churches underwent several significant changes. First, the introduction of the Roman Rite (replacing the venerable Augsburg Rite) in the late sixteenth century had a wide-ranging effect on chant, polyphony and church ceremony in general, and reflected a desire

---

[1] Catholicism and Calvinism, the two great antagonists to Lutheran orthodoxy in the late sixteenth century, are comparable developments in as much as those at the top levels of society – theologians, academics, jurists and church and secular leaders – espoused these dogmas first and most fervently. For example, the Jesuits placed great emphasis on conversions of highly placed figures; see Hsia, *Social Discipline in the Reformation*, pp. 44–45. Furthermore, the imposition of religious orthodoxy by elites was an aspect of the linkage between confessionalization and the expansion of secular authority; see, for example, Schilling, 'Die Konfessionalisierung im Reich', pp. 11–13.

on the part of the diocese's higher clergy to standardize liturgical practice on a Roman model. Second, church services at the cathedral and SS Ulrich and Afra were increasingly embellished by instrumental music and large-scale polychoral repertories, adding a degree of ostentation consistent with other contemporary religious displays like processions, pilgrimages and public supplications. At the same time, the Jesuits of St Salvator called for regular polyphonic music in their own services (and especially litanies) despite statutory injunctions against the cultivation of church polyphony by leaders of the order. In the cathedral, at least, vernacular song became an accepted part of church services on a limited basis, as Catholic leaders realized its value in terms of popular devotion and its already proven success among the Protestants. Finally, the nature of the liturgical polyphony composed and published by Augsburg's major Catholic composers underwent a decisive shift around the turn of the seventeenth century, as collections of masses and motets for general liturgical use gave way to publications with a Marian or Eucharistic tendency, or to publications reflecting the overall move towards Roman standardization. If Counter-Reformation ideology in itself was not directly responsible for all these changes (the fashionability of Venetian music also encouraged the adoption of polychoral repertories, for example), the profile of music in Augsburg's Catholic churches by the early seventeenth century echoed the Catholic renewal that shaped Augsburg's religious life in this period.

Music at the Cathedral in the Wake of the Peace of Augsburg (1555)

When the Peace of Augsburg in 1555 created a new basis for Augsburg's religious and political structure after several decades of sectarian conflict, it would have been difficult to speak of an ongoing tradition of Catholic music in the city, liturgical or otherwise. The Catholic clergy had been expelled from the city for a period of ten years between 1537 and 1547, and again during the spring and summer of 1552. The recovery of Catholicism in Augsburg began under the auspices of Bishop Otto Truchseß von Waldburg and the fiery Jesuit Petrus Canisius, who served as cathedral preacher between 1559 and 1566. Their reform efforts, however, were seriously hindered not only by the still precarious position of Augsburg's Catholic community at mid-century, but also by entrenched opposition from the noble members of the cathedral chapter, who tended to see the centralized reform measures of Trent as an unacceptable abrogation of their traditional rights. A permanent Jesuit settlement in Augsburg was not established until the early 1580s, and then only with the generous financial assistance of the Fugger family.

In this atmosphere of slow recovery, Catholic music in Augsburg remained tied to traditional institutions – mainly the cathedral and the Benedictine abbey of SS Ulrich and Afra – and functions. The cathedral was only able to support a cantorate from 1561, thanks to a sum of 800 Gulden willed for this purpose by the canon Jakob Heinrichmann.[2] In that year a choir of 26 singers was established, consisting of six each of altos, tenors and basses, and eight choirboys singing the discant parts.[3] The chapter also drew up an ordinance for the cultivation of polyphonic music and organ playing on specific occasions. Several major feasts of the church year (including Easter, Christmas, Pentecost and Corpus Christi) were to feature complete polyphonic settings of the Mass as well as the *Ave Regina*; for a larger group of lesser feasts (including Epiphany, Ascension, Trinity Sunday and several saints' days of local importance) the chapter called for a polyphonic sequence and Credo, as well as the replacement of the Offertory by a motet on Epiphany and the Nativity of the Virgin; and other feasts were to feature chant and organ only.[4]

This ordinance largely determined the scope of music at the cathedral for the next several decades, and was modified only around the edges by a reorganization of the cathedral cantorate in 1616 by the *Kapellmeister* Georg Metzler.[5] While the *Choralen* or *Chorschüler* were responsible for singing figural music in church, a larger number of boys known as the *Scholaren* helped to sing liturgical plainchant and supported themselves in part by singing on city streets, forming a Catholic counterpart to the street choirs of St Anna.[6] Beyond this, however, there is little evidence to suggest an abundance of contexts for non-liturgical or para-liturgical music at the cathedral before the turn of the seventeenth century, when

[2] See Hermann Fischer and Theodor Wohnhaas, 'Miscellanea zur Augsburger Dommusik', in Brusniak and Leuchtmann, eds, *Quaestiones in musica*, pp. 127–28. The cathedral had already attempted to find new 'readers or choristers' [*leser seu cantores*] by 1555, and presumably these persons would have been in place by the time of the cantorate's organization in 1561. See Otto Ursprung, *Jacobus de Kerle (1531/32–1591): Sein Leben und seine Werke* (Munich: Hans Beck, 1913), pp. 57–58, and *DR* (Augsburg Domrezessionalien), 24 May 1555.

[3] Ursprung, *Jacobus de Kerle*, p. 63.

[4] For the following see ibid., 63–64. With respect to the last-named group of feasts, Ursprung interprets 'musicam manualem in organis' as implying chant and organ alone.

[5] See Ursprung, 'Die Chorordnung von 1616 am Dom zu Augsburg: Ein Beitrag zur Frage der Aufführungspraxis', in *Studien zur Musikgeschichte: Festschrift für Guido Adler zum 75. Geburtstag* (Vienna: Universal Edition, 1930), pp. 137–42.

[6] This choir was accustomed to singing in Latin, a practice banned by the city council, which insisted that they sing in German and restrict the number of occasions upon which they were found on the streets; see Ursprung, *Jacobus de Kerle*, pp. 71–72. Given the continuining marginalization of Augsburg's Catholic minority at this early stage, it is possible that the city council feared Protestant protest against this group. From time to time cathedral singers were also hired by wealthy patricians for weddings and other

the cathedral became one focus for the activities of new or revived Catholic confraternities and played a prominent role in the organization of public processions.

The lack of surviving musical sources such as manuscript choirbooks from this period makes it difficult to speculate on the music actually cultivated by the cathedral cantorate in its first few decades. Publications by Johannes de Cleve (c.1529–82) and Jacobus de Kerle (1531/32–91), the two most prominent musicians that can be associated with the cathedral during these years, were marketed widely and betray no overt connections to the liturgical needs of the cathedral. We may pass quickly over Cleve, who only lived in Augsburg for a few years before his death in 1582 and probably had little, if any, influence over the cathedral's repertory.[7] Jacobus de Kerle, however, is of greater interest due to his association with one of the great Tridentine reformers, Bishop Otto Truchseß von Waldburg.

Otto engaged Kerle as his own music director between 1562 and 1565 and later arranged a benefice and a position as organist for him at Augsburg Cathedral (1568–75).[8] Kerle is best known today, of course, for his *Preces speciales* (1562), polyphonic settings of the ten responsories in the *Preces speciales pro Salubri generalis Concilii Successu ac Conclusione*, a collection of prayers for the success of the Council of Trent by Petrus de Soto, a Dominican monk and professor of theology at the university of Dillingen.[9] Otto Truchseß commissioned Kerle in late 1561 or early 1562 to compose these settings, which were

---

entertainments. For example, in 1585 the *Kapellmeister* Bernhard Klingenstein and his cathedral singers were paid 80 Gulden for performing at the wedding of Ursula von Liechtenstein and Georg Fugger in the church of SS Ulrich and Afra. See Layer, *Musik und Musiker der Fuggerzeit*, p. 34.

[7] Cleve received a payment from the cathedral chapter on 18 March 1580 for instructing the new *Kapellmeister*, Bernhard Klingenstein, in composition (see *DR*); otherwise I have found no evidence of any official attachment to the cathedral.

[8] The most authoritative work on Kerle's life and work remains Ursprung, *Jacobus de Kerle*. On Kerle's participation in religious and political events at Otto's court in Dillingen, see pp. 39–40; on Otto's intercession on his behalf with the Augsburg cathedral chapter, see p. 50; see also Singer, 'Leben und Werke des Augsburger Domkapellmeisters Bernhardus Klingenstein', p. 15, and Adolf Layer, 'Musikpflege am Hofe der Fürstbischöfe von Augsburg in der Renaissancezeit', *JVAB*, **10** (1976), p. 204.

[9] Jacobus de Kerle, *Preces speciales pro Salubri generalis Concilii Successu, ac Conclusione ... collectae: & ... ad Figuras & Modos musicos accommodatae, cum quatuor Vocibus* (Venice: Antonio Gardano, 1562; RISM A/I, K445). On de Soto, see esp. H. Lais, 'Petrus de Soto, Mitbegründer der Universität Dillingen', *Jahrbuch des Historischen Vereins Dillingen an der Donau*, **52** (1950), pp. 145–58. Otto Truchseß von Waldburg himself composed a similar set of prayers for the success of the Council of Trent that may also have served as an inspiration for Kerle's work, the *Selectae Preces in Usum Piorum pro Successu ac Conclusione generalis Concilii et Populi christiani Unione atque Salute ex sacra*

printed by Gardano in Venice and were already being performed before the Council of Trent by Easter 1562.[10] The extent of its influence on church fathers with respect to the retention of polyphony in the divine service remains unclear, although Otto's musical sophistication and advocacy, along with the music's remarkable textual clarity in a polyphonic context, suggests that it may have provided an acceptable model for church polyphony.[11]

With respect to the text, however, the *Preces speciales* has a unique position in Kerle's output. The two books of masses (1562 and 1583) and seven books of motets (1571–85) that followed the *Preces* reflect Kerle's career aspirations in their dedications, but do not embrace the overt confessional symbolism of his most famous work.[12] Among the dedicatees of these publications were institutions and individuals whose discretion may have obtained a permanent position in Augsburg for the composer: the cathedral chapter (the *Selectae quaedam Cantiones* of 1571), the abbot of the Augustinian monastery of St Georg (the *Liber Modulorum sacrorum* of 1572) and the new bishop of Augsburg, Johann Egolph von Knöringen (the *Liber Mottetorum* [sic], *quatuor et quinque Vocum* of 1573). These prints were not organized to be liturgically useful, nor do they emphasize any particular devotional theme.

If Kerle was hoping that these works would lead to his appointment as *Kapellmeister* upon the retirement of Anton Span in 1574, he was sorely to be disappointed. The choice of Bernhard Klingenstein over Kerle for the position reflects the chapter's preference for an 'inside candidate' who had been a choirboy and a student at the cathedral

---

Scriptura et Ecclesiae Usu collectae pro Usu et Commoditate suae Dioecesis (Dillingen: Sebald Mayer, 1561). See Friedrich Zoepfl, *Das Bistum Augsburg und seine Bischöfe im Reformationsjahrhundert* (Munich: Schnell & Steiner, 1969), pp. 328–29 n.

[10] On the performance of Kerle's *Preces speciales* at Trent, see esp. Ursprung, *Jacobus de Kerle*, p. 19.

[11] The bishop and Kerle left Trent in 1563, but the issue of music was not reopened until two years later by Cardinals Vitellozzo Vitellozzi and Borromeo. Thus the influence of Kerle's *Preces* may well have been indirect. See Lewis Lockwood, 'Vincenzo Ruffo and Musical Reform after the Council of Trent', *Musical Quarterly*, **43** (1957), pp. 343–44. For more on Otto's role at the Council, and the *Preces speciales* of Kerle, see Ursprung, *Jacobus de Kerle*, pp. 19–20; Zoepfl, *Das Bistum Augsburg*, pp. 328–29; and Layer, 'Musikpflege am Hofe der Fürstbischöfe von Augsburg in der Renaissancezeit', p. 202.

[12] RISM A/I, K445–K455. Ursprung noted Kerle's increased productivity during his Augsburg years (*Jacobus de Kerle*, pp. 76–77), but added that he never dedicated a work to members of the Fugger family, who were among Europe's most important musical patrons in this period (ibid., pp. 89–90). Octavian II Fugger, however, did receive a manuscript codex of music for a double wedding in 1579 from Johannes Dreer, the choir director of SS Ulrich and Afra: this *Officium Missae nuptialis* included music by Kerle, Orlando di Lasso and Melchior Schramm. See Wolfgang Boetticher, *Orlando di Lasso und seine Zeit, 1532–1594* (Kassel: Bärenreiter, 1958), p. 163.

school.[13] It is possible that Kerle was hedging his bets by 1573, the year he dedicated his *Liber Modulorum sacrorum* for four to six voices to Abbot Johann Habnitzel of the Benedictine monastery at Weingarten, which later would host the composers Jakob Reiner and Michael Kraf. Although he did not obtain a position at Weingarten, the abbot recommended him for a similar position at the Benedictine monastery of Kempten two years later.[14] Kerle also failed to gain a position there, despite the dedication of his *Sacrae Cantiones* to Abbot Eberhard von Stein.[15] Kerle spent his remaining years in positions in Cambrai, Cologne, Vienna and Prague, but did not remain active in publishing new music. The only surviving large-scale collection of his music in manuscript was a hymn cycle copied around 1577 by Johannes Dreer, the choir director at SS Ulrich and Afra in Augsburg. Purely liturgical needs determined the nature of these hymns, whose texts were appropriate for the Benedictines' use of the Italian monastic breviary combined with feasts of local patron saints like St Ulrich, St Afra and St Narcissus.[16]

Music, Liturgy and the Counter-Reformation in Augsburg

The works of Cleve and Kerle on liturgical texts demonstrate little relationship with the changes in Catholic spirituality that later would be

---

[13] The cathedral chapter strongly supported music education in the late sixteenth and early seventeenth centuries as a means of creating musical talent that would perpetuate itself; see below. The chapter may also have heard about Kerle's conflicts with the church authorities in Ypern in Flanders in the mid-1560s, when the composer was in fact excommunicated for having struck a priest (he later successfully had this sentence revoked in Rome); see Ursprung, *Jacobus de Kerle*, pp. 47–48.

[14] On Kerle's relationship to the Weingarten monastery, see Ursprung, *Jacobus de Kerle*, pp. 81–82; on his bid for a position at Kempten see ibid., pp. 92–93, and Adolf Layer, in *Musikgeschichte der Fürstabtei Kempten* (Kempten: Verlag für Heimatpflege, 1975), pp. 15–16, who suggests that Kerle may in fact have worked at Kempten before moving to Cambrai, where he held a prebend.

[15] On links between Kempten and Augsburg composers, including Kerle, Aichinger and Erbach, see Siegfried Gmeinwieser, 'Kirchenmusik', in Brandmüller, ed., *Handbuch der bayerischen Kirchengeschichte*, p. 992, and Franz Krautwurst, 'Musik in Reichsstadt und Stift', in Volker Dotterweich et al., eds, *Geschichte der Stadt Kempten* (Kempten: Verlag Tobias Dannheimer, 1989), p. 315.

[16] These stylistically conservative hymns, some of which originally appeared in Kerle's *Hymni totius Anni* (Rome: Valerio Dorico, 1558; 2nd edn, Rome: Antonio Barre, 1560; RISM A/I, K441 and K442) were sung at SS Ulrich and Afra at least until 1624; see Ursprung, *Jacobus de Kerle*, p. 86. On the German hymn cycle and the cycles of Kerle and Lasso, see Daniel Zager, 'Liturgical Rite and Musical Repertory: The Polyphonic Latin Hymn Cycle of Lasso in Munich and Augsburg', in Ignace Bossuyt, Eugeen Schreurs and Annelies Wouters, eds, *Orlandus Lassus and his Time: Colloquium Proceedings, Antwerpen 24–26.08.1994* (Peer: Alamire, 1995), pp. 215–31.

of great importance to the profile of Catholic polyphony in early seventeenth-century Augsburg. In the final decade of the sixteenth century, for the first time in many decades, Catholic processions left the immediate confines of the ecclesiastical quarter of the city and extended throughout the city. By the first decade of the seventeenth century, Augsburg's Catholics were establishing or reviving confraternities in honour of the Virgin Mary, the Eucharist and patron saints, and the traditional pilgrimage to the nearby shrine of Andechs blossomed. All of these phenomena led to the creation of new contexts for Catholic devotional polyphony and monophony, contexts that were all but unthinkable only 30 years previously. While the consequences of the Catholic revival for non-liturgical, devotional music in the city were dramatic, the nature of liturgical music also began to change in response to a new emphasis on Roman standardization and on specific objects of veneration (especially the Virgin Mary and the Eucharist) that were central to the formation of a specifically Catholic religious identity.

The Introduction of the Roman Rite and the Catholic Liturgy

By the time that Bishop Johann Otto von Gemmingen resolved in the late 1590s to introduce the Roman Rite formally in the diocese of Augsburg, the Augsburg Rite had been in use for several centuries, even if its form and content had varied considerably. The Augsburg Rite, in fact, had roots extending back to the Carolingian period and was a legacy of Frankish attempts to promote liturgical uniformity across their realm.[17] In any case, the similarities between the Augsburg and Roman Rites were significant, although gradual modifications to the Roman liturgy itself over the course of the Middle Ages as well as the persistence of local devotional traditions led to divergences, especially with respect to the Sanctorale.[18] The Council of Trent mandated universal acceptance of the Roman Rite in the mid-sixteenth century, and in the following decades many dioceses acknowledged the renewed centrality of Rome by

---

[17] F.A. Hoeynck, the chronicler of the Augsburg liturgy from its origins to its dissolution during the Counter-Reformation, called the rite 'Roman-Augsburg' in recognition of its original dependence on the Roman model, even though he felt that 'Roman-German-Augsburg' was a better description due to the Augsburg Rite's similarity to other contemporary German rites. See Hoeynck, *Geschichte der kirchlichen Liturgie des Bisthums Augsburg. Mit Beilagen: Monumentae liturgiae Augustanae* (Augsburg: Litterar. Institut von M. Huttler [Michael Seitz], 1889), pp. 36–39. For the sake of clarity I shall use the term 'Augsburg Rite' to describe the diocesan liturgy before the late sixteenth century.

[18] The organization and content of this Proper is far too complex to be discussed here. The reader is directed to Hoeynck's detailed breakdown of the Proper according to month; see ibid., pp. 235–88.

supplanting their traditional rites with the Roman one. However, rites that were over 200 years old were exempted from the mandate and, indeed, the bishops of Augsburg ordered the publication of liturgical books for the Augsburg Rite well into the late sixteenth century: the last Augsburg Missal was ordered by Bishop Otto Truchseß von Waldburg in 1555, while Bishop Marquard von Berg ordered a new Augsburg Ritual in 1580 and a new Augsburg Breviary in 1584.[19]

On 24 May 1597 Johann Otto promulgated his decision to mandate the adoption of the Roman Rite in the diocese of Augsburg, to take effect on the first Sunday of Advent in that year. The decision was a nod to the spiritual authority of Rome, although it was also a practical expedient.[20] Copies of the Missal of 1555 were becoming scarce and worn out, and a decision had to be taken either to reprint the Augsburg Missal (which also would have required a new Breviary) or to replace the Augsburg Rite with the Roman outright. Johann Otto cited the numerous inconsistencies and errors that had crept into the Augsburg liturgical books over the years, making it necessary to revise and reprint liturgical books frequently. The Roman liturgy (which was made available through the official Tridentine Breviary of 1568, Missal of 1570, and Pontifical of 1596; a Ceremonial would follow in 1600 and a Ritual in 1614) offered a standard liturgical format that would obviate this need. Johann Otto mandated the use of the Roman Missal and Breviary only, but for the moment he allowed the retention of the Augsburg chant repertory, albeit with some adjustments:

> nevertheless we wish that the chant in the cantionals or chant books, which along with the tones of the church of Augsburg has been customary up to now, should be retained, [but] some substitution is necessary. Indeed certain Graduals, Responsories, Hymns, Antiphons and others of this type only require transposition, which can easily be identified and assigned by numbers.[21]

---

[19] Hoeynck provides detailed descriptions of these and other printed liturgical books from the fifteenth to eighteenth centuries (ibid., pp. 335–50). The 1580 Ritual, entitled *Ritus ecclesiastici Augustensis episcopatus* (Dillingen: Johann Mayer, 1580), is provided with a catechism by the prominent Jesuit preacher Petrus Canisius, who had been a close associate of Marquard's predecessor Otto Truchseß von Waldburg. Marquard mandates in his preface that Canisius's catechism be used throughout the diocese, not only in schools but also publicly in churches, particularly on Sundays and feast days, as well as at meals.

[20] See Hoeynck, *Geschichte der kirchlichen Liturgie des Bisthums Augsburg*, p. 294.

[21] 'in Cantionalibus tamen seu libris cantum choralem continentibus, quem iuxta tonum Ecclesiæ Augustanæ hactenus consuetum, planè retineri uolumus, aliqua immutatio est necessaria. Quasdam enim Gradualia, Responsoria, Hymni et Antiphonæ et alia id genus, transpositionem tantum requirunt, quæ per numeros facile significari et assignari poterunt.' Mandate quoted in 'Historia episcoporum Augustanorum usque ad annum 1611', ABA, Hs 64, fols. 200r–201r. See also Hoeynck, *Geschichte der kirchlichen Liturgie des Bisthums Augsburg*, pp. 294–95, and Zoepfl, *Das Bistum Augsburg*, pp. 724–25. The

The bishop surely recognized that this concession was necessary so as not to throw local musical establishments into disarray, for a new chant repertory would require a more gradual period of introduction.[22]

Of course, the liturgical changes did not happen instantly. The cathedral and the collegiate chapters accepted the changes in theory, but not in practice, while parishes in the countryside lagged significantly due to the lack of books and the weight of local traditions.[23] Elected upon Johann Otto's death in 1598, the new bishop, Heinrich V von Knöringen, was deeply dissatisfied with the progress of change during his first decade on the episcopal throne. If some of Johann Otto's motivations for the introduction of the Roman Rite had been practical, Heinrich's were political, and were directed towards the cementing of the Augsburg diocese to the Roman hierarchy. Heinrich ordered a diocesan

---

bishop also allowed clerics in the diocese to continue using the Augsburg Breviary for a temporary period.

[22] Even under Johann's successor Heinrich, the older Augsburg chant was retained for certain functions; for example, Heinrich commissioned a new printing of the Office for the Dead in 1599 (*Officium Defunctorum accomodatum Cantui ecclesiastico Diocesis Augustanae* [Dillingen: Johann Mayer, 1599]) that held to the older tradition. The impracticality of imposing a new chant repertory in 1597 recalls the appearance of a collection of Gregorian chant issued by the Augsburg Cathedral schoolmaster Johann Holthusius 30 years earlier, the *Compendium Cantionum ecclesiasticarum* (Augsburg: Matthäus Franck, 1567). In the preface to his *Compendium* Holthusius complained of widespread irregularity in the performance of liturgical chant and decried priests' lack of training in chant singing. 'No doubt from such inexperience', he writes, 'not rarely to be found even in the divine service, great abuses, scandals, errors and confusion arise in the church of God, and the greater part of the Christian people is not only greatly scandalized on account of this, but also made less devout and pious, and is indiscriminately alienated from things divine. And it would be for this reason that church music likewise with the divine service is considered in these days more and more vile, and is despised, and since it is horrendous spoken or heard, it is an object of mirth: and not only among the enemies of the church, but also sometimes among those who declare themselves to be adherents of the venerable Catholic faith.' Bishop Johann Otto's reluctance to mandate Gregorian chant 30 years later may well reflect the clergy's continuing inability to successfully practise the repertory with which it was already familiar.

[23] Hoeynck, *Geschichte der kirchlichen Liturgie des Bisthums Augsburg*, p. 295. A manuscript Roman antiphoner, based on the Roman Breviary of 1568, from the Augustinian church and monastery of St Georg in Augsburg suggests that a lack of uniformity in chant performance persisted there into the early seventeenth century. In his preface, dated 1607, brother Simpert Fischer noted that a new and uniform repertory was necessary to alleviate 'confusion and errors': 'Idcirco mente sepe tractaui, tum unum modum et antiquum ritum psallendi in ecclesia maxime esse deceat, ad tollendum tedium requirendi, ne vt hactenus confusiones erroresque irreverent verus ordo ritusque in conquirendo recompensaretur ad dei laudem hoc opus laboriosum in antiphonis et responsoriis: recolligendis et simul rescribendis aggregi et ex antiquioribus varijs antiphonarijs unum sumarium sicut decet nostrum chorum Antiphonarium quod omnino accepto Breuiario Romano responderet, vtrumque contexere.' From D-As, 2° Cod. 509.

synod in 1610, at which he insisted on full implementation of the Roman
Rite. 'Let all say the Mass from the Roman Missal and the prescribed
ceremonies for anointing found within it,' he states in the synodal decree,
'and let no one use other [rites] for any reason'.[24] Between 1597 and
1610 the Roman Rite had not even been implemented at the cathedral,
where, as a contemporary chronicle records, 'the canons and vicars were
obliged to accept the Roman Missal and Breviary [*Officium et
Breuiarium Romanum*] after 12 years, none of the ceremonies hitherto
having been observed'.[25] Unlike Johann Otto's original decree of 1597,
the synodal statutes from 1610 now mandated the complete
displacement of the Augsburg Rite by the Roman, including the
introduction of Gregorian chant throughout the diocese:

> therefore, in order to eliminate irregularity in the divine service and
> in the ceremonies of the church, it has been mandated that the
> Roman Missal and Breviary shall be used by all of our clergy, just as
> it has been accepted by all others; likewise we have considered it
> necessary to revise the old Ritual in order to bring it into agreement
> with the Roman Use as much as possible, so that the same order may
> be observed in the administration of the sacraments, and in the other
> mystical rites [*ritibus mysticis*], both in the tones and in polyphonic
> singing [*& in tonis ac figuris cantandi*], which are customarily used
> in the divine Office.[26]

Thus reads the preface to the new Ritual published at Heinrich's
direction in 1612, which contains a separate section for 'sung tones and
formulas according to the Roman Rite';[27] here the new psalm tones are
given, as are tones for the Chapter, epistles, Gospels, the four Marian
antiphons and other formulas. Echoing the Tridentine discussions
concerning intelligibility of the text, the reader of the epistles and Gospel
is admonished to 'sing [them] gravely, distinctly, with prolongation,
slowly and attentively, so that devotion and piety towards God shall
shine forth, and the Christian faithful shall be moved to piety'.[28]

---

[24] Quoted in Hoeynck, *Geschichte der kirchlichen Liturgie des Bisthums Augsburg*, pp. 295–96.

[25] ABA, Hs 64, fols. 218v–219r. The chapter formally implemented the Roman ceremonies by December 1610. In the minutes of the chapter meeting on 20 December the notary writes that 'following on the report by the cathedral dean, it pleases the chapter to begin using the Roman ceremonies for today's Vespers, as has been recently decided'. *DR*, 20 December 1610.

[26] From preface to *Liber Ritualis, Episcopatus Augustensis, distinctus in tres Partes, et ad Usum Romanum accommodatus. Continens Canones et Ritus sacros, qui in Administratione Sacramentorum, & cæteris Munijs ecclesiasticis, præsertim pastoralibus ritè obeundis, obseruari debent* (Dillingen: Johann Mayer, 1612).

[27] Ibid., pp. 251–80.

[28] 'In cantando autem seriò caueant Presbyter nimias vocum elationes, præcipitationes, ostentationes, necnon vociferationes: sed assuescant grauiter, distinctè, tractim, lentè &

While the 1597 decree and 1610 synod streamlined liturgical rites according to the Roman model, Johann Otto and Heinrich were nevertheless loath to eliminate the traditional Augsburg Sanctorale entirely. In fact, Johann Otto issued a new Augsburg Proper [*Proprium Augustanum*] at the same time as his decree introducing the Roman Rite, thus preserving the observance of locally important saints like Ulrich, Afra and Hilaria (the hymn *Gaude civitas Augusta*, appearing in the Offices for Saints Afra, Hilaria and Narcissus, was a local speciality).[29] A new edition of the Proper in 1605 restored many of the traditional feasts that in 1597 had been omitted or provided with the simple Roman commemoration. In 1626, however, Heinrich finally decided in favour of full Romanization and many of the feasts of local importance were eliminated or scaled back.[30] The minutes of the cathedral chapter also suggest that the copying and purchase of Roman liturgical books began to accelerate only after the 1610 synod.[31] While Romanization was one of Heinrich's top priorities in the early seventeenth century, the traditional veneration of Augsburg's patron saints and the practical difficulties of replacing an entire liturgy hindered his efforts.

While recognizing the symbolic value of local feasts (at least until 1626), Heinrich stressed the celebration of feast days of more general importance to the political standing of the Catholic church. In September 1605, for example, he expanded the observance of feasts for the Virgin

---

attentè cantare; vt deuotio, & erga DEVM religio eluceat, Christique fideles ad pietatem excitentur.' Ibid., p. 251. Heinrich's introduction of a new Ritual was poorly timed, for only two years later Pope Paul V brought out a Roman Ritual, the last of the new series of Tridentine liturgical books. See Hoeynck, *Geschichte der kirchlichen Liturgie des Bisthums Augsburg*, p. 298.

[29] See Hoeynck, *Geschichte der kirchlichen Liturgie des Bisthums Augsburg*, pp. 302–3.

[30] Ibid., p. 305.

[31] See *DR*, 7 September 1601, 26 August 1608, 31 July 1609, 7 December 1610, 13 February 1617, 8 April and 20 May 1620, 15, 17 and 19 February 1621, 1 and 8 July 1624, 16 May and 14 November 1625, and 4 May 1627. These records, the bulk of which occur after 1620, tend to concern payments to copyists or the outright purchase of printed liturgical books. Before the 1610 synod it appears to have been common for the choir-vicars to own copies of both Augsburg and Roman liturgical books, suggesting that the two rites were mixed in varying degrees for some time. A contemporary description (1605) survives of the conditions of and items (including books, vestments, candles and the like) belonging to the various benefices at the cathedral; among the liturgical books belonging to the St Barbara benefice, held by the *Kapellmeister* Bernhard Klingenstein, were 'two books for the Mass, one of which is Roman', and 'two old chant books' [*zwaÿ allte Coral büecher*]. See BSA, Hochstift Augsburg/Münchner Bestand, Lit. 1025, fol. 33r. The cathedral's clergy seems to have been more diligent about using the Roman ceremonies after the 1610 synod. Apart from the references to the copying of Roman liturgical books cited above, a sumptuous manuscript codex survives from the choir library, ABA, Hs 30, which is dated 1616 and contains a complete set of Roman antiphons and Invitatory psalms for the Offices of the Temporale, Sanctorale and the Common of the Saints.

Mary, the Guardian Angels, and St Michael Archangel. After assuring his subjects of the importance of the Virgin's intercession in those troubled times, his mandate continues:

> We wish, moreover, that by the ancient example of the Catholic church and by the customs of our ancestors the festal days of the Virgin Mary be observed with more ardent piety, reverence and sanctity ... thus we command ... that in the future throughout our diocese of Augsburg the particular yearly venerations and feast days of the angelic guardians of these provinces and parts, and of the sole protectors of men, should be held in solemn and perpetual ceremony. We declare, moreover, that on the festal Sunday of the Nativity of the Virgin Mary immediately preceding ... those in all parishes or colleges or chapels who have not been in the habit of coming solemnly to first Vespers ... should be assembled, and that this Vespers should be sung with greater solemnity, or where this is impossible due to lack of music, should be prayed by the parish priest or by another priest in the church, and finally the Litany of the Angels should be similarly sung or prayed, and sung or prayed the previous day by the parish priest. Moreover we wish and decree these things also to be observed more diligently and reverently on the feast day of Saint Michael Archangel ... mindful of this leader of the heavenly army, and commander designated by God of the Church militant, and strongest defender of the Roman Empire.[32]

Heinrich's language suggests the perceived threats to the diocese's Catholic community as well as the need to assume a vigilant, if not militant, stand against them. In calling for special observance of the feast of St Michael, Heinrich invokes the potent image of the archangel as defender of the Catholic Church, an image that had gained currency in Augsburg as well as in the wider Catholic world.[33] Heinrich's 1629

---

[32] From StAA, KWA B10[11]. Further references by the cathedral chapter to the introduction of the feast of the Guardian Angels in 1605 may be found in DR, 25, 27, and 30 October, and 15 November 1604. Stetten also remarked on this mandate in his chronicle; see Stetten, *Geschichte der Heil. Röm. Reichs Freyen Stadt Augspurg*, vol. 1, p. 872.

[33] In Augsburg, the portrayal of St Michael as defender of the (Catholic) Church militant was heightened by the dedication of a new chapel in the Catholic graveyard to the archangel in 1600 (Stetten, *Geschichte der Heil. Röm. Reichs Freyen Stadt Augspurg*, vol. 1, p. 871). The placement of Hans Reichle's sculptural group featuring St Michael on the Zeughaus during this period drew criticism from a Protestant chronicler, Georg Kölderer. He feared that people viewing the sculptures would see 'how this angel treads on the Devil and strikes at him with his sword; thus all Lutherans must be crushed and destroyed by the sword – this will soon come to pass'. Quoted in Roeck, *Eine Stadt im Krieg und Frieden*, pp. 187–88; see also Wolfram Baer, 'Michaelsgruppe am Zeughaus (vollendet 1607)', in Mai, ed., *Sankt Michael in Bayern*, p. 88. Stetten noted in his chronicle (*Geschichte der Heil. Röm. Reichs Freyen Stadt Augspurg*, vol. 1, p. 872) that in 1608 Heinrich augmented the celebration of the feast of St Michael by ordering all churches in Augsburg to bring their relics to the cathedral on that day to be exhibited to the public (see also the cathedral

mandate of the celebration of the feast of the Conception of the Blessed Virgin Mary, as Stetten reported, had explicit political overtones: he did it at the behest of Emperor Ferdinand II, who sought to celebrate this feast 'out of particular devotion, and because he attributed the happy success of his arms and his victories to the supplication of the Holy Virgin, as well as of God'.[34]

Liturgical standardization and emphasis of certain feasts were the order of the day, but churches could also become stages for public supplications that fell outside the normal liturgy. On numerous occasions in this period, for example, the bishop of Augsburg ordered the holding of the Ten- and Forty Hour Prayers in the diocese's churches. The Forty Hour Prayer and its shorter counterpart were originally Italian Lenten devotions, introduced in Milan in 1577 by Cardinal Carlo Borromeo and in Germany (in Cologne) by a papal nuncio in 1591; in Rome it was extended as the Perpetual Prayer in 1592.[35] Churches observing the Forty Hour Prayer were to assign specific individuals or groups (such as canons, vicars, members of the choir and so forth) to pray in the church before the exposed Sacrament during predetermined times, so that the prayer would extend uninterrupted for the duration of 40 hours. Bishop Johann Otto von Gemmingen seems to have first called for the Forty Hour Prayer on 1 September 1594 as a means of averting God's wrath, embodied especially in the threats of the 'bloodthirsty Turks' [*Blutdürstigen Türcken*]. The musical embellishment of the opening hour of the devotion was to include sung verses, the hymn *O salutaris hostia*, the penitential responsory *Emendemus in melius*, the seven Penitential Psalms and litanies.[36]

chapter's discussion of this mandate, *DR*, 4 August 1608). During Heinrich's reign other parishes in the diocese commissioned paintings of St Michael and priests were directed to deliver sermons concerning him; see Lothar Altmann, 'Michaelskirchen im Bistum Augsburg', in Mai, ed., *Sankt Michael in Bayern*, p. 76. The association between St Michael and the Counter-Reformation was explicit in Bavaria, where the new Jesuit church was consecrated in the archangel's honour in 1597. Count Wolfgang Wilhelm of Pfalz-Neuburg also appropriated this image in the wake of his re-Catholicization of that territory after 1614. Peter Paul Rubens received commissions for a number of paintings from Wolfgang Wilhelm for his court chapel in the late 1610s and 1620s, including the well-known large-format of *The Last Judgment* and two versions of the *Descent of the Fallen Angels into Hell*, all of which feature a heavily armed St Michael driving the damned into the flaming pit; see Merkl, 'Kunst und Konfessionalisierung', pp. 204–5.

[34] Stetten, *Geschichte der Heil. Röm. Reichs Freyen Stadt Augspurg*, vol. 2, p. 155.

[35] Erwin Iserloh, Joseph Galzik and Hubert Jedin, *Reformation and Counter Reformation*, trans. Anselm Biggs and Peter W. Becker (New York: Seabury Press, 1980), p. 563.

[36] StAA, KWA E45[8], printed ordinance of Bishop Johann Otto von Gemmingen, 1 September 1594. An episcopal ordinance for the Ten Hour Prayer in 1596 is also extant, and differs from the former only in minor details; see ABA, BO 2234. *Emendemus in*

It is not always easy to tell from the distribution of the subsequent hours of the Prayer itself exactly which groups may have sung, but it is all but certain that the '*Kapellmeister* with his students and choirboys, along with the church's lay instrumentalists' [*Herr Capellmaister sampt seinen Discipulis vnnd Chorschulern auch des Stiffts wältlichen Instrumentiste[n]*], who were assigned to be present from 6.00 to 7.00 a.m. on Friday morning and from 7.00 to 8.00 p.m. on Friday evening, performed sacred vocal music with some sort of instrumental accompaniment. After completion of the Prayer all the participants were to reassemble in the cathedral and hear an Office for the Blessed Virgin Mary and a sung Litany of Loreto. Finally, as the officiant gave his benediction, the choir was to sing the Eucharistic hymn *Ecce panis Angelorum*. The music in honour of the Virgin Mary and the Eucharistic hymns and verses underscore the emphasis placed on these confessional symbols by the clergy in this period.

Although the 1594 ordinance laid down strict rules for the cultivation of the Forty Hour Prayer, Johann Otto's successor, Heinrich V, allowed for greater flexibility in other churches. In 1641, for example, he permitted churches without trained singers to replace the usual music with 'some German sacred songs, to be sung for a quarter-hour'. Afterwards the priest was to intone German litanies of the Sacrament, the Name of Jesus, the saints, or others, during which the congregation was to say the appropriate responses. At the end of his ordinance Heinrich adds that:

> If it serves to awaken the devotion of the common man to sing sacred songs in the German language during the first or last quarter-hour [of the Prayer], that is, various litanies, the Our Father in the form of a song, the Seven Last Words of our Lord, the Magnificat, the Ten Commandments or other songs appropriate for that time of year, the pastor should select these songs from the general songbook or else from approved sacred Catholic books.[37]

It is clear that music, whether chant, instrumental music or German songs and litanies, played an important role before, after and during the Forty Hour Prayer. Although the Prayer was, to a certain extent, an opportunity for individuals to pray to God at a critical moment, its embellishment with processions, music and displays of the Sacrament

---

melius, whose normal liturgical position is in Matins for the first Sunday of Lent, is a penitential responsory and serves here as a suitable introduction for the subsequent praying of the seven Penitential Psalms. On the 'Catholic' symbolism of this reponsory for William Byrd, see Joseph Kerman, 'On William Byrd's *Emendemus in melius*', in Dolores Pesce, ed., *Hearing the Motet: Essays on the Motet of the Middle Ages and Renaissance* (New York and Oxford: Oxford University Press, 1997), pp. 329–47.

[37] ABA, BO 130, 3 April 1641, fol. 1v.

ensured a theatrical projection of Catholic devotion to its observers and participants. In the early decades of the seventeenth century, the Forty Hour Prayer and its lesser variants became a regular fixture in Augsburg (particularly in the cathedral[38] and in the Jesuit church of St Salvator), and were ordered for outbreaks of plague, war and for political events.

We can only speculate whether local musicians composed music for the Forty Hour Prayer, but Heinrich's embrace of liturgical Romanization and renewed emphasis on the feast of the Guardian Angels moved at least two Augsburg composers to respond with appropriate music. Christian Erbach's three volumes of *Modorum sacrorum tripertitorum* (1604–06), comprising a complete cycle of Introits, Alleluias and Communions for the Mass Propers of Roman feasts, must have been directly inspired by the bishop's efforts. Furthermore, both Erbach and Gregor Aichinger responded to the higher status of the feast of the Guardian Angels with special polyphonic compositions: Aichinger brought out his *Officium Angeli Custodis* in 1617, containing Vespers and Mass music for four voices and continuo, in addition to the Litany of the Angels; Erbach composed a five-voice setting of the Litany of the Angels that was entered in manuscript at the end of a series of bound prints probably belonging to the music library of SS Ulrich and Afra.[39] However, the introduction of the Roman ceremonies also resulted in the elimination of the customary music for other feasts, resulting in complaints from the cathedral choir and instrumental musicians that their incomes were being curtailed. On 23 March 1615 the chapter decided to deliberate privately after the 'four canons [*Vierherren*], levites and vicars reported that, since the introduction of the Roman ceremonies, certain members of the choir have seen a great reduction in their payments [*Præsentz*] and ask that the

---

[38] In the cathedral, the Forty Hour Prayer and related devotions were ordered on numerous occasions beginning with Johann Otto's ordinance in 1594. See *DR*, 2 May 1595, 8 June 1601, 25 August 1601, 8 May 1602, 7 June 1602, 9 August 1602, 3 July 1604, 2 June 1606, 3 August 1618, 23 November 1619, 20 March 1620, 1 July 1620, 12 July 1630 and 15 July 1630; few of these entries in the chapter minutes make explicit references to music, however. Apart from the 1594 ordinance in StAA, KWA E45[8], more detailed descriptions of and ordinances for these devotions may be found in ABA, BO 130, 791, 818, 2234 and 2296.

[39] D-As, 8° Tonk. Schl. 297–301; see also Richard Charteris's description of this series of prints in 'An Early Seventeenth-Century Manuscript Discovery in Augsburg', *Musica disciplina*, 47 (1993), pp. 35–70. The music was probably bound in the 1590s or early 1600s; the most recent print therein is Jakob Reiner's *Selectae piaeque Cantiones* (1591; RISM A/I, R 1084). The cathedral chapter minutes confirm that Erbach also provided litanies for that institution. On 22 May 1619 the chapter asked the dean to decide how much to pay Erbach for certain hymns, antiphons and litanies that he had composed; on 1 July the dean responded that he should be paid the considerable sum of 100 Gulden (see *DR*, 22 May 1619, 1 July 1619).

old system of payments be restored'.[40] Heinrich's streamlining of the
Augsburg liturgy, then, was a mixed blessing for local musicians.

Polyphonic Repertories in Augsburg's Catholic Churches

At the same time that Erbach was composing his polyphonic Propers
around the turn of the seventeenth century, elaborate instrumental and
polychoral music after the Venetian model was finding an ever greater
presence in Augsburg's Catholic churches. While musicians at the
cathedral and at SS Ulrich and Afra partook of a general transalpine
enthusiasm for Venetian music after the turn of the century, the
cultivation of polychoral and instrumental music required more than
efforts of the *Kapellmeister* alone. This music was a large financial
investment for musical institutions, which had to compensate not only
their own singers, but also organists and instrumentalists. As the overall
economic situation of Augsburg worsened after the turn of the century,
affecting individuals and institutions alike, the cathedral chapter and the
clergy of SS Ulrich and Afra maintained and even increased the scope
and ostentation of the music heard in church services.

Unfortunately, the cathedral's choirbooks do not survive, and
descriptions of actual musical performances in extant chronicles are rare.
Some conclusions can be drawn, however, from the records of the
chapter, which purchased and received music, hired singers and
instrumentalists and encouraged the choirboys to learn various musical
instruments. These documents suggest that the period between 1600 and
1630 saw a significant expansion in instrumental music at the cathedral.
At the same time, surviving choirbooks and scores from SS Ulrich and
Afra confirm that the choir there was performing polychoral music by

---

[40] *DR*, 23 March 1615. On 4 June the chapter resolved to increase the choir's payments
for the feasts that remained, but a long-term solution was found only after the
Kapellmeister, Georg Metzler, took it upon himself to suggest a complete reorganization of
the choir in March 1616 that attempted to return to the original 1561 ordinance for
liturgical music. According to Metzler's supplication, dated 22 March 1616, figural and
organ music was originally established (1561) for ten feasts, Christmas, Epiphany, St
Hilaria, Easter, Pentecost, Assumption of the Virgin, Trinity Sunday, Corpus Christi,
Dedication of a Church and All Saints. However, to these ten, four had been added as feasts
of the first rank, namely Ascension, Nativity of John the Baptist, Apostles Peter and Paul
and St Ulrich (one of the diocesan patrons). Metzler suggests that the chapter pay the choir
and musicians equally for all 14 feasts, and eliminate extra music that had been customary
for feasts of lower rank. He also proposed reforms in the administration of the choir
students. See BSA, Hochstift Augsburg/Neuburger Abgabe 5282, 22 March 1616. On the
same day the chapter agreed to provide the same music for all 14 feasts, and to deliberate
on Metzler's other suggestions privately. *DR*, 22 March 1616. On the 1616 ordinance, see
also Otto Ursprung, 'Die Chorordnung von 1616 am Dom zu Augsburg'.

Giovanni Gabrieli and others in the early seventeenth century. Although it is impossible to discern whether a desire for aural ostentation consistent with the spirit of the Counter-Reformation inspired the adoption of this repertory, the embrace of instrumental and polychoral music in these churches in the early seventeenth century was entirely of a piece with the theatrical displays of the contemporary processions and devotional exercises to be described in Chapters 6 and 7.

On 7 March 1596 the cathedral chapter drew up a contract with a cornettist, Jakob Baumann, which obliged him, among other duties, to teach the cornetto to one of the choirboys or another suitable student and to oversee the maintenance of the musical instruments owned by the cathedral.[41] Before this time neither the *Kapellmeister* nor the organist seem to have taught instrumental music on a regular basis; on occasion, however, students were sent to musicians employed by the Fugger family or the Munich court chapel for instruction.[42] Baumann was joined in 1609 by the cornettist and composer Philipp Zindelin, whom the chapter had previously engaged as a performer (the terms of Zindelin's contract were identical to those of Baumann's). Together they were responsible for the teaching of wind instruments, and later, string instruments.[43] Numerous references in the chapter minutes to the purchase or refurbishing of musical instruments confirm the commitment of these men and the chapter to the expansion of instrumental music.

---

[41] BSA, Hochstift Augsburg/Neuburger Abgabe 5282, 7 March 1596, 'Obligation. Jacob Paumanns *Cornetistens* vff dem Thumbstifft alhie'. Bauman previously had been a cornettist in the Munich court chapel and at the time of his Augsburg appointment was serving in the Fugger household (Layer, *Musik und Musiker der Fuggerzeit*, p. 26).

[42] A certain 'Fugger cornettist' taught the cornetto to choirboys in 1580 (*DR*, 11 April 1580), probably Martin Boets (Bods), as Layer indicates in *Musik und Musiker der Fuggerzeit*, p. 34; in 1581 the chapter increased his salary, in return for which he was to teach the dulcian (*DR*, 15 July 1581). In 1589 and 1591 respectively Klingenstein sent the students Hans Schmidt and Bernard Messenhauser to Munich to learn the cornetto (*DR*, 13 October 1589 and 9 October 1591; see also Singer, 'Leben und Werke des Augsburger Domkapellmeisters Bernhardus Klingenstein', p. 18). In 1592 one of the choir-vicars, Peter Sartorius, was paid to teach the trombone to Andreas Hitzelberger, one of his colleagues (*DR*, 25 September 1592); such an arrangement seems to have been unusual, however. Ursprung claimed that instrumental music was performed at the cathedral from 1572, but does not specify his sources; see *Jacobus de Kerle*, p. 73.

[43] Christian Erbach's well-known role as a teacher of both organ and composition – he not only founded what Adolf Layer called an 'Augsburg organ school' (*Musik und Musiker der Fuggerzeit*, pp. 6 and 71) but also taught composition to the cathedral *Kapellmeister* after Klingenstein's death – is not directly relevant to the cantorate's repertory and so can be passed over here. For more details on Erbach's duties and reputation as a pedagogue, see esp. Ernst von Werra's edition of *Ausgewählte Werke von Christian Erbach (um 1570–1635)*, Jahrgang 4, vol. 2 of *Denkmäler der Tonkunst in Bayern* (Leipzig: Breitkopf & Härtel, 1903), pp. xvi–xvii.

Significantly, there seems to be no record of the purchase of new instruments before 1601, although in 1581 the chapter obtained a regal from the estate of the deceased organist Christoph Klingenstein.[44] There are indications that the cathedral chapter hired outside musicians from the *Stadtpfeifer* on special occasions, but there is no evidence for a continuous tradition of instrumental music before the seventeenth century.[45] Beginning in 1601 and extending to the outbreak of war in the early 1630s, the cathedral obtained numerous instruments on at least fifteen different occasions, including trombones, dulcians, regals and string instruments.[46] For example, on 23 February 1609 the chapter reimbursed 'the cornettist Baumann in the amount of 39 Gulden, 48 Kreutzer for the purchase of two new trombones in Nuremberg, and for the repair of two older ones'.[47] In May of 1628 alone the chapter approved payments for a 'large bass violin' [*grosse Paßgeigen*] and 'two dulcians from Venice'.[48] The chapter even purchased a clavichord in 1625 at the request of the student Felix Zimmermann, ordering the *Kapellmeister* Johann Aichmiller to 'place the chapter's insignia on the instrument, record it in the inventory, and lend it to Zimmermann for as long as he wants it'.[49]

The chapter not only approved the requests of Baumann and the *Kapellmeister* for new instruments, but also encouraged the interests of the choirboys in learning how to play them. A few students requested organ and composition lessons with Erbach,[50] but many others asked to learn cornetto, trombone, dulcian and string instruments from Baumann

---

[44] Klingenstein in turn had purchased the regal for 20 Gulden from his predecessor, Jacobus de Kerle. This instrument was 'to be used in the choir with the viols' [*so in Choro zu den Violen zu gebrauchen*], suggesting that string instruments and the regal were played to accompany the choir, probably *colla parte*. See Layer, *Musik und Musiker der Fuggerzeit*, p. 34.

[45] In 1586, for example, the chapter temporarily hired the trombonist Thomas Lang, a *Stadtpfeifer*; see Layer, *Musik und Musiker der Fuggerzeit*, p. 51.

[46] DR, 26 January 1601, 5 October 1601, and 23 February 1609 (for trombones); 3 August 1618, 25 June 1627, 11 October 1627, 31 May 1628 and 30 October 1629 (for dulcians); 2 May 1609 and 5 April 1628 (for regals); 12 May 1628 and 27 April 1629 (for string instruments and replacement strings); 3 November 1625 (for a clavichord); and 28 January 1619 and 6 October 1627 (for unspecified instruments).

[47] DR, 23 February 1609.

[48] DR, 12 May and 31 May 1628.

[49] DR, 3 November 1625.

[50] Among these was a Johann Mozart, perhaps an ancestor of Leopold and Wolfgang, who requested in 1612 to take composition along with the organ lessons he was currently receiving from Erbach. DR, 14 November 1612. Mozart later became an Augustinian monk and entered the monastery of Heilig Kreuz in Augsburg (see Layer, *Musik und Musiker der Fuggerzeit*, p. 37). Between 1613 and 1616 Erbach taught Johann Klemm, who later became court organist in Dresden; see ibid., p. 37.

and Zindelin. One student, Matthias Pliem (Bluem), was taught several instruments around 1610; he would later become vice-*Kapellmeister* at the court of Pfalz-Neuburg.[51] In May 1618, the choirboy Johann Braun's voice broke, and he asked the chapter to be allowed to learn an instrument. The chapter agreed, assigning Baumann to teach the boy trombone and dulcian.[52] On 13 January 1627 another student, Johann Mantsch, asked the chapter if he could learn the 'small violin' [*klaine Geiglen*] from Baumann. Apparently the chapter approved his request, for two weeks later Mantsch asked the chapter to purchase a violin for his use, and two years later the chapter minutes confirm that he was still studying the instrument.[53] The chapter had a vested interest in the quality of this instruction, since they expected these children eventually to participate regularly in the performance of instrumental music during church services. 'The instrumentalists who are obliged to teach one or more students at no extra cost', the chapter resolves in May 1630, 'shall report to the chapter on their progress and whether they show sufficient talent.'[54] The obligation of the cathedral musicians to instruct the choirboys in instrumental music, the rapid acquisition of instruments and the vigorous support for instrumental instruction all point to a dramatic expansion of instrumental music at the cathedral after 1600. Together with the cultivation of liturgical processions and other special observations like the Forty Hour Prayer, the performance of this music reflected the greater emphasis placed on the embellishment of the liturgy.

Since the cathedral's choirbooks do not survive, it is difficult to generalize about the vocal repertory available to the *Kapellmeister* in the late sixteenth and early seventeenth centuries. We do know that the chapter sometimes paid their own musicians for the composition of new polyphonic works, sometimes quite handsomely: the chapter gave Klingenstein 100 Gulden, equivalent to the entire yearly salary of an organist, for the compositions he offered in 1581 and again in 1586.[55] As for music acquired from the outside, one must rely on the minutes of the chapter meetings, which contain frequent references to the purchase

---

[51] Ibid., p. 36.

[52] *DR*, 25 and 28 May 1618.

[53] *DR*, 13 and 27 January 1627, 4 April 1629.

[54] *DR*, 10 May 1630.

[55] Klingenstein's offering of 1581 prompted accolades from the chapter, which was impressed by his industry and expressed its hope that he would continue to provide music for the cantorate and maintain good order among the choirboys. See *DR*, 31 October 1581 and 28 July 1586. There are evidently no surviving compositions by the cathedral's organist, Erasmus Mayr, who served from 1581 to his death in 1624 (see Ursprung, *Jacobus de Kerle*, p. 93). Although Mayr's successor Christian Erbach was a prolific composer, it appears that only the *Kapellmeister* was expected to provide new compositions.

of music or the dedication of music to the chapter. Table 4.1 shows the
known acquisitions of music by the chapter between 1580 and 1630.
From this list alone one certainly cannot reconstruct the range of

Table 4.1   Music acquired by the cathedral chapter, 1580–1630

Date	Composer[a]
23 Sept. 1580	Johannes Lotter, mass
1 Feb. 1581	Blasius Tribauer, masses, 5vv
21 June 1586	Conrad Stuber
24 Oct. 1586	Johann Fischer
25 Mar. 1587	Jacobus de Kerle, *Selectorium aliquot modulorum, qui in sacris templis … decantari solent*[b]
9 Sept. 1587	Orlando di Lasso
29 Mar. 1589	Johannes Gallus Stein
4 May 1589	Heinrich Leutgeb, 'Beatae Virginis' and 'Canticum eucharisticum'
23 June 1589	Orlando di Lasso, masses[c]
15 Oct. 1592	Martin Langgreder and Nikolaus Zangius
19 Dec. 1603	Ferdinand di Lasso offers motets by his father
8 Mar. 1604	Orlando di Lasso, *Magnum Opus musicum*
3 July 1608	Music book from a 'bass from Graz'
21 June 1610	Orlando di Lasso, *Missae posthumae*
13 Feb. 1612	Rudolph di Lasso, *Triga musica qua Missae Odaeque Marianae*
7 Oct. 1613	Lambert de Sayve
21 Oct. 1616	Georg Victorinus (possibly his anthology *Siren cœlestis*)
13 Feb. 1617	Georg Victorinus
10 Nov. 1617	Hieronymus Praetorius, *Opus Musicum novum et perfectum*, vol. IV; Abraham Schadæus, *Promptuarium musici*, vol. IV
14 Jan. 1619	Rudolph di Lasso, Magnificats (possibly the *Jubilus B. Virginis* by Orlando di Lasso)
12 May 1625	Ferdinand II di Lasso
5 Dec. 1629	Bernardino Borlasca, 'Italian music'

[a] Names of works are given if known.

[b] Jacobus de Kerle, *Selectorium aliquot Modulorum, qui in sacris Templis … partim quatuor, partim quinque et octo Vocibus, decantari solent* (Prague: Georg Nigrinus, 1585; RISM A/I, K455).

[c] Probably his *Patrocinium musices, Missae aliquot quinque Vocum* (Munich: Adam Berg, 1589; RISM A/I, L990).

repertory available to Klingenstein and his successors, but it does suggest certain patterns. With respect to the composers whose identities are known, the chapter tended to accept music only from those employed by Catholic courts and churches.[56] Unsurprisingly, composers from the nearby Munich court are very well represented in the list, including members of the Lasso family, Georg Victorinus (the *Kapellmeister* of the Jesuit church of St Michael) and Bernardino Borlasca (an Italian who served as *Kapellmeister*, *Vizekapellmeister* and *Konzertmeister* at the court). The large fourth volume of Abraham Schadaeus's *Promptuarii musici* (1617, edited posthumously by Caspar Vincentius) would have been a major acquisition.[57] Consisting of 132 pieces for five to eight voices (and with an added basso continuo part that functions mainly as a *basso seguente*), this anthology of Latin-texted music by Italian and German composers provides material for Trinity, Corpus Christi and for the Sundays after Trinity. The largest portion of the volume, however, is given over to the general category of 'prayers, sighs, praises, and songs, with psalms and spiritual consolations' [*Preces, Suspiria, Laudes, & Cantica, cum Psalmis & Spiritualibus consolationibus*] and a 'Marian wood' [*Sylva Marialis*] with about two dozen compositions devoted to the Virgin Mary. The musical output of many of the composers represented both in this anthology and in the other acquisitions by the cathedral, especially after the turn of the seventeenth century, is in fact oriented towards Marian themes and the idiom of the few-voiced concerto.[58]

---

[56] There is little information, unfortunately, on Johannes Lotter, Blasius Tribauer or Johann Fischer. Conrad Stuber (*c.*1550–*c.*1605) attended the University of Freiburg and by 1587 was a priest and chorister at the court of Count Eitelfriedrich IV von Hohenzollern-Hechingen, at Hechingen in Swabia. Several of his works, all sacred, turn up in printed anthologies and manuscripts around the turn of the seventeenth century. His patron was a zealous partisan of the Counter-Reformation. See Anthony F. Carver, 'Stuber [Stuberus, Stueber], Conrad', in *New Grove II*, vol. 24, pp. 618–19.

[57] *Promptuarii musici, sacras Harmonias V. VI. VII. & VIII. Vocum ... Pars quarta* (Strasbourg: Anthonius Bertram, sumptibus Paul Ledertz, 1617; RISM B/I, 1617¹).

[58] Late in 1603 Ferdinand di Lasso, Orlando's first son and *Kapellmeister* at the court, offered a 'body of motets' [*Corporis Motetarum*] by his father to the chapter; the latter initially hesitated to accept the offer since they already had 'many of these motets and many others, indeed an excess' (*DR*, 19 December 1603). However, Klingenstein indeed purchased the *Thesaurus Orlandi* (almost certainly a reference to the gigantic *Magnum Opus musicum*) in March and the chapter agreed to reimburse him for the purchase (*DR*, 8 March 1604). The chapter's acceptance of music by Georg Victorinus (*DR*, 21 October 1616 and 13 February 1617) suggests that newer *concertato* pieces may have found a way into the cathedral's performance repertory by this time. At least one of these entries could well refer to Victorinus's anthology *Siren cœlestis* (Munich: Adam Berg, 1616), a large collection of early sacred *concertato* music for two to four voices and continuo by Italian and German musicians. Much of the music of Rudolph di Lasso, Orlando's second son,

The chapter, however, seems to have exercised greater caution with music by composers from Protestant areas. In 1589 Heinrich Leutgeb, a musician from the Protestant Württemburg court, offered Eucharistic and Marian music to the chapter. They instructed Klingenstein not only to judge the musical quality, but also to ensure that the text was not 'corrupted' [*corrumpiert*]. Three weeks later, the *Kapellmeister* found it acceptable and the chapter approved a payment of 25 Gulden to Leutgeb.[59] The *Opus Musicum novum et perfectum* of Hieronymus Praetorius (indicated in the chapter minutes of November 1617 as *pretorij operum musicorum tomum quartum*) would represent the only other known Protestant exception to the Catholic repertory acquired by the cathedral during this period.[60] On the whole, the surviving evidence suggests that the cathedral acquired a much narrower range of music than its Protestant counterpart, the cantorate of St Anna (see Chapter 3), preferring Latin-texted music by composers in Catholic areas. How much of this music was actually performed by the cathedral cantorate remains an open question.[61]

The polyphonic repertory heard at SS Ulrich and Afra is somewhat better known, since numerous choirbooks and scores from its music library survive. A sophisticated, if conservative, musical tradition was well entrenched by the late sixteenth century, as numerous choirbooks in the hand of Johannes Dreer (or Treer) attest.[62] Beginning in the 1560s and extending into the early seventeenth century, this series of

---

also draws on the *concertato* idiom and may have been used by Klingenstein and his successors; the chapter accepted 'Masses and Magnificats' by him in 1612, almost certainly referring to his *Triga musica qua Missae Odaeque Marianae triplice fugantur* (Munich: Nikolaus Heinrich, 1612; RISM L1039), which are subtitled 'in Viadanae modos' (*DR*, 13 February 1612). Although there is no evidence that the chapter purchased it, Lasso's *Virginalia Eucharistica* (1615) shows the stylistic direction of the composer's work (see the recent edition by Alexander J. Fisher (Madison, Wis.: A-R Editions, 2002)). The 'mass book' accepted by the chapter in 1610 (*DR*, 21 June 1610) is almost certainly the *Missae posthumae* of Orlando di Lasso (Munich: Nikolaus Heinrich, 1610; RISM L1024).

[59] *DR*, 4 October and 25 October 1589. See also Singer, 'Leben und Werke des Augsburger Domkapellmeisters Bernhardus Klingenstein', pp. 29–30.

[60] It is clear, however, that the Praetorius volume and the Schadaeus anthology were intended for the use of the *Marianer* (children's choir), and probably not for the church liturgy itself.

[61] Rudolf Flotzinger has suggested that the nature of liturgical texts tended to militate against the introduction into the church liturgy of monody, which proved more effective in setting highly emotive and/or poetic texts; see 'Die kirchliche Monodie um die Wende des 16./17. Jahrhunderts', in Fellerer, ed., *Geschichte der katholischen Kirchenmusik*, vol. 2, p. 79.

[62] Theodor Wohnhaas suggests that this vitality may be attributed to the slow recovery of music printing in Augsburg in the late sixteenth century; see Wohnhaas, 'Der Augsburger Musikdruck', p. 301.

choirbooks points to the dominating influence of Orlando di Lasso, the best-represented composer in these sources with numerous Magnificats, Mass ordinary cycles and hymns.[63] Heinrich Isaac and Jacobus de Kerle account for the majority of polyphonic Mass proper settings up until 1614, when the choir presented Johannes Dreer with a transcription of proper settings from Erbach's *Modorum sacrorum tripertitorum* (1604–6; see above).[64] With the exception of Giovanni Croce's *Vespertina omnium Solemnitatum Psalmodia* (1597), a set of psalms in eight-voice *cori spezzati* copied into a choirbook in 1608,[65] and the music by Giovanni Gabrieli and Asprilio Pacelli described below, the choirbooks of SS Ulrich and Afra tend to favour imitative music for four to six voices.[66]

Although this conservative repertory probably held sway for most occasions,[67] there is some evidence that polychoral music found its way into SS Ulrich and Afra's musical repertory by 1600. This is not surprising, since the abbot, Johann von Merk, was the dedicatee of Giovanni Gabrieli's second volume of *Sacrae Symphoniae* in 1615.[68] At least two extant manuscripts testify to the presence of polychoral music at the church. One contains manuscript organ basses for all the pieces from Andrea and Giovanni Gabrieli's *Concerti* of 1587 and from

---

[63] The first surviving choirbook from the abbey, dated 1568, is devoted to Lasso's Magnificats (D-As, Tonk. Schl. 13), while Lasso's music is represented more than 40 years later in a volume of Requiem Masses dated 1613 (D-As, Tonk. Schl. 21). Wolfgang Boetticher has recognized the importance of these sources for our understanding of Lasso's oeuvre; Lasso made at least one trip to Augsburg in the company of his copyist Franz Flori, in 1582; see *Orlando di Lasso und seine Zeit*, pp. 162–63, 314, 342, 506, 614, and 646 n. Daniel Zager, in 'Liturgical Rite and Musical Repertory', pp. 215–31, has argued that the hymn cycles by Kerle and Lasso, copied by Dreer in 1577 and 1584/85 respectively, reflect the modification of the Roman liturgy by a local sanctoral tradition, including observances of the feasts of SS Ulrich, Afra, Narcissus and so forth.

[64] Isaac's and Kerle's Mass propers appear in D-As, Tonk. Schl. 23 (1575) and 7 (1576). Another volume of Mass propers for four to six voices, copied in 1578 (Tonk. Schl. 6), contains settings by Ippolito Chamatero (probably copied from his *Li Introiti fondati sopra il canto fermo del basso* of 1574), Gianmatteo Asola (probably from his *Le messe a quattro voci pari* of 1574) and Johannes Eccard.

[65] D-As, Tonk. Schl. 2 (*primus chorus*) and 3 (*secundus chorus*).

[66] Other sixteenth-century composers well represented in Dreer's choirbooks include Andrea Gabrieli, Jakob Handl, de Monte, Palestrina, Jakob Regnart, Jakob Reiner, Rore, Scandello, Utendal, Vaet, Victoria and others.

[67] One of Johannes Dreer's codices contains a hymn cycle in a mostly imitative style by Jacobus de Kerle (most of which are drawn from his *Hymni totius anni secundum ritum Sanctae Rom. Eccl.* (Rome: Antonio Barre, 1560; RISM A/I, K442)) that was performed at SS Ulrich and Afra at least until 1624. See Ursprung, *Jacobus de Kerle*, p. 86.

[68] Layer noted that Merk received at least a part of Gabrieli's estate (*Nachlaß*) upon the latter's death in 1615; see Layer, *Musik und Musiker der Fuggerzeit*, p. 43.

Giovanni Gabrieli's *Sacrae Symphoniae* of 1597.[69] The other score contains complete and mostly untexted manuscript scores copied from Giovanni Gabrieli's *Sacrae Symphoniae* of 1597 and from the first book of Asprilio Pacelli's *Motectorum et Psalmorum Liber primus* for eight voices (1597).[70] According to the title page the manuscript was presented to the abbot in 1616 by the local publisher, bookdealer and organist Caspar Flurschütz; he or one of his apprentices may well have copied the music from prints available in his shop.[71] Gabrieli's and Pacelli's music may have formed an impressive musical counterpoint to Johann von Merk's massive redecoration scheme for the interior of the church, which included covering the walls with white marble (1601), adding at least three splendid altars in honour of the church's patron saints, erecting a bronze sculptural group of the Crucifixion in 1605 (which may have been related to some music by the organist Gregor Aichinger; see below, p. 197), and expanding the Fugger organ by 13 registers and repainting its wings (1607–08).[72] In a few short years, the visual and aural impact of services at SS Ulrich and Afra was greatly augmented.

Vernacular Song in the Church

In 1563 the Augsburg printer Philipp Ulhart reissued a small book of German translations of Latin Mass and Office texts, compiled and edited by Christophorus Flurhaim of Kitzingen.[73] The recent iconoclasm of the

---

[69] D-As, 2° Tonk. Schl. 200ᵃ. The manuscript attests to the widespread practice in both Italy and Germany of improvising or writing organ basses (generally in the nature of a *basso seguente*, where the organ mirrors the lowest sounding part at any given time) to accompany sacred vocal music in the late sixteenth century. See Richard Charteris, 'Two Little-Known Manuscripts in Augsburg with Works by Giovanni Gabrieli and his Contemporaries', *R. M. A. Research Chronicle*, 23 (1990), pp. 125–26.

[70] D-As, 2° Tonk. Schl. 39ᵃ.

[71] The page is inscribed 'Reuerendissimo & Amplissimo Patri I D. IOANNI I Celeberrimi Monasterij SS: Vdalricj I et Afra Aug. Vind. Abbatj I Totiq[ue] Venerabili eiusdem Monasterij I Conuentui I Diuûm Honori Sacra Musica commodo I communi vsui I Hanc Musicam operam Xenij loco I libens merito offert, consecratq[ue] I *Caspa: Flurschüz* I A°. I [1616].' The Gabrieli *Sacrae symphoniae* was available in Flurschütz's shop in 1613, 1615, 1616, 1618 and 1619; the Pacelli, *Motectorum et psalmorum liber primus* in 1613 and 1615; see Schaal, *Die Kataloge des Augsburger Musikalien-Händlers Kaspar Flurschütz*, nos. 7, 84, 259, 260, 340, 801, 1404 and 1904.

[72] See Layer, *Musik und Musiker der Fuggerzeit*, pp. 27 and 42, and Stetten, *Geschichte der Heil. Röm. Reichs Freyen Stadt Augspurg*, vol. 1, p. 872.

[73] Flurhaim's translations may have been based on those by Peter Ernst I von Mansfeld (1517–1604/06), who, as Flurhaim explains in his preface, had published a similar series of translations for the use of those who could not understand Latin. The full title of Flurhaim's book is *Alle kirchen Gesäng vnd Gebeet des gantzen Jars, von der hailigen*

Protestants still fresh in his mind, Flurhaim railed against Protestant depredations of Catholic images and their disrespect for the traditional ceremonies of the Catholic Church. Among the changes that the Protestants had introduced into their services, Flurhaim wrote, was the increased use of German texts not only to supplement the traditional liturgy but also to replace certain items of the Latin Mass. He then mounted a spirited defence of the Latin language in the divine service:

> I do not doubt that we Germans ... previously sang everything in Latin in church, and not in German, so that we and particularly the clergy would not despise the Latin language, in which the entire body of divine Scripture from Hebrew and Greek has been transmitted. And Luther himself (who is the chief leader of the rebellious host) now writes that it is good that one sings Latin in the church, so that youth may become accustomed to the language. Who would doubt that the singing of everything in German in the church will lead to the demise of the Latin language? And therefore to the demise of Christian belief? For then everyone would speak solely in German. But since most of the Doctors of the Church [wrote] in Latin, how would we then understand their writings? The gifts of God are many, and not all is revealed to any one man. So we have seen with our own eyes what trouble has resulted from this change [of language].

Flurhaim's book embodies a fundamental paradox in the Catholic Church's attitude towards the use of the vernacular tongue. On the one hand, many Catholics saw the Latin language as crucial to the church's identity for practical as well as symbolic reasons. As Flurhaim reminds his readers, knowledge of Latin was indispensable for understanding Scripture and the writings of the Church Fathers. More generally, Catholic reformers of the late sixteenth and early seventeenth centuries saw Latin as a symbolic link not only to the pre-Reformation traditions of the Church, but also to the seat of the Church in Rome. Even given the continued (albeit limited) presence of the Latin language in the Lutheran church throughout the early modern era, the equation of *Latinitas* and *Romanitas* by German Catholics helped to make Latin a marker of their own religious identity.[74]

Christenlichen Kirchen angenommen, vnd bißher in löblichem brauch erhalten Vom Jntroit der Mess, biß auff die Complent. Darneben die benedeyung der Liecht, der Palm, des Feürs, des Osterstocks, der Tauff/ vnd der Kreütter. Alles verteutscht, vnd längest durch M. Christophorum Flurhaim von Kitzingen gemehret. Yetzt fleissig nachgetruckt, für die, so die Lateinischen Gebeet mit andern Ceremonien zu verstehn vnd nachzubeten begeren (Augsburg: Philipp Ulhart, 1563). Exemplar in D-As, 8° Th Lt K 290, Bbd. 1. An earlier edition of this book may have been published, but does not appear to have survived.

[74] Both Wolfgang Reinhard ('Was ist katholische Konfessionalisierung?', p. 444) and R. Po-Chia Hsia (*Social Discipline in the Reformation*, p. 103) stress that the Catholic promotion of Latin reflected the traditional propagation of the Catholic faith by literate elites.

On the other hand, Catholic officials could hardly ignore the positive role of vernacular song in the spread of the Lutheran faith. A well-established body of vernacular chorales and psalms, disseminated widely through the relatively new technology of print, transmitted Lutheran doctrine directly to the common people; as seen in Chapter 2, this body of German music could become a cultural marker of Protestant identity in the same way that Latinity became associated with Catholicism.[75] The Austrian Catholic theologian David Gregor Corner spoke of the seductive power of Protestant song in his *Groß Catolisch Gesangbüch* of 1625:

> Above all ... Godly blessings and devotion have been driven from the earth through the lovely sweetness of singing, in that the heretics have made use of this means and have betrayed true belief through cheerful, yet false and corrupting songs; at the same time they have been able to spread their false, damnable errors. Most heretics [throughout history] have used this method, that is, to spread heresy through the charm of music.[76]

Adam Contzen, the Jesuit confessor of Duke Maximilian I of Bavaria, expressed this sentiment more famously when he encouraged his patron in his *Politicorum Libri decem* (1620) to promote Catholic song in the vernacular, for 'the hymns of Luther kill more souls than his writings or declamations'.[77] These songs were so popular that in the mid-sixteenth century even Catholic congregations in some areas of Germany were singing them. Duke Albrecht V of Bavaria warned in a school ordinance of 1569 that 'in our time many new and seductive songs and falsified psalms [*gefelschter Psalmen*] have become popular among the common man, and have even been found in the Christian, Catholic divine service'.[78] A few years later, in the preface to a songbook for the diocese

---

[75] An important recent contribution to the political usage of Lutheran song is Oettinger, *Music as Propaganda in the German Reformation*.

[76] From David Gregor Corner, *Groß Catolisch Gesangbüch Darinen in die vierhundert Andechtige alte vnd newe gesäng vnd rüff, in eine gute vnd richtige ordnung zusäm gebrach, so theils zu Hauß theils zu Kirchen auch beÿ Procesionen vnd Kirchenfesten, mit grosen nütz konnen gesungen werden* (Nuremberg: Georg Endtner d.J., 1625; RISM B/VIII, 1625⁰⁵). Corner (1585–1648) was a theologian, hymnologist and poet, and was one of the most prominent figures in the Austrian Counter-Reformation. See Robert Johandl, 'David Gregor Corner und sein Gesangbuch', *Archiv für Musikwissenschaft*, 2 (1920), pp. 447–64, and Walther Lipphardt and Dorothea Schröder, 'Corner, David Gregor', in *New Grove II*, vol. 6, pp. 479–80.

[77] From Contzen's *Politicorum Libri decem* (Mainz, c.1620), vol. 2, p. 19, quoted in Hsia, *Social Discipline in the Reformation*, p. 100.

[78] From Albrecht V's *Schuel-Ordnung In den Fürstenthumben Obern und Niedern Bayerlands* (1569), quoted in Otto Ursprung, *Münchens musikalische Vergangenheit: Von der Frühzeit bis zu Richard Wagner* (Munich: Bayerland-Verlag, 1927), pp. 55–56. Concerns about the political content of Protestant psalm translations led the Catholic priest

of Bamberg, the anonymous author claimed that 'in many places German lieder or songs are sung in the Mass before and after the sermon, but many of them are not Catholic, but rather of suspicious origin'.[79]

Catholic officials in Augsburg, too, understood the dangers of heretical songs to which their flocks would have been exposed on a daily basis. Bishop Otto Truchseß von Waldburg, whose own involvement with musical questions at the sittings of the Council of Trent is well known, held a diocesan synod in 1567 that dealt in part with the question of music. 'We wish that the songs of the heretics [*cantiones haereticorum*] be excluded from our church ... however much they flatter [the ear] with the appearance of measure and piety', the synodal decree states. However, 'we allow the public [to sing] ancient and Catholic songs, especially, those which have been used for greater feasts in most German churches, and we deem it fitting that they be retained both in the church and in processions'.[80] Recognizing the advantages of vernacular song for public understanding of and participation in the divine service, Otto deemed it a valuable tool, yet one that had to be carefully controlled.

Later bishops of the diocese persisted in their concern about the

---

Caspar Ulenberg to issue his own 'purified' translations of the psalms in his *Die Psalmen Dauids in allerlei Teutsche gesangreimen bracht* (Mainz: Köln: G. Calenius & J. Quentels Erben, 1582, with many later editions). These translations would receive polyphonic settings by Orlando and Rudolph di Lasso (their *Teutsche Psalmen geistliche Psalmen mit dreyen Stimmen* (Munich: Adam Berg, 1588; RISM B/I, 1588[12])) and Konrad Hagius (his *DJe Psalmen Dauids, Wie die heibeuor in allerlej art Reymen vnd Melodejen, durch den Herrn CASPARVM VLENBERGIVM in Truck verfertigt, newlich abgesetzt* (Düsseldorf: Albert Buyß, 1589; RISM B/VIII, 1589[04])).

[79] From the preface to the *Kurtzer Außzug: Der Christlichen vnd Catholischen Gesäng, deß Ehrwirdigen Herrn Joannis Leisentritij, Thümdechants zü Budessin, Auff alle Sontag, Fest vnd Feyertäg, Durch das gantz Jar, in der Catholischen Kirchen sicherlich zusingen. Auß Bevelch des Hochwürdigen in Gott Fürsten und Herren, Herrn Veiten, Bischoffen zü Bamberg, sampt eines Ehrwürdigen Thüm Capitels daselbsten, für derselbigen Hochlöblichen und Kayserlichen Stifft also auß zuziehen und zusingen verordnet* (Dillingen: Sebald Mayer, 1575; RISM B/VIII, 1575[04]). As the title indicates, this is an abridgement of Johann Leisentrit's well-known *Geistliche Lieder und Psalmen* (Bautzen: Hans Wolrab, 1567; RISM B/VIII, 1567[05]). The Bamberg songbook was reissued in 1576 by the same printer (RISM B/VIII, 1576[01]).

[80] 'A nostris ecclesiis arceri volumus ... cantiones haereticorum, quantalibet modulationis et pietatis specie vulgo blandiantur. Antiquas vero et Catholicas cantilenas, praesertim, quas pii majores nostri Germani majoribus Ecclesiae Festis adhibuerunt, vulgo permittimus et in Ecclesiis, vel etiam Processionibus retineri probamus.' Quoted in Zoepfl, *Das Bistum Augsburg*, p. 363. The Salzburg diocese took a similar position two years later, allowing for popular songs [*cantiones vulgares*] in the Mass, as long as they were drawn from an officially approved repertory; see Michael Härting, 'Das deutsche Kirchenlied der Gegenreformation', in Fellerer, ed., *Geschichte der katholischen Kirchenmusik*, vol. 2, p. 60.

presence of Protestant songs in Catholic churches. On 26 October 1591 Bishop Johann Otto von Gemmingen ordered a sweeping campaign against heresy in the town of Füssen, at the southern end of the diocese in the Alpine foothills.[81] His banning of Lutheran psalm-singing in that town, along with his mandate that local officials search households for and confiscate banned books, writings and pictures, was an early precedent for steps taken by the Catholic city council in Augsburg after the Edict of Restitution was promulgated in 1629 (see Chapter 8). A few years later Bishop Heinrich V, alarmed by the continuing tendency of Catholic parents in his diocese to send their children to Augsburg to attend Protestant schools and to work for Protestant tradesmen, directed his religious agents to clamp down on such practices and to ensure that Catholic children were adhering to the Church's doctrines and rituals. Heinrich showed special concern for children who could not be expected to adhere to Catholicism when surrounded by Protestants:

> Children who are sent in their immature youth to Augsburg to learn a trade or for other reasons cannot help but to have to hear constantly the Protestant song *Daß Brott ich iß, das Lied ich sing*, and are often resistant when their parents or pastoral fathers try to hold them to the practice of the Catholic religion.

He goes on to condemn his Catholic subjects who secretly adhere to Protestant doctrine:

> But from this evil we have also seen that in many Catholic territories and regions, there are not a few persons who, even if they espouse some Catholic beliefs out of fear of punishment, show themselves to adhere [to Protestantism] because they own and read heretical books, send their children or servants into sectarian, dangerous places, arrange marriages in foreign lands, hold contempt for the Catholic Mass and ceremonies, sing Lutheran psalms and songs and do other things contrary to Catholic belief and doctrine.[82]

As Catholic officials like these began to recognize the value of vernacular song for popular indoctrination, German songs began to appear in diocesan liturgical books in the second half of the sixteenth and early seventeenth centuries. The first liturgical book to provide for German songs was an *Obsequiale* for the diocese of Regensburg, printed

---

[81] See Zoepfl, *Das Bistum Augsburg*, pp. 715–16.

[82] BSA, Hochstift Augsburg / Neuburger Abgabe 522, 10 March 1603, 'Getrewe Erinnerung vnd Bericht/ Welcher massen der Catholischen Herrschafften vnnd Obrigkeiten Vnterthanen/ so lernens-dienens- Handwercktreibens- oder anderer Vrsachen halber sich ausser ihrer Herrschafften Land vnd Gebiet in Augspurg befinden/ bey Catholischer Religion zuerhalten. Item/ was eben zu disem Gottseligen End/ mit denen Vnterthanen diser Zeit fürzunemmen/ die sich nicht zu Augspurg/ sondern an andern Orthen auß obgemelter Vrsachen auffhalten.'

in 1570 by Alexander Weissenhorn in Ingolstadt.[83] Bishop Marquard von Berg of the Augsburg diocese followed suit in his *Ritus ecclesiastici Augustensis Episcopatus* of 1580, which contains a separate section for German songs to be sung before the sermon. In his preface he refers to a lengthy tradition of vernacular song in the liturgy, and indeed there is evidence to suggest that Augsburg congregations had been accustomed to singing in church previously.[84] Marquard, however, explicitly permits only ten songs:[85]

Der Tag der ist so frewdenreich	From Christmas to Purification of the BVM
Ein Kind geborn zu Betlehem	Christmas
Mitten vnsers lebens zeyt	Lent
Siesser Vatter Herre Gott (the Ten Commandments)	Lent, or in any season
Christ ist erstanden	From Easter to Ascension
Erstanden ist der heylig Christ	Easter
Christus für mit schallen	From Ascension to Pentecost
Komb heyliger Geist Herre Gott	From Pentecost to Corpus Christi
Der zart Fronleichnam der ist gut	Octave of Corpus Christi
Jesus ist ein süsser nam	'Ein schöner Ruff' [no season given]

---

[83] An *Obsequiale* served the same purpose as a 'Ritual' (*Rituale* or *Ritus*) or 'Agenda': it provided directions for the parish priest for the administration of the sacraments and the conduct of various paraliturgical actions, such as exorcisms and processions. The full title of the Regensburg book is *Obsequiale, Vel liber Agendorum, circa Sacramenta, Benedictiones, & Ceremonias secundum antiquum Vsum, & Ritum Ecclesie Ratisbonensis* (Ingolstadt: Typographia Weissenhorniana, 1570; RISM B/VIII, 1571[10], later edns as 1624[03], 1626[03] and 1629[11]). A facsimile edition of the German songs contained therein has been edited by Klaus Gamber in *Cantiones Germanicae im Regensburger Obsequiale von 1570: Erstes offizielles katholisches Gesangbuch Deutschlands* (Regensburg: Pustet, 1983). Alexander Weissenhorn was the last Catholic printer in Augsburg until the early seventeenth century, fleeing to Ingolstadt in 1540; see Hans-Jörg Künast, 'Entwicklungslinien des Augsburger Buchdrucks von den Anfängen bis zum Ende des Dreißigjährigen Krieges', in Gier and Janota, eds, *Augsburger Buchdruck und Verlagswesen*, p. 19.

[84] For his sermon at Augsburg Cathedral on Christmas 1561, the Jesuit Petrus Canisius opened with the following words: 'The church makes song in this feast more than in any feast of the year, not only by the clergy, but also by the laity; not only by adults but also by boys and girls. Thus these beautiful and ancient songs are sung in church and in the home: *Gelobet seyst du Jesu Christ das du mensch geboren bist; Der tag der ist so freudenreich allen creaturen;* and *In dulci jubilo, nu singet vnd seyt fro, vnsers Hertzen wonne, ligt in presipio, vnd leuchtet als die sonne matris in gremio, α es et ω.*' Quoted in Ursprung, *Jacobus de Kerle*, p. 53.

[85] *Ritus ecclesiastici Augustensis Episcopatus, tribus Partibus siue Libris comprehensi, nuncque primûm recogniti, editi atque promulgati* (Dillingen: Johann Mayer, 1580; RISM B/VIII, 1580[02]), pp. 95–104.

This Augsburg Ritual is similar to other contemporary liturgical books of other dioceses in the relative narrowness of its song repertory, although not all the listed songs were exclusive to Catholic songbooks.[86] The pioneering Regensburg *Obsequiale* only contains 13 songs, of which ten are also found in the Augsburg Ritual.[87] Furthermore, nine of the Augsburg songs are found among the 12 given in a *Pastorale* for the Freising diocese, first published in 1611.[88] In 1586 the Jesuits of Ingolstadt published a book of 12 song texts appropriate for church services, the *Zwölf Geistliche Kirchengesäng, für die Christliche Gemein*.[89] Here, likewise, nine of the 12 songs are those found in other liturgical books. The relatively small number of approved songs in these books contrasts strikingly with other non-liturgical Catholic songbooks, which provide a much broader repertory. Catholic officials realized the necessity for German songs in church services, but also felt the need to control their usage strictly, insisting on a small repertory for use at particular times of the liturgical year. Any large-scale introduction of vernacular song in Catholic services remained out of the question; as the preface to the Bamberg diocesan songbook of 1575 reads, 'nothing from the celebration of the Mass, that is, from the Latin chant, is to be omitted on account of these songs'.[90]

The cathedral had hired a *Vorsinger* (literally, a singer who stood before the congregation and led them in songs) as early as 1589 to lead the congregation in German songs before the sermon at Sunday Mass, although this duty was assigned in 1609 to one of the cantors, who otherwise helped with the instruction of the choirboys and themselves sang the normal chant repertory during services.[91] Unfortunately, no

---

[86] Of the ten songs listed, only five, *Mitten vnsers lebens zeyt, Siesser Vatter Herre Gott, Christus für mit schallen, Der zart Fronleichnam der ist gut* and *Jesus ist ein süsser nam* were generally exclusive to Catholicism. The remaining songs, and especially the popular *Der Tag der ist so freudenreich*, make frequent appearances in contemporary Protestant songbooks, although none of them contains text praising Lutheranism or criticizing the Catholic church.

[87] The additional songs are the Latin *Resonet in laudibus, Künigin in dem Himmel* (a German version of the antiphon *Regina caeli*) and *Da Jesus zu Bethanien war*.

[88] *Pastorale ad usum Romanum accomodatum. Canones et Ritus ecclesiasticos, qui ad Sacramentorum Administrationem aliaque Pastoralia Officia in Diœcesi Frisingensi, ritè obeunda pertinent complectens* (Ingolstadt: Wilhelm Eder, 1611; RISM B/VIII, 1611[05]).

[89] *Zwölf Geistliche Kirchengesäng, für die Christliche Gemein in Druck verfertigt. Jn ihren eigenen Melodeyen* (Ingolstadt: David Sartorius, 1586).

[90] From *Kurtzer Außzug: Der Christlichen vnd Catholischen Gesäng/ deß Ehrwirdigen Herrn Joannis Leisentritij* (Dillingen: Sebald Mayer, 1575; RISM B/VIII, 1575[04]), quoted in Theo Hamacher, *Beiträge zur Geschichte des katholischen Deutschen Kirchenliedes* (Paderborn: im Selbstverlag, 1985), p. 15.

[91] *DR*, 18 December 1589. Also see Singer, 'Leben und Werke des Augsburger Domkapellmeisters Bernhardus Klingenstein', p. 2. On 26 October 1609 [*DR*] the chapter

evidence survives concerning the actual selection of songs, although it is unlikely that the *Vorsinger* strayed far from the approved body of Catholic songs outlined above. The song *Christ ist erstanden*, one of the tunes approved for church usage, was called for during Easter vigil by Heinrich V in the 1612 Ritual, although it is unclear that he intended it for congregational singing;[92] in the cathedral processional from around 1620 we read that during the Easter vigil the *Marianer* (a group of mature choirboys) and the readers were to alternate verses of *Christ ist erstanden* and the Sequence *Victimae paschali laudes*.[93] Although we have little other evidence for specific German songs in contemporary descriptions or accounts of services, we can be confident that they were a common feature in the diocese of Augsburg in the late sixteenth and early seventeenth centuries. In the 1612 Ritual, Heinrich V felt it unnecessary to add a separate section for German songs:

> In this place [in the Ritual] were previously German songs, which were long ago and laudably introduced by most of our [clergy] in the church. However, we have seen that such songs have been printed separately in diverse locations and in a suitable fashion; hence we have decided to omit them here, for it would be senseless and inconvenient to bring out such a book unnecessarily. We wish, in the meantime, that priests and rectors of church parishes should see to it that no songs are permitted that have not been approved and accepted previously in the church.[94]

The rising tide of Catholic diocesan and general songbooks made German songs available for the Mass, but parish priests, *Vorsinger* and the congregation could also be expected to know the songs well enough to obviate the need for their reprinting in the 1612 Ritual. Heinrich's final warning to the priests of his diocese makes clear, however, that the vernacular song repertory within the church was to be carefully limited and controlled. In the synodal decrees two years previously, he had made this explicit:

> In the churches none of the songs of the heretics, regardless of their appearance of harmony and piety, may be allowed; nor may any profane, frivolous or lascivious songs be used. Rather, let there be grave, pious and distinct songs and tones, suitable for the house of God and for divine praises, so that the words shall clearly be

---

granted the cantor (who is unnamed in the minutes) an extra 45 Kreutzer per week to sing before the sermon. In 1631 the salary of the *Vorsinger* was fixed at 4 Gulden per year, amounting to only one-tenth of the amount spent by the chapter in 1609 (from StAA, KWA A38[14]). The poor economic situation by 1630 surely accounts in part for the reduction.

[92] *Liber Ritualis, Episcopatus Augustensis*, vol. 3, p. 121.

[93] ABA, Hs 31a, p. 103: 'incipiuntur et canitur à Lectoribus Sequentia: Victimæ Paschali: &c et à Marianis cantio Germanica: Christ ist erstanden: alternatus versibus ac vocibus.'

[94] *Liber Ritualis, Episcopatus Augustensis*, vol. 3, p. 279.

understood and listeners be excited to piety. In our churches we permit the retention of those ancient and Catholic songs in the vernacular which have been collected in the greater part of German [churches], to be used on more solemn feasts in the church and in public supplications.[95]

Whatever its value for involving the congregation more directly in the celebration of the Mass, church officials were careful not to allow German song to displace the Latin liturgy, which maintained its symbolic importance as a marker of confessional identity.

Sacred Music at the Jesuit Church of St Salvator

In his monumental *Geschichte der Jesuiten in den Ländern deutscher Zunge in der ersten Hälfte des XVII. Jahrhunderts* Bernhard Duhr catalogued many of the official reservations about the use of music in the Jesuit order.[96] In the original Constitutions of the order Ignatius Loyola wrote that

> Since the occupations which are undertaken for the help of souls are of such great moment, proper to our Institute, and very time-consuming, and, moreover, since our place of dwelling, either in this or that place, is so uncertain, our [men] will not use choir for singing the canonical hours, or Masses and other offices.[97]

Ignatius's successors shared the founder's view that music was an unnecessary distraction from pastoral duties. In 1562 the visitor Jerónimo Nadal forbade Petrus Canisius (then the provincial of the Jesuits' Upper German Province) to allow anyone in the order to receive musical instruction, and, with a few exceptions, disallowed music in the Mass and the use of rented organs (the order forbade ownership of organs by its members).[98] The fourth General of the Order, Eberhard Mercurian, took a less restrictive view of singing (he allowed it for Easter week, Christmas and other major feasts) but continued the ban on organ

---

[95] Quoted in Ursprung, *Jacobus de Kerle*, p. 54.

[96] See Bernhard Duhr, *Geschichte der Jesuiten in den Ländern deutscher Zunge in der ersten Hälfte des XVII. Jahrhunderts* (Freiburg im Breisgau; St Louis, Mo.: Herder, 1913), esp. vol. 1, pp. 443–46 and 536; and vol. 2/2, pp. 52–53. For another account of the initial restrictions on and changing attitude towards music among the Jesuits, see Dietz-Rudiger Moser, *Verkündigung durch Volksgesang: Studien zur Liedpropaganda und -katechese der Gegenreformation* (Berlin: Erich Schmidt Verlag, 1981), pp. 69–70.

[97] Quoted in Thomas D. Culley, *Jesuits and Music*, vol. 1: *A Study of the Musicians connected with the German College in Rome during the 17th Century and of their Activities in Northern Europe* (Rome: Jesuit Historical Institute; St Louis, Mo.: St Louis University, 1970), p. 104.

[98] Duhr, *Geschichte der Jesuiten in den Ländern deutscher Zunge*, vol. 1, p. 443.

playing.[99] Mercurian's successor, Claudius Aquaviva, continued to oppose the organ in particular, directing that Jesuit churches having organs should sell them to other institutions.[100]

Reports from the Jesuit colleges that had sprung up in Germany demonstrate official opposition to music, but also suggest that it was in widespread use by the 1580s.[101] Indeed in Rome itself Jesuit musical practice was not always consistent with their official policies, as Thomas Culley has argued in his study of the elaborate music at the Collegium Germanicum.[102] Despite his forbidding of musical performance in the order's Constitutions, Ignatius himself was known to enjoy music in private settings, and his successors often made dispensations for music on special occasions.[103] Although the General Congregations of the

---

[99] Mercurian oversaw the production of a catalogue of Latin, German and Italian *Cantiones probatae et prohibitae* in 1575; in the latter category fall some of the works of Orlando di Lasso. See D-Mbs, Clm 9237, fol. 31; also Duhr, *Geschichte der Jesuiten in den Ländern deutscher Zunge*, vol. 1, p. 443.

[100] Ibid.

[101] Music could become so elaborate that Jesuit leaders were compelled to issue more specific injunctions. A 1585 report from the Jesuit college at Molsheim, under the direction of Jakob Ernfelder (who was provincial of the Rhenish Province), stated that some of the Jesuits there spent an inordinate amount of time on music, disturbing prayer and confession and wasting time on rehearsals that could be better spent in pastoral activities (ibid., vol. 1, p. 444). Ernfelder reported to Aquaviva in 1589 that he had enforced restrictions on singing in Würzburg, Koblenz and Cologne, although he eventually allowed music in the Mass on major feasts since the practice was common in other provinces (ibid., 444–45). The objections to music by Paul Hoffaeus, the visitor to the Upper German Province (which included the Jesuit college in Augsburg) from 1594 to 1597, were particularly strong, yet imply an active and diverse musical life in the Jesuit colleges there. He explicitly forbade Jesuits to keep musical instruments, either at church or at home, excepting only one 'to help the bass' [*excepto unico ... quo Bassus iuvetur*] and a small regal or portative organ that had to be rented. The rectors of the colleges were to remove all 'madrigal-like songs' [*cantus madrigales*] from colleges and churches, and were not permitted to buy new ones or accept them as gifts, even if the texts were acceptable. Especially annoying to Hoffaeus was the participation of paid singers and instrumentalists in Masses at Jesuit churches, where performances included dance-madrigals, multiple choirs, organs, horns, and violins (ibid., pp. 445–46).

[102] The Collegium Germanicum in Rome was undoubtedly one of the premier musical institutions in the city by the turn of the seventeenth century; between 1570 and 1670 the college employed such talented musicians as Tomás Luis de Victoria, Annibale Stabile, Ruggiero Giovanelli, Asprillo Pacelli, Stefano Landi and Giacomo Carissimi as *maestri di capella*. In his detailed study of the college, Culley has demonstrated its significance not only as a context for the early development of sacred monody, but also as source for well-trained German Catholic musicians who helped to establish the new idiom north of the Alps. German musicians who graduated from the Collegium Germanicum included Philipp Friedrich von Breiner from Vienna, Johannes Wetzel from Mainz, Johannes Lohr from Neisse, Johann Melschede and Friedrich Gramaye from Cologne and J.C. Härtlin. See Culley, *Jesuits and Music*, pp. 15–16 and 169–70.

[103] Ibid., pp. 15–16.

Society in 1558, 1565 and 1573 all stressed a limited role for music, the number of requests for dispensations was so great by the turn of the seventeenth century that the original rules were no longer enforced. By this time a number of Jesuit colleges had become important musical centres, notably those in Graz, Vienna, Munich, Prague, Cologne, Dillingen and Augsburg.[104]

Already in 1588, four years after the opening of the Jesuit Gymnasium at St Salvator, the Augsburg college issued a detailed ordinance governing the performance of church polyphony by their students. They made the following provisions: (1) the litany with the usual antiphons and collects was to be sung after school on all Sundays and feast days, and on the vigils of the same; (2) the *Miserere* was to be sung every day in the evening during Lent; (3) the Mass was to be sung on New Year's Day, on the Feast of the Dedication of a Church, on Good Friday and Holy Saturday, at the beginning of the school year, on All Souls Day and on the Feast of St Sebastian; furthermore, both first and second Vespers were to be sung on New Year's Day and on the Feast of the Dedication of a Church; (4) the antiphon *Surrexit Christus hodie* was to be sung daily between Easter and Pentecost, *Puer natus* was to be sung between Christmas and the Feast of the Purification of the Blessed Virgin Mary, *O salutaris hostia* was to be sung during the octave of Corpus Christi and the litany was to be sung after the transubstantiation of the Eucharist during Holy Week and on the Feast of St Mark; and (5) psalms and motets were to be sung continuously before the Holy Sepulchre.[105] The students were to perform all this music polyphonically, but, contrary to official policies, the priests themselves were occasionally permitted to help in the singing if necessary. Furthermore, one of the fathers was instructed to conduct the choir until one of the students was able to assume this duty.[106] Organs and other musical instruments were indeed permitted during Mass and Vespers, as long as they were played by outside musicians.[107] 'Not only is nothing to be taken away from this order in the Augsburg college,' the chronicler Placidus Braun relates, 'but it is to be expanded depending on the time and place, to serve as a means

---

[104] Ibid., p. 16.

[105] Described in Braun, *Geschichte des Kollegiums der Jesuiten in Augsburg*, pp. 120–21. It is unclear from Braun's account how often the last-mentioned music was performed. The Holy Sepulchre [*heiliges Grab*] was a representation of Christ's tomb that was erected in many south German Catholic churches and served as a setting for quasi-theatrical recreations of Christ's deposition in and resurrection from the tomb; an analogue may be found in the Viennese tradition of the *sepolcro*. This was one of several types of 'folklorized ritual' or *functiones sacrae* that developed in the shadow of the official liturgy; see Scribner, *Popular Culture and Popular Movements in Reformation Germany*, pp. 23–24.

[106] Braun, *Geschichte des Kollegiums der Jesuiten in Augsburg*, p. 121.

[107] Ibid.

of general edification and strengthening of the Catholicism.'[108] The Augsburg Jesuits recognized the utility of religious music well before the turn of the seventeenth century, regardless of any objections from Rome.[109]

A manuscript catalogue of the library of St Salvator survives, although it is rather unhelpful as far as music is concerned.[110] Begun in 1591, the catalogue includes a large amount of religious and devotional literature dating mainly from 1560–1600. Both Jacobus de Kerle and Orlando di Lasso are listed in the index of authors, but no publications by either composer actually appear in the pages of the catalogue. Only a handful of other composers are found in the catalogue itself, including Palestrina, Gumpelzhaimer, Hassler, Utendal and Reiner.[111] In addition, we find Caspar Ulenberg's *Psalmen Davids* (1582)[112] and the *Catholische Creütz gesäng, vom Vatter vnnser, Aue Maria* by Johann Haym, a cleric at Augsburg cathedral and a prominent member of the Trinity Confraternity (see Chapter 5). Several prints appear by Johannes Holthusius, a schoolmaster at the cathedral, but not his collection of liturgical chant, the *Compendium Cantionum ecclesiasticarum* (1567).[113] The composer Gregor Aichinger is represented in the catalogue by his devotional book for priests, the *Thymiama sacerdotale*

---

[108] 'Von dieser Ordnung soll im Kollegium zu Augsburg nicht nur nichts vermindert, sondern vielmehr nach Erforderniß des Orts und der Zeiten zur allgemeiner Erbauung und Stärkung der Katholiken vermehrt werden.' See ibid. Like the remainder of Braun's account of the 1588 ordinance, it is unclear whether he is paraphrasing the original source.

[109] As late as 1602, Jesuits from the Lower Rhenish Province sought Aquaviva's approval in 1602 for singing on all feasts of the church calendar, a request that the General rejected except for the colleges in Cologne and Münster, where the performance of music was thought beneficial for the retention of new converts to Catholicism (see Duhr, *Geschichte der Jesuiten in den Ländern deutscher Zunge*, vol. 2, pt. 2, p. 52). By contrast, the Augsburg college may have enjoyed music more frequently from 1588 onward, since the ordinance from that year called for the performance of litanies, antiphons and collects on every feast day.

[110] D-As, Cod. Cat. 15 (I–II), 'Catalogus Librorum Bibliothecae Collegii S. J. Augustae'.

[111] The specific prints are Palestrina's *Hymni totius Anni* (1589), a '*Musica Lat[inogerm].*' (1595) by Adam Gumpelzhaimer (perhaps his *Contrapunctus quatuor et quinque Vocum*), Hans Leo Hassler's *Missae* (1599), volumes 2 and 3 of Alexander Utendal's *Cantionum sacrarum* (1573) and Jakob Reiner's *Cantiones sex et octo Vocum* (1600).

[112] Dietz-Rudiger Moser has suggested that the heavy use of the Ulenberg Psalter, a German translation of the psalms 'purified' of Lutheran doctrine, by the Jesuit Marian Congregations helped to account for its eleven editions up until 1710; see Moser, *Verkündigung durch Volksgesang*, pp. 80–84.

[113] The other Holthusius prints listed in the catalogue are his *De Modo examinandi Ordinandos* (Dillingen, 1564), *Grammatica* (Dillingen, 1572) and *Examen Ordinandorum* (Venice, 1567).

(see below), but music by him is lacking.[114] The lack of a music library that would serve the musical needs of St Salvator as outlined in the 1588 ordinance is odd, although there might be at least three explanations: the music library may have been entrusted to the outside music director (possibly Bernhard Klingenstein, the cathedral *Kapellmeister*); the Jesuit fathers may not have wished to betray the presence of a substantial music library in writing, given the official restrictions against the cultivation of music; or the music collection (including liturgical books) was kept entirely separate. The lack of any liturgical books whatsoever in the catalogue provides some support for the latter possibility.[115]

Regular church music at Jesuit colleges required a corresponding music pedagogy, and by the early seventeenth century evidence from Augsburg and elsewhere points to the Jesuits' desire to provide basic singing instruction, whether to improve the condition of church music at the colleges themselves or to provide future priests with proper musical training. Some Jesuits argued for this instruction in singing to address complaints about the poor state of Gregorian chant in divine services. In 1625, for example, the Congregation of the Rhenish Province directed that 'since many complain that our students obtain their benefices without being able to sing, a singing teacher shall henceforth train the students, particularly candidates for the priesthood'.[116] In Mainz local Jesuits asked the visitor Ferdinand Alber in 1609 whether they might be able to establish a singing school with an instructor hired from outside the college; Aquaviva approved of this measure, with the reservation that it not take anything away from the students' regular studies.[117] In the early seventeenth century many German and Austrian Jesuit colleges opened special schools [*Armenkonvikte*] in which poor boys were required to learn music and participate in church music as a condition of their upkeep.[118]

---

[114] The publication of Aichinger's *Thymiama sacerdotale* in 1618 is noted in the Jesuit chronicle: 'Iam de re libraria, prodiêre in lucem hoc anno opera nostratium, ethica ouidiana cum commentariolo, Atticorum bellariorum pars secunda, Promptuarium Germanicolatinum libellus cui inscriptio Thymiama sacerdotale, Officium corporis Xpi latinogræcum et Eucharistico dedicatum sodalitio'; *HCA*, vol. 1, p. 518 [1618].

[115] The Jesuits did in fact own at least one liturgical book: their ex-libris with a date of 1636 appears on an exemplar housed at D-As (8° Aug 1688) of the *Officium hebdomadæ sanctæ* (Augsburg: Valentin Schönig, 1594), a book containing the Proper liturgy from Palm Sunday to Easter Sunday. An exemplar of the Ulenberg Psalter mentioned above, also at D-As (8° Th. Lt. K. 557), also contains the Augsburg Jesuits' ex-libris.

[116] From the Archivium Collegii Bambergensis, quoted in Duhr, *Geschichte der Jesuiten in den Ländern deutscher Zunge*, vol. 2, pt. 1, p. 507.

[117] Ibid.

[118] The Jesuits opened such schools in Linz, Neuburg, Amberg, Ingolstadt, Dillingen, Vienna, Glatz, Hall, Graz and elsewhere. Boys at the Jesuit school in Munich, which

At St Salvator, the Jesuits may have employed outside musicians to provide thorough musical instruction: Lipowsky claimed that Octavian II Fugger, a supporter of the college, lent his chamber musician Hans Leo Hassler to the seminarians for this purpose, while Singer identified the cathedral *Kapellmeister* Bernhard Klingenstein as the college's choir director.[119] By the early seventeenth century the Jesuit Gymnasium had even attracted some students from the cathedral school. A chronicle of the college notes in 1611:

> when the Society [of Jesus] began to instruct the youth of Augsburg, that [cathedral] school gradually fell into decline, until finally, reduced to only a few students, it came entirely under our auspices. Twenty-four students are trained in the divine service and for use in the choir, who likewise learn letters from us in their spare time.[120]

The music at St Salvator was further augmented by the gift of organs and musical instruments, some of which were donated by members of the Fugger family. Sibylla Fugger, whom Petrus Canisius had converted to Catholicism years before, donated an organ in 1586;[121] for the members of the college who had remained in Augsburg during a plague in 1592, Octavian II Fugger donated a 'musical instrument, or very elegant organ', perhaps a regal or portative organ.[122] Again in 1621, a Martin Huber from the chapter of St Moritz donated an organ for the student meeting hall.[123] Although the Jesuits were prohibited from purchasing such items themselves, they gladly accepted them from their enthusiastic patrons.

A surviving description of the customs of St Salvator from 1623 shows that the occasions for music in the context of the liturgy had been

---

boasted a particularly active musical life, enjoyed musical instruction by Orlando di Lasso and his colleagues from the ducal court as early as the 1570s. See ibid., vol. 1, p. 317, and vol. 2, pt. 1, pp. 641–42 and 648–54.

[119] Although their employment by the Jesuits is not unlikely, I have not been able to verify this information. See Felix Joseph Lipowski, *Geschichte der Jesuiten in Schwaben* (Munich: I. I. Lentner, etc., 1819), p. 93 n; and Singer, 'Leben und Werke des Augsburger Domkapellmeisters Bernhardus Klingenstein', p. 29.

[120] 'Sed ubi Societas docere Augustæ iuuentutem occepit, illa sensim decreuit; donec tandem ad paucos redacta, ad nos tota migrauit. Viceni quaterni ad cultum diuinum, et usum chori, ab eisdem aluntur, qui apud nos itidem uacuis horis literas discunt'; *HCA*, vol. 1, pp. 488–89 [1611].

[121] Krautwurst, 'Die Fugger und die Musik', p. 44.

[122] 'Sodalitum propè dissociatum pestilitate fuit, usque adeo numerus est imminutus. qui reliqui fuêre, officium et partes sodalium, egregiè prestiterunt, quibus Octauianus Fuggerus instrumentum musicum, seu organum perelegans, donauit.' *HCA*, vol. 1, pp. 337–38 [1592].

[123] Braun, *Geschichte des Kollegiums der Jesuiten in Augsburg*, p. 48.

expanded since 1588.[124] One striking example is the feast of Corpus Christi, music for which was not mentioned in the 1588 ordinance: on the eve of this feast, a 'great host' [*magna hostia*] was to be consecrated for the monstrance. At Vespers, before litanies were sung, the host was to be carried in a procession out of the sacristy accompanied by bells and torches; at the beginning of this procession the hymn *Ecce panis Angelorum* was to be sung, accompanied by a benediction. Following the singing of litanies and motets [*Lytanijs cum Motetis*], the priest was to sing the versicle *Tantum ergo sacramentum* and return the host to the high altar. On the feast day itself, the Jesuits were to participate in a public procession with the sacrament during which the Gospel of St John was to be sung. During the octave of Corpus Christi, the students were to sing Eucharistic music [*cantatur aliquid de Venerabili Sacramento*], and the Sunday within the octave featured a sung Mass of the sacrament.[125] In this case, the Jesuits' elaboration of the music for Corpus Christi reflected the greater status of this feast in Augsburg after the turn of the seventeenth century, when the annual Corpus Christi procession through the city was greatly expanded (see Chapter 6). The frequent performance of litanies for this and other occasions points to a broader tradition of paraliturgical and non-liturgical performances that will be discussed further in Chapter 5.

Augsburg's Catholic Composers and Liturgical Polyphony in the Counter-Reformation: Klingenstein, Aichinger, Erbach and Zindelin

Specific collections of music published by individual composers in

---

[124] D-As, 4° Aug 195, 'Consuetudines Collegii Augustani Soc: Iesu. 1623', a manuscript booklet of 38 folios.

[125] 'Pridie Festi Corporis Christi, consecratur magna hostia pro Monstrantia; Quo die Vesperi ante Lytanias cantandas, defertur Venerabile Sacramentum ex Sacristia cum cymbalis & facibus: & cantantur in principio Ecce panis Angelorum: cum benedictione: & finitis Lytanijs cum Motetis, iterum cantantur aliquid à Sacerdote, V. Tantum ergo Sacramentum, cum benedictione, & relinquitur Venerabile Sacramentum in Altari sum[m]o.

Ipso die festo dicuntur sacra more solito in ordine usque ad horam decimam. Et instruitur Altare propter Processionem publicam extra in ædibus censualibus pro Venerabili Sacramento, quod hic in solennj Processione deponitur & cantat[ur] Euangelium Vltimum S. Joannis, ornatur tota domus, quà longa est tapetibus & Poëmatis Rhetorum & Poetarum nostrj Gymnasij. Dum procedit Processio pulsatur nostra magna campana. Post prandium nulla est Concio in n[ostro] templo, nec aliquid aliud.

Per totam Octauam sub sacro discipulorum (qui tum nostrum templum aduent) cantatur aliquid de Ven[erabili] Sacr[amento]. Et die Dominico infra Octauam, cantat[ur] sacrum de Venerabilj Sacr[amento].' D-As, 4° Aug 195, fol. 31r–v.

this period point to the blurry boundaries between 'liturgical', 'para-liturgical' and 'non-liturgical' musical practice. Whereas most of the polyphonic collections of Cleve and Kerle, for example, bring together liturgical texts of general utility, composers in Augsburg around the turn of the seventeenth century preferred a certain thematicism in their prints that often reflected the broader flowering of Marian and Eucharistic devotion in the region. Gregor Aichinger's *Solennia augustissima Corporis Christi* (1606), for example, consists exclusively of settings of liturgical texts, yet the full title ('... in sanctissimo sacrificio missae & in eiusdem festi officijs, ac publicis supplicationibus seu processionibus cantari solita') and its dedication to the Corpus Christi Confraternity suggest that the cathedral cantor was not necessarily the print's intended audience. More traditional collections like Aichinger's *Vespertinum Virginis* (1603), a set of five-voice Magnificat settings, could have been heard as easily in the devotional gatherings of the Marian Congregation as in the Vespers services of the cathedral.

Even if collections of 'liturgical' music such as these cannot be assigned, as it were, to the repertories of the established churches, it is nonetheless useful to consider them together as a barometer of the changes taking place in musical composition and publication around the turn of the seventeenth century. The following section offers an introduction to the biographies of Augsburg's chief composers of Catholic polyphony – Bernhard Klingenstein, Christian Erbach, Gregor Aichinger and Philipp Zindelin – and examines their music setting liturgical texts (their devotional music will be discussed in Chapter 5). The handful of prints considered here point to the Counter-Reformation's influence on the thematics and organization of this repertory.

Bernhard Klingenstein (1545–1614)

It is a great irony that the one musician charged with the composition of liturgical music for the cathedral left not a single published collection reflecting his duties. When Anton Span retired from the position of *Kapellmeister* at Augsburg Cathedral in 1574, the cathedral chapter passed over Jacobus de Kerle and offered the position to the relatively inexperienced Bernhard Klingenstein, who had spent most of his life to that point under the care of the chapter, first as a choirboy in the cathedral school and then as a minor cleric.[126] That Klingenstein was

---

[126] Klingenstein was probably born in Peiting bei Schongau in 1545, and probably was accepted as a choirboy by Augsburg Cathedral by the late 1550s. On his early biography,

engaged despite his lack of compositional training is consistent with the chapter's tendency, also expressed in later appointments, to prefer the cathedral school's own products; in any case Klingenstein had the opportunity to learn composition with Johannes de Cleve when the latter arrived in Augsburg in the late 1570s.[127] As *Kapellmeister* Klingenstein was required to be ordained, and in connection with his post the chapter granted him an ecclesiastical benefice, and indeed appointed him as parish priest for the village of Lorch in 1578.[128] The foundational ordinance for the cathedral cantorate in 1561 prescribed Klingenstein's musical duties:

> He shall be learned, trained, and experienced in singing, and especially in figural singing. ... He shall at all times keep the boys or choirboys of our foundation with him in his house at his expense, and instruct and train them in singing. He shall also diligently look after the choirbooks, and draw the finest pieces out of them and bring them together; these shall be sung on high feasts, each according to its proper time. ... He shall also exert himself at all times to compose new and good music, and provide it to embellish the musical chapel.[129]

Although Klingenstein was expected to compose, his tasks were not unlike those of his Protestant counterpart Adam Gumpelzhaimer (see

---

see Kroyer, 'Gregor Aichingers Leben und Werke', in his edition *Ausgewählte Werke von Gregor Aichinger (1564–1628)*, Denkmäler der Tonkunst in Bayern, Jahrgang 10, vol. 1 (Leipzig: Breitkopf & Härtel, 1909), pp. xlix–l; Singer, 'Leben und Werke des Augsburger Domkapellmeisters Bernhardus Klingenstein', pp. 24–26; and Martina Schmidmüller, *Die Reihe der Augsburger Domkapellmeister seit dem Tridentinum bis heute* (Augsburg, 1989), pp. 75–78. Singer's dissertation remains the only lengthy study on Klingenstein's life and work.

[127] See Singer, 'Leben und Werke des Augsburger Domkapellmeisters Bernhardus Klingenstein', pp. 26, 28–29 and 34–35. In 1580 the chapter paid Cleve 40 Gulden for compositions as well as for his instruction of the young *Kapellmeister*: 'Fl: dl. Erzthörzogs Carls ~ geweßnen Capellmaister Johann de Cleue, Isst seiner *offerierter* gesanng, auch meiner gl: herrn Capellmaisters villfeltiger getreuer *Instruction* halb[er] mit vngefarlich 40 R zuuerehren beuolhen.' *DR*, 11 March 1580.

[128] Klingenstein, however, was not required to reside in the village, and in any case transferred the position to another cleric in 1589. During his career at the cathedral he held several different benefices, each with different terms and conditions. These somewhat complicated arrangements are described in Singer, 'Leben und Werke des Augsburger Domkapellmeisters Bernhardus Klingenstein', pp. 40–42; some references to them appear in the *DR* on 20 January 1576, 14 June 1577 and 20 October 1589. As early as 1584 Klingenstein agitated to have his benefice allocated to the *Kapellmeister*, so that the house, which came with the benefice, could be made into a permanent residence for the music director. This request was finally granted in the early seventeenth century and confirmed by Rome. See Singer, 'Leben und Werke des Augsburger Domkapellmeisters Bernhardus Klingenstein', pp. 41–42, and *DR*, 9 April 1584, 23 March 1604 and 15 December 1606.

[129] Quoted in Singer, 'Leben und Werke des Augsburger Domkapellmeisters Bernhardus Klingenstein', pp. 33–34.

Chapter 3) in that much of his energy was consumed with the care and instruction of his students. This aspect of his post became increasingly difficult for Klingenstein as he grew elderly, and several entries in the cathedral chapter minutes from the early seventeenth century suggest that both the *Kapellmeister* and his superiors were becoming frustrated with the students' unruliness.[130]

Klingenstein began to offer his own compositions to the chapter in 1581, and entries from the chapter minutes in that year and again in 1586 confirm that his superiors were entirely satisfied with his efforts.[131] Although Klingenstein probably had some kind of musical association with the nearby Jesuit college of St Salvator, there seems to be no direct evidence to support Kroyer's assertion that he was the choir director there, nor Singer's assumption, based on the subject matter of his *Rosetum Marianum* (see Chapter 5), that he was a member of the Marian Congregation.[132] Even though his own published music did not appear until after 1600, Klingenstein seems to have enjoyed a good reputation among his contemporaries: motets of his appeared in a lute book by Hans Kaspar Kärgel in 1586, Friedrich Lindner included three of his works in the anthology *Corollarium Cantionum sacrarum* of 1590 and Georg Victorinus included an eight-voice litany of the saints by Klingenstein in the *Thesaurus Litaniarum* of 1596.[133] Klingenstein's style varies depending on the number of voices called for: works for six or more voices exhibit

---

[130] In 1599 and again in 1600 the chapter reprimanded Klingenstein for his students' misbehaviour in public, and the *Kapellmeister* demanded in 1603 that he be relieved of the care and housing of the students, or else he would ask to be released. Subsequent negotiations between Klingenstein and his superiors were successful, the chapter engaging Abraham Pliemle [Blüm] as his 'Substitut' and assigning a curator to the instruments and music. See Singer, 'Leben und Werke des Augsburger Domkapellmeisters Bernhardus Klingenstein', pp. 43–46, and *DR*, 12 March 1599, 17 April 1600, 19 March, 25 and 27 August, 1603 and 18 September 1606.

[131] The chapter granted Klingenstein the impressive sum of 100 Gulden – roughly equivalent to the entire yearly salary of an organist – for his music in 1581 and again in 1586. The 1581 payment was accompanied by a commendation. See Singer, 'Leben und Werke des Augsburger Domkapellmeisters Bernhardus Klingenstein', pp. 34–35, and *DR*, 13 October 1581 and 28 July 1586.

[132] See Kroyer, 'Gregor Aichingers Leben und Werke', pp. xlix–l, and Singer, 'Leben und Werke des Augsburger Domkapellmeisters Bernhardus Klingenstein', pp. 37–38.

[133] Singer, 'Leben und Werke des Augsburger Domkapellmeisters Bernhardus Klingenstein', p. 51. Klingenstein did not set the standard *litaniae maiores* or *litaniae minores* called for on the feast of St Mark and on Rogation Days, but rather a shorter version of the text that included supplications to local saints such as Ulrich, Afra and Narcissus. The work is homophonically and antiphonally conceived, following the leads of Giovanni Gabrieli and Hans Leo Hassler. See ibid., pp. 132–34. On other works by Klingenstein that appeared in contemporary anthologies and manuscripts, see ibid., pp. 146–52.

the homophonic and antiphonal influences of the Venetian school (mediated, perhaps, through figures like Hassler and Aichinger, who had studied in Venice during the 1580s), while more modest works follow the lead of Orlando di Lasso in their exploration of different voice groupings.[134]

None of Klingenstein's three published collections seems to have been intended for normal liturgical use, although one, the *Triodia sacra* (1605), may have a distinct connection to the liturgy performed at the cathedral (see below).[135] The *Rosetum Marianum* (1604), an anthology of settings of the devotional text 'Maria zart' by 33 different composers, and the *Liber primus s. Symphoniarum* (1607), containing numerous settings in honour of its dedicatee, Johann Conrad von Gemmingen, bishop of Eichstätt, along with an idiosyncratic collection of other settings honouring the Virgin Mary, the Eucharist, and patron saints of local importance, will be discussed in Chapter 5. The 41 sacred tricinia of the *Triodia sacra*, drawn from existing compositions by Augsburg composers (Klingenstein, Aichinger, Erbach, Zindelin), composers attached to the Bavarian court (Orlando di Lasso, Johann à Fossa), the Habsburg court (Philippe de Monte, Jakob Regnart) and others, include a large proportion of internal Mass Ordinary and Magnificat sections for reduced voices, as well as a number of Proper items that are largely *unica* in this source. The collection represents an exclusively sacred version of a pedagogical genre that previously had been typified by secular texts, and may reflect the influence of the Jesuit fathers of the University of Dillingen, two of whose students (the brothers Johann Wolfgang and Johann Egolph von Leonrod) were the dedicatees of the print. At the same time, the collection hints at some of the musical repertory available to Klingenstein at the cathedral, music that was gradually acquired by the chapter and probably copied into manuscripts that are no longer extant. The circumstance that most of the *unica* belong to the Mass Proper may indicate that Klingenstein had intended to assemble a new cycle of polyphonic Propers for use at the cathedral, but the evidence is inconclusive.[136] In the course of his lengthy career Klingenstein never placed great emphasis on the publication of his own music; this, combined with the lack of extant manuscript sources from the cathedral, makes it difficult to draw firm conclusions about

---

[134] On general stylistic features of Klingenstein's music, see ibid., pp. 102, 112–13 and 119.

[135] For a recent study of this source see Christian Thomas Leitmeir, 'Catholic Music in the Diocese of Augsburg c. 1600: A Reconstructed Tricinium Anthology and its Confessional Implications', *Early Music History*, **21** (2002), pp. 117–73.

[136] See ibid., p. 160.

the nature of the repertory there. Like his counterpart at St Anna, Adam Gumpelzhaimer, Klingenstein's energies may have been consumed by the day-to-day demands of his position, not only as a composer, but also as a pedagogue who had to see to the needs of his students. With respect to music publication, at least, his colleagues Christian Erbach and Gregor Aichinger could afford to be more prolific.

Christian Erbach (c.1570–1635)

Like his older colleague Klingenstein, Christian Erbach spent most of his career employed in Augsburg churches, first as organist to the church of St. Moritz (from 1602), then as assistant organist at Augsburg Cathedral (from 1614), and finally as the cathedral organist upon the death of the long-serving Erasmus Mayr in 1624.[137] Erbach, however, also enjoyed the direct patronage of Marcus Fugger the younger (1564–1614), who employed him as a chamber musician between 1564 and his death in 1614. It was probably through the influence of the Fugger family, in fact, that Erbach was appointed as Hans Leo Hassler's successor at St Moritz in 1602, since the organ itself and the organist position had been donated by Jakob Fugger in 1587.[138] The organist position at St Moritz shared one important characteristic with that of SS Ulrich and Afra, which was also controlled by the Fugger family: the organist 'had to belong to the true, Roman Catholic religion'.[139] Erbach's patron Marcus Fugger may also have had certain religious expectations of him, since the latter was actively involved in the city's Catholic renewal through the foundation of the Corpus Christi Confraternity in 1604 (see Chapter 5). Erbach's Catholic profession is further confirmed by his election to the greater chamber of the new, entirely Catholic city council in 1631 during the period of the Edict of Restitution.[140] In addition to his organist

---

[137] The most significant literature on Erbach's life and works remains Werra's introduction to *Ausgewählte Werke von Christian Erbach*.

[138] Layer, *Musik und Musiker der Fuggerzeit*, p. 44.

[139] 'Namlich vnnd Erstlich, hat wolernanter Herr Jacob Fugger, auß sonderem Catholischem Christenlichem Eifer, freÿer Naÿgung, Gnaden, vnnd wolnaÿgung, dem berüerten Stifft, vnd der kirchen Sanct Moritzen, ain herrliche Orgel geschenckt ... darzue wöllen wir auch ain taugenlichen (so der wahren Römischen Catholischen Religion, sein solle) Organisten, zue disem hieoben gemelten werckh, an vnnd aufnemen'; from 'Herrn Jacob Fuggers vbergab brieff der orgel so er ainem stifft S Mauritien geschenckt A. 1587', StAA, KWA B8¹⁶. Given this condition, however, it is odd that Hans Leo Hassler had previously been granted this position by Jakob I Fugger, as stated by Krautwurst in 'Musik der Blütezeit', p. 390.

[140] ABA, Hs 52, 'Annales Augustani Reginbaldi Moehneri', vol. 2, p. 1353. See also Werra, *Ausgewählte Werke von Christian Erbach*, p. xvi, and Bernhard Paumgartner, 'Zur Musikkultur Augsburgs in der Fuggerzeit', in Götz Freiherr von Polnitz et al., eds, *Jakob*

duties, Erbach was also in charge of the city *Stadtpfeifer*, a position that he also took over from Hassler after the latter's departure for Nuremberg in 1602. Erbach continued his organist's duties at the cathedral until 9 June 1635, when the cathedral chapter decided to release him due to lack of funds. Within four days he was dead, and the chapter approved his burial in the *finsterer Grad*, the covered walkway connecting the cathedral with the chapel of St. Johannes.[141]

Perhaps the most extensive musical legacy of Bishop Heinrich V's efforts to Romanize the diocesan liturgy were the three volumes of Erbach's *Modorum sacrorum tripertitorum* (1604–06), comprising a complete cycle of Introits, Alleluias and Communions for the Mass Propers of Roman feasts.[142] Volume 1 (1604) covers the liturgical calendar from Pentecost to Advent, Volume 2 (1606) covers the liturgical calendar from Christmas to Pentecost, and Volume 3 (1606) provides music for the Sanctorale. Erbach takes an unusually conservative approach, composing imitative four-voice counterpoint over the Gregorian melody, presented as a long-note cantus firmus in the fifth voice. Although Erbach was the organist of St Moritz at the time of publication, he dedicated the three volumes to the prelates of local and regional monasteries: Abbot Johann von Merk of SS Ulrich and Afra, Prince-Abbot Johann Adam of Kempten and Urban, provost of the Augustinian monastery of St Georg in Augsburg.[143] In addition to the financial support (or consideration for employment) he might have expected to receive from these three men, Erbach certainly would have expected that his polyphonic Propers would have been appropriate for these institutions' choirs as well as that of his own church. However, the contents of the three volumes, as well as the timing of their composition and publication, suggest that the introduction of the Roman Rite in the Augsburg diocese by Bishops Johann Otto and Heinrich around the turn of the seventeenth century inspired their creation. In choosing an archaic cantus-firmus approach to the setting of these Gregorian melodies, Erbach provided a musical counterpoint to the historicism embodied in the embrace of the Roman liturgy.

Likewise intended for liturgical use, whether specifically for the

---

Fugger, Kaiser Maximilian und Augsburg 1459–1959 (Augsburg: Stadt Augsburg, 1959), p. 88.

[141] *DR*, 9 June and 13 June 1635. Curiously, Erbach was denied a burial in the cathedral's cloister. Wolfgang Agricola was appointed as the new organist at this time.

[142] Christian Erbach, *Modorum sacrorum tripertitorum* (Dillingen: Adam Meltzer, 1604–06); RISM A/I, E728, E729 and E730.

[143] See Werra, *Ausgewählte Werke von Christian Erbach*, pp. x–xii, although the three exemplars I examined from the British Library (filmed at D-Mbs, fp. 138-1, 2 and 3) lacked dedications.

Roman liturgy or not, are three additional books of motets, the two volumes of the *Modi sacri* (1600 and 1604) and the *Sacrarum Cantionum ... Liber tertius* (1611), composed variously for four to nine voices; the first of these volumes is explicitly subtitled 'ad ecclesiae catholicae usum'.[144] Despite the Marian or Eucharistic orientation of a significant minority of the texts chosen by Erbach, neither the dedications (to his patron Marcus Fugger in the first book, to the two Augsburg *Stadtpfleger* in the second, and in the third to the bishop of Wettenhausen, who is known to have sent students to study with Erbach[145]), nor the overall text selection indicates an interest in overt confessional propagandizing. Entirely different from any of these collections are the *Mele sive Cantiones sacrae ad Modum Canzonette* for four voices (1603), a set of sacred canzonettas with mostly devotional texts in praise of Christ and the Virgin Mary;[146] and the *Acht vnderschiedtliche Geistliche Teutsche Lieder* (1610), a simple, vernacular collection of music for use during Holy Week.[147] The non-liturgical texts and the largely homophonic tendency of both of these works, which are discussed in Chapter 5, would have made them suitable for musical amateurs in Catholic devotional contexts.

Gregor Aichinger (1564–1628)

Of all the composers active at Catholic musical institutions in Augsburg in the early seventeenth century, Gregor Aichinger alone was demonstrably an ardent partisan of the Counter-Reformation. In spite of (or perhaps because of) his lack of a position that obliged him to compose on a regular basis, he turned his energies towards the composition of polyphony that was not only specifically Catholic in subject matter – emphasizing Marian and Eucharistic devotion – but also

[144] *Modi sacri sive Cantus musici, ad Ecclesiae catholicae Usum, Vocibus quaternis, quinis, VI, VII. VIII. et pluribus, ad omne Genus Instrumenti musici accomodatis ... Liber primus* (Augsburg: Johannes Praetorius, 1600; RISM A/I, E725); *Modorum sacrorum sive Cantionum, quaternis, quinis, senis, 7. 8. & pluribus Numeris compositarum, Lib. secundus* (Augsburg: Johannes Praetorius, 1604; RISM A/I, E727); and *Sacrarum Cantionum quaternis & quinis Vocibus factarum, Liber tertius* (Augsburg: Johannes Praetorius, 1611; RISM A/I, E731).
[145] Werra, *Ausgewählte Werke von Christian Erbach*, pp. xvi–xvii.
[146] *Mele sive Cantiones sacrae ad Modum Canzonette ut vocant, quaternis Vocibus factae, quibus accessit ... Hymnus Mariae, cum Mariana senum Vocum Cantione* (Augsburg: Johannes Praetorius, 1603; RISM A/I, E726).
[147] *Acht Vnderschiedtliche Geistliche Teutsche Lieder/ von den fürnembsten Geheimnussen deß bittern Leydens vnd Sterbens vnsers HErrn vnd Seligmachers Jesu Christi/ nutzlich zu gebrauchen (sonderlich) in der H. Kharwochen. Mit 4. Stim[m]en zusam[m]en gesetzt/ durch Christianum Erbach* (Augsburg: Johann Schultes, 1610; RISM A/I, E732).

stylistically fashionable and, in many cases, suitable for the needs of musical amateurs in private or public devotional contexts. Aichinger is best known for his *Cantiones ecclesiasticae* of 1607, the first major musical publication by a German composer that includes basso continuo. Despite his undeniable significance as, perhaps, the earliest German composer to experiment with this new technical idiom, his importance with respect to the cultural and musical landscape of Counter-Reformation Augsburg lies in his effort to create, seemingly *ex nihilo*, a substantial body of music that was unmistakably Catholic in inspiration and intention.[148] More than other masses, motets, songs and litanies that adorned Catholic devotional activities in this period, Aichinger's works form the most vivid musical symbol of Augsburg's Catholic revival.

The thesis, first advanced by Theodor Kroyer, that Aichinger was a convert from a Protestant family in Regensburg is compelling but lacks firm evidence.[149] An entry in a Munich court chapel document from 1577, in which a son of one Georg Aichinger is paid 4 Gulden for a musical composition ('Georgen Aichinger khnaben für ein verehrt gesang fl. 4.'), hints that the family may have moved to Munich and the young Gregor Aichinger may have been a choirboy under Orlando di Lasso's tutelage.[150] Whether or not Aichinger had his earliest musical training in Regensburg or Munich, Kroyer noted that passages in his later dedications imply that he had studied music from an early age.[151] If indeed Aichinger was born into a Protestant family, he probably would have converted to Catholicism by the time he matriculated in 1578 at the University of Ingolstadt, which was firmly under the control of the Jesuit

---

[148] William E. Hettrick and Anne Kirwan-Mott have explored Aichinger's concertos in detail; see esp. Hettrick, 'The Thorough-Bass in the Works of Gregor Aichinger' (Ph.D. diss., University of Michigan, 1968), and his editions of Aichinger's concertos *The Vocal Concertos* (Madison, Wis.: A-R Editions, 1986) and *Cantiones ecclesiasticae* (Madison, Wis.: A-R Editions, 1972); see also Kirwan-Mott, *The Small-Scale Sacred Concertato in the Early Seventeenth Century* (Ann Arbor: UMI Research Press, 1981), vol. 1, pp. 48–55. For a recent overview of Aichinger's life and works see Hettrick's article 'Aichinger, Gregor', in *New Grove II*, vol. 1, pp. 249–50.

[149] See Kroyer, 'Gregor Aichingers Leben und Werke', pp. xii–xiii; no such claim is made in Bettina Schwemer, 'Aichinger, Gregor', in *MGG²*, vol. 1, cols 265–68.

[150] Kroyer, 'Gregor Aichingers Leben und Werke', pp. xiii–xv; Schmid, 'Aichinger, Gregor', p. 177; Boetticher, *Orlando di Lasso und seine Zeit*, p. 432.

[151] See Kroyer, 'Gregor Aichingers Leben und Werke', p. xv. Aichinger writes in his first book of *Divinae Laudes* (1602), 'Though I cultivated the study of music continually from when I was a child, and fervently loved the elegant harmony of song, I cannot begin to believe that those melodies that I have contemplated and completed until now would be pleasing to all.' See also the preface to his *Quercus Dodonae* (1617), in which he writes that despite his advancing age, 'still I know not how to remain silent, for since my childhood I have trained myself in that [art] which I learned through practice'.

order.[152] Kroyer supposed that Aichinger became a member of the Jesuit-organized Marian Congregation during his years in Ingolstadt (he matriculated twice, in 1578 and 1588), a fact that would help to explain his later compositions devoted to the Virgin.[153] Aichinger's membership in the sodality is not unlikely, although no proof of this has yet surfaced.

At Ingolstadt Aichinger befriended Jakob II Fugger (1567–1626), who would later become the Bishop of Konstanz (1604–26) and an active supporter of the Counter-Reformation in that diocese. This friendship proved decisive, as Jakob's father, Jakob I Fugger (1542–98), engaged Aichinger as organist at the Benedictine church of SS Ulrich and Afra in Augsburg in 1584. The elder Fugger had donated a new organ to SS Ulrich and Afra in 1580, with the important stipulation that the organist 'should be a Catholic, and the organ should be played by no one else'.[154] From this time forward Aichinger seems to have forged close relationships with the Benedictine leadership and brothers at the abbey; three of his publications, the first book of *Divinae Laudes* (1602), the *Corolla eucharistica* (1621) and the *Flores musici* (1626) would be dedicated to them, while his *Lacrumae D. Virginis* (1604) is thematically related to a sculpture of the weeping Virgin and St John at the foot of the cross that was erected in the church in 1605 (see Chapter 5).

In 1584 Jakob I Fugger furthered Aichinger's education by financing a trip to Italy that took him to Venice, Siena and Rome over the space of

---

[152] The Ingolstadt Jesuits, however, by no means turned away Protestant students. Adam Gumpelzhaimer, who later was to become the cantor of the Protestant church of St Anna in Augsburg, matriculated at Ingolstadt in 1582. The Jesuits' success at conversions depended in no small measure on their welcoming of Protestant students into their midst. Other students of the university went on to have musical careers, such as Georg Victorinus, the musical director (1591–c.1624) at the Jesuit college in Munich, who published two important collections of sacred concerti, the *Siren coelestis* in 1616 and the *Philomela coelestis* in 1624. On music at the university see Karl Batz, 'Universität und Musik', pp. 111–24. At the Jesuit university in nearby Dillingen (also the episcopal seat for the diocese of Augsburg), singing preceded instruction in both morning and afternoon, and despite occasional protests on visitations by officials of the order, elaborate instrumental music accompanied important events. For example, at the celebration of the feast of St Ignatius in July 1619, Heinrich V presided over a service involving the contributions of viols, regals, winds, a bassoon and an organ ('Musica fuit gravis, magnifica, ab omnibus laudata, etiam a R. Rectore. Missa fuit P. Wolfgangi Schörifleder super Laudate. Intersonuerunt perpetuo duae cheles Bassi, 2 Regalia, 2 Tibicines, et fistula una maioris Bassi Fagott, et subinde ipsa organa'). Quoted in Ursprung, *Jacobus de Kerle*, pp. 44–45.

[153] Kroyer, 'Gregor Aichingers Leben und Werke', p. xviii.

[154] The organist should be someone 'der catholisch sein soll, und sonsten von keinem andern solle geschlagen werden'. Quoted in Krautwurst, 'Die Fugger und die Musik', pp. 43–44. This was not entirely unprecedented: at the cathedral the appointment of Servatius Roriff as organist in 1560 was delayed, since he had married a Protestant woman and the chapter wished to know 'what his marital status is, and which religion [i.e., confession] he wished to espouse'. See Ursprung, *Jacobus de Kerle*, p. 68, and *DR*, 2 January 1560.

four years.[155] Aichinger was one of the earliest, if not the earliest, German composer to study with Giovanni Gabrieli; Hans Leo Hassler, who travelled to Venice in the same year from Nuremberg, in fact studied with Giovanni's father Andrea.[156] The choice of Venice can be accounted for, on one level, by the waxing economic and cultural connections between south German cities and northern Italy in this period, connections that were actively furthered by the Fugger family's trade relationships. On another level, musical developments in northern Italy and especially in Venice were exerting an ever greater influence over German musicians and patrons.[157] Aichinger himself obtained a large number of Venetian madrigal prints for his own library, perhaps during his stay in Venice in the 1580s. A set of five partbooks, labelled 'Ex libris Gregorij Aichinger' and preserved in the Staats- und Stadtbibliothek Augsburg, contain three madrigal prints by Cipriano de Rore, two by Orlando di Lasso, two by Giaches de Wert, and five volumes of madrigal anthologies.[158] Aichinger, then, knew mid-century Italian madrigal

---

[155] According to Hettrick ('Aichinger, Gregor', vol. 1, p. 249), Aichinger matriculated at the University of Siena in November 1586, and then visited Rome.

[156] See Paumgartner, 'Zur Musikkultur Augsburgs in der Fuggerzeit', pp. 86–87. For more details on Aichinger's first Italian trip, see Kroyer, 'Gregor Aichingers Leben und Werke', pp. xxxi–xxxiv. While in Venice, Aichinger also purchased a substantial amount of music, which he subsequently brought back to Augsburg. On later musicians to study with Giovanni Gabrieli, and especially Heinrich Schütz, see Siegfried Schmalzriedt, *Heinrich Schütz und andere zeitgenössische Musiker in der Lehre Giovanni Gabrielis: Studien zu ihren Madrigalen* (Stuttgart: Hänssler, 1972).

[157] The nearby Bavarian capital Munich, for example, played host to both Andrea and Giovanni Gabrieli (see Gmeinwieser, 'Kirchenmusik', pp. 981–82). It is also significant that the latter's two main publications of *Symphoniae sacrae* were dedicated to Augsburg figures: the four sons of Marcus Fugger (1597) and Johann von Merk, abbot of SS Ulrich and Afra (1615).

[158] D-As, Tonk. Schl. 411–415. The full contents, in order of appearance, are as follows:

Cipriano de Rore, *Li Madrigali Cromatici* (Venice: Girolamo Scotto, 1562; RISM A/I, R2484)

Cipriano de Rore, *Li Madrigali cinque voci libro secondo: insieme con alcuni di M. Adriano et de altro auttori, nouamente ristampato* (Venice: G. Scotto, 1562; RISM B/I, 1562[20])

Cipriano de Rore, *Il terzo libro di madregali* (Venice: A. Gardano, 1560; RISM A/I, R2492; RISM B/I, 1560[21])

Orlando di Lasso, *Il primo libro di madrigali* (Venice: A. Gardano, 1557; RISM A/I, L759)

Orlando di Lasso, *Il secondo libro di madrigali* (Venice: A. Gardano, 1559; RISM A/I, L762)

Il primo libro de le muse (Venice: A. Gardano, 1555; RISM B/I, 1555[25], including music by Arcadelt, Berchem, Ruffo and Barre)

Il secondo libro de le muse (Venice: A. Gardano, 1559; RISM B/I, 1559[16])

Il terzo libro delle muse (Venice: A. Gardano, 1561; RISM B/I, 1561[10], including works by Palestrina, Lasso, Finot, Donato, Corsini and others)

repertories well, but in his own music the influences of the polychoral motet, the canzonetta, and the villanella are also plainly evident. It was in cities like Augsburg, Munich, and Nuremberg, which lay along the major transalpine trade routes, that much of this music entered Germany, encouraging an enthusiastic engagement among local composers with modern Italian styles and genres.

For most of the remaining years of the century Aichinger remained in Augsburg as organist at SS Ulrich and Afra (he did briefly rematriculate at Ingolstadt in 1588), during which time he brought out his first three motet books (1590, 1595, 1597).[159] In these early prints he followed his teacher's model closely in his preference for the genres of the madrigal and polychoral motet; the texts, moreover, do not anticipate his later turn to confessionally specific themes. A second trip to Italy beginning in 1598 seems to have been a turning point, not only for his development as a composer but also for his religious stance, which may be discerned in the dedications and texts of nearly all his subsequent publications. He matriculated at the University of Perugia in 1599 and was in Venice for some time as well, but his stay in Rome during the Holy Year of 1600 may have had religious motivations and it is likely that he took priestly vows during this time.[160] Having negotiated the benefice of St Mary Magdalene and a position as vicar-choral at the cathedral by the time he returned to Augsburg in 1601, Aichinger publicly renounced the composition of secular music in his sacred canzonetta collection entitled *Odaria lectissima*, echoing previous vows by composers influenced by the Catholic renewal such as Palestrina and Marenzio (see Chapter 5).

Although one cannot follow Aichinger's subsequent biography in great detail, a few facts survive that shed some light on his religious preoccupations. First of all, in 1617 the cathedral chapter paid him for two paintings, one representing a sitting of the Council of Trent, and another showing an assembly of Cardinals in the Sistine Chapel. Both paintings probably originated around 1600 and were very likely

---

Giaches de Wert, *Madrigali del fiore*, bks. 1 and 2 (Venice: G. Scotto, 1561; RISM A/I, W856, W861)

I dolci et harmoniosi concenti, bks. 1 and 2 (Venice: G. Scotto, 1562; RISM B/I, 1562[5], 1563[6])

For more on these partbooks, see Bernstein, 'Buyers and Collections of Music Publications', p. 25; and Mary S. Lewis, *Antonio Gardano, Venetian Music Printer, 1538–1569: A Descriptive Bibliography and Historical Study* (New York: Garland, 1988), vol. 1, pp. 128–29.

[159] The *Sacrae Cantiones*, 4–10vv (Venice: Gardano, 1590; RISM A/I, A517); the *Liber tertius sacrarum cantionum*, 4–6vv (Venice: Gardano, 1595; RISM A/I, A518); and the *Liber sacrarum Cantionum* (Nuremberg: Paul Kauffmann, 1597; RISM A/I, A519).

[160] 'Reverendus' is found in all of his publications from 1603 onward, suggesting that he may not have been ordained immediately.

obtained during his Roman pilgrimage.[161] Secondly, in 1618 Aichinger
published a small prayer book, the *Thymiama sacerdotale* ('priestly
incense'), which contains prayers and meditations [*considerationes*] for
priests immediately before or after the celebration of the Mass.[162] He
drew these texts from the works of the Carthusian monk Anthony da
Molina and Jacobus Pontanus, the rector of the Jesuit college in
Augsburg and most likely a personal acquaintance. The texts, designed
to deepen the piety and mystical understanding of the reader, are
meditations on the mysteries of Christ's death and redemption for each
ferial day of the week, as well as for the period between Advent and
Pentecost.[163] Finally, we have a series of political commentaries and
verse on the events leading to the Catholic victory at the Battle of White
Mountain in 1620.[164] Some of these materials are in Aichinger's hand; of
particular interest are two dialogues in Italian, one between Emperor
Ferdinand II and his vassal armies just before setting off for battle, and
one between the Devil and Ernst von Mansfeld, a Catholic mercenary
leader who sided with the Protestant Bohemian Union, and was thus
considered a traitor to the Catholic cause. It is unclear whether these
dialogues were ever set to music, nor is the context obvious in which they
may have been recited or sung. However, they suggest that Aichinger was
aware of the political events that threatened the European peace, and
that he was indeed a partisan of the Catholic side.

The lengthy series of publications that followed Aichinger's return to
Augsburg were not, as a rule, intended for general liturgical use, even if
from time to time he chose to set texts from the liturgy. Instead, these
collections tend to be topical in nature: sets of Marian music (the
Liturgica sive sacra Officia and the *Vespertinum Virginis*), Eucharistic
music (the *Solennia augustissimi Corporis Christi* and the *Flores musici
ad Mensam SS Convivii*), music concerning Christ's Passion (the *Vulnera
Christi* and the *Lacrumae D. Virginis et Ioannis*), or various

[161] Denis A. Chevalley, *Der Dom zu Augsburg* (Munich: B. Oldenbourg Verlag, 1995),
p. 352.

[162] Gregor Aichinger, *Thymiama sacerdotale, Hoc est, Meditationes piae, a Sacerdotibus
ante Celebrationem Missae per singulos Hebdomadae Dies devote exercendae* (Augsburg:
Sara Mang, 1618).

[163] This book found its way, at least, into the libraries of SS Ulrich and Afra (the printed
books portion of 'Catalogus Codicum Manuscriptorum Bibliothecae Benedictinorum
Liberi ac Imperialis Monasterii ad SS Udalrici et Afrae Augustae Vindelicorum ... a
P. Placido Braun ... 1786', StAA, KWA G39) and St Salvator ('Catalogus Librorum
Bibliothecae Collegii S. J. Augustae', D-As, Cod. Cat. 15 [I–II]; see also *HCA*, vol. 1,
p. 518).

[164] Uncovered by Theodor Kroyer in 'Gregor Aichinger als Politiker', in Karl Weinmann,
ed., *Festschrift Peter Wagner zum 60. Geburtstag* (Leipzig: Breitkopf & Härtel, 1926),
pp. 128–32, referring to D-Mbs, Fol. Ms. Chart. 735.

combinations of these kinds of devotional texts dominate his output. Two basic styles of writing prevail in his music after 1600: the sacred canzonetta and the vocal concerto with basso continuo. The former type, of course, represented a simplification of Renaissance counterpoint, a turn to a lighter, simpler, mostly homophonic style of writing that appealed to musical amateurs in its fashionability and relative ease of execution. In his approach to the vocal concerto, too, Aichinger adopted this ideal. Eschewing the virtuosic flights that characterized the early vocal concerto in Italy, his vocal writing often resembles that of his tricinia of the 1590s: light imitation with occasional homophonic passages. The devotional and identifiably 'Catholic' quality of his texts, combined with the contrapuntal simplicity and clear text declamation of his writing, all suggest the new kinds of performance contexts for Catholic music in Augsburg that were beginning to flourish at the turn of the seventeenth century: devotional exercises of the Jesuits, confraternities and private individuals, public processions and pilgrimages. These were settings in which Catholic musical amateurs (rather than trained, professional choirs) would have required music suited to their abilities and devotional interests.

Much of this music can be left for the following chapter, but here we can consider a few collections setting explicitly liturgical texts, whether or not they were intended for the official liturgy. Broadly speaking, few of Aichinger's collections setting liturgical texts seem well suited for the general repertory of churches. Among them might be his setting for 8–12 voices of the *Miserere* (1605), suitable, as he states in his dedication to Abbot Petrus of the Cistercian abbey of Salem, for Vespers services during Lent.[165] The setting, in which each verse receives a different scoring, exhibits a mixture of imitative and polychoral writing that may be said to typify the prevailing style of church polyphony just before the advent of the sacred vocal concerto. The shift in stylistic direction may be seen in another print containing liturgical texts of a general nature, the *Sacrae Dei Laudes* (1609), dedicated to the two Augsburg *Stadtpfleger* Marcus Welser and Johann Jakob Rembold.[166] The subtitle

---

[165] 'Iam pridem in multas ecclesias introducta est consuetudo per sacros Quadrigesimæ dies omnes sub vesperam symphonia, siue concentu musico decantandi Psalmum illum quinquagesimum, quo Dauid Rex & Propheta flebiliter peccata suæ accusans, à clementissimo DEO misericordiam piè efflagitat.' From the dedication to Aichinger's *Psalmus L. Miserere mei Deus, musicis Modis ad IIX. IX. X. XI. XII. Voces varie compositus* (Munich: Nikolaus Heinrich, 1605; RISM A/I, A532).

[166] *Sacrae Dei Laudes sub Officio divino concinendae, quarum Pars prior V. VI. VII. VIII. posterior vero II. III. IV. & V. Vocum* (Dillingen: Adam Meltzer, 1609; RISM A/I, A540 and A541). Welser, who held the office of *Stadtpfleger* from 1600 to his death in 1614, was a Catholic deeply committed to the cause of the Counter-Reformation, although

'sub officio divino concinendae' certainly suggests an intention for liturgical use, while the text selection – befitting a collection dedicated to the leading officials of the biconfessional city government – reveals no emphasis on the Marian and Eucharistic imagery so common in his other music. Aichinger probably refers to his recent experiments with the thoroughbass concerto when, in the dedication, he defends his music from the 'poisonous tongue of the jealous' [*aemulorum lingua venenata*], but his own ambivalence about the new style may be reflected in the print's division into two halves, the *Sacrae Dei Laudes* proper, consisting of more traditional motets for five to eight voices, and the *Cantiones nimirum*, which includes accompanied 'Concerti' for two to four voices as well as five instrumental *Canzoni per sonare*. Basso continuo, although of the *seguente* variety, also appears in the 1616 *Triplex Liturgiarum Fasciculus*, a set of three imitation masses for four to six voices dedicated to three younger members of the Fugger family who may have received instruction from the composer. It is difficult to determine the intended audience for this print, but its modest size is suggestive more of a presentation work than a collection for general use in the liturgy. Aichinger's last print that seems to have been intended explicitly for the church liturgy is the *Officium Angeli Custodis* (1617), a collection of Vespers and Mass music for the feast of the Guardian Angels, whose celebration had been mandated by Bishop Heinrich V in 1605.[167]

Unlike his colleague Erbach, then, Aichinger did not feel compelled to publish music of great utility for the official church liturgy. Other prints of his containing settings of liturgical texts, furthermore, strongly suggest the currents of Marian and Eucharistic devotion embodied in the devotions of Catholic confraternities. Aichinger refers directly to such groups with the subtitle 'in usum tum sodalium, tum aliorum cultorum & amantium matris Dei' on the title page of his *Tricinia Mariana* (1598), a collection of three-voice settings of mostly liturgical texts in praise of the Virgin.[168] The inclusion of an image of the Jesuit seal – the motto

---

he remained neutral in matters of official policy. He maintained close contacts, for example, with the Protestant leadership of the St Anna church and *Gymnasium*; see Katarina Sieh-Burens, *Oligarchie, Konfession und Politik im 16. Jahrhundert: Zur sozialen Verflechtung der Augsburger Bürgermeister und Stadtpfleger, 1518–1618* (Munich: E. Vogel, 1986), pp. 189–90. Welser and Rembold would also receive the dedication of Gumpelzhaimer's *Sacrorum Concentuum … Liber secundus* (1614).

[167] *Officium Angeli Custodis a S. Romana Ecclesia approbatum & concessum quaternis Vocibus ad Modos musicos concinatum … cum Basso ad Organum ubi Opus erit* (Dillingen: Gregor Hänlin, 1617; RISM A/I, A545).

[168] *Tricinia Mariana, quibus Antiphonae, Hymni, Magnificat, Litaniae, et variae Laudes ex Officio Beatiss. Virginis suavissimis Modulis decantantur* (Innsbruck: J. Agricola, 1598; RISM A/I, A521).

'IHS' superimposed on a cross, surrounded by a blazing sun – over a
Latin epigram praising the Virgin suggests a connection to the Jesuit
Marian Congregation, which probably counted the composer as well as
the dedicatee (Jakob II Fugger, the prince-bishop of Konstanz and
Aichinger's former schoolmate at Ingolstadt) among its members.[169] The
settings of Marian antiphons, the Litany of Loreto, and other Latin texts
in the volume would very likely have been fitting for the liturgical or
para-liturgical devotional services of these sodalities, and would have
pleased its dedicatee, a fervent supporter of the Catholic renewal who
would zealously promote the Counter-Reformation in the diocese of
Konstanz.

The *Tricinia Mariana* anticipates Aichinger's Marian output to come,
not least in the epigram's rejection of pagan harmonies and embrace of
the Virgin and her son in resounding song:[170]

> SOmniet Ascræus Parnassi in vertice Musas,
>   Vanaque Latonæ numina Callimachus.
> Dorica Pindarico rumpatur pollice phorminx,
>   Nec resonet Latia barbitos icta manu.
> Ite profana cohors, melior mihi carminis auctor.
>   Nasceris et virgo, Virginis atque puer.
> Hanc atque hunc mecum præsago pectore vates,
>   Dicunt; hanc atque hunc nulla Sibylla tacet.
> Isacidæ celebrant Mariam, psalteria Regis,
>   Et Solomonæi cantica diva chori.
> Plurima te mecum populorum millia cantant,
>   Milleque te gentes regnaque mille sonant.
> Omnia certatim te secula virgo loquuntur,
>   Omne genus superûm terrigenumque canit.
> Da mihi pro nostro spectandum carmine natum.
>   Mater, et æterno carmine utrumque canam.

> Let Hesiod of Parnassus dream of the high Muses,
> Callimachus of the feigned deity of Latona.

---

[169] The *Tricinia Mariana*, in fact, was not the first time Aichinger had composed music
suitable for the Marian Congregations. In 1596 he had contributed an eight-voice Marian
litany to the *Thesaurus litaniarum* (1596), an anthology of litanies for the Virgin, the
saints, and the Name of Jesus compiled by Georg Victorinus, the music director at the
Jesuit college of St Michael in Munich. Victorinus dedicated his volume to the Marian
Congregations of the Jesuits' Upper German Province, including sodalities in Munich,
Ingolstadt, Dillingen and Augsburg. Like Aichinger, Victorinus had also attended the Jesuit
university at Ingolstadt; he matriculated in 1588, only two days after Aichinger's second
matriculation. See Batz, 'Universität und Musik', p. 117. Kroyer mentions the dedication
of the *Tricinia Mariana* to Jakob II Fugger (see 'Gregor Aichingers Leben und Werke',
p. li), but it is missing from the exemplar I have examined from the Staats- und
Stadtbibliothek Augsburg (Tonk. Schl. 11).

[170] Aichinger would explicitly reject the composition of secular music in his *Odaria
lectissima* (1601).

Let the Dorian lyre be broken by Pindar's thumb,
And let not the barbitos be struck by Latin hand.
Go, profane cohort; I have a better song composer.
You are born, Virgin, and the son of the Virgin.
The prophets join me in talking of them with visionary inspiration.
No Sibyl remains silent about them.
The sons of Isaac celebrate Mary, as do the psalteries of the King,
And the divine songs of the Solomonic choir.
With me thousands of people sing of thee,
A thousand men and kingdoms resound.
All generations rival one another in speaking of you, virgin,
Every nation in heaven and earth sings.
For our singing grant us the sight of your son.
Mother, I shall sing an eternal song to you both.

The pieces in this volume are relatively modest in scope and complexity, suiting the abilities of singers with a basic musical training. Aichinger gave these tricinia a strong contrapuntal basis that may be indebted to the example of Lasso; the bass voice, for example, lacks the harmonic functionality that would characterize his later music. However, occasional episodes of homophony and sections in triple metre lend these pieces a folklike quality that Aichinger would exploit more fully in his canzonetta collections in the next decade.[171] Homophony marks the opening of his setting of the hymn *Memento salutis auctor* (see Example 4.1),[172] although more imitative textures prevail until a mostly homophonic passage in triple time at the close. It is in these passages that the 'bass' voice (scored, however, in the alto range with a C_3 clef) shows the most functionality in the prevalence of chord roots and dominant-to-tonic leaps (see bars 22 ff). Here as elsewhere, Aichinger places special emphasis on the clarity and audibility of the text, a feature often associated with the influence of the Counter-Reformation, but which was in fact endemic to polyphony in this era. Syllabic text-setting prevails, broken up by occasional melismatic passages over important words. Although the tricinia of this volume could naturally have been used in a variety of circumstances, their Latin, Marian texts and some-what simplified polyphony point to the 'usum sodalium' indicated by Aichinger on the title page. Furthermore, the consistently high cleffing (a typical combination is G_2, G_2 and C_3) would have suited the Marian Congregations, composed largely of students at Jesuit colleges; naturally other groups of singers would have opted for downward transposition.

Aichinger's Roman pilgrimage in the Holy Year of 1600 was a decisive

---

[171] See Kroyer, 'Gregor Aichingers Leben und Werke', pp. li and cxxxiii.

[172] 'Mary, mother of grace, / mother of mercy, / shield us from our enemy, / and receive us in the hour of death. / Glory be to you, O Lord, / who was born of the Virgin, / with the Father and the Holy Spirit / for ever and ever.'

moment, as his subsequent publications would embrace devotional imagery more explicitly and emphasize the Italianate forms of the sacred canzonetta and, in time, the sacred vocal concerto. Those volumes setting liturgical texts, however, tended to remain more firmly anchored in the older, imitative idiom. Such is the case with his *Liturgica sive sacra Officia ad omnes Dies festos magnae Dei Matris* (1603), dedicated not to an earthly patron but to the Virgin Mary herself, embodied at the popular Marian pilgrimage shrine of Einsiedeln in Switzerland.[173] Addressing the Virgin directly, Aichinger writes that 'I ... have been led to you by zeal and veneration, indeed toward reverence, by whose

Example 4.1   Aichinger, *Memento salutis auctor*, from *Tricinia Mariana* (1598), adapted from the edition by August Scharnagl (Regensburg: Feuchtinger & Gleichauf, 1979)

---

[173] *Liturgica sive sacra Officia, ad omnes Dies festos magnae Dei Matris per Annum celebrari solitos, quaternis Vocibus ad Modos musicos facta* (Augsburg: Johannes Praetorius, 1603; RISM A/I, A528).

Example 4.1 *concluded*

guidance my life so far has happily run its course.' He may have previously gone as a pilgrim to Einsiedeln, perhaps in the company of his old university friend Jakob II Fugger, who as cathedral provost at Constance may have been expected to make such a journey.[174] It is not unlikely that Aichinger would travel there later as a member of

---

[174] Kroyer, 'Gregor Aichingers Leben und Werke', pp. lxxxii–lxxxiii.

the Corpus Christi Confraternity at the church Heilig Kreuz: a contemporary manuscript chronicle of the city's confraternities records that members of that group went on pilgrimage to Einsiedeln in 1607 and 1614.[175] In any case, given the lack of a separate dedication to one or another of his earthly patrons, it is likely that a visit to the shrine by the composer himself was the inspiration for the *Liturgica*.[176]

This is not, however, music that would have been especially suitable for pilgrimages. Aichinger provides settings of liturgical texts for the Offices of the Annunciation, Assumption, Nativity and Purification of the Virgin Mary, along with an Office for the Dedication of a Church (a reference to the shrine itself), a Mass for the Virgin, various motets (including the four Marian antiphons) and a setting of the Litany of Loreto. The collection does not, however, fully embrace the Roman Rite. In a brief note to the reader following the dedication Aichinger acknowledges its primacy, but insists that other, older rites should not be neglected. 'Do not simply praise the new, and condemn the old', he writes. 'If the living, ancient customs are esteemed by Favorinus, according to Gellius, why should we not undertake the singing of the traditional music from time to time?'[177] A closer examination of Aichinger's Gloria reveals the presence of Marian tropes (given here in italics), as follows:

> Domine Fili unigenite Jesu Christe, *spiritus et alme orphanorum paraclete*. Domine Deus, Agnus Dei, Filius Patris, *primogenitus Mariae virginis matris*. Qui tollis peccata mundi, miserere nobis, *ad Mariae gloriam*. Qui sedes ad dexteram Patris, miserere nobis. Quoniam tu solus sanctus, *Mariam sanctificans*. Tu solus Dominus, *Mariam gubernans*. Tu solus Altissimus, *Mariam coronans*, Jesu Christe.

---

[175] The entry from 1607 reads, 'Anno 1607. Multi fratres et sorores pietatis causa usque ad Divam Virginem in Einsidlen peregrinati, ut Indulgentiarum possent fieri participes', while that from 1614 reads 'Anno 1614. Multi fratres et sorores devotionis gratia iuerunt usque ad Divam Virginem Einsidlensem'. From 'De initijs ac progressu omnium Fraternitatum, quæ in alma hac vrbe Augustana fuerunt diversis temporibus erectæ à Christi fidelibus, narratio MDCXVII', D-As, 2° Aug 346, fols 27r, 29v.

[176] Franz Fleckenstein certainly errs, though, in suggesting that Aichinger dedicated the work during a return trip from Rome via Einsiedeln in 1603 (see 'Marienverehrung in der Musik', in Wolfgang Beinert and Heinrich Petri, eds, *Handbuch der Marienkunde* (Regensburg: Pustet, 1984), p. 186); Aichinger had assumed his position at Augsburg Cathedral no later than 1601.

[177] 'Si priscis moribus viuendum censet apud Gellium Phauorinus, cur antiquis subinde modulis canendum non putemus?' The second-century writer Aulus Gellius relates in his *Attic Nights* (bk. 1, ch. 10) that the philosopher Favorinus told a young man who used obsolete words out of admiration for ancient morality, 'Live by all means according to the manners of the past, but speak in the language of the present.' Translation by John C. Rolfe in Aulus Gellius, *The Attic Nights of Aulus Gellius* (London: William Heinemann; New York: G.P. Putnam's Sons, 1927), vol. 1, p. 51.

O Lord the only-begotten son Jesus Christ, *O spirit, nourisher and protector of the orphaned.* O Lord God, Lamb of God, Son of the Father, *first-born of Mary the virgin mother.* Thou that takest away the sins of the world, have mercy upon us, *for the glorification of Mary.* Thou that sittest at the right hand of the Father, have mercy upon us. For thou only art holy, *blessing Mary.* Thou only art the Lord, *guiding Mary.* Thou only art most high, *crowning Mary*, Jesus Christ.

This is a version of the *Gloria Marianum*, the 'Marian Gloria' that was commonly used in many Catholic areas before the Tridentine era.[178] In his note to the reader Aichinger may have been referring to a practice in which song and speech alternated between the main texts and the tropes. In allowing for pre-Tridentine practice Aichinger acknowledges, perhaps, that the Marian music contained in this volume was suitable not only for the church liturgy, but also for the gatherings of Marian brotherhoods, in which the Roman liturgy was not mandated. It is also possible that his preface reflects the uncertain status of the liturgy in the Augsburg diocese. It will be remembered that while Bishop Johann Otto von Gemmingen had officially introduced the Roman Rite in 1597, it took years, even at the cathedral, for the new liturgy to be fully implemented (see above).

Befitting the liturgical character of this collection, Aichinger employs a style closer to his motet publications of the 1590s than to his recent canzonettas and tricinia. Although syllabic text declamation prevails, homophony is relatively infrequent; imitative textures are far more common. The same is true for his other Marian print of 1603, the *Vespertinum Virginis*, which consists of six Magnificats in a traditional, imitative style. All except the first appear to be imitation Magnificats, although the composers of the models remain to be identified.[179] He directed his dedication to Prince-Abbot Johann Adam von Kempten, whom he had met during his Roman pilgrimage, and suggested the content of this publication was inspired by the Virgin Mary herself. 'I believe', he writes, 'no melody to be better than that which I have composed for the cult of the Virgin, of whom you and I declare and shall

---

[178] See Hoeynck, *Geschichte der kirchlichen Liturgie des Bisthums Augsburg*, p. 44.

[179] *Vespertinum Virginis Canticum sive Magnificat quinis Vocibus varie modulatur* (Augsburg: Dominicus Custos, 1603; RISM A/I, A529). Further research will clarify the exact models, whose incipits (as given by Aichinger in his table of contents) are as follows: *Oncques amours, Liquide perl'amor, Maria Virgo, Vienne Montan* and *Poi che il camin.* *Oncques amours* may be one of Thomas Crecquillion's four settings of that text; Marenzio was probably the author of the two models *Liquide perle Amor* (in 1588[21]) and *Vienne Montan* (from his first book of four-voice madrigals, 1585); *Poi che'l camin m'e* may be the setting by Vincenzo Ruffo (in 1557[25]). All are scored for five voices except for the last, which is scored for six.

always declare ourselves followers.'[180] A fruitful comparison may be made with Orlando di Lasso's imitation Magnificats, which Aichinger almost certainly would have known through the repertories of the cathedral or SS Ulrich and Afra, where he was the organist. Like Lasso's Magnificats, the motivation for these works was at least in part religious; Aichinger also follows his predecessor in not shying away from secular models, which are found in four out of the six settings. Composers may have justified this practice in the belief that the holiness of the canticle's text transformed the originally secular model into a sacred gift.[181]

The notoriety of Aichinger's *Cantiones ecclesiasticae* (1607), scored for combinations of two to four voices, can be attributed to its status as the first print by a German composer to employ basso continuo, but its textual orientation underlines the strong Marian tendencies in the composer's output after 1600.[182] The commonplace title gives no hint of the print's topical content, but the large proportion of Marian pieces – 11 out of 20 texted works (he also appended a single instrumental canzona) – makes it appropriate to consider this print in tandem with the previously discussed ones. Aichinger acknowledged this emphasis in his preface to the reader by stating that 'I have wanted to follow Viadana in the present little work, to the glory of God and the God-bearing Virgin Mary [*ad laudem Dei & Deiparæ virginis Mariæ*], [and] also for my own amusement and recreation.'[183] Magnificats in the successive modes form the core of the collection (in this case, two Magnificats in mode 1, one each in modes 2, 4, 6 and 8, and a *Magnificat Ascendit Deus* in mode 1).[184] The remaining Marian motets include a Marian antiphon (*Salve Regina*), two pieces based on biblical verses (*Exsurgens Maria*, from Luke 1: 39–43, 46; *Mansit autem Maria*, from Luke 1: 56), and one piece, *Ave gratia plena*, based on an unknown source.[185] Since liturgical texts like the Magnificat and the *Salve Regina* are balanced by numerous settings of biblical verses in the volume as a whole, it occupies a middle

---

[180] 'Ego certè, siue quadam animi opinatione inductus, siue reipsa persuasus, nunquam mihi felicius vllum melos meditari videor, quàm cum ad Virginis cultum aliquid conari incipio, cuius ego me, Tuæque iuxta C. clientem æternum profiteor, semperque profitebor.' From preface to *Vespertinum Virginis*.

[181] As argued by Crook in *Orlando di Lasso's Imitation Magnificats*, pp. 80–82.

[182] *Cantiones ecclesiasticae, trium et quatuor Vocum Cuivis Cantorum Sorti accomodatae, cum Basso generali & Continuo in Usum Organistarum* (Dillingen: Adam Meltzer, 1607; RISM A/I, A538). Edition by William E. Hettrick in *Cantiones ecclesiasticae* (1972).

[183] Translation by Hettrick in *Cantiones ecclesiasticae*, p. ix.

[184] Ibid., pp. ix–x. Hettrick noted that all but the first three and the last four compositions are paired according to mode and scoring.

[185] Sources ibid., pp. xii–xiii.

ground between the 'liturgically' oriented collections cited above and devotional music.

Aichinger directs his brief dedication to Johann Heinrich von Rohrbach, a canon at the cathedrals of Augsburg and Passau, and also provides a lengthy note to the reader that contains the first discussion of thoroughbass practice in the German language, following closely and explicitly upon the example of Viadana.[186] It is important to note that the new idiom in no way compromises Aichinger's ideal of clear and precise text declamation, a feature common to most of his music. With the exception of occasional melismatic passages at the ends of phrases or at words of particular significance, he adheres to a syllabic style keyed closely to the accents of the Latin texts. He frequently turns to entirely homophonic textures, making these concertos at times indistinguishable from the sacred canzonettas prevalent in his other contemporary prints. Furthermore, he does not embrace the virtuosic flights characteristic of Italian monody. This music, emphasizing melodic motion in semibreves, minims and semiminims (smaller note values are rare), remains unpretentious and relatively easy to perform. Although the *Cantiones ecclesiasticae* does represent a ground-breaking step in the adoption of thoroughbass practice north of the Alps, Aichinger does not abandon his ideal of providing music for a variety of Catholic contexts in which the clear perception of the text is paramount.

Like the *Cantiones ecclesiasticae*, Aichinger's *Solennia augustissimi Corporis Christi* (1606) displays a characteristic ambivalence between liturgical and non-liturgical performance, and betrays the composer's devotional commitments even within the context of a notionally 'liturgical' collection.[187] He dedicated the volume to the leaders of the Corpus Christi Confraternity, of which he was a member, and seems to have intended its contents for the services of such a group: the title page indicates that this set of 'solemn rites of the most venerable body of Christ' is 'customarily to be sung in the most holy sacrifice of the Mass, and in the Offices of the same feast, as well as in public supplications or processions', assigning this music a range of functions consistent with the devotional activities of the brotherhood. The music includes a complete Office of Second Vespers for the feast of Corpus Christi, a set of Propers for the Mass of Corpus Christi and a set of procession hymns. The

---

[186] For more detailed information on Aichinger's thoroughbass practice see esp. Adam Adrio, *Die Anfänge des geistlichen Konzerts* (Berlin: Junker und Dünnhaupt, 1935), pp. 13–14; Hettrick, ed., *Cantiones ecclesiasticae*, pp. viii–xi; and Kirwan-Mott, *The Small-Scale Sacred Concertato*, pp. 48–55.

[187] *Solennia Augustissimi Corporis Christi, in sanctissimo Sacrificio Missae & in eiusdem Festi Officijs, ac publicis Supplicationibus seu Processionibus cantari solita* (Augsburg: Johannes Praetorius, 1606; RISM A/I, A533).

polyphonic style and complexity in this print varies widely. At one extreme lies a piece like the responsory *Homo quidam fecit*, which features a long-note plainchant cantus firmus in the uppermost voice accompanied with rather traditional melismatic polyphony in the remaining three voices (see Example 4.2).[188] With the exception of brief

Example 4.2   Aichinger, *Homo quidam fecit*, from *Solennia augustissimi Corporis Christi* (1606)

---

[188] 'A certain man made a great supper; and he bade many: and he sent forth his servant at supper time to say to them that were bidden, Come.'

Example 4.2 *concluded*

passages like that at 'dicere invitatis' (bars 18–20), Aichinger largely
dispenses with the syllabic style he developed in his other music,
preferring longer-spun phrasing and a more complex polyphonic web.

At the other extreme lie the final three strophic hymn settings, *Sacris
solemniis, Ave panis Angelorum* and *Pange lingua gloriosi* (the other two
hymns, *O sacrum convivium* and *Domine non sum dignus*, consist of a

single stanza only and resemble the more traditional music in the volume stylistically). *Ave panis Angelorum*, given as Example 4.3,[189] illustrates the wide stylistic gap in this book: the five-voice texture is entirely homophonic with the exception of some light counterpoint in the final bars; unlike *Homo quidam fecit*, furthermore, the bass voice assumes a more functional role harmonically, tracing a clear localized tonal progression from C to G in bars 1–7, C to C in bars 8–13 and F to G to C in bars 14–25. The style of *Ave panis Angelorum* would clearly have been more suitable for processions, in which the harmonic and rhythmic

Example 4.3   Aichinger, *Ave panis angelorum*, from *Solennia augustissimi Corporis Christi* (1606)

---

[189] 'Hail, bread of the Angels, / Hail Jesus, teacher of morals, / Healer of sins, / everlasting sacrifice.'

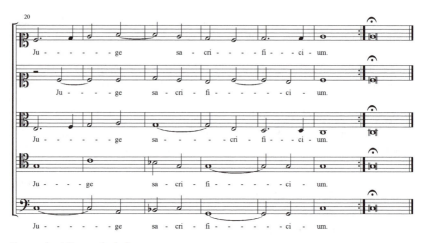

Example 4.3 *concluded*

regularity would have been well synchronized with the rhythm of walking.

The relative sophistication of the polyphony and the lack of vernacular music in Aichinger's *Solennia* raises the question of whether the collection would have been suitable for a confraternity that very likely embraced persons who were literate neither in the Latin language nor in polyphonic music. A partial answer is suggested by a 1618 publication of Office texts for Corpus Christi (including many of the same texts set by Aichinger, along with a sacramental litany and the sequence *Lauda Sion salvatorem*) in both Latin and Greek by the Augsburg Jesuit Georg Mayr, who dedicated the small duodecimo volume to the Corpus Christi Confraternity.[190] In the dedication Mayr tells of the great erudition of many of the group's members, who 'excel in their knowledge of languages, and truly have prayed to Christ the Lord ... in so many other languages'.[191] Although the Corpus Christi

---

[190] Georg Mayr, *Officium Corporis Christi, De Festo et per Octauam Latinè et Græcè editum, ac Fraternitati Eucharisticæ Augustanæ dedicatum* (Augsburg, 1618). Mayr, from Rain, a small city on the Danube north of Augsburg, served as a preacher at the church of St Moritz between roughly 1600 and 1620; see Layer, *Musik und Musiker der Fuggerzeit*, p. 44. The book is of a piece with others of Mayr's publications in the early seventeenth century, which provide liturgical and devotional texts in Latin and Greek translation for the benefit of Jesuit students. See, for example, his *Officium Beatæ Mariæ Virginis Latino-Græcum* (Augsburg: Ad insigne pinus, imprimebat David Francus, 1612); *Fasciculus sacrarum Litaniarum* (Augsburg: Christophorus Mang, 1614); and *Officium Angeli Custodis Pauli V. Pont. Max. Authoritate publicatum* (Antwerp: Apud Heredes Martini Nutij, & Ioannem Meursium, 1617).

[191] 'Cùm enim hæc Fraternitas tam Augustæ quàm alibi non paucos complectatur, qui, vt in alijs scientijs, ita linguarum cognitione excellunt, imò verò cùm tot aliæ linguæ

Confraternity most certainly included many members for whom Latin texts, much less Greek texts, would have been opaque, Mayr's preface implies the continuing presence of an elite cadre – including patricians like the Fugger, clerics and other educated persons like Aichinger – who may have been responsible for the organization of the brotherhood's ceremonies. Even if, as is likely, members of the confraternity sang German songs and litanies in the course of public processions and pilgrimages, the Latin language (Mayr's Greek texts would have been mainly of academic interest) still prevailed in the services attended by the group at Heilig Kreuz. Although there is no firm evidence that the Latin polyphony of Aichinger's *Solennia* was performed before the brothers and sisters, the collection stands as an artful expression of the rise of Eucharistic devotion in early modern Augsburg.

Philipp Zindelin (1570–c.1625)

Of the four chief Catholic composers in Augsburg, Philipp Zindelin was the least prolific, yet his career path and music resemble that of the others in certain ways.[192] Born in Constance in 1570, Zindelin may have spent some length of time as a child at the court of Königsegg-Aulendorf (a short distance north of Constance), as the later dedication of his first published collection, the *Primitiae Odarum sacrarum* in 1609, implies.[193] He matriculated at the Catholic university at Freiburg im Breisgau in 1589, and subsequently served Bishop Andreas of Constance as a musician for 11 years; during his stay at the episcopal court he would probably have become acquainted with Jakob Fugger, who headed the cathedral chapter from 1593 and would eventually ascend to the bishop's throne in 1604. Jakob's brother Marcus seems to have taken an interest in Zindelin's fortunes, for the latter's appointment as an

---

Christum Dominum in sanctissimo Eucharistiæ Sacramento verè presentem confiteantur, & vel publicâ vel priuatâ precum recitatione laudent (nam Augustæ idem Officium iam etiam Germanicè editum est) haud æquum fuerit solam linguam Græcam huic cultui, & multorum virorum ac iuuenum eruditæ pietati deesse.' From the dedication of Mayr, *Officium Corporis Christi*.

[192] On Zindelin's biography, see Adolf Layer, 'Zindelin, Philipp', in *MGG*, vol. 14, cols 1301–2; A. Lindsey Kirwan and Stephan Hörner, 'Zindelin, Philipp', in *New Grove II*, vol. 27, pp. 843–44, and Wohnhaas, 'Der Augsburger Musikdruck', p. 316.

[193] The dedicatees of this print are Ulrich (*c*.1558–1620), Marquard (*c*.1559–1626) and Georg (*c*.1566–1622) von Königsegg-Aulendorf, all three the sons of Johann Jakob von Königsegg (1508–67). In his dedication Zindelin claims to have enjoyed the family's generosity during his childhood ('ab usque propè infantia crevi, vestra liberalitate adolevi, artemque canendi perdidici') and wishes to allow them to enjoy the first fruits of his labours ('par est ergo, ut has primitias odarum mearum, nominibus vestris inscriptas & consecratas in orbem emittam, quo fructum aliquem benignitatis vestrae … degustetis').

Augsburg *Stadtpfeifer* in 1604 followed partly from Marcus's intercession. It is not inconceivable, furthermore, that Zindelin's engagement as a musician by the Augsburg cathedral chapter around 1600 was partly attributable to his connections with the regional nobility. These connections would again be in evidence in November 1609, when the chapter granted him a salary increase at the behest of Johann Conrad von Gemmingen, the Bishop of Eichstätt (and dedicatee of the *Kapellmeister* Klingenstein's *Liber primus s. Symphoniarum* two years previously). In return for this doubling of his salary the chapter obligated Zindelin to teach the cornetto to a qualified student.[194] Little more is known about his biography, but it is certain that as a *Stadtpfeifer* and cathedral musician he would have participated in a wide variety of musical contexts. Even before his first official appointment as *Stadtpfeifer* in 1604, Zindelin was active as a musician in private circles (an extant criminal case from 1601, briefly discussed in Chapter 2, contains a reference to Zindelin making polyphonic and monophonic music with two other men, including a Jesuit student, in a house; see p. 67, note 62). The dedications of his published music, furthermore, suggest that he was employed as an occasional musician by a number of German Catholic nobles and prelates. He may have visited the Munich court chapel on occasion, although his silence about any protracted connection with the court in the dedication of his *Traurigs Klaglied* of 1612 (directed to Duchess Magdalena of Bavaria, the sister of Duke Maximilian I) would argue against a close association with that institution.[195] On the other hand, Archduke Leopold's standing as

---

[194] See Layer, 'Zindelin'. His salary increase is noted in *DR*, 2 November 1609: 'Philip Zindelin Cornetisten alhie, Ist auf sein *supplication*, vnd meines genedigen fürsten vnd herrn bischouens zue Eÿstett *intercession* zu den zuuor jerlichs habenden 50R. noch mit 50R. *addition* auf seinen khönfftigen fleis vnd wolhaltten, auch dergestaltt zuwilfaren beuohlen, das Er sich auf gleichen schlag, wie der Pawman verobligiern solle, ainen qualificieren Knaben auf dem Zinckhen abzurichten, auch den Gottsdienst wan man figuriert nicht zuuersaumen. Sonnsten werde man Ime laut *Recessus*, von 29. Martij A.º 608. an der besoldung abziehen.' On Zindelin's engagement to teach the cornetto, see 'Obligation Philips Jacoben Zindelins, Burgers vnd *Cornetisten* zue Augspurg, vmb 100R. soldt, Anno 1609', dated 9 September 1609, in BSA: Hochstift Augsburg/Neuburger Abgabe, 5282. Zindelin was also called upon from time to time to give instrumental instruction to students at the Protestant church of St Anna. In 1621, for example, he taught the cornetto, dulcian and trombone to a certain Caspar Hainlin or Haimlin, at the school's expense. See Mayr, in Gumpelzhaimer, *Ausgewählte Werke*, p. 20. Layer, in *Musik und Musiker der Fuggerzeit*, p. 78, noted that Zindelin applied for the post of *Kapellmeister* on Klingenstein's death in 1614, but was rejected on the grounds that he was not a priest.

[195] Layer pointed to Zindelin's connection with the Munich court chapel; see 'Zindelin'. Among the dedicatees of his other published music are Prince-Abbot Heinrich of the Benedictine abbey of Kempten (his *Symphonia Parthenia* of 1615) and Heinrich and

THE CATHOLIC LITURGY IN AUGSBURG

godfather for two of Zindelin's sons may suggest a closer connection with the Habsburg court at Innsbruck.[196]

Zindelin brought out four music prints between 1609 and 1615, three with Latin texts and one with German texts. Three of these are liturgical in nature. His first collection, the *Primitiae Odarum sacrarum* (1609), contains settings mainly of Gregorian antiphons for various feasts in the Roman calendar, in stylistically conservative settings for four voices.[197] Far more significant from the standpoint of contemporary Catholic devotion is the *Lugubria super Christi Caede et Vulneribus* (Laments over Christ's death and wounds, 1611), which despite the affectation of its title is a collection of liturgical music for five voices, namely for the service of the Veneration of the Cross, a liturgical devotion that took place in the context of the Mass of the Presanctified in the Good Friday liturgy.[198] In this service (according to the Tridentine Rite) the cross was carried into the middle of the choir, where it was unveiled by the priest during the singing of the antiphon *Ecce lignum crucis* (Behold the wood of the cross). Those present were to kneel before and kiss the cross while the cantors sang a series of antiphonal 'reproaches'.[199] Zindelin's polyphonic setting includes the refrain 'Populue meus' along with the reproaches themselves, a concluding antiphon *O admirabile commercium*, and five short hymns on the wounds to Christ's hands, feet and side, pieces that may have traditionally concluded the Veneration.[200] The surviving partbooks suggest a relatively traditional imitative texture, but one in which syllabic declamation is the norm. Homophonic passages are generally found in triple-metre sections, while brief episodes

---

Frobenius von Waldburg (his *Lugubria* of 1611), the latter both members of the dynasty that produced Otto Truchseß von Waldburg, the mid-sixteenth-century bishop of Augsburg and powerful cardinal.

[196] Three letters from Zindelin to the Archduke, dated 1618, 1619 and 1625 respectively, have been preserved. See Walter Senn, *Musik und Theater am Hof zu Innsbruck: Geschichte der Hofkapelle vom 15. Jahrhundert bis zu deren Auflösung im Jahre 1748* (Innsbruck: Österreichische Verlagsanstalt, 1954), pp. 237–38. The date of the final letter, a supplication for money, proves that Zindelin died later than 1622, the death year given by Layer in *Musik und Musiker der Fuggerzeit*, p. 38, and Kirwan-Mott in 'Zindelin, Philipp', p. 843.

[197] *Primitiae Odarum sacrarum quaternis Vocibus ad praecipuos totius Anni Dies festos accomodatae* (Augsburg: Johannes Praetorius, 1609; RISM A/I, Z236).

[198] *Lugubria super Christi Caede et Vulneribus, Vocibus quinis ad Modos musicos facta* (Dillingen: Gregor Hänlin, 1611; RISM A/I, Z237).

[199] An example of such *improperia* is 'Ego te exaltavi magna virtute: et tu me suspendisti in patibulo crucis', or 'I have exalted you by great virtue, and you hung me from the pillory of the cross'), answered with a refrain of 'Populue meus, quid feci tibi?' ('O my people, what have I done to you?') by the choir.

[200] In the Tridentine Rite the service is concluded with the hymn *Pange lingua gloriosi*, to each verse of which the versicle *Crux fidelis* is appended.

of *falsobordone* and madrigalistic word-painting lend occasional emphasis.[201] Since this was music probably intended for church choirs in a specific liturgical service, Zindelin does not embrace the more fashionable canzonetta-type writing typical of Aichinger's para-liturgical and non-liturgical music. On the other hand, its subject matter aligns it closely with other Christological devotional music composed in early seventeenth-century Augsburg, including Aichinger's *Lacrumae D. Virginis et Ioannis* (1604) and *Vulnera Christi* (1606), and Erbach's *Acht underschiedtliche Geistliche Teutsche Lieder* (1611) (see Chapter 5).

Collections of Magnificat settings and Vespers music were, of course, common coin in Catholic sacred music in this era. However, Zindelin's *Symphonia Parthenia* of 1615, a collection of Magnificats in the eight modes, Marian antiphons, litanies and other motets, is musically notable for its adoption of the basso continuo and inclusion of two-voice concertos and even monodies.[202] This book suggests the penetration of the concerted style into liturgical contexts; if surviving documents do not indicate whether this type of music in particular was performed at Augsburg Cathedral, it is clear that instruments – whether in the form of polychoral choirs or basso continuo groups – were granted a larger role in liturgical music there after 1600 (see above, pp. 100–103). Zindelin's dedication of the print to Prince-Abbot Heinrich of the Benedictine abbey of Kempten suggests that he may once have been in the prince's employ.[203]

It must be stressed that churches in Augsburg like the cathedral and SS Ulrich and Afra would very likely have continued to use a relatively conservative and established repertory of liturgical music, despite the new trends represented by some of the prints discussed in this chapter. Bernhard Klingenstein seems not to have attempted any radical revision of the cathedral's liturgical music, although the lack of surviving sources makes any conclusions difficult. On the other hand, surviving choirbooks from SS Ulrich and Afra demonstrate the continued viability of older polyphonic repertories at that church, including music by Lasso, Kerle and even Isaac, notwithstanding the introduction of large-scale

---

[201] Both the tenor and bass partbooks are missing from the only known exemplar, at D-Rp, B 183.

[202] *Symphonia Parthenia qua in Aedibus Zachariae Vatis et Elisabethae Coniugum ... quaternis Vocibus* (Augsburg: Johannes Praetorius, 1615; RISM A/I, Z239).

[203] 'Me verò non solum anni tempus & mos receptus, sed & grandia insuper pro beneficijs debita, in te Reu: ᵐᵉ Præsul: Ill:ᵐᵉ Princeps, non tam liberalem esse, aut munificum quam gratum exhibere cogunt, grauem mihi & seriam legem fixerunt, tua in me, imò & tuorum tot beneficia, iam inde à primis annis tui me parentes inter suos numerarunt. Hanc tu parentum tuorum in me beneuolentiam perseuerasti, imò & cumulasti.' From the preface of Zindelin, *Symphonia Parthenia*.

polychoral music shortly after 1600. New liturgical music by Augsburg's Catholic composers may gradually have found a home in their own city, but apart from certain prints that directly responded to local liturgical changes (like Erbach's *Modorum tripertitorum*), much of this music seems to have been inspired by a rising interest in specifically Catholic devotional imagery: above all, the Virgin Mary, the Eucharist and the crucified Christ. It is this characteristic that aligns Catholic liturgical music in Augsburg closely with the larger number of devotional prints discussed in the next chapter.

CHAPTER FIVE

Devotional Music in Counter-Reformation Augsburg

The prints discussed in the previous chapter contained settings almost exclusively of liturgical texts, but their actual use could not have been circumscribed so easily. In an era characterized by consolidation of the main confessional churches and the enforcement of sectarian ideologies, the boundaries between the 'official' liturgy and 'popular' religious beliefs and practices remained contested and often ambiguous. Even the celebration of the liturgy itself included a number of actions, including the tolling of bells, the holding of processions, the display of relics and the adornment of altars, not all of which were prescribed in liturgical books. In the course of an entire ritual year, the official liturgy was in fact only a skeleton, around which a large and complex body of ritual practices developed, in other words, 'the "popular" side of ritual life'.[1] Churches in Augsburg played host to a variety of religious activities beyond the liturgy, not all of which are well documented. However, a few types of observances of special significance from the standpoint of the Counter-Reformation may be singled out for discussion, including the observance of the Ten- or Forty Hour Prayer, the vigils and devotional services of confraternities and the public devotions, catechism instruction and theatrical productions of the Jesuit order. Catholic processions and pilgrimages, two highly visible phenomena of central importance to Counter-Reformation spirituality, demand separate treatment and will be discussed in Chapters 6 and 7.

To varying degrees, vocal or instrumental music contributed to the theatricality of many of these activities, heightening the solemnity of the occasion and exciting the piety of participants and onlookers. The end of this chapter will examine selected collections of devotional music by Augsburg's Catholic composers, music that could have found a home in any number of these para-liturgical or non-liturgical venues. In these prints Marian, Eucharistic and Christological themes come to the fore,

---

[1] See esp. Scribner, *Popular Culture and Popular Movements in Reformation Germany*, pp. 22–23 and 41. Ritual life in sixteenth-century Catholic Germany, according to Scribner, had three overlapping components: the formal liturgy prescribed by the church hierarchy; a body of *functiones sacrae* or 'ceremonies', including processions, benedictions and exorcisms; and a third area of folk and magical beliefs and practices, including the popular belief in the magical properties of holy water or the Eucharist, for example.

with musical styles reflecting a range of different aptitudes and interests among contemporary performers. The flexible nature of this music, bound neither by ecclesiastical ordinances nor liturgical propriety, facilitated a more explicit embrace of fashionable Italian idioms ranging from the simple canzonetta to the concerto for few voices and basso continuo. First, however, it is necessary to explore the religious, political, and social conditions under which such a repertory could emerge and flourish.

Patronage and Catholic Music in Augsburg: the Fugger Family

At least two factors paved the way for the strengthening of the Catholic position by 1600 and the subsequent self-assertion of the Catholic community: the emergence of the Jesuits and the embrace of Counter-Reformation Catholicism by elements in the city's patriciate. By the late sixteenth century certain patrician families that were well represented in the city oligarchy – chief among them the Fugger family – began more openly to embrace the defence of Catholicism. The political controversies of the 1580s (primarily the *Kalenderstreit* and the *Vokationsstreit*, a conflict over the right to name new Protestant preachers) were exacerbated by confessional tensions within the city council, tensions that had been slowly rising since the 1560s.[2] The Fugger family's overt support of Catholicism may be attributed in part to the influence of the Jesuits, who sought influence among and conversions of highly placed persons such as Sibylla von Eberstein (wife of Marcus Fugger), Ursula von Liechtenstein (wife of Georg Fugger) and Elisabeth von Montfort (wife of Johann Fugger).[3] Certain members of the family involved themselves more directly with Catholic institutions. Jakob Fugger (1567–1626) was consecrated as the Bishop of Konstanz in 1604, and tirelessly promoted the Counter-Reformation in his diocese.[4] Jakob's oldest brother Marcus (1564–1614) was the

---

[2] On confessionalism in the city oligarchy, see Sieh-Burens, *Oligarchie, Konfession und Politik*, pp. 187–207.

[3] See Rummel, 'Petrus Canisius und Otto Kardinal Truchseß von Waldburg', pp. 54–55; and Warmbrunn, *Zwei Konfessionen in einer Stadt*, pp. 240–21. It was Sibylla Fugger who invited Petrus Canisius to Augsburg in 1569 to perform an exorcism on Anna von Bernhausen, a lady-in-waiting who was suspected of being demonically possessed. The subsequent pilgrimage of Anna, Canisius and various members of the Fugger family to Altötting in 1570 became the centrepiece of Martin Eisengrein's *Unser liebe Fraw zu Alten Oetting* (1571), the most significant published apologia for Counter-Reformation pilgrimage in Germany. See Soergel, *Wondrous in His Saints*, pp. 119–26.

[4] On Jakob Fugger in Konstanz, see esp. Konstantin Holl, *Fürstbischof Jakob Fugger von Konstanz (1604–1626) und die katholische Reform der Diözese im ersten Viertel des 17.*

co-founder of the Corpus Christi Confraternity (1604), a Eucharistic brotherhood which contributed to a more public profile of Counter-Reformation Catholicism through the organization of processions and pilgrimages (see Chapters 6 and 7).[5]

The family, of course, had long been among the most significant patrons of composers in Europe, both locally and internationally, a legacy of their economic success as well as of their artistic interests.[6] Although their financial fortunes began to suffer in the late sixteenth century (a result, among other things, of the splitting of the family business and the extension of credits to the empire that could not be repaid),[7] the family continued to patronize artists and musicians, who increasingly produced work showing a more overtly Catholic profile. Altarpieces commissioned by the family, for example, no longer emphasized central themes of redemption, but tended towards the glorification of God, the Virgin Mary and the saints.[8] Jakob Fugger the elder donated a new organ for the St Michael's chapel of the church of SS Ulrich and Afra in 1580; however, this organ was to be played 'by a Catholic, and shall not be played by any other'.[9] The music dedicated to the Fugger family after the turn of the seventeenth century took on a more explicitly Catholic cast, rejecting liturgical texts of a general nature in favour of devotional, and at times mystical texts honouring the Virgin Mary, the Eucharist or Christ.

Nevertheless, Octavian II Fugger's employment of the Protestant Hans Leo Hassler as his chamber organist in 1586 suggests that with respect to musical patronage there was still room for toleration. Octavian's frequent and generous monetary donations to the Augsburg Jesuits leaves little doubt that he was a devout Catholic, but this zeal did not extend to the confessional makeup of his

---

Jahrhunderts (Freiburg im Breisgau: im Commission der Geschäftstelle des 'Caritasverbandes für das katholische Deutschland', 1898).

[5] For other examples of the Fugger family's confessional turn in the late sixteenth century, see Sieh-Burens, *Oligarchie, Konfession und Politik*, pp. 188–89.

[6] Franz Krautwurst has provided a lengthy list of musical dedications to members of the family in 'Die Fugger und die Musik', pp. 47–48. The Fugger family's musical interests are too broad and multifaceted to be addressed fully in this study; an important recent volume on this subject is the volume in which Krautwurst's essay appears, edited by Renate Eikelmann, *Die Fugger und die Musik: Lautenschlagen lernen und ieben: Anton Fugger zum 500. Geburtstag: Ausstellung in den historischen Badstuben im Fuggerhaus Augsburg, 10. Juni bis 8. August 1993* (Augsburg: Hofmann Verlag, 1993).

[7] See Karg, 'Die Fugger im 16. und 17. Jahrhundert'.

[8] Bruno Bushart, 'Kunst und Stadtbild', in Gottlieb et al., eds, *Geschichte der Stadt Augsburg*, pp. 381–82.

[9] Krautwurst, 'Die Fugger und die Musik', pp. 43–44.

household.[10] Hassler obliged his patron not only with the secular German songs and Italian madrigals prized by the family, but also with Latin sacred music for the Catholic Mass. He dedicated to Octavian both his book of four- to twelve-voice motets for the principal feasts of the church year (*Cantiones sacrae*, first issued in 1591 and reprinted in 1597) and a book of masses for four to eight voices, some of which were based on motets from the earlier collection.[11] The masses were almost certainly heard in the private services of the Fugger family, and a copy of the volume was also owned by the Augsburg Jesuits.[12] The general liturgical nature and high quality of the motets made them suitable for Protestant contexts as well, and indeed a copy of the motet book appears in the inventory of St Anna's music library.[13] Broadly speaking, Hassler's output during these years represented a skilful compromise between the demands of his Catholic patrons and the need to provide practical and saleable editions for use across confessional boundaries.

The Jesuits

The Jesuits, not surprisingly, were also major contributors to the Catholic revival in Augsburg, and benefited heavily from Fugger family support. Although they did not introduce confessional tension in the city, they certainly helped to widen the confessional divide, agitating against mixed marriages, demanding that Catholic citizens release their Protestant servants and carrying out spectacular public conversions and exorcisms.[14] While acting, in effect, as Catholic missionaries to Augsburg's Protestant population, they sought to draw the lines between

---

[10] Octavian and his brother Philipp Eduard Fugger were particularly generous, together donating some 16 000 florins to the Jesuits in 1586 alone. See Braun, *Geschichte des Kollegiums der Jesuiten in Augsburg*, pp. 35–36.

[11] *Cantiones sacrae de Festis praecipuis totius Anni 4. 5. 6. 7. 8. et plurium Vocum* (Augsburg: Valentin Schönig, 1591; RISM A/I, H2323; reissued as H2324); and the *Missae quaternis, V. VI. et VIII. Vocibus* (Nuremberg: Paul Kauffmann, 1597; RISM A/I, H2327). A second volume of motets, the *Sacri Concentus quatuor, 5, 6, 7, 8, 9, 10 & 12 vocum* (Augsburg: Valentin Schönig, 1601; RISM A/I, H2328), though written in Augsburg, was dedicated to the town council of Nuremberg, which employed Hassler beginning in 1601.

[12] See D-As, Cod. Cat. 15 (I–II), the *Catalogus Librorum Bibliothecae Collegii S.J. Augustae*, a book-list from the library of St Salvator.

[13] See Bernstein, 'Buyers and Collections of Music Publications', pp. 31–33.

[14] The Jesuit college in Augsburg was established in 1582 with the help of a sum of 30 000 florins from the estate of Christoph Fugger, with further funds provided by his brothers Philipp and Octavian. In subsequent decades members of the family lavished the Jesuits with money and decorations; see Braun, *Geschichte des Kollegiums der Jesuiten in Augsburg*, pp. 35–38, and *passim*. The extant chronicle of the Augsburg Jesuits [HCA] emphasizes efforts to convert local Protestants. For a recent broader study of conversion

the two faiths more clearly through the promotion of public and at times dramatic expressions of Catholic ritual. It was partially through the Jesuits' influence that public supplications, processions, pilgrimages, theatrical productions and confraternities were transforming Augsburg's religious landscape by the turn of the seventeenth century.

In the light of the Jesuits' missionary emphasis, it is unsurprising that they designed many of their ceremonies and exercises for public consumption as well as for religious expression. Litanies and other types of music certainly played a role in these public events, which embraced both visual and aural stimuli to dramatize Catholic ritual for onlookers. In 1602, for example, the Jesuits held public supplications including music upon the return of pilgrims from the shrine of Andechs. On the feast of the Ascension of the Virgin,

> the Marian Congregation from our church, after the well-attended sermon, betook themselves with the whole people and the retinues of the chief princes to the cathedral of the Blessed Virgin with rejoicing and song, for the sake of the indulgences that had been granted by the Pope; they persevered in their prayers for four hours, and finally left the way they came in order and with music.[15]

By the early seventeenth century the Jesuits were embracing music for other kinds of public religious activities. Although little evidence survives from Augsburg itself, German Jesuit fathers at large began to use vernacular songs in catechism instruction by the late sixteenth century, an acknowledgement of the great success enjoyed by the Protestants in this area previously.[16] In 1586 Claudius Marschall, the rector of the Jesuit college in Fulda, reported the spectacular success of music in helping students memorize the catechism:

> Already our people are teaching catechism in eleven towns, and it is amazing to see the advantages conferred by the singing of the catechism. I had worked with a few boys for almost an entire year, and they barely learned the Our Father. Now, however, they are able to learn the Creed and the Ten Commandments exactly in only a few hours through singing.[17]

---

and confessionalism in southern Germany (and in early modern Augsburg in particular), see Duane J. Corpis, 'The Geography of Religious Conversion: Crossing the Boundaries of Belief in Southern Germany, 1648–1800' (Ph.D. diss., New York University, 2001).

[15] *HCA*, vol. 1, pp. 397–98 [1602].

[16] The appearance of published songbooks for Jesuit catechism instruction by the 1620s indicates the extent to which vernacular song was considered a part of this practice.

[17] 'Schon in elf Dörfern geben die Unsrigen jeden Sonntag Katechismusunterricht und wunderbar sind die Dienste, welche das Absingen des Katechismus dabei leistet. Ich hatte mich mit nur wenigen Knaben vom Lande fast ein ganzes Jahr abgemüht, kaum das Vaterunser hatten sie gelernt. Jetzt aber prägen sie sich durch Singen das Glaubensbekenntnis und die zehn Gebot ein wenigen Stunden exakt ein.' Quoted in Duhr, *Geschichte der Jesuiten in den Ländern deutscher Zunge*, vol. 1, pp. 459–60.

Marschall went on to say that the visitor Oliver Manare wished to introduce the singing of the catechism in the entire Rhenish Province. 'To some', Marschall continued, 'this practice may seem new and unfamiliar. But this was also true of the introduction of the Marian Congregations, and see how they now flourish.'[18] Already in 1569, Viennese Jesuits were giving catechism instruction to both boys and girls, who were expected to sing the catechism in front of the congregation on feast days.[19] Unfortunately there seems to be little direct evidence for these practices in Augsburg, but given the proven success of song as a vehicle for the memorization of texts elsewhere, it is not unlikely that vernacular song played a role in catechism instruction in Augsburg as well. At the very least, the Augsburg Jesuits owned a copy of the most widely circulated collection of German catechism songs, Georg Vogler's *Catechismüs Jn aüsserlesenen Exempeln, kürtzen Fragen, schönen Gesängern, Reÿmen vnd Reÿen für Kirchen vnd Schülen*, published in Würzburg in 1625.[20] In this manual for the catechist Vogler described the proper usage of song in children's catechism, directing the students to be divided into two groups on each side of the classroom; the songs, which sought to inculcate proper Catholic doctrine, then were to be performed antiphonally. Vogler also provided many of his songs with instrumental basses in case an organ was available.[21]

The Marian Congregation, a body of students and lay devotees organized by the Jesuits, practised other types of free devotions, such as are found in a collection of prayers and meditations on the Virgin, ΠΑΡΘΕΝΟ ΜΗΤΡΙΚΑ [*Partheno Metrika*], dedicated to the group by Jacobus Pontanus, the probable founder of the Augsburg Marian Congregation.[22] Designed 'for the use of the Augsburg Marian

---

[18] 'Der P. Visitator [Oliver Manare] will das Singen des Katechismus in der ganzen [rheinischen] Provinz einführen.... Freilich scheint einigen die Sache gar zu neu und ungewohnt. Doch war es auch so bei der Einführung der Marianischen Kongregationen, und wie blühen diese schon.' Quoted ibid., vol. 1, pp. 459–60.

[19] Ibid., pp. 455–56.

[20] Würzburg: Johann Volmar, 1625; RISM B/VIII, 1625[24]. The title page of the exemplar preserved in the Staats- und Stadtbibliothek Augsburg (D-As, 8° Th. Pr. 2727) gives the inscription 'Societatis JESV ad S. Anna Aug.ᵃᵉ 1637' and the name 'Joannes Traber'.

[21] 'Der Generalbaß welcher bey etlichen zufinden/ ist dahin vermeint/ daß man vnderweylen die Orgel darzu gebrauchen könde.' From the preface to Vogler, *Catechismüs Jn aüsserlesenen Exempeln*.

[22] ΠΑΡΘΕΝΟ ΜΗΤΡΙΚΑ [*Partheno Metrika*], id est, Meditationes, Preces, Laudes in Virginem Matrem, potissimùm ex Ecclesiasticis Græcorum Monumentis. Ad Usum Parthenianæ Sodalitatis Augustanæ (Augsburg: David Frank, 1606). Dietz-Rudiger Moser has pointed to catechism instruction, missionary work, the meetings of [Marian] congregations and mealtimes as important venues for Jesuit singing. See Moser, *Verkündigung durch Volksgesang*, pp. 71–72.

Congregation', the collection contains no musical notation, but some of the contents suggest musical genres, such as a Marian litany and a series of seven Marian hymns for the feasts of the Conception, Nativity, Presentation, Annunciation, Visitation, Purification and Assumption of the Virgin respectively. Significantly, these are precisely the same seven hymn texts that Gregor Aichinger set polyphonically in his *Encomium Verbo incarnato* of 1617 (see below).[23] Even if it is impossible to say whether Aichinger's canzonetta-like hymn settings would have been sung by members of the Marian Congregation, the publication does testify to the close relations between Pontanus and the composer.[24]

Finally, music was also performed in the context of Jesuit theatre, which was perhaps the best artistic expression of the order's goal of converting souls, combining drama, costume, scenery, poetry, dance and music in service of a religious message. Theatrical productions were common especially in south German Jesuit establishments such as Augsburg, Munich, Ingolstadt, Dillingen, Neuburg, Konstanz and elsewhere, and were performed as a fixed part of the school year, often at the beginnings and ends of academic periods.[25] In some cases, theatrical presentations, often involving Christ's Passion or the Nativity, were performed in church services.[26] Apart from the undeniable potential for propaganda, Jesuit theatre also provided opportunities for Jesuit students to practice rhetorical, gestural and also musical techniques. In Augsburg, Jesuit theatre began as early as 1583 with Pontanus's *Josephus Aegyptius* and extended through hundreds of dramas, melodramas and even *Singspiele* by the end of the eighteenth

---

[23] Ingolstadt: Gregor Hänlin, 1617; RISM A/I, A546. The hymn texts, according to Pontanus's original publication, were composed by Cornelis Musius (1500–72), a priest at the church of St Agatha in Delft who was executed in Leiden by rebel forces at the onset of the siege of Haarlem. See Alastair Duke, *Reformation and Revolt in the Low Countries* (London and Ronceverte: The Hambledon Press, 1990), p. 206.

[24] Aichinger set texts by Pontanus on other occasions as well: see in particular his *Divinae Laudes ex Floridis Iacobi Pontani* (Augsburg: Dominicus Custos, 1602; RISM A/I, A525), a set of canzonettas based entirely on texts from Pontanus's *Floridorum libri octo* (Augsburg: Johannes Praetorius, 1585).

[25] On the geographical scope of Jesuit theatre, see Wüst, *Das Fürstbistum Augsburg*, pp. 344–45; at the Jesuit university in Dillingen, for example, theatre became a fixed part of the curriculum from an early stage.

[26] See Duhr, *Geschichte der Jesuiten in den Ländern deutscher Zunge*, vol. 2, pt. 2, p. 50, although he does not provide more specific information. Hsia has argued (in *The World of Catholic Renewal, 1540–1770* (Cambridge and New York: Cambridge University Press, 1998), pp. 160–61) that the spacious interiors, large frescoes, and numerous windows in Jesuit architecture contributed to the 'theatricality' of Catholic sacraments; churches became, in effect, stages for the drama of the liturgy and sacraments.

century.[27] Perhaps the most famous of these plays was *Cenodoxus* (concerning St Bruno's founding of the Carthusian Order in medieval Paris) by Jakob Bidermann, premiered by the Marian Congregation in 1602 and still popular into the twentieth century. Although the specific kind of music performed as a part of *Cenodoxus* is unknown, the libretto does call for both spoken and sung choruses, including a 'chorus angelorum lugentium' and a 'chorus diabolorum'; like Greek choruses, these would have served as a means of heightening dramatic tension at critical moments in the narrative.[28]

The libretto for one drama by the Augsburg Jesuit Matthäus Rader, entitled *Didymus* (1613), survives today in the Staats- und Stadtbibliothek Augsburg and contains two polyphonic choruses by Christian Erbach.[29] Didymus the Blind (310/13–395/98) was the head of the catechetical school in Alexandria and a follower of Origen, highly praised by St Jerome before the official repudiation of Origenist doctrines by the church. Rader's drama, however, does not make specific reference to Didymus' historical circumstances, but rather presents him as the protagonist in a morality tale pitting the seductive influences of such allegorical characters as Mundus, Grossus and Anarchus against the wisdom of Conscientia, Charistius, Pœnitentia and 'Genius Bonus'. Typically for most Jesuit dramas of this period, direct references to confessional politics are avoided. As Didymus abandons the devilish seductions of his friends and embraces a true life of piety, a group of children dressed as angels (*Chorus puerorum cultum Angelico*, presumably students at St Salvator) sing verse in praise of Didymus and of God. Two four-voice choruses by Erbach are embedded, 'Ter maximo, ter optimo' and 'Vobis datur Didymus', the first of which is shown in Example 5.1.[30] The chorus strongly suggests the style of the homophonic canzonetta, with little contrapuntal activity and clear declamation of the words, not at all dissimilar to many contemporary sacred canzonettas by Erbach, Aichinger and others. This type of style would have suited the Jesuits' needs well, as it places emphasis squarely on the projection of the text and on stylistic accessibility as opposed to contrapuntal complexity. Erbach's contribution was not unusual: in other cities as well, prominent

---

[27] For an overview of Jesuit theatre at St Salvator, see Adolf Layer, 'Musik und Theater in St. Salvator', in Baer and Hecker, eds, *Die Jesuiten und ihre Schule St. Salvator in Augsburg 1582*, pp. 69–74.

[28] See Ruth Hofmann, 'Jesuitentheater in Ingolstadt', in Hofmann, ed., *Musik in Ingolstadt*, p. 172.

[29] D-As, 8° H 1840.

[30] 'To the thrice greatest, to the thrice best let this triumph turn, who has converted his comrade Didymus in so blessed a way. Out of the most horrid of his companions he made a devotee of the heavens. Lo, for us a dance, Lo, for us a triumph.'

composers were engaged for such material, such as Lasso in Munich and Palestrina in Rome.[31]

The musical needs of catechism instruction and Jesuit theatre, along with the rising demand for vocal and instrumental music in Jesuit churches and colleges, led to an active musical life in many institutions

Example 5.1   Erbach, *Ter maximo, ter optimo*, from Matthäus Rader, *Didymus* (1613)

[31] See Helmuth Osthoff, 'Einwirkung der Gegenreformation auf die Musik des 16. Jahrhunderts', *Jahrbuch der Musikbibliothek Peters*, **41** (1934), p. 46. For two other choruses from Jakob Gretser's *Timon*, for the Jesuit college in Dillingen, see Sonja Fielitz, *Jakob Gretser Timon. Comoedia Imitata (1584). Erstausgabe von Gretsers Timon-Drama mit Übersetzung und einer Erörterung von dessen Stellung zu Shakespeares Timon of Athens* (Munich: Wilhelm Fink Verlag, 1994), pp. 385–92. Franz Körndle (in '"Ad te perenne gaudium": Lassos Musik zum "Vltimum Judicium"', *Die Musikforschung*, 53 (2000), pp. 68–71) recently has shown that six of Lasso's motets were performed for a Jesuit drama in Graz in 1594. Apart from their larger scoring these works seem to preserve a greater role for contrapuntal activity – true to Lasso's style – than do Erbach's homophonic choruses. Nonetheless Lasso's choruses are highly syllabic and closely attuned to textual accent. See, for example, *Heu, quis armorum*, edited by David Crook in Lasso, *Cantiones sacrae sex vocum (Graz, 1594)*, The Complete Motets, 16 (Madison, Wis.: A-R Editions, 2002).

Example 5.1 *concluded*

that was at odds with the original intentions of the order's founders. The practical experiences of many Jesuits had confirmed the utility of music as an important medium for the propagation of religious messages; by the early seventeenth century music formed an essential component not only of their missionary work, but also of their own devotional exercises. As in other types of religious settings, the Jesuits promoted music not as an end in itself – this would have been contrary to the mission of the Society – but rather as a component of larger rituals involving visual as well as aural stimuli. Even if by the seventeenth century the Jesuits had recognized the value of music, it remained for them a limited, yet effective tool in the service of propaganda.

Confraternities

Even if the Augsburg Jesuits were able to adapt their mission to suit the local context, fundamentally they remained an organization whose structure and aims were largely determined by their Roman leadership. Catholic confraternities, by contrast, were far better integrated into the

economic and social fabric of the city, since many of them were
associated with specific guilds of lay tradesmen (note, for example, the
establishment of a weavers' confraternity at the church of St Georg in
1596 and a soldiers' confraternity at St Moritz in 1603)[32] and all
included members from a relatively wide cross-section of the Catholic
populace. The most prominent of these groups – the Trinity
Confraternity based at the cathedral and the Corpus Christi
Confraternity based at the church of Heilig Kreuz – counted hundreds of
people from various walks of life among their members and organized
some of the most elaborate public displays of Catholic devotion; they
also met privately on a regular basis, observing feast days of significance
to them and commemorating deceased members with processions,
prayers and music. The social organization of confraternities reflects
their position in a vital middle ground between the 'top-down'
confessionalization promoted by the ecclesiastical hierarchy and Jesuits
on the one hand, and the 'bottom-up' confessionalization manifested at
lower social levels on the other.

The musical activities of Italian confraternities have been researched
in great detail by Noel O'Regan and Jonathan Glixon in the cases of
Rome and Venice respectively, but corresponding documentation of
music in Catholic German confraternities is much more spotty and
reflects the more turbulent religious history of southern Germany.[33]
Confraternities, even if endorsed by the bishop and endowed with
indulgences from Rome, were largely independent organizations whose
records, it seems, were not preserved in a systematic manner; those
documents that remained in church archives were probably dispersed
after secularization in the early nineteenth century and may or may not
be extant. Nevertheless, scattered surviving evidence from statutes,
expense sheets, chronicles and musical compositions suggests that the
sacred music cultivated by confraternities was as varied as their
membership: contrapuntal polyphony, simple sacred canzonettas and
vernacular devotional songs addressed the spiritual and musical needs of

---

[32] See Ch. 1 n. 16.

[33] Although Catholic confraternities are known to have existed in Augsburg in the pre-
Reformation era, the disruptions of the Reformation meant that many of these
brotherhoods had to be established anew in the later sixteenth century; by contrast, many
Italian confraternities had lengthy histories and well-entrenched institutional structures
and cultures that provided fertile ground for active systems of music patronage. On Roman
and Venetian confraternities see especially Denis Arnold, 'Music at a Venetian
Confraternity in the Renaissance', *Acta musicologica*, 37 (1965), pp. 62–72; Noel
O'Regan, *Institutional Patronage in Post-Tridentine Rome: Music at SS. Trinità dei
Pellegrini 1559–1650* (London: Royal Musical Asssociation, 1995); and Jonathan Glixon,
Honoring God and the City: Music at the Venetian Confraternities, 1260–1806 (New
York: Oxford University Press, 2003).

the educated and uneducated alike, and provided a vivid aural component to public and private devotional activities.

The confraternity of SS Sebastian and Barbara was originally instituted for the cathedral's personnel in 1506 and included the *Kapellmeister*, organists and other persons responsible for regular music. A list of the confraternity's members survives[34] that indicates the membership, approximate dates of entry and death dates of such figures as Bernhard Klingenstein (joined between 1576 and 1579), the organist Erasmus Mayr (joined in 1584 or 1585), Gregor Aichinger (joined in 1595 or 1596),[35] Jakob Baumann (joined in 1603), Christian Erbach (joined in 1607) and others; death dates, but no dates of entry into the brotherhood, are given for Johann Haym, a prominent member of the Trinity Confraternity and composer (see below; died 10 May 1593), and for Johannes Holthusius, the schoolteacher and compiler of the chantbook *Compendium Cantionum ecclesiasticarum* of 1567 (died 9 July 1578). By the end of the sixteenth century the brotherhood included prominent laypersons, including members of the Fugger family and Catholic members of the city council. The brotherhood was similar to other lay confraternities in its organization of regular sung funeral services for deceased members; a surviving but undated expense list for these *Besingnusen* in Advent and Lent indicates payments for priests and singers. In addition to this evidence, a leaf of parchment has been inserted into the paper manuscript containing the text for the antiphon *Media vita*, labelled 'antiphon for use during time of plague'. It is unclear whether or not this antiphon would have required the hiring of singers.[36]

Music also played a role in the vigils and devotional services held by the Trinity Confraternity in the cathedral or in the adjoining chapel of St Johannes. Four times yearly the group held sung memorial services [*vigilias mortuorum*] at the altar of St Michael at St Johannes for recently deceased members, as provided for in the original statutes of the group. Each member who 'would devotedly help, sing, or

---

[34] BSA, Hochstift Augsburg / Münchner Bestand Lit. 1061, fols. 14v–56r.

[35] Aichinger's entry into this brotherhood in 1595 or 1596, as much as seven years before his return from Italy and acceptance of a benefice at the cathedral, suggests that he may have been intending such a move at an early stage. In any case, many members of the Fugger family, by whom he was employed, were also members of the brotherhood.

[36] The expense list appears on the back cover of the manuscript containing the above-mentioned membership roll. Among the expenses for these vigils were 10 Kreutzer for the priest who sang the Office of the Dead and 10 Kreutzer for the priest who sang an Office of St Sebastian. A further 6 Kreutzer were paid to unspecified 'singers' [*cantori*]. Similar amounts were paid for a remembrance day for one Herr Sturmfelder in the first week of Advent.

attend with devotion shall obtain and enjoy ten years' indulgence for his sins'.[37] Furthermore, in honour of the Holy Trinity, the brotherhood was to attend an Office of the Holy Trinity, with collects for the deceased and for the health of the living, on the second day after the Octave of Pentecost each year.[38] Further Offices were to be held in the cathedral, where the choirboys received payments for singing.[39] On some occasions, the confraternity paid choirboys from the cathedral and outside instrumentalists for music-making in their services. On the feast of St Sebastian in 1627, for example, the Trinity Confraternity and the Confraternity of SS Sebastian and Barbara joined forces for the observance of the Ten Hour Prayer in the chapel of St Johann. The two groups were to split the costs of hiring musicians for the occasion: Caspar Stern, schoolmaster at the cathedral, along with the *Marianer* (a choir consisting of 16 older boys from the cathedral), was paid 1 Gulden, 30 Kreutzer 'for singing in the morning of the procession with the most Worthy Sacrament, and [for singing] for some hours during the prayer'; 40 Kreutzer were paid to the remaining choirboys; and 2 Gulden were paid to the 'four instrumentalists, who were at the service'.[40] Two years later, a similar service was held in which the same number and type of

---

[37] 'Item welcher ain affttermontag aines jeden *Quattember* Zeÿtt, in Sankt Johannis Kirchen die *Vigilias mortuorum*, andechttig wurdt helffen, singen, oder mitt andachtt beÿnen, der soll erlanngen, vnd geniessen zehen Jar ablaß seiner sundten.' StAA, KWA E45[8]. Wilhelm Holder, a Lutheran preacher from Stuttgart, published a response to the Pope's granting of indulgences to the Trinity Confraternity. He criticized the preceding point as follows (from *Bericht welchermassen Papst Sixt, der fünffte dises Namens, die neue Augspurgische Bruderschafft, des H. Bergs Andex, mit Gnad vnd Ablaß bedacht, auch was von solchem Ablaßkrom zuhalten. Gestellet Durch M. Wilhelm Holdern, Stifftspredigern zu Stutgarten* (Tübingen: Georg Gruppenbach, 1588), p. 31): 'What is more, in the tenth article it reads that whoever, on the Tuesday before each quarter-year, helps to sing the vigils of the dead in St Johann's church in Augsburg, or whoever only devotedly attends such bawling, shall have ten years' indulgence. But he who makes his prayers for the praise and honour of the Holy Trinity only receives five years, that is, only half as much indulgence. Thus the Pope does not hold the honour of God any higher, in that he values funeral song just as much as God's honour. You pilgrims might consider among yourselves whether this is right.'

[38] From 'Augsburg Dompfarrei Bruderschaft des heil: berges Andechs zuerst errichtet A° 1543', StAA, KWA C8[1], fols. 7v–8r.

[39] Ibid.

[40] 'Herrn Caspar Steern Stiffts Schuelmaistern, sambt seinen *Marianis*, vmb daß er am Morgens der *Procession*, mit dem Hochwürdigen *Sacrament* beigewohnt, gesungen etliche stundt vnnder dem Gebett verehrt 1R 30K–' ... 'den Chorschuelern mit einander 40K' ... 'Vier *Musicis Instrumentalibus* so den Gottsdiensten beigewohntt indem zuer Præsenz geben 30K t. 2R'. From 'Vncosten: Sobeÿ dem Zehentstündigen Gebett Welches am fesst deß H. Martrers *Sebastianj* vnsers lieben *Patronen Anno* 1627. in *S*. Johannß Pfarrkürchen gehalt[en], vfgewendt, vnd von beeden *Fraterniteten*, alß erstgemelten *S. Sebastianj*, vnd *Sanctissimæ Trinitatis* ist zue gleichem tail bezalt worden.' StAA, KWA L404.

musicians were hired, except that an organist was also paid 30 Kreutzer for 'playing between Vespers and the Mass'.[41]

It is likely, however, that the members of the confraternities themselves participated in the music during such services. On numerous occasions the brotherhood received gifts of or obtained liturgical books for their use, and even a regal. The following entries are taken from an inventory of gifts to the brotherhood between 1581 and 1615:[42]

[1581]
5. Cardinal Otto [Truchseß von Waldburg], in his blessed memory, has willed to this brotherhood two new Mass books [for the pilgrimage] to the Holy Mountain.
6. Herr Johann Haym von Themar, vicar in the cathedral, has also donated and given a new Passau Mass book, which shall belong to the brotherhood ...
7. Further, the aforesaid brotherhood has received a black chest, in which is a Mass book which Herr Johann Haym has given to the brotherhood.
8. Further, Haym has also donated a new manuscript vigil book in parchment, which costs 15 Kreutzer.
...
10. Herr Thomas Agricola, Herr Caspar Faÿglin and Herr Matthias Midenmann, all three cathedral vicars, have also donated a manuscript vigil book in parchment to this brotherhood, costing 12 Kreutzer. Also, [they have given] four printed vigil books.
...
17. On 15 October 1597, the Brotherhood of the Holy Mountain ordered and obtained a lovely regal for the divine service, costing altogether 17 Gulden, 18 Kreutzer.
...
[1605]
25. In this year Herr Michael Schmidtner, sealer, gave six new Roman vigil books for the brotherhood's vigils, which were bound together in white, and cost along with the case 3 Gulden, 20 Kreutzer.

Presumably the 'vigil books' would have been copies of the Breviary, providing appropriate chants and texts for certain Offices celebrated by the confraternity. The donation of a regal in 1597 suggests, however, that the group may have performed more than just plainchant on occasion.

Since commoners as well as educated lay and clergy joined groups like the Trinity Confraternity by the early seventeenth century, German songs as well as Latin music would have found a place in their devotional activities. The six published songsheets by Johann Haym von Themar

---

[41] 'ainem Organisten, so zwisch[en] der *Vesper* vnd hochambtt geschlagen ehrtt 30K'. Ibid.
[42] 'Ornamenta oder Kirchenzier der Brüderschafft zum Heÿligen Berg, in vnser liebenn Fraüwen Thümbstifft zü Augspurg'. StAA, KWA C8¹, fols. 34v–37v.

(d. 1593), a choir-vicar at Augsburg Cathedral and a member of the group, demonstrate this coexistence of Latin- and German-texted music. On the one hand we find the *Litaniae Textus triplex* (1582), a set of three simple polyphonic Latin litanies for Christ, the Virgin Mary and saints designed for pilgrimages (discussed in greater detail in Chapter 7); but the remainder of his songs set German texts, like the *Christenliche Catholische Creutzgesang* (1584), consisting of German paraphrases of the Our Father, *Ave Maria* and Apostles' Creed 'for the praise and honour of God, and of the lay, praiseworthy brotherhood of the Holy Mountain in the Cathedral of Our Lady in Augsburg; and also for the benefit of other Catholic Christians when one processes with the cross, or sings in church' (see Example 5.2).[43] This print in particular enjoys a close relationship to the rituals of the Trinity Confraternity itself. None of the three songs is among the ten approved by Bishop Marquard von Berg in the 1580 *Ritus ecclesiastici Augustensis Episcopatus* (see p. 113); however, in 1587 Pope Sixtus V had granted indulgences to members of the Trinity Confraternity for reciting the Our Father, *Ave Maria* and Apostles' Creed, precisely the texts of Haym's *Creutzgesang*, during pilgrimages and on feasts of Jesus and the Virgin Mary.[44]

Example 5.2   Haym, *Vater unser der du bist*, from *Christenlich Catholische Creutzgesang* (1584)

---

[43] 'Our Father, who (Kyrie eleison) art in heaven, where there is eternal joy, O Father mine, forgive us here on earth, that we may become your beloved children.' *Christenliche Catholische Creutzgesang/ vom Vatter vnser vnnd Aue Maria, von denn zwölff stucken deß Apostolischen Glaubens/ &c. Durch einen Catholischen Priestern/ Gott zu lob vnd ehr/ vnnd der gemainer lobwürdigen Brüderschafft zum Hayligenberg/ inn vnser lieben Frawen Thümbstifft inn Augspurg/ &c. Auch sonst anderen Catholischen Christen zu gütter wolfart/ wann man mit dem Creutz gehet/ wie auch inn der Kirchen zusingen ist/ inn den Truck gegeben worden* (Augsburg: Johann Haym [Josias Wörli], 1584; RISM B/VIII, 1584[12]).

[44] StAA, KWA E45[8]. Members received a one-year indulgence for praying the Our Father and *Ave Maria* thrice each, and reciting the Apostles' Creed during the brotherhood's annual pilgrimage to Andechs; in addition, they received a hundred days' indulgence for praying the Our Father and *Ave Maria* on feasts of Jesus and the Virgin Mary.

Apart from its regular processions, the Corpus Christi Confraternity also participated in divine services and celebrations of the Ten- and Forty Hour Prayers, and held vigils including music. The first Thursday of every month members processed around the church (presumably that of Heilig Kreuz) with the Eucharist and then heard a sung Mass with music appropriate for the feast of Corpus Christi.[45] Like other lay confraternities this group held vigils with music in memory of recently deceased members. Its statutes state that 'the brothers and sisters should accompany the [procession] of the corpses to the grave, and also attend their sung memorial services [*Besüngckhnussen*] and funeral services four times yearly'.[46] The devotees seem to have performed the Masses and Offices for the Dead themselves, or at least contributed to the singing, but for the deaths of prominent members money would have been available to hire outside musicians.[47] In 1616, for example, Johann Ernst Fugger took over the leadership of the confraternity upon the death of his father Christoph, the previous head. Johann and his cohorts, in memory of his father and of Marcus Fugger (the founder), established a yearly service involving a sung Vespers and Office for the Dead, as well as an Office and Mass on a second day, for which he donated 50 Gulden per year;[48] such a sum would have been more than sufficient to hire a priest and a number of musicians, although it is unclear precisely how the money was spent.

---

[45] 'Alle Monat den ersten donnerstag oder den mitwoch zuuor, da ein fest am donnerstag einfiele, solle an statt der Meß, ein hochambt *De corpore Christi* gestern Gsungen, vnd vorher ein *procession* vnd vmbgang, in welcher ein Priester deß hochwürdigist *Sacrament* vnder einem him[m]ell welche die Bruderschafft vmbwechslendt füehren trag[en] solle, gehallten werden. Beÿ diser Monatlichen *procession* vndt ambt, sollen sich alle brueder vnd schwestern, sie werden dann durch erhebliche billiche vhrsachen, daran verhindert, mit iren angezündten kherzen befinden, den heilig[en] fronleichnamb beglaitten, vnd dem ganzen Gottsdienst, wo möglich, so lang beÿwohnen bis daß heilig[en] *Sacrament* wider an sein orth erwürdigckhlich getragen vnd gesetzt würdt.' From '*Instruction* für die andechtige Bruederschafft des heylig[en] fronleichnambs welche zue Augspurg beym Heyligen Chreuz am donnerstag den 11 thag Monats Martij A°~ sechzehenhundert vier wider ist aufgericht worden. ~ Von aufnemung der Brüeder vnd schwestern.' StAA, KWA L74.

[46] 'Die brueder vnd schwestern sollen dern so auß der bruederschafft absterben leichnamb, zur begräbnuß helffen beglaiten, deßgleichen auch Irn Besüngckhnussen, vnd *Quattember*lichen seelämptern beiwohnen.' From 'Satzungen bei Aufnahme der Mitglieder', StAA, KWA L74. These quarterly funeral services were to supplant the regular Mass on the first Thursday of the month.

[47] The scribe of the manuscript 'De initijs', noting a change in the procedures for celebrating the funeral services of deceased members (1611), writes that '*we* should sing an Office for the Dead each month for the deceased brothers and sisters' [emphasis mine]. 'De initijs ac progressu omnium Fraternitatum', 2° Aug 346, fol. 29v.

[48] 'Anno 1616. Joannes Ernestus Fuggerus filius Christophori fuit in defuncti sui parentis locum Præfectus electus, qui unà cum Assistentibus haud immemor Domini Marci Fuggeri, piæ memoriæ, auctoris et fundatoris huius fraternitatis, singulis annis pro anima ipsius

Music Printing

A regional revival of Catholic music printing, spearheaded by local entrepreneurs but also by the Jesuit presses in nearby Dillingen and Ingolstadt, also aided in the production and dissemination of Catholic devotional music. Earlier in the sixteenth century music printing in Augsburg was dominated by Protestant tradesmen who did not hesitate to print Catholic as well as Protestant commissions. Church leaders entrusted Valentin Schönig, for example, with the printing of a monastic Diurnale for the Benedictines of SS Ulrich and Afra in 1572, and the last diocesan Breviary of the Augsburg Rite in 1584.[49] The last Catholic printer, Alexander Weissenhorn, had departed for Ingolstadt in 1540, and in the subsequent decades the bishop was forced to turn to printers in the episcopal seat of Dillingen for the production of liturgical books.[50] By 1600, however, printers in Augsburg began to emerge who concentrated mainly on Catholic literature and music, including Christoph Mang, Chrysostomus Dabertzhofer, Andreas Aperger, Dominicus Custos and Johannes Praetorius (otherwise known as Hans or Johann Schultes); Praetorius was especially prolific as a music printer, bringing out at least 18 music prints between 1600 and 1621.[51] Despite their relatively small numbers compared with Protestant printers, by the early seventeenth century local Catholic printers accounted for some 40 per cent of the total print market in Augsburg, a striking achievement.[52]

More significant from a musical standpoint were the entirely Catholic

---

Anniversarium cum Vesperis et Vigilijs defunctorum cantatis, nec non altero die cum Officio et aliquot Missis peragendum solenniter instituit, pro quibus laboribus nobis et futuris fratribus quindecim florenos quotannis se daturum ex ærario fraternitatis promisit.' Ibid., fol. 30r.

[49] Theodor Wohnhaas, 'Notizen zu Druck und Verlag katholischer Kirchenmusik in Augsburg', *JVAB*, **31** (1997), pp. 154–55. For an excellent overview of printing in Augsburg through the period of the Thirty Years War, see Künast, 'Entwicklungslinien des Augsburger Buchdrucks'. On the Schönig family and printing in Augsburg, see Wohnhaas, 'Die Schönig, eine Augsburger Druckerfamilie', *Archiv für Geschichte des Buchwesens*, 5 (1964), pp. 1473–84.

[50] Wohnhaas, 'Notizen zu Druck und Verlag', pp. 154–55.

[51] At the same time, it is interesting to note that the two main Protestant composers in Augsburg during this period, Adam Gumpelzhaimer and Hans Leo Hassler, published their music almost exclusively with Valentin Schönig and his son Johann Ulrich Schönig. One must be wary, however, of imputing too much confessional significance to this, especially in the light of Valentin Schönig's occasional acceptance of Catholic commissions. Furthermore, Praetorius (Schultes) had previously been accused of printing materials critical of the city government's pro-Catholic position in the wake of the Augsburg *Kalenderstreit*; see Ch. 2, p. 64–65.

[52] Künast, 'Entwicklungslinien des Augsburger Buchdrucks', p. 19.

printing operations in nearby Dillingen.[53] Bishop Otto Truchseß had called the printer Sebald Mayer to Dillingen in 1549. Mayer sold his press to the bishop in 1560, who leased it back to him; eight years later Otto donated the press to the Dillingen Jesuits. As the official printers of the Jesuit university, Sebald Mayer, his son and daughter-in-law Johann and Sabina Mayer and their successors dominated printing in Dillingen well into the seventeenth century. The Dillingen music printers Adam Meltzer (fl. 1603–09) and Gregor Hänlin (fl. 1610–17) brought out at least 44 music prints between 1603 and 1617. Twenty-one of these prints were by Augsburg composers, including Gregor Aichinger, Christian Erbach, Bernhard Klingenstein and Philipp Zindelin, making Meltzer and Hänlin the most prolific sources for Catholic polyphony in Augsburg in the early seventeenth century (the press also brought out prints by other Catholic composers like Jakob Reiner, Christian Keifferer, Konrad Hagius, Michael Tonsor, Michael Kraf and Johann Simon Kruog).[54] The membership of Adam Meltzer and his wife Sabina (who continued her husband's printing operation after his death in 1609) in the Dillingen Corpus Christi Confraternity from 1605 suggests their personal commitment to the Catholic cause.[55] Hänlin moved to Ingolstadt in 1617, where he continued printing music, but on a smaller scale.[56]

These Catholic music printers must be seen in the wider context of the revival of Catholic music printing in Germany at large in the late sixteenth and early seventeenth centuries, a phenomenon that has mostly escaped scholarly attention. Adam Berg's activity in Munich, emphasizing the works of Orlando di Lasso, was continued by Nikolaus Heinrich, who printed music by Aichinger and Klingenstein, as well as numerous works by Orlando di Lasso and his two sons, Rudolph and Ferdinand. Also significant for Catholic polyphony were the shops of Johann Gäch and Michael Wagner in Innsbruck (printing music by the Innsbruck *Kapellmeister* Johann Stadlmayr and Christoph Sätzl of Brixen), and that of Johann Schröter in Ravensburg (specializing in the

---

[53] Paul B. Rupp gives an overview in *Fünfhundert Jahre Buchdruck in Lauingen und Dillingen: Ausstellung anläßlich des 100jährigen Bestehens des Historischen Vereins Dillingen* (Dillingen: Studienbibliothek, 1988).

[54] See Otto Bucher, 'Adam Meltzer (1603–1610) und Gregor Hänlin (1610–1617) als Musikaliendrucker in Dillingen/Donau', *Gutenberg-Jahrbuch*, 31 (1956), pp. 217–25.

[55] See ibid., p. 216.

[56] See Rupp, *Fünfhundert Jahre Buchdruck in Lauingen und Dillingen*, p. 9; however, in 1617 he did bring out Aichinger's *Encomium Verbo incarnato*, a set of sacred concertos, and in 1618 and 1624 he printed music by Christian Keifferer, his *Flores musici seu divinae Laudis Odores suavissimi* (RISM A/I, K238), and his *Flores musicales, in Totum Iubilum D. Bernardi* (RISM A/I, K239).

music of Michael Kraf of the Weingarten monastery and Matthias Spiegler of Jakob Fugger's episcopal court at Constance). This production of Catholic polyphony was balanced by a flood of Catholic songbooks and songsheets that emerged from presses in Dillingen, Ingolstadt, Innsbruck, Cologne, Konstanz, Mainz, Munich, Würzburg and elsewhere; in many cases Jesuits from local colleges or universities served as authors, editors or compilers of this material. In contrast to Protestant presses, which were concentrated in free cities and depended more on market forces for their survival, Catholic presses were usually located near Jesuit establishments, the seats of bishoprics or Catholic courts, and often enjoyed the direct patronage of Catholic religious or secular leaders. Unsurprisingly, they reflected the devotional and political aims of the Counter-Reformation in their prints, which ranged from bare polemics against Protestantism, to pilgrimage and procession songs, to Catholic polyphony in honour of the Virgin Mary, the Eucharist, the Passion of Christ or the saints. Without the existence of such presses, the rise of a specifically Catholic musical repertory in late sixteenth- and early seventeenth-century Germany would have been unthinkable.

Given the growing market for Catholic music in Germany during the Counter-Reformation, it is important to bear in mind that Augsburg composers intended their music to be sold and performed regionally, even if the local expansion of devotional contexts prompted composers to orient their music towards Catholic themes. Much of this music, indeed, was published not in Augsburg but in the episcopal seat and Jesuit stronghold of Dillingen, from where it would have been distributed throughout Catholic Germany by means of book fairs and other channels. The role of the prominent Augsburg bookseller Georg Willer should not be underestimated, as music prints by Augsburg composers turn up consistently in his catalogues for the biannual Frankfurt book fair, especially from 1600 onwards; the Leipzig fair catalogues of Abraham Lamberg during the same period suggest a pathway for dissemination to the north and east.[57] The confessional nature of the texts chosen by Augsburg composers, then, certainly reflects their immediate experience of the Catholic revival in that city,

---

[57] A survey of the Frankfurt and Leipzig book fair catalogues during this period shows that Augsburg music prints were most likely to be found in Willer's catalogues for the Frankfurt fair, the Frankfurt 'public catalogue', and Lamberg's catalogues for the Leipzig fair. Of the 48 music publications by Augsburg's Catholic composers between 1590 and 1626, only a small handful (mostly Aichinger's prints before his arrival in Augsburg) were not advertised by Willer. See Karl Albert Göhler, *Verzeichnis der in den Frankfurter und Leipziger Messkatalogen der Jahre 1564 bis 1759 angezeigten Musikalien* (Leipzig, 1902; repr., Hilversum: Frits A.M. Knuf, 1965).

but it is also a response, in fact, to broader changes in devotional life that swept Catholic Germany around the turn of the seventeenth century.

Augsburg's Catholic Composers and Devotional Polyphony in the Counter-Reformation

There is little doubt that the liturgy and liturgical changes – notably the mandate of the Roman Rite in the Augsburg diocese in 1597 – represented a significant motivation for Augsburg's Catholic composers, who responded with a variety of publications implicitly or explicitly for liturgical use (see Chapter 4). However, the demands of a burgeoning culture of Marian and Eucharistic devotion partly determined the character of that repertory (see Aichinger's *Tricinia Mariana* and *Solennia augustissimi Corporis Christi*, both ostensibly collections of liturgical music), and arguably encouraged the most telling musical expression of Catholic renewal in Augsburg, the proliferation of devotional music aimed not primarily at church choirs but at devotees in both public and private circumstances. The rapid increase in such publications after the turn of the seventeenth century suggests a growing market for music that was accessible, fashionable in style and confessionally specific, and their appearance coincides with the formation of new Catholic confraternities, the extension of processions even into Protestant areas of the city and the expansion of pilgrimages to local shrines. The process of Catholic confessionalization in Augsburg's musical culture is reflected in the preference for specific devotional objects in extant collections of music: the Virgin Mary, the Eucharist and Christ, particularly his Passion and crucifixion.

Marian Polyphony

For many Catholics in late sixteenth- and early seventeenth-century Germany, the Virgin Mary was the most recognizable and universal symbol of their faith and of the Roman Church. Much of the credit for the revitalization of Marian devotion can be attributed to the Jesuits, who promoted the cult of the Virgin in particular by founding branches of the Marian Congregation and by supporting important Marian pilgrimage shrines (including Loreto, Einsiedeln and Altötting) through sermons and propagandistic literature. The Marian cult flourished nowhere more strongly than in the nearby duchy of Bavaria, where the Virgin – the so-called *Patrona Boiariae* – became the object of an official state cult. Although Marian devotion was hardly a new phenomenon in nearby Augsburg, it also underwent a renewal in the late sixteenth century, spurred by the religious interests and efforts of the Jesuits, Catholic patricians and church leaders. The most visible expression of this trend was the establishment of a branch of the Marian Congregation (given the title Annunication of the Virgin Mary) at the Jesuit church of St Salvator in 1584, a group that organized devotional services and public processions in honour of the Virgin. Other Marian sodalities followed, many of them founded by Jesuit priests, including brotherhoods in honour of the Virgin's Nativity (1589), of Mary as Queen of the Angels (1609) and of the Purification of Mary (1622).[58] Another confraternity in honour of the Rosary (an important Marian symbol) had been established at the Dominican church in 1574, and was active in organizing public processions.

While the devotional gatherings, processions and pilgrimages of these groups created suitable contexts for Marian music, the religious interests of Augsburg's most significant patrons of Catholic polyphony, above all the Fugger family, also helped to shape this repertory. Fervent devotion to the Virgin among certain members of the family may be traced back at least to 1570, when the Jesuit preacher Petrus Canisius, in the company of several family members, embarked on a well-publicized pilgrimage to the Marian shrine of Altötting in Bavaria in order to perform an exorcism on one of the family's maidservants.[59] A number of members of the Fugger family would later receive the dedications of Marian musical prints, including Jakob II Fugger (Aichinger's *Tricinia Mariana* of 1598), Georg Fugger (Aichinger's *Lacrumae D. Virginis* of 1605), Maximilian Fugger (Aichinger's *Encomium Verbo incarnato* of 1617) and Johann M., Johann Ernst, and Ottheinrich Fugger (Erbach's *Mele sive Cantiones* of 1603). More generally, other dedicatees of this music were strong supporters of the Catholic renewal, including Prince-Abbot Johann Adam of Kempten (Aichinger's *Vespertinum Virginis* of 1603) and especially Bishop Heinrich V von Knöringen (Klingenstein's *Rosetum Marianum* of 1604). Although the religious preoccupations of the composers themselves (and particularly Gregor Aichinger) played a role in the selection of Marian themes for these prints, the overall atmosphere of musical patronage was also highly favourable for such music.

Judging from the diversity of styles and texts in this music, Aichinger, Erbach, Klingenstein and Zindelin wrote for a variety of possible musical contexts, ranging from the church liturgy to the non-liturgical devotional practices of Marian confraternities. The setting of the Magnificat or the

---

[58] The latter group was intended for young or single laymen; see Braun, *Geschichte des Kollegiums der Jesuiten in Augsburg*, pp. 127–36.

[59] See Ch. 5, p. 258, and Soergel, *Wondrous in His Saints*, pp. 119–26.

four Marian antiphons, of course, had had a long history in polyphonic composition, a tradition that continued in the works of these composers. On the other hand, a considerable proportion of new Marian polyphony in Augsburg shortly after 1600 was not intended for the liturgy; it consisted instead of settings of devotional texts, often rhymed poetry, in Latin or German. Stylistically, one observes a shift away from the imitative polyphony of the sixteenth-century tradition towards a simpler, more schematic style of writing that was influenced by Italian genres, especially the canzonetta and the early vocal concerto. Although the preference for this style of writing was certainly not limited to Catholic composers, it was indeed well suited to the abilities of musical amateurs in Catholic brotherhoods or in private household devotions. The religious interests of composers and patrons, combined with the demand for appropriate music by Catholic devotees, created a powerful impetus for the creation of a Marian musical repertory.

It was a sign of the times, perhaps, that a composer who was responsible mainly for the day-to-day liturgical music of the cathedral chose a Marian topic for his first musical print. Bernhard Klingenstein's *Rosetum Marianum* (1604) is an anthology of settings of the Marian popular song *Maria zart* by 33 different composers, all of whom were solicited by Klingenstein to provide a five-voice setting of a different stanza of text.[60] Anthologies of this kind – compositions by numerous composers on a single given subject – were not altogether new; Giulio Gigli's *Sdegnosi ardori* (1585) and the *Il Trionfo di Dori* (1592) are possible antecedents.[61] However, the Marian subject matter was new; the print, in fact, may have been intended for the devotions of the Jesuit-organized Marian Congregation, although this is difficult to

---

[60] *Rosetum Marianum. Unser lieben Frawen Rosengertlein von drey und dreyssig lieblichen schönen Rosen oder Lobgesangen Gott dem Almechtigen, und dessen würdigsten Mutter und Junckfrawen Marie, durch drey und dreyssig beriembte Musicos und Componisten, mit sondern Fleiss auff ein Subiectum, mit fünff Stimmen componirt, und letzlich zusammen getragen* (Dillingen: Adam Meltzer, 1604; RISM B/I, 1604[7]). William Hettrick has edited a complete edition of the work, in *Rosetum Marianum*, Recent Researches in the Music of the Renaissance, vols 24–25 (Madison, Wis.: A-R Editions, 1977).

[61] See Singer, 'Leben und Werke des Augsburger Domkapellmeisters Bernhardus Klingenstein', pp. 54–55, referring to *Sdegnosi ardori: Musica di diversi auttori, sopra un istesso soggetto di parole, a cinque voci, raccolti insieme da Giulio Gigli da Immola* (Munich: Adam Berg, 1585; RISM B/I, 1585[17]); and *Il trionfo di Dori, descritto da diversi, et posto in musica, à sei voci, da altretanti autori* (Venice: Angelo Gardano, 1592; RISM B/I, 1592[11]). For a later Protestant anthology also based around a single subject (in this case Ps. 116), see *Angst der Hellen und Friede der Seelen* (Jena: J. Weidner, 1623; RISM B/I, 1623[14]), in an edition by Christoph Wolff and Daniel R. Melamed (Cambridge, Mass.: Harvard University Press, 1994).

prove.[62] Klingenstein at least could have expected his collection to please the dedicatee of the volume, Bishop Heinrich V von Knöringen, who was simultaneously the highest ecclesiastical official in the diocese and perhaps the most fervent promoter of the Counter-Reformation in Augsburg and in surrounding areas. Klingenstein's dedication to Heinrich links the Marian image of the rose together with the idea of his anthology as a cultivated garden:

> Thus it has happened, according to my wish and desire, that, but of the particular grace of generous persons, I have received a very fine old and devout song, which is full of all kinds of sweet, pleasant fruit, spiritual joy, and useful reflections, and which, perhaps, a youth, during a lingering illness, wrote in praise and honor of God and His most worthy Mother Mary, and through which, as I am informed, he wonderfully obtained health of body and soul. Since the aforementioned song, comprising thirty-three fine little stanzas, gives me much pleasure, I have made it my business to bring into print and communicate this polyphonic song, well embellished for the consolation of all God-loving hearts. I have well considered that, because the subject is lengthy and the theme is repeated several times and also out of necessity must be reiterated, many people might therefore find it more pleasing if this work were decorated and worked out with the manifold flowers and talents of many excellent musicians. Thus, I easily obtained an agreement from several distinguished musicians, who are named below in this work, voluntarily to help me to decorate and work the little pleasure garden that I began, with such diligence and seriousness that I could reserve for myself only a single little bud to embellish according to the best of my ability.[63]

The devotional character of the collection is heightened by two quotations from Bernard of Clairvaux's sermons on the Assumption of the Virgin Mary that appear on the verso side of the title page, given in both Latin and German.[64] This is but a small taste of a broader

---

[62] See Fleckenstein, 'Marienverehrung in der Musik', p. 186, and Forkel Göthel, in *Musik in Bayern. II. Ausstellungskatalog. Augsburg, Juli bis Oktober 1972* (Tutzing: Hans Schneider, 1972), p. 222.

[63] From the preface of Klingenstein, *Rosetum Marianum*. Translation by William E. Hettrick in his edition, pp. viii–ix.

[64] Hettrick translates these passages as follows: 'Our pilgrimage sent on before an advocate, who, as mother of the judge and mother of mercy, will seek and further the cause of our salvation humbly and very efficiently.' The second quotation from the same sermon itself includes a quotation from 1 Cor. 2: 9: 'For eye has not seen nor ear heard, neither have entered into the heart of man, what God has prepared for them that love him. Who, then, would speak of what he has prepared for her that bore him and also – as is known to everyone – loved him more and deeper than every other?' See *Rosetum Marianum*, ed. Hettrick, p. viii. Klingenstein's quotations of Bernard were entirely of a piece with a fervent revival of interest in his mystical writings (or writings attributed to him) that seized Catholic Germany in the early seventeenth century. Klingenstein himself would publish a

enthusiasm for Bernard's writings that would manifest itself in several musical and non-musical Catholic publications in south Germany (see below).

Whatever truth lies in Klingenstein's anecdote about the song's origins, *Maria zart* was probably the product of fifteenth-century *Meistersinger* and was one of few *Meistergesänge* to insinuate themselves into popular consciousness by the sixteenth century.[65] The tune was frequently included in Catholic songbooks such as Leisentrit's well-known *Geistliche Lieder und Psalmen* of 1567, from which Klingenstein probably derived the song (see Example 5.3).[66] However, it has been more recently argued that the most direct model for Klingenstein's text was an unnotated songsheet entitled *Hie folget der Schöne andächtige Text, Lied, und Gedicht, welches ein reicher Jüngling, in seiner schweren Kranckheit, Gott dem Allmächtigen und dessen würdigsten Mütter Mariæ zu Lob und Ehrn gedichtet, und nach vollendung dessen, Leibs und der Seelen gesundheit erlangt und wider empfangen* which, according to Hettrick, may have been printed by Adam Meltzer in Dillingen, the printer of the *Rosetum Marianum*.[67] The editor (unnamed in this print) was Renwart Cysat of Luzern (1545–1614), an exact contemporary of Klingenstein who was a Catholic censor and ardent promoter of the Counter-Reformation.[68]

Given the devotional subject of Klingenstein's anthology, composers from Catholic courts and churches around southern Germany are well represented, and attest to the *Kapellmeister*'s extensive connections. It is probably no accident that the *Rosetum* begins with settings of individual

---

motet, *Sanctus Bernardus*, in his *Liber primus s. Symphoniarum* (1607; see below), while texts by Bernard (or Pseudo-Bernard) figured prominently in two publications by Gregor Aichinger, the *Odaria lectissima* of 1601 and the *Vulnera Christi* of 1606.

[65] On the origins of *Maria zart*, see Singer, 'Leben und Werke des Augsburger Domkapellmeisters Bernhardus Klingenstein', pp. 56–62, and *Rosetum Marianum*, ed. Hettrick, p. x.

[66] 'Mary tender, of noble kind, a rose on all thorns. Through Adam's fall, St Gabriel did promise to you. Help that my sin and guilt shall not reek. Grant me grace, for there is no comfort that through my merit I might obtain mercy. At the very end, [I] beg you not to turn from me in my death.' Singer provides a list of Catholic songbooks containing *Maria zart* in 'Leben und Werke des Augsburger Domkapellmeisters Bernhardus Klingenstein', pp. 60–62. Despite its age the song appears most commonly in the songbooks of the early seventeenth century, which otherwise tend to emphasize a new and more catechetical repertory.

[67] Another version of this text survives as *Ein schon andächtigs Liedt und gedicht, von unser lieben Frawen* (Dillingen: Johann Mayer, 1593), present at D-Mbs. Copies of the *Schöne andächtige Text*, which probably were a part of a larger publication, are bound in the tenor partbook of the Brussels exemplar of the *Rosetum Marianum*. See *Rosetum Marianum*, ed. Hettrick, pp. xi–xii.

[68] Ibid.

Example 5.3   *Maria zart*, from Leisentrit, *Geistliche Lieder und Psalmen* (1567)

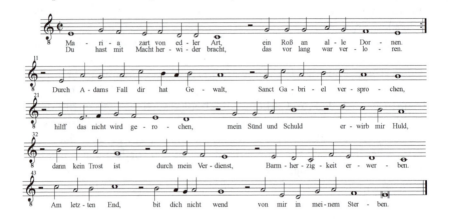

stanzas of *Maria zart* by composers from Munich (including Johann à Fossa, Rudolph and Ferdinand di Lasso and Fileno Cornazzano), where the Marian cult was especially strong.[69] Also significant here is the number of settings by composers employed by the Imperial courts at Prague (Franciscus Sale, Karel Luyton, Lambert de Sayve, Jakob Regnart) and Innsbruck (Georgius Flori, Simon Kolbanus). Klingenstein procured settings by his Augsburg colleagues Gregor Aichinger, Christian Erbach, Philipp Zindelin and Hans Leo and Jakob Hassler. The Protestant cantor Adam Gumpelzhaimer may have been reluctant to contribute music to such an openly Catholic collection, while it was probably no coincidence that the brothers Hans Leo and Jakob Hassler, Protestants who had previously been in service of the Fugger family in Augsburg, chose to set the stanzas beginning with the more confessionally neutral 'Jesu ich bitt'.[70]

If the musical subject of the *Rosetum Marianum* was derived from popular religious culture, the same cannot be said for the five-voice polyphonic settings themselves, which range from traditional Nether-landish counterpoint to a more Italianate idiom involving homophonic passages and antiphonal implications. The overall stylistic profile of the book, then, is not unlike that of contemporary motet collections with liturgical texts, and indeed the influence of Orlando di Lasso's motets is

---

[69] The absence of a setting by Orlando di Lasso, who died in 1594, and the presence of a setting by Fossa, who died in 1599, suggests that Klingenstein began his solicitations between those two years. See Singer, 'Leben und Werke des Augsburger Domkapellmeisters Bernhardus Klingenstein', pp. 62–63.

[70] See *Rosetum Marianum*, ed. Hettrick, pp. xiii–xiv.

discernible in many of the settings.[71] In his own setting of 'Maria süss' (see Example 5.4)[72] Klingenstein prefers motif-based imitation, as is immediately evident in the opening bars, which gradually develop a rising-fifth figure and a variant that returns to the original pitch of *e'* (mm. 1–5; see Example 5.4(*a*)). His only concession to pictorialism is a

Example 5.4 Klingenstein, *Maria süss, hilf dass ich büss*, from *Rosetum Marianum* (1604): (*a*) bars 1–9; (*b*) bars 28–32

[71] However, Singer noted that the pieces by Augsburg composers show a simplification of counterpoint that can be attributed to Hans Leo Hassler's Venetian influences: see 'Leben und Werke des Augsburger Domkapellmeisters Bernhardus Klingenstein', pp. 66–68. Aichinger could equally well have been responsible for such influence, however.

[72] 'Mary sweet, help me to atone for my sins on this earth ... of joy so great, in the tree of Abraham.'

Example 5.4 *concluded*

florid melismatic passage at 'der Freuden groß', opening the second half of the piece (mm. 28–34; see Example 5.4(b)).

If Klingenstein's *Rosetum Marianum* represents the union of a complex musical idiom with a popular Marian text, Aichinger's *Virginalia* of 1607 reverses these terms, joining Latin poetry on the mysteries of the Rosary with simple, canzonetta-like settings for five voices.[73] The influence of contemporary Roman repertories in this collection is clear: Aichinger dedicated the *Virginalia* to Marquard von Schwenden, a canon of Augsburg Cathedral who evidently had been with Aichinger during his stay in Rome and aided the composer in unspecified ways; Aichinger excuses himself before him, who 'so warmly embraced such an importune man in Germany as well as in Italy, and offered so many benefits and favours'.[74] The preface also states that Simone Verovio (fl. 1575–1608), a Roman editor, engraver and calligrapher, sent Aichinger the Marian texts for this collection. Verovio moved from the Netherlands to Rome in 1575 and played an important role in the dissemination of the sacred canzonetta through the publication of anthologies such as the *Diletto spirituale* of 1586, containing a largely Roman repertory by Anerio, Giovanelli, Marenzio,

---

[73] *Virginalia: Laudes aeternae Virginis Mariae, Magnae Dei Matris complexa, et quinis Vocibus modulata* (Dillingen: Adam Meltzer, 1607; RISM A/I, A539).

[74] 'ignosce tibi ipsi, qui tam importunum hominem tantopere & in Italia & Germania semper tam amicè complexus es, & tibi tot officijs & beneficijs deuinxisti'. From preface to Aichinger, *Virginalia*. Kroyer speculated that Marquard may have introduced Aichinger into certain social circles, or provided him with financial assistance. See Kroyer, 'Gregor Aichingers Leben und Werke', pp. liv–lv.

Nanino and Soriano.[75] The sacred canzonetta's domination of Aichinger's output in the first decade of the century, then, can be attributed in part to Verovio's influence.

The volume contains settings of 20 Latin poems (perhaps penned by Verovio himself), each with the text incipit 'Virgo'. After an introductory *Virgo Dei, mater pura* follow poetic interpretations of the 15 mysteries of the Rosary, divided into the five joys, sorrows and glories of the Virgin, respectively; a set of four additional Marian poems concludes the publication. While the Marian emphasis of the *Virginalia* is consistent with much of his other music, the structure of the volume is rather unusual for Aichinger in that it corresponds to a specific type of devotional exercise, and thus would probably have appealed to a somewhat narrower circle of devotees. On the other hand, Rosary devotions were becoming increasingly common in the era of the Counter-Reformation and were probably practised in Augsburg as early as 1574, when a Confraternity of the Rosary was founded at the Dominican church. Aichinger's *Virginalia*, furthermore, was not an isolated phenomenon: the contents strongly echo Palestrina's collection of Marian litanies 'which are said everywhere in the chapels of the Society of the Rosary of the Virgin Mary' [*quae in sacellis societatis S. Rosarii Mariae Virginis ubique dicatis*] (Rome, 1593).[76] Aichinger's collection also recalls the title of Klingenstein's anthology *Rosetum Marianum*, although the latter is not based directly on the devotional exercise.

The Latin texts of the *Virginalia* may have been incomprehensible to uneducated performers and listeners, but the polyphony, inspired by the example of the homophonic canzonetta, is stylish and unpretentious, and

---

[75] The *Diletto* was also the first large-scale example of copperplate engraving in music printing; Verovio would also apply this technique to the Luzzasco Luzzaschi's 'luxuriant' madrigals (1601), which lent themselves more easily to this more flexible, but expensive, technique. See Tim Carter, *Music in Late Renaissance and Early Baroque Italy* (Portland, Ore.: Amadeus Press, 1992), p. 149 n. On Verovio's publications in general see Gary L. Anderson, 'The Canzonetta Publications of Simone Verovio' (DMA diss., University of Illinois, 1976).

[76] Palestrina, *Litaniae deiparae Virginis, quae in Sacellis deiparae Virginis ubique dicatis concinnuntur, liber primus* (Rome, 1593; now lost). The devotional connection between litanies and the praying of the Rosary may be seen clearly in the Augsburg Rosary confraternity, whose members processed around the church on the first Sunday of every month singing a Litany of the Virgin in honour of the church and of the recently deceased: 'Allweg an dem ersten Sontag eines jeden Monats/ helt man sonderlichen Creutzgang/ inn der Brüderschafft Kirchen/ allda für alle Brüder vnd Schwesteren/ sie seyen lebendig oder abgestorben/ wie auch vmb glückseligen Stand der Christenlichen Kirchen/ gesungen werden die Letaney von vnser lieben Frawen.' From *Kurtzer Bericht, Von der Gnadenreichen Bruderschafft deß H. Rosenkrantzs, oder Psalter vnser lieben Frawen* (Augsburg: Christoph Mang, 1616), p. 11.

suggests an intention for devotional exercises involving educated amateurs. Example 5.5 shows the first piece in the volume.[77] Despite the five-voice setting (it is tempting to speculate that the number of voices also symbolizes the fivefold nature of the devotion), the influence of the canzonetta is clear in the work's brevity, two-part repeated structure, homophonic texture and word-based accent patterns, all of which contribute to the clarity of the text declamation. Aichinger reserves one lengthier imitative passage for the image of flowers ('cum floribus') that are prepared in honour of the Virgin (bars 22–27); otherwise, the verticality of the texture is striking, with a strong melodic profile shared

Example 5.5   Aichinger, *Virgo Dei, mater pura*, from *Virginalia* (1607)

[77] 'Virgin of God, mother most pure, unique splendour of virginity, take care of me as I desire to praise you, and prepare roses and flowers in your honour.'

Example 5.5 *concluded*

between the cantus and quintus voices, and a harmonically driven bass line. With the exception of the scoring for five voices – normally Aichinger prefers a three- or four-voice texture – the style here closely resembles that of his other sacred canzonettas in collections like the *Odaria lectissima* and *Divinae laudes*.

   Less bound to a specific type of Marian devotion is Aichinger's *Encomium Verbo incarnato, eiusdemque Matri augustissimae Reginae Coelorum* [Eulogy to the Incarnate Word, and to Its Mother, the Most Exalted Queen of Heaven], a set of vocal concertos published in 1617.[78] Apart from the obvious stylistic gap between the two prints, the

---

[78] *Encomium Verbo incarnato, eiusdemque Matri augustissimae Reginae Coelorum Musicis Numeris decantatum* (Ingolstadt: Gregor Hänlin, 1617; RISM A/I, A546).

Encomium shows a somewhat different profile from the *Virginalia* in that veneration of Christ (as the Word Incarnate) is joined to that of the Virgin Mary: Aichinger sets seven Marian hymns by the Jesuit rector in Augsburg, Jacobus Pontanus, and a series of Marian antiphons, along with several poems praising both Christ and the Virgin. Even if the specific occasion for such music is unknown, Aichinger may have compiled it with the Jesuit Marian Congregation in mind, for the seven hymns in honour of the Conception, Nativity, Presentation, Annunciation, Visitation, Purification and Assumption of the Virgin, respectively, are precisely the same as those given in Pontanus's ΠΑΡΘΕΝΟ ΜΗΤΡΙΚΑ [*Partheno Metrika*], a collection of prayers and meditations on the Virgin dedicated to the Marian Congregation of Augsburg (see above, p. 159). It is unclear whether the musical abilities of the Augsburg Marian Congregation were sufficient for the performance of these concertos for four voices and continuo, but the group is known to have sung polyphonic litanies on a regular basis and thus included some members with musical training.[79]

Eucharistic Polyphony

While aspects of Marian devotion – for example, the regular performance of the Magnificat – persisted in many Protestant churches well into the early modern era, devotion to the Eucharist became a more tangible symbol, both literally and figuratively, of Catholic doctrine. The transsubstantiation of the host was among the most divisive confessional issues of the age, not only in that it reinforced the sacramental role of the priesthood, but also because it exploited popular and pre-existing beliefs about the magical properties of the host, beliefs that found expression in the form of Eucharistic processions and pilgrimages (see Chapters 6 and 7). Popular Eucharistic devotion had emerged in thirteenth- and fourteenth-century Europe and occupied a middle position between the older physicality of grave cults and the newer emphasis on visual and imagistic forms of piety.[80] Some of this fervency was harnessed by late

---

[79] For example, members of the Jesuit Marian Congregation performed polyphonic litanies daily in 1593, perhaps during the octave of Corpus Christi when the sacrament was displayed publicly (from *HCA*, vol. 1, p. 342 [1593]): 'The congregation, diminished in size last year due to the plague, now is growing again, and consequently seethes with zeal for piety and for the practice of good deeds. There are 50 members; they have considered amongst themselves which hours to celebrate the memory of Our Lord in the tomb for the greater part of a week, so that they may establish daily prayers in our church. In those days in which the publicly displayed Eucharist is adored, the members sing litanies in harmonious music daily after afternoon classes in front of the main way. From the same [group] two joined [our] religious brotherhood.'

[80] Soergel, *Wondrous in His Saints*, p. 23.

sixteenth-century church leaders, resulting in official patronage of and literary propaganda on behalf of elaborate Corpus Christi processions and pilgrimages to Eucharistic shrines. In Bavaria, for example, Corpus Christi processions in Munich reached massive proportions (often involving thousands of participants) under the support and encouragement of the Bavarian dukes, while Eucharistic shrines such as Deggendorf and Passau were celebrated in polemical tracts by Johann Nass, Johann Rabus and Johan Sartorius.[81] For these men devotion to the Eucharist was not simply a pious expression, but rather a potent and even militant symbol of the victory of Catholic truth over heresy.

In Augsburg, too, Catholics seized upon the Eucharist as an unambiguous symbol of confessional identity. Among the numerous Catholic confraternities that were revived or established around the turn of the seventeenth century, the Corpus Christi Confraternity, founded in 1604 by Marcus Fugger and the Capuchin Ludwig Sax [Sachs], was particularly fervent in its promotion of public religious spectacles, designed not only to bolster the faith of local Catholics, but also to impress the city's Protestant majority. This group met regularly at the church of Heilig Kreuz, which housed the famous *Wunderbares Gut*, an allegedly miraculous host that was the focus of local and regional devotion.[82] Although it did not reach the proportions of its Munich counterpart, the annual Corpus Christi procession in Augsburg was probably the most elaborate regular procession in the city, involving clergy, religious orders, confraternities and laypersons; much of the music associated with this event, furthermore, had a militaristic character (see Chapter 6). Furthermore, this period saw the revival of the biannual pilgrimage from Augsburg to the shrine of Andechs in Bavaria, where hundreds of pilgrims from various stations in life expressed their devotion to three holy hosts that were believed to have miraculous properties (see Chapter 7).

All three collections of polyphonic music that are explicitly associated with Eucharistic devotion were composed by Gregor Aichinger, himself a member of the Corpus Christi Confraternity. The *Solennia augustissimi Corporis Christi* (1606), as discussed above, is a mainly liturgical collection that nevertheless includes some hymns suitable for para- or

---

[81] On Eucharistic devotion in Bavaria in general, see Adolf Wilhelm Ziegler, ed., *Eucharistische Frömmigkeit in Bayern* (Munich: Seitz, 1963); on Nass, Rabus and Sartorius, see Soergel, *Wondrous in His Saints*, pp. 91–95, 176 ff., and 178 ff. Mitterweiser's *Geschichte der Fronleichnamsprozession in Bayern* (Munich: Knorr & Hirth, 1930) provides a detailed account of the Munich Corpus Christi processions; see also Soergel, *Wondrous in His Saints*, pp. 81–90.

[82] For a list of contemporary literature concerning the *Wunderbares Gut*, see Ch. 6 n. 69.

non-liturgical processions. Less connected to any specific liturgical service is his *Corolla eucharistica* (1621), consisting of vocal concertos for two and three voices with continuo, setting a series of Latin Eucharistic texts as well as an eight-part hymn in honour of the Virgin Mary.[83] Aichinger dedicated the collection to the Benedictines of SS Ulrich and Afra, where he had been employed as an organist since Jakob I Fugger granted him the position in 1584. In his preface Aichinger explicitly refers to the garland [*corolla*] brought by people in honour of the Eucharist (perhaps in the course of Corpus Christi processions), and suggestively calls it a *corolla agonistica*, or 'garland of victory'.[84] On one level, this can be read as the victory of the crucified Christ over death, but also suggests the militant overtones of Corpus Christi processions as they were conducted in Augsburg (see Chapter 6). The first 12 pieces in the volume – seven for two voices and continuo, five for three voices and continuo – are settings of Latin texts concerning the Eucharist; only a few, like *O sacrum convivium* (an antiphon for Second Vespers on Corpus Christi) and *Ave vivens hostia* (a hymn for Corpus Christi) are properly liturgical, while many are derived from biblical passages and would have been more suitable as liturgical substitutes or for devotional contexts (for example, *Hic est panis*, from John 6: 59 [6: 58], *Discubuit Jesus*, adapted from Luke 22: 14–15, and *Caro mea*, from John 6: 56, 59 [6: 56, 58]). These are followed by a lengthy Marian hymn in eight sections, *Mater supremi numinis*, for three voices (the final part, 'Regina caeli', is scored for two voices) and continuo. The presence of Marian music in an explicitly Eucharistic collection is unsurprising; Aichinger's *Encomium Verbo incarnato*, described above, joins veneration of Christ as the Word Incarnate with that of the Virgin, while his *Lacrumae* (see below) gives Mary a central place in the drama of Christ's crucifixion. Many of these prints, then, emphasize the Virgin's role as the chief intercessor on behalf of the sinful.[85]

The first piece in the volume, *Hic est panis* (Example 5.6), may be taken as representative of the collection, and indeed, of Aichinger's general approach to the vocal concerto.[86] The scoring for two equal

---

[83] *Corolla eucharistica, ex Variis Flosculis et Gemmulis pretiosis Musicarum sacrarum, binis ternisque Vocibus contexta. Cui etiam aeternae Virginis Uniones quidam de Tessera Salutis affixi* (Augsburg: Johannes Praetorius, 1621; RISM A/I, A548).

[84] 'Demus unâ cælesti Regi, Matrique Reginæ hanc COROLLAM EVCHARISTICAM; accepturi olim ab illis Corollam Agonisticam.' From the preface to *Corolla eucharistica*.

[85] A contemporary collection of vocal concertos by Rudolph di Lasso at Munich, the *Virginalia Eucharistica* (1615; RISM A/I, L1040), is another interesting analogue. See the edition by Alexander J. Fisher.

[86] 'Here is the bread that came down from heaven, not as the manna that the fathers ate, and died. He who eats this bread shall live for ever.' Transcription adapted from Gregor Aichinger, *The Vocal Concertos*, ed. Hettrick.

voices over basso continuo is a common feature of Aichinger's concertos of the 1620s and reflects broader trends as well in the contemporary concerto literature; in fact all the two-voice concertos in the *Corolla* are scored similarly (the three-voice concertos feature paired sopranos or tenors with a bass). This, along with Aichinger's tendency to turn to homophonic writing, leads frequently to passages in parallel thirds, such as in bars 11–12 and 18–21. The prose text leads Aichinger to a through-composed form, distinct from the strophic canzonettas of his earlier career. He sometimes turns to word-painting to express textual ideas, such as the descending melodic lines in bars 5–13 at 'qui de caelo descendit', and the full stop accompanied by a deceptive cadence in bars 21–22 at 'et mortui sunt' (black notation is used to provide visual emphasis to the idea of death);[87] however, these remain limited in scope

Example 5.6   Aichinger, *Hic est panis*, from *Corolla eucharistica* (1621)

---

87 Noted by Hettrick, ibid., p. xv.

Example 5.6 *concluded*

and Aichinger avoids virtuosic passagework for this purpose, only once
turning to fusae to illustrate the manna falling from heaven in bar 19. On
the other hand, *Hic est panis* is an excellent example of his emphasis on
clarity of text declamation, a concern that pervades all his work. He pays
careful attention to the accentuation of the Latin text, giving strong
metrical and rhythmic emphasis to the appropriate syllables in 'PA-nis'
(bars 2–5), 'de-SCEN-dit' (bars 6–13) and 'MOR-tu-i' (bars 20–21). This
clarity is heightened by the syllabic declamation, occasional homophony
and a tendency to use the vocal lines antiphonally. Typically, he never
overinterprets his texts; instead he allows them to be heard clearly by
listeners and performers, who very likely would have been talented
amateurs in devotional contexts such as confraternities or private
households, rather than church choirs.

Aichinger's next and final publication was the *Flores musici ad
Mensam SS. Convivii* (1626), settings of Eucharistic (and a few more
generally Christological) texts for five and six voices with basso
continuo.[88] Like the *Corolla eucharistica*, this book was dedicated to the
fathers of SS Ulrich and Afra, and specifically to Abbot Johann von
Merk, who had supported the cultivation of music at the church and had

---

[88] *Flores musici ad Mensam SS. Convivii quinque & sex Vocibus concinendi, & in
Xenium praeparati dicatique, reverendissimo in Christo P. Dno. Dn. Ioanni, incliti
Monasterii ad SS. Vdalricum et Afram Praesuli, etc.* (Augsburg: Johannes Udalricus
Schönig [C. Flurschütz], 1626; RISM A/I, A549).

thoroughly recast the interior decoration of the church in the spirit of the Counter-Reformation.[89] The *Flores musici* was, however, not the first musical publication with this title to be dedicated to the abbot. In 1618 Christian Keifferer, a composer and subprior at the Premonstratensian monastery of Weissenau, had also dedicated to Johann his *Flores musici seu divinae Laudis Odores suavissimi*, a collection of six-voice motets with basso continuo on Marian, Eucharistic and other Latin texts. Aichinger may have been influenced by Keifferer's precedent in the choice of his title; however, the two composers' approaches to scoring are also similar: both collections call for a full complement of at least five voices and continuo, a rather unusual format in a period when the concerto for few voices was gaining ascendancy.[90]

While the example of Keifferer's *Flores musici* may have influenced Aichinger to use a fuller scoring in his own print, he may also have been motivated to do so by the five- and six-voice madrigals attributed to Luca Marenzio (*Deh come potrò io dirui, Parto da voi, La dipartita è amara* and *Crudel perché mi fuggi*) and Orlando di Lasso (*S'io esca vivo*) that he parodied in five of his compositions. This procedure of sacred contrafacture of secular music certainly was prefigured in his own Magnificats of 1603 (the *Vespertinum Virginis*), as well as in numerous

---

[89] Bushart, 'Kunst und Stadtbild', p. 382.

[90] A full stylistic comparison of the two prints is difficult since certain partbooks are no longer extant (the first cantus part of Keifferer's *Flores musici* does not seem to have survived; the most complete exemplar (including first alto, tenor and bass, and second soprano and tenor) is found at D-Rp, A.R. 579–581. A sixth partbook, containing cantus and quintus parts, is also missing from Aichinger's *Flores musici*), it appears that Keifferer favours a homophonic, bass-driven texture and harmony resembling that of Aichinger's canzonettas of the previous decade. Keifferer's *Flores musici*, like most of his other surviving printed works, were printed by Gregor Hänlin in Ingolstadt, who had previously brought out at least three prints of Aichinger's music between 1609 and 1617 (the *Zwey Klaglieder vom Tod und letzten Gericht* [1613], the *Officium Angeli Custodis* [1617] and the *Encomium Verbo incarnato* [1617]). Keifferer's other works are the two parts of *Parvulus Flosculus, ex melitissimo D. Bernardi Iubilo delibatus Modisque musicis tribus Vocibus* (Dillingen: Sabina Meltzer, 1610; and Dillingen: Gregor Hänlin, 1611; RISM A/I, K234 and K235 respectively); the *Odae soporiferae; ad Infantium Betlehemiticum sopiendum Vocibus quatuor aequalibus factae; quibus accesseret Christi Dni, D. Virginis, S. Crucis, SS. Synaxeos, Consolationes, Adorationesque piae* (Dillingen: Gregor Hänlin, 1612; RISM A/I, K236); and *Sertum, tum Hybernis, tum Aestivis Floribus; Hymnis scilicet, toto Anni Curriculo in Ecclesiae, partim Romana, partim Praemonstratensi, decantari solitis, Musicis Modulis 4. & 5. Vocibus concinnatis* (Dillingen: Gregor Hänlin, 1613; RISM A/I, K237). Like Aichinger, the Catholic Keifferer seems also to have been inspired by poetry attributed to Bernard of Clairvaux. On Keifferer's biography and works, see Leon Goovaerts, *Écrivains, artistes et savants ... de l'orde de Prémontré: Dictionnaire bio-bibliographique* (Brussels: Société belge de librairie, 1899–[1920]); Georg Reichert, 'Keifferer, Christian', in *MGG*, vol. 7, col. 779–80, and A. Lindsey Kirwan and Stefan Hörner, 'Keifferer, Christian', in *New Grove II*, vol. 13, p. 446.

Magnificats by Orlando di Lasso,[91] but in this case the new texts were drawn from the liturgy (*O quam suavis*, a contrafactum of *Parto da voi*) or were devotional texts in praise of the Eucharist (*Ave verbum incarnatum*, a contrafactum of *Deh come potrò io dirui*). I have already mentioned in connection with the Magnificat prints that such contrafacture could be entirely unproblematic, given that the sacred words could be seen as 'purifying' the originally profane music (see p. 143).[92] While the continuo generally plays the conservative role of a *basso seguente*, two prominent exceptions that more closely resemble the contemporary Italian vocal concerto of the 1620s are the pieces for cantus, tenor, bass and continuo, *Angelus Domini* and *Paratum cor meum*, in which Aichinger has added two obbligato instrumental parts that play interpolated *sinfonie* at regular intervals.[93] Despite this, in his approach to the three vocal parts he maintains his usual emphasis on syllabic text declamation and relative ease of execution.

Christological Polyphony

Given the number of monophonic and polyphonic prints in this period devoted to the Virgin Mary and to the Eucharist, it is perhaps surprising that an almost equal number take Christ as their theme, one which at face value may seem less of a confessional symbol than the others. To many Catholics in the era of the Counter-Reformation, the Virgin Mary emerged as their most significant intercessor, the greatest among the panoply of saints; it was her role as a mediator between the sinner and God (rather than simply as a model of virtue) that set her apart as a confessional marker. The divisiveness of Eucharistic devotion stemmed from the doctrines of transsubstantiation, an idea that exploited entrenched popular beliefs in the magical properties of consecrated hosts and found expression in pilgrimages and processions for the feast of Corpus Christi processions. By contrast, devotion to Christ as the ultimate redeemer of the sins of men crossed confessional boundaries. Catholic Christology in this era, however, encouraged a personal relationship to and identification with Christ's Passion in particular, not only the abstraction of the redemption of sin, but especially the physical instruments and circumstances of the Passion: the crucifix, the Mount of Olives, the Holy Sepulchre.[94]

---

[91] See Crook, *Orlando di Lasso's Imitation Magnificats*.

[92] See also Crook, ibid., 80–82, who cites the many secular models for Lasso's litanies for the Munich court.

[93] See Hettrick, in Gregor Aichinger, *The Vocal Concertos*.

[94] Zeeden, 'Aspekte der katholischen Frömmigkeit', p. 326. Although a closer identification with the person of Christ as intercessor can be seen in Protestant song by the

In Augsburg as elsewhere, Catholics exploited these tangible and emotionally charged aspects of Christ's Passion in their devotional activities, which in the period of Catholic revival took on a distinctly public profile. In Good Friday processions, representations of Christ's Passion could be especially vivid, and indeed, bloody (see Chapter 6). By the early seventeenth century scenic representations of the Mount of Olives and the Holy Sepulchre had been constructed in both the cathedral and in the Jesuit church of St Salvator; both types of scenes were the focus of musical events and quasi-dramatic plays illustrating the events of the Passion.[95] Such displays encouraged in their audiences an emotional identification with the sufferings of Christ. In Passion songs and in the Christological music of Aichinger, Erbach and Zindelin, styles, texts and functions often point to this devotional embrace of Christ's Passion; even when the music does not concern the Passion *per se*, the texts tend to suggest the kind of emotional subjectivity and individual relationship to the person of Christ that was characteristic of Catholic devotion in this period.

The poetry of Bernard of Clairvaux, who found many adherents among Catholic literati of the early seventeenth century, was an ideal vehicle for this type of devotion. In the early sixteenth century Bernard was praised across confessional boundaries as a representative of the late medieval *devotio moderna*, but in time he came to be seen as a symbol of the Roman Church through Catholics' fervent embrace of his writings.[96] Gregor Aichinger was one of Bernard's devotees, and

---

early seventeenth century (see Hans-Georg Kemper, 'Das lutherische Kirchenlied in der Krisen-Zeit des frühen 17. Jahrhunderts', in Alfred Dürr and Walther Killy, eds, *Das protestantische Kirchenlied im 16. und 17. Jahrhundert: Text-, musik- und theologiegeschichtliche Probleme* (Wiesbaden: in Kommission bei O. Harrassowitz, 1986), pp. 105–7), Catholic music tends to focus much more closely on the bodily sufferings of Christ as an example for imitation.

[95] In 1592 Octavian II Fugger contributed 150 fl. to the construction of a *Heiliger Grab* in St Salvator that was the focus of dramas during Holy Week; this was replaced in 1613 (Braun, *Geschichte des Kollegiums der Jesuiten in Augsburg*, pp. 41 and 46–47). In the 1620s cathedral choirboys received payments from the chapter for singing before the cathedral's *Heiliger Grab* during Holy Week (see *DR*, 15 April 1622, 7 July 1623, 7 April 1625 and 12 April 1627). A representation of the Mount of Olives, or *Ölberg*, was constructed in the cathedral in the early seventeenth century (see Chevalley, *Der Dom zu Augsburg*, pp. 144–45).

[96] On the cult of Bernard in general, see Adriaan Hendrik Bredero, *Bernard of Clairvaux: Between Cult and History* (Grand Rapids, Mich.: William B. Eerdmans, 1996), pp. 160–62 and 173–76. Contemporary polyphonic prints setting Bernard's texts included Aichinger's *Odaria* (discussed presently) and Christian Erbach's *Mele sive Cantiones sacrae* (1603), both of which were published by Johannes Praetorius (Hans Schultes) in Augsburg; in Dillingen, Adam Meltzer brought out the *Rythmus, et Suavissimà D. Bernardi Oda, vulgo Iubilus dicta* in 1607, a collection of four-voice settings in Latin and German by

signalled his affection for the latter's poetry by setting 34 poems of the *Jubilus* in the *Odaria lectissima* (1601), presumably his presentation work upon joining the clergy at Augsburg Cathedral after returning from his Roman pilgrimage.[97] In his dedication to the newly elected bishop of Augsburg, Heinrich V von Knöringen, Aichinger publicly renounced the composition of secular music (and, indeed, would remain true to his word thereafter):

> Although today there are, as there always have been, those who abuse the Deity through their service, not so much to their own ruin, but to that of many; they move many to weakness, and, I would say without any offence, turn [them] to profane frivolity, and more to the drunken Thalia than to the sober Melpomene. From afar I have always observed this perverse use of such a noble and elegant art, and I see well how God, the creator of the art of music, has defined it for composers and masters, so that through the sweetness and allure of measure and harmony, the souls of men may be inflamed with the love for divine things.

For Aichinger the poetry of Bernard was ideally suited for such an undertaking. 'I think ardently of that mind of Bernard', he writes, 'desirous of heavenly things, whose speech flowed no less sweetly from his mouth than honey; he made the sweetest hymns, by which he spread the flames of divine ardour in our hearts and in his own.' In a separate epigram Aichinger called on the poet to fill him with his 'nectar of nectars, so that it will seem that you have sung my songs'.

The 34 texts, most of which consist of only four identically rhymed lines, are brief and concentrated expressions of devotion to Christ and/or the Virgin Mary, and Aichinger's musical responses are equally succinct. Most of these pieces are only several dozen measures in length, and tend to fall into the form ABCDC'D', in which the music for the final two lines is repeated, either literally or as a paraphrase. Like his *Tricinia Mariana*, this collection straddles the boundary between imitative and

---

Johannes Feldmayer (see Bucher, 'Adam Meltzer (1603–1610) und Gregor Hänlin (1610–1617)', pp. 217–21; no exemplar seems to have survived); three years later, Meltzer's widow Sabina would print Keifferer's *Parvulus Flosculus* (see above). The latter print, consisting of lightly imitative and homophonic three-voice settings, is demonstrably related to the example of Aichinger's *Odaria*. The Catholic interest in Bernard should not obscure the fact of Bernardine influence on Protestant reformers; for example, Franz Posset (in *Pater Bernhardus: Martin Luther and Bernard of Clairvaux* (Kalamazoo, Mich. and Spencer, Mass.: Cistercian Publications, 1999)) has argued for the influence of Bernard on Luther's Christological understanding, while Anthony N.S. Lane (in *Calvin and Bernard of Clairvaux* (Princeton: Princeton Theological Seminary, 1996)) has accepted a distinct, though limited, role of Bernard's writings in the formation of Calvin's literary style.

[97] *Odaria lectissima ex melitissimo D. Bernardi Iubilo delibata. Modisque musicis partim quatuor partim et tribus Vocibus expreßa* (Augsburg: Dominicus Custos, 1601; RISM A/I, A523). The attribution of the *Jubilus* poems to Bernard is insecure.

homophonic writing; typical is a shift to homophony accompanying a change to triple metre, as can be seen in Example 5.7.[98] Regardless of the texture, however, syllabic text declamation prevails, with melismas generally reserved for phrase endings. Madrigalisms, whether created through harmonic tension or illustrative melodic figures, are rare; in these works Aichinger seeks to let these texts speak for themselves by

Example 5.7   Aichinger, *Cum Maria diluculo*, from *Odaria lectissima* (1601)

[98] 'With Mary at daybreak I shall seek Jesus at the grave; with the plaintive cry of the heart, I shall seek him with the soul, not the eye.'

Example 5.7 *concluded*

providing modest, attractive settings in which the text is clearly audible. The ease of execution is heightened by a straightforward harmonic profile: in *Cum Maria diluculo*, the *cantus mollis* harmony pivots exclusively between tonal centres on D minor and F, although a genuinely tonal harmonic plan is discernible neither in the profile of the bass voice nor in the overall harmonic scheme. In the *Odaria*, it is Bernard whose words are emphasized, while the composer seeks only to provide a clear, attractive and unassuming vehicle for these words.

The Latin mystical poetry of Jacobus Pontanus, the rector of the Jesuit college of St Salvator, was not unlike that of Bernard in style and content. Pontanus was a well-regarded Latinist who probably founded the Marian Congregation at St Salvator in the 1580s; he dedicated to the group two of his major publications, the *Floridorum Libri octo* (1596) and the *Meditationes, Preces, Laudes in Virginem Matrem* (1606).[99] Aichinger's next publication, the *Divinae Laudes* for three voices (1602), mostly drew upon the *Floridorum*, choosing Christological or

---

[99] See Theodor Rolle, *Heiligkeitsstreben und Apostolat: Geschichte der Marianischen Kongregation am Jesuitenkolleg St. Salvator und am Gymnasium der Benediktiner bei St. Stephan in Augsburg 1589–1989* (Augsburg: im Eigenverlag St Stephan, 1989), pp. 17–18.

Eucharistic texts, except for the three-part *Augusta civitas Dei*, an ode to the city of Augsburg.[100] The texts are longer than those of the *Odaria*, and Pontanus's sensuous imagery led Aichinger to provide somewhat more artful and stylistically flexible settings, with occasional madrigalisms to illustrate certain images. The high cleffing of the print (two sopranos at G_2 and a 'bassus' at C_3) could certainly have called for singing in downward transposition, but he may also have had in mind the Marian Congregation, in which boys' voices were well represented and where the Latin, devotional texts of Pontanus would have been especially welcome. Aichinger dedicated the book to his superior at SS Ulrich and Afra, Abbot Johann von Merk, who after his appointment in 1600 had embarked on an ambitious programme for the redecoration of the church. In his dedication Aichinger expressed his admiration of Johann's efforts, and indeed the redecoration would directly implicate one of Aichinger's own works a few years later, the *Lacrumae D. Virginis et Ioannis* (see below).[101]

If the style of the Italian canzonetta was only occasionally visible in his earlier work, Aichinger's *Ghirlanda di canzonette spirituali* of 1603 made it explicit. Of the 21 three-voice settings, 14 are of Italian texts; the remaining seven are Latin hymns of praise. Aichinger directed a brief dedication in Italian to his old patron Jakob Fugger, who at the time was only one year away from being elected as the bishop of Konstanz. It is likely that Jakob, who had spent considerable time in Italy in the previous decade (and who remained active as a musical patron after his consecration), would have been familiar with the spiritual canzonetta as a genre. Aichinger's dependence on the Italian model extends to the mostly Christological texts, many of which had also been used by Paolo Quagliati in a collection of spiritual canzonettas.[102] While Aichinger had frequently turned to madrigalisms to express Pontanus's textual imagery

---

[100] *Divinae Laudes ex Floridis Iacobi Pontani potissimum decerptae, Modisque musicis ad Voces ternas factae* (Augsburg: Dominicus Custos, 1602; RISM A/I, A525). Aichinger also brought out a second book of *Divinae Laudes* in 1608 (A527), which are similar in musical style to the first book but consist of settings of hymn texts for a variety of feast days.

[101] 'Ritè certè me facturum arbitrabar, si Amplitudine vestra in opere templi nobilissimi & ante non pauca secula cœpto cum omnium gratulatione rursus suscepto, moxque absoluendo occupata, ego diuinas ad eam rem laudes meditarer, tanto quidem, vt meum fert ingenium, humiliores, quanto amplius & excelsius religiosissimi templi est opus.' From preface to *Divinae Laudes*. The redecoration of SS Ulrich and Afra was carried out in the spirit of Catholic reform, which may well have impressed the staunchly Catholic composer. See Bushart, 'Kunst und Stadtbild', p. 382.

[102] See Kroyer, 'Gregor Aichingers Leben und Werke', p. xliii. He almost certainly refers to the anthology *Canzonette spirituali de diversi a tre voci* (Rome: Alessandro Gardano, 1585; RISM B/I, 1585[7]).

in the *Divinae Laudes*, he preferred a more syllabic and homophonic profile for the *Ghirlanda*, emphasizing the accentuation of the language over word-painting.

Perhaps the finest expression of this turn towards textual subjectivity may be found in Aichinger's *Lacrumae D. Virginis et Ioannis in Christum a Cruce depositum*, or 'Tears of the Blessed Virgin and John at the deposition of the crucified Christ', published in 1604.[103] This collection consists of eight Latin motets for five voices, representing a mournful dialogue between the Virgin Mary and John the Evangelist at the foot of the cross. Despite the Latin text, the closest model for the *Lacrumae* was the *madrigale spirituale*, a genre closely identified with the Italian Counter-Reformation and cultivated especially in Rome; particularly well-known examples include collections by Palestrina (1594) and Marenzio (1584).[104] In Catholic Germany the *madrigale spirituale* was cultivated in Prague by the Imperial court composer Philippe de Monte, and more famously in Munich by Orlando di Lasso, whose *Lagrime di San Pietro* (1595) was a landmark of the genre. Aichinger may also have been aware of the growing tradition of quasi-dramatic madrigals involving dialogue, cultivated by Alessandro Striggio, Adriano Banchieri and especially Orazio Vecchi; furthermore, the didactic dialogues advocated by the Jesuits may also have left their mark on this work.

Although the theme of Mary and John at the foot of the cross was well known, Aichinger's madrigals may also be related to the erection of a bronze sculptural group of Mary, Mary Magdalene, John and the crucified Christ in SS Ulrich and Afra in 1605 (see Figure 5.1). This group was made by Hans Reichle, a prominent Augsburg sculptor with ties to the Fugger family, and who was also responsible for the sculpture of St Michael Archangel on the façade of Augsburg's Zeughaus (an image that in this period was laden with Counter-Reformation symbolism).[105] In the SS Ulrich and Afra group, Mary is at the left of the

---

[103] *Lacrumae D. Virginis et Ioannis in Christum a Cruce depositum, Modis musicis expressae* (Augsburg: Johannes Praetorius, 1604; RISM A/I, A531).

[104] Palestrina, *Delle madrigali spirituali a cinque voci … libro secondo* (Rome: Francesco Coattino, 1594; RISM A/I, P764); Marenzio, *Madrigali spirituali … a cinque voci … libro primo* (Rome: Alessandro Gardano, 1584; RISM A/I, M525). On the significance of the *madrigale spirituale* to the Counter-Reformation and the support of Cardinal Borromeo for this genre, see Lockwood, 'Vincenzo Ruffo and Musical Reform', pp. 351–52. Although most works in this genre set vernacular texts, Latin was used in isolated instances, as in the anthology *Madrigali de diversi auttori accomodati per concerti spirituali* (1616), containing Latin contrafacta of madrigals by Marenzio, Andrea Gabrieli and others. See Suzanne G. Cusick and Noel O'Regan, 'Madrigale spirituale', in *New Grove II*, vol. 15, p. 572.

[105] In its imagery of St Michael slaying a dragon, Wolfram Baer has seen a link to a similar group on the façade of the Jesuit church of St Michael in Munich, a clear reference to the church's triumph over heresy. See 'Michaelsgruppe am Zeughaus', p. 88.

5.1   Hans Reichle sculptural group from SS Ulrich and Afra (1605). Photo
courtesy of the Basilica of SS Ulrich and Afra

cross, John at the right; both are standing facing the viewer, seemingly
declaiming with open mouths and gestures. At the centre a kneeling
Mary Magdalene embraces the cross, looking up to the crucified Christ
above. Directly beneath the cross on the stone foundation is inscribed
ALTARE PRIVILEGIATVM, or 'altar of the justified'. The inscriptions beneath

Mary and John are drawn from John 19: 26–27, when Jesus addresses the two at the foot of the cross. Underneath Mary is the inscription MVLIER, ECCE FILIVS TVVS, or 'Woman, behold your son' (John 19: 26), while the inscription (IOANNES) ECCE MATER TVA, or '(John), behold your mother' (John 19: 27) is found underneath John (in the biblical narrative John subsequently took Mary into his home). On the back side of the group, underneath the Virgin, reads the inscription TORCVLAR CALCAVIT DOMINVS VIRGINI FILIAE IVDA ('the Lord hath trodden the winepress for the virgin daughter of Juda'), an excerpt from the Lamentations of Jeremiah (1: 15) that may be taken to represent Mary's despair at the crucifixion of her son. Beneath John on the same side is an excerpt from the last chapter of the Gospel of John (21: 22) in which the risen Jesus castigates Peter for asking about the fate of the Beloved Disciple (i.e., John): SIC EVM VOLO MANERE DONEC VENIAM or '[What is it to you] if I wish him to remain until I return?'

None of the four gospels contains the words spoken between Mary and John at the foot of the cross, so the dialogue presented between them in Aichinger's *Lacrumae* is cut from whole cloth and does not seem to include biblical text. Aichinger may have penned the texts himself, which, like Tansillo's texts in Lasso's *Lagrime*, are intense and subjective in expression rather than dramatically conceived. The eight madrigals take the form of a large-scale dialogue, as Mary's five utterances alternate with John's three. John's first utterance, 'Mater ita enim pietas' (Example 5.8), provides an example of the vivid and at times gruesome nature of Aichinger's texts, as well as the composer's approach to the setting:

> Mater (ita enim pietas iubet fari atque amor)
> Non gemitibus, non fletibus iam suadeam
> Parcere, dolori fræna laxa liberè,
> Effunde quicquid in te lacrumarum latet,
> Vetet quis? Ille sanguinem fudit prior.
> Eia aspice. Ah! spectaculum illætabile!
> Et sanguine et cute viduum corpus, patent
> Vacua ossa, flagris nuda defluxit caro.
> Complectere artus, pectore incumbens foue
> Fossum latus, fossos pedes ferro, et manus.

> Mother (for indeed piety and love command me to speak thus),
> I would not longer urge either sighs or tears
> be spared; release the reins of sorrow freely,
> pour out any tears that are hidden within you;
> who would forbid it? That man poured out his blood first.
> Ah, behold, o unhappy sight!
> The body bereft of blood and skin, the empty bones lie exposed,
> the bare flesh has peeled away.
> Embrace his limbs, prone on his breast, caress
> his side laid open, his feet and hands pierced with iron.

Example 5.8   Gregor Aichinger, *Mater ita enim pietas*, from *Lacrumae* (1604)

Example 5.8 *concluded*

The vivid imagery of the text does not lead Aichinger, however, to overindulge in word-painting; as in other collections the composer allows the text to be heard clearly by means of largely syllabic declamation and textures that at times approach a *parlando* style (see especially bars 7–9 and 29–34). He does, however, add some pictorial and rhetorical touches at crucial points, such as flowing melismas as John urges Mary to 'release the reins of sorrow' and 'pour out any tears' within her (bars 13–16); a simultaneous semibreve in four voices setting apart the exclamation 'Ah!', the effect of which is heightened by a cross-relation between the previous C♯ in the Cantus II and the C♮ in the Cantus I (bars 27–28); and a similar gesture involving all five voices in bar 31.

The particularly 'Catholic' sensibility of the *Lacrumae* texts is paralleled in the texts and dedication of Aichinger's *Vulnera Christi* (1606), a set of Latin sacred canzonettas for three and four voices on Bernard's poetry concerning the wounds of Christ.[106] His dedication to Abbot Urban of the Benedictine monastery of Ochsenhausen (near Ulm) demonstrates his close connection with yet another German Catholic prelate, but also typifies the subjective, emotionally charged language preferred by the composer:

> I give you, most dignified prelate, these wounds of Christ, a theme not so much of sorrow as of love. However much they once afflicted the author of our salvation, now they bring forth Christ to those burning with love, when from these [wounds] full, holy fountains of nectar come forth, in which that great servant of Christ, Bernard, was steeped. Whence from his mouth these honeyed liquors of tears have also flowed down to us, which I pass on to you, most dignified prelate, not after the fashion of Trimalchio, but to be enjoyed in the manner of the saints. Drink, most worthy Father, this philtre of love, and offer it to your charges to drink, and indulge your ears with my singing of pious songs; this drink seeks not the head, but the mixture fills the breast with celestial sweetness.[107]

The same emphasis on the individual's subjective relationship with the crucified Christ, as well as the strongly visual and graphic understanding of his suffering, pervades the 39 texts that follow, divided into seven groups corresponding to Christ's feet, knees, side, hands, breast, heart and face respectively (the sevenfold division, naturally, also corresponds with the Seven Last Words of Christ on the cross). A typical example that illustrates the sensibility of the texts as well as Aichinger's compositional approach is no. 34, *Salve caput cruentatum*, the first of five settings

---

[106] *Vulnera Christi, a D. Bernardo salutata, et nunc quaternis et tribus Vocibus musice defleta* (Dillingen: Adam Meltzer, 1606; RISM A/I, A534).
[107] From the preface to *Vulnera Christi*.

devoted to the face of Christ (see Example 5.9).[108] The text, though brief, is graphic and unsettling, and Aichinger adds small touches that bring out certain key words, such as a running semiminim passage in the tenor at 'spinis' (bar 7) and a series of sharp dissonances followed by a minim rest in all voices (bars 13–20) at 'arundine verberatum', lending special stress to the image of Christ's face being struck. Otherwise he does not waver from his usual emphasis on syllabic text declamation and light, homophonic textures, although the penitential character of the texts leads to a marked emphasis on the minor mode.

The texts of Bernard also attracted Aichinger's slightly younger colleague Christian Erbach. Two years after the appearance of Aichinger's *Odaria*, Erbach brought out his own *Mele sive Cantiones sacrae ad Modum Canzonette* for four voices (1603), a set of sacred canzonettas with many of the same texts of (Pseudo-)Bernard selected by Aichinger for the earlier book.[109] A relationship, both textually and

Example 5.9   Aichinger, *Salve caput cruentatum*, from *Vulnera Christi* (1606)

---

[108] 'Hail, bleeding head, all crowned with thorns and rent with wounds, struck with rods, the face spat upon.'

[109] *Mele sive Cantiones sacrae ad Modum Canzonette ut vocant, quaternis Vocibus*

Example 5.9 *concluded*

stylistically, between the two prints is certain: like Aichinger, Erbach joins the Latin, mystical poetry attributed to Bernard with a fashionable and accessible musical vehicle in which the simplicity and penetration of Bernard's insights is mirrored by the transparency of the music, which through homophony and syllabic declamation allows the text to be

factae, quibus accessit ... Hymnus Mariae, cum Mariana senum Vocum cantione (Augsburg: Johannes Praetorius, 1603; RISM A/I, E726).

heard clearly. In his dedication to Johann, Johann Ernst and Ottheinrich Fugger, Erbach reveals that he may have been personally motivated to write music in honour of Christ and the Virgin, to whom he attributed his recovery from a serious illness. 'I rose not just from the bed but also from the grave', he writes, 'and with this music in celebration of my recovery I sang praises to the Virgin my helper, and to the son of the Virgin my protector, to the author of life who rightly delivers salvation and health.'[110] Although many of the texts are Christological rather than Marian in orientation, this statement demonstrates the indistinct boundaries between these two forms of devotion.

Contrasting with the general nature of Bernard's texts in the *Mele sive Cantiones*, Erbach's *Acht underschiedtliche Geistliche Teutsche Lieder von den fürnembsten Geheimnussen deß bittern Leydens und Sterbens unsers Herrn und Seligmachers Jesu Christi* (1610) more specifically targets Holy Week devotions.[111] Given that this vernacular music may have had a larger market than Erbach's Latin polyphony (much of which was intended strictly for liturgical usage), it lacks a dedication entirely, suggesting that either the composer or the printer, Hans Schultes (i.e., Johannes Praetorius), financed the publication himself. Erbach set eight German poems on the theme of Christ's Passion, and short directions following each piece indicate that these songs were to be performed in front of specific images – whether paintings or devotional prints – of the Passion story. A sample appears below:

'Vor dem Oelberg'
(Before [an image of] the Mount of Olives)

O Mensch betracht/	O Man, take heed
Wie angst gemacht/	Of how your impure sin
dein Sünd vnrein/	Has troubled
Dem allr getrewsten Heyland dein.	Your most faithful saviour.

'Vor der Geyßlung'
(Before the Scourging)

Ach führ zu hertzn/	O Man, feel in your heart
O Me[n]sch die pein/	the pain and anguish
Auch sondern schmertzn/	that Christ your Lord
de[n] Christus dein Herr gnummen ein.	has suffered.

---

[110] 'Surrexi ego non tam de lectulo quam tumulo, & hæc musica soteria Auxiliatrici Virgini, Virginisque filio sospitatori, vitæque auctori lubens merito saluus sanusque cecini.' From the preface to *Mele sive Cantiones sacrae*.

[111] *Acht Vnderschiedtliche Geistliche Teutsche Lieder/ von den fürnembsten Geheimnussen deß bittern Leydens vnd Sterbens vnsers HErrn vnd Seligmachers Jesu Christi/ nutzlich zu gebrauchen (sonderlich) in der H. Kharwochen. Mit 4. Stimen zusamen gesetzt/ durch Christianum Erbach* (Augsburg: Johann Schultes, 1610; RISM A/I, E732).

'Vor der Krönung'
(Before the Crowning with Thorns)

Mensch thue erwegn/	O Man, be moved
Wie dein Herr zart/	by how your sweet Lord
Von deinetwegn/	Was crowned with thorns
Mit dörneren gekrönet ward.	For your sake.

The chronological series of pieces suggests an exercise in which a four-voice choir would accompany devotees' viewing of the Stations of the Cross; alternatively, one can imagine a small group in private circumstances contemplating printed woodcut images, perhaps, of Christ's Passion. Although we cannot be sure whether Erbach had in mind a specific set of images, a surviving late Gothic painting of the crowning of thorns from the altar of the Holy Trinity in Augsburg Cathedral (Figure 5.2) suggests a type of painting that could have been an object of the exercise.

Erbach's polyphony for the eight songs consists entirely of rhythmic formulas corresponding to the 4/4/4/8 syllabic structure of each stanza; in each song only the melodic lines, and thus the harmony, changes. The first song is shown in Example 5.10, with a reconstructed tenor part. In

5.2   Anonymous late Gothic painting of Christ crowned with thorns, Augsburg Cathedral. Photo courtesy of Augsburg Cathedral

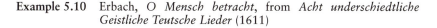

Example 5.10 Erbach, *O Mensch betracht*, from *Acht underschiedtliche Geistliche Teutsche Lieder* (1611)

their brevity, syllabic declamation, homophony, narrow range and clear phrase endings, these pieces embody a kind of repertory that would have suited the abilities of amateur musicians in Catholic brotherhoods or in private households. The formulaic character of this music, furthermore, would have made it easy to memorize and execute, an important trait given that the singers' attentions would have been divided between the music on the one hand and the contemplation of Passion images on the other. The appearance of this music ultimately cannot be understood outside of Catholic visual culture. As the Jesuits and Catholic confraternities promoted a more tactile understanding of the holy mysteries through visual and aural spectacles, Catholic printing houses produced an ever-greater quantity of devotional music and images that would have penetrated private spaces as well as the public arena of the church. Erbach's lieder represent a direct correlation of musical and visual culture, but the same can be assumed for much of the other music discussed in this chapter in which the prescription is not so explicit.

Erbach's Latin canzonettas of the *Mele sive Cantiones sacrae* and eight German Passion songs are mirrored in Philipp Zindelin's two Christological publications. In the *Lugubria super Christi Caede et Vulneribus* (1611; see above, p. 151) he provides madrigalistic five-voice settings of a series of Latin, meditative texts on Christ's Passion and wounds, suited for the liturgy of the Veneration of the Cross. A year later he brought out a collection of German Passion songs for three voices, the *Traurigs Klaglied auß den siben Worten* (1612), which, like Erbach's Passion songs, would have been suitable for non-liturgical Holy Week devotions.[112] Zindelin dedicated these songs to Magdalena, the Duchess of Bavaria, who in the following year would marry Count Palatine Wolfgang Wilhelm of Neuburg, a convert and ardent supporter of the Counter-Reformation who embarked on a radical re-Catholicization of his territory when he assumed power in 1614. In the dedication Zindelin praised Magdalena's piety and love for music, and wrote how important it was 'to praise and honour the triumphant battle and splendid, glorious victory of the innocent, most holy [redeemer's] bitter suffering and death on the wood of the holy cross, which saved all men'.[113] These 19 short texts, as the title implies, are based on the seven last words of Christ on the cross drawn from the Gospels of Luke (23: 34, 43 and 46), Matthew (27: 46), and John (19: 26–28, 30). Although there seems to be a strong imitative component to Zindelin's writing, as in the *Lugubria*, the light homophony of the canzonetta is more prevalent, broken up occasionally by decorative melismas.

Catholic Devotional Song in Augsburg

That composers such as Gregor Aichinger and Christian Erbach chose to address the needs of lay devotees with suitable music should be seen less as a sign of musical decline than an indication that Catholic elites were beginning to take seriously the need to speak accessibly to a broader segment of the laity. The relatively simple and accessible nature of much

---

[112] *Traurigs Klaglied auss den siben Worten, welche Christus der Herr am stammen dess heiligen Creutzes geredt, gezogen, mit drey Stimmen componirt* (Augsburg: Johann Schultes, 1612; RISM A/I, Z238).

[113] 'wievil billicher ist der Sigreiche kampff vnd stattliche Glorwirdige auch dem gantzen Menschlichen Geschlecht heylsame *Victori*, deß vnschuldiges allerheiligstes bitters Leiden vnd Sterben am Stammen deß heiligen Creutzes gewaltigklich vberwunden/ nicht allein auff dergleichen weiß zu beschreiben/ sondern mit worten vnd gesangen höchlich zu Loben vnd zu Preisen.' From the dedication to *Traurigs Klaglied auss den siben Worten*.

of the polyphony discussed above suggests that Catholic devotional music in Augsburg cannot easily be categorized into 'high' and 'low' forms. Singers of varying aptitudes came together in confraternity devotions, processions and pilgrimages, performing a continuum of music ranging from sacred canzonettas in several parts to the simplest monophonic songs. As Lutheran leaders had discovered many decades previously, the medium of monophonic, vernacular song was ideally suited both for propaganda and for individual and collective religious expression. In the late sixteenth and early seventeenth centuries Augsburg experienced a flowering of Catholic vernacular song that paralleled the polyphony discussed above in its embrace of the Virgin Mary, the Eucharist and the Passion of Christ; in addition, some extant songs also point to continuity with older and more popular traditions of sanctoral devotion.

Especially after 1600, monophonic songs meant to accompany the praying of the Rosary appeared in Catholic songbooks. A large songbook published in Augsburg in 1638 provides valuable insight into the public organization of Rosary devotions, one of the most important types of Marian devotion in this period, and the important role of songs in it. The Viennese Dominican priest Eustachius Mayr had brought out at least one previous edition of his *Andächtige Vbung/ Vnd Geistliche Gesäng deß Heyligen Rosenkrantzes IESV MARIÆ* (Ingolstadt, 1637), but his 1638 edition was financed by the Augsburg Dominicans and he referred in his preface specifically to Rosary devotions in Augsburg. Mayr's title page establishes that his book was intended 'to be used throughout the year, before and after the praying of the Rosary in the brotherhood's church, in pilgrimages and at home'.[114] Furthermore, he organized the book specifically with the devotions of Rosary confraternities in mind ('In dise Form allen der Bruderschafft deß heyligen Rosenkrantzes IEsu Mariæ Mitglidern zugefallen gestellt'). After arguing for the spiritual value of the Rosary devotion, he explained his motivation for publishing such a collection in his preface:

> and since this wonderful pleasure-garden of the holy Rosary is ever more frequented and attended everywhere, and especially here in Augsburg, where people often assemble each Sunday for the public praying of the Rosary, I desired to bring together the Rosary [prayer] with the songs that usually accompany it, put them in this form and

---

[114] *Andächtige Vbung/ Vnd Geistliche Gesäng deß Heyligen Rosenkrantzes. IESV MARIÆ, Durch das gantze Jahr/ vor vnnd nach dem Rosenkrantz/ in den Bruederschafft Kirchen/ bey Wallfahrten/ vnnd im Hauß/ zugebrauchen. In dise Form allen der Bruderschafft deß heyligen Rosenkrantzes IEsu Mariæ Mitglidern zugefallen gestellt* (Augsburg: Andreas Aperger, 1638; RISM B/VIII, 1638¹⁴). The earlier edition is given in RISM B/VIII as 1637¹¹.

prepare them for publication, for the benefit of [these assemblies], the devotees of God and Mary and for the pleasure of many zealous hearts.

Mayr's *Andächtige Übung* remains an imperfect – and perhaps wholly prescriptive – guide to the conduct of the Rosary devotion, for no corroborating documentation of this service appears to have survived. However, the details he provided are intriguing and suggest ways in which vernacular songs were interwoven with the prayers of the Rosary itself.[115]

Omitting notated melodies, probably in the expectation that the tunes would have been well known to devotees, Mayr indicates appropriate songs for the various seasons of the liturgical year, from Advent to Corpus Christi, as well as a number specifically for Marian feasts and in honour of the Dominican Order and its founder.[116] Taking the season of Advent as an example, Mayr's directions for the conduct of the Rosary service are as follows: at the opening of the service the people sing a 'song of the joyous Rosary', *Gleich wie der Hirsch*. The priest mounts the pulpit or stands before the altar, and exhorts the congregants to the praying of the Rosary and the veneration of the Virgin Mary; he then may briefly instruct the congregation in the order of the service.[117] After making the sign of the cross, he begins by reciting the *Salve Regina* in a loud, slow voice, and the congregation responds by reciting the German version, *Gegrüsset seyest du Königin*, in response. Then the priest recites a litany of the Virgin (probably the Litany of Loreto), and the congregation recites the short responses (in most cases, *Ora pro nobis* ['pray for us'], or *Bitt für uns, Maria*, in the vernacular). Then the

---

[115] Another direct connection with Augsburg may be seen in the imprimatur of Caspar Zeiller, the vicar-general of the Augsburg diocese, which appears on the last page: 'ADmodum Reuerend. Nobilis ac Magnifici Domini, Domini Caspari Zeileri, SS. Theol: Doctoris, Reuerendiss. & Illustriss. Principis Episc. August. Consiliarij, & in Spiritualibus Vicarij Generalis, nec non Collegiatæ Ecclesiæ S. Mauritij August. Canonici.' | *Imprimatur*. | Alles zu Gottes vnd Mariæ deß H. Rosenkrantzes Königin/ auch deß H. Vatters Dominici/ vnd aller Heyligen/ grösserer Ehr vnd Glory.'

[116] At least one other previous book with musical references had been dedicated to the Rosary devotion, the *Geistlicher Psalter/ Von dreyen Rosenkräntzen: in 15. Decurias/ oder Geistlich Ordnungen außgetheylt vnd vnderschiden* (Konstanz: Leonhard Straub, 1598; RISM B/VIII, 1598[17]). However, the compiler, Johann Georg Tibianus, a Latin schoolmaster from Überlingen (near Konstanz), provided only one song, *Vns sagt die Gschrifft gantz offenbar*, whereas Eustachius Mayr provided his *Andächtige Übung* with several dozen, keyed to the different seasons of the liturgical year.

[117] 'Dann steigt der Priester auff die Cantzel/ oder vor dem Altar/ ermahnet mit kurtzen Worten menigklich zur Andacht deß H. Rosenkrantzes/ vnnd verehrung der Mutter Gottes/ zaiget auch an/ vor wem/ vnnd vor was Anligen der Rosenkrantz zubetten sey/ wie andern dardurch geholffen worden'. From Mayr, *Andächtige Vbung/ Vnd Geistliche Gesäng deß Heyligen Rosenkrantzes*.

praying of the Rosary proper begins, divided into meditations by the priest on the five joys, five sorrows and five glories of the Virgin Mary respectively. After each mystery has been explained (the five joys include the Annunication, the Visitation, the Nativity of Jesus, the Presentation of Jesus in the Temple and the Finding of Jesus in the Temple), the congregation, broken into a 'left choir' and 'right choir' [*linker Chor* and *rechter Chor*], answer each other antiphonally in the recitations of the requisite Our Father, Apostles' Creed and Hail Mary. Preceding each group of five meditations is a song, led by a *Vorsinger*: *Gleich wie der Hirsch* serves this function for the first five mysteries, and these are ended by the song *O Gott im höchsten Throne* (there is no direct evidence that these were sung antiphonally, however). This pattern is maintained for the five sorrows and five glories respectively, with different songs indicated for the various seasons of the year. Although the *Andächtige Übung* itself gives no evidence for it, it is plausible that polyphonic music, such as the sacred canzonettas on the Rosary mysteries of Aichinger's *Virginalia*, could have been performed as well.

It is neither easy nor advisable to make a firm distinction between Marian songbooks and songsheets and the large amount of Marian devotional literature that circulated in Counter-Reformation Augsburg. There were, naturally, books for Rosary devotions that did not contain music but were similar in other ways to Mayr's *Andächtige Übung*, such as the *Psalterium Mariæ, Der heyligsten Junckfraw vnd Gottes gebererin* (1611), a vernacular guide to that service.[118] Isolated songs, with or without musical notation, could turn up in Marian devotional books: an example is an anonymous prayer book published in 1611 with the title *Erscheinung vnd Offenbarung der allerheiligsten vnd glorwürdigsten Mutter Gottes*, a collection of devotional prayers to the Virgin Mary to which 'a very pious Catholic song' was attached, *O Maria dich heben wir an zu loben*. The pamphlet contains neither musical notation nor an indication of the appropriate tune, suggesting that this song was well known.[119] Popular devotional literature, vernacular songs and polyphony in honour of the Virgin were by no means separate spheres. Instead, they reflect different aspects of a

---

[118] *Psalterium Mariæ, Der heyligsten Junckfraw vnd Gottes gebererin* ... (Augsburg: Christoph Mang [Chrysostomus Dabertzhofer?], 1611). This 'Marian psalter', which also contains no melodies, is in fact a Rosary devotion, consisting of a series of meditations on the Virgin divided into the customary three sections.

[119] *Erscheinung vnd Offenbarung der allerheiligsten vnd glorwürdigsten Mutter Gottes/ so die heylig Königin Elisabeth (wie gottselig geglaubt wirdt) gehabt hat. Aus den Opusculis deß H. Kirchen Lehrers Bonauenturæ ins Teutsch gebracht. Sampt einem Geistlichen Gesang/ zu höchstgemeldter Mutter Gottes* (Augsburg: Chrysostomus Dabertzhofer, 1611).

single continuum of devotional culture that characterized Catholic society as a whole.[120]

Compared with the variety of songs in honour of the Virgin Mary and patron saints that appear in German Catholic songbooks in this period, the Eucharistic song repertory seems narrower, and may reflect the relative novelty of organized Eucharistic devotion as a major component of Counter-Reformation religious culture. Supplicatory music in honour of the Virgin or the saints, in fact, still figured prominently in pilgrimages to Eucharistic shrines: the biannual pilgrimage to Andechs, for example, featured the repeated singing of the *Regina cæli* and litanies of the Virgin or the saints.[121] A 1642 ordinance for a pilgrimage to the *Wunderbares Gut* at Heilig Kreuz in Augsburg by the Munich Corpus Christi Confraternity called explicitly for the singing of the Litany of Loreto and the *Salve Regina* along the route (see Chapter 7).[122] However, at least one Eucharistic song, *Der zart Fronleichnam der ist gut*, was a staple of Catholic songbooks and diocesan rituals by the late sixteenth century. A translation of the Latin hymn for Corpus Christi *Ave vivens hostia*, it was allowed by Bishop Marquard von Berg in his 1580 *Ritus ecclesiastici Augustensis Episcopatus* to be sung during the octave of that feast in church (see Chapter 4, p. 113). *Der zart Fronleichnam* and another translation of the *Ave vivens hostia*, *Gegrüßt seystu heilig opffer rain*, appeared in Johann Haym's *Drey Gaystliche vnd Catholische Lobgesang* (1584), a small collection of Marian and Eucharistic songs dedicated to his own Trinity Confraternity of Augsburg Cathedral. As he states on the title page, both texts (sung to the same melody) were 'to be sung on the feast of Corpus Christi during the procession, as well as throughout the year after the transsubstantiation of the

---

[120] R. Po-Chia Hsia has identified three main types of Catholic devotional prints in this era: *suffragia*, or images of patron saints used in devotional exercises; literature for use in catechism classes; and votive prints for pilgrims. See Hsia, *The World of Catholic Renewal*, pp. 159–60. Any of these kinds of literature could have included simple vernacular songs, notated or unnotated.

[121] Explicitly Eucharistic litanies seem to have been rare.

[122] '3. Vor gemeltem Bruck herauß/ wird man ein weil verziehen/ biß das Volck zusamen kombt/ alßdann vngefehr vmb 5. Uhr zu Abendts in der ordnung in die Pfarrkirchen gehn/ allda vnser Lieben Frawen Letaney singen/ vnd in gemeltem Marckt vber Nacht verbleiben.

'4. Den andern Tag/ als am Pfintztag wird man Morgens frühe von 3. biß auff 4. Uhr etliche Messen halten/ hernach auff Fridberg raisen/ allda vor dem Thor in die Ordnung tretten/ in die Kirchen gehn/ vnd ein *Salue Regina* singen/ folgends das Mittagmal nemmen/ vnd auff gegebenes Glockenzaichen sich in gedachter Kirchen widerumb versamblen/ vnd biß zum alten Zollhauß vor der Lechbrucken bey Augspurg begeben.' From StAA, KWA A42[13], 'Ordnung/ Der *Procession* oder Wallfahrt/ welche deß zarten Fronleichnam[m]s ErtzBruderschafft zu München/ nacher Augspurg zu dem Wunderbarlichen Hochheiligsten Sacrament auff den 2. 3. 4. 5. vnd 6. Julij 1642. Jahr angestellet.'

host'.[123] The songs, then, reflect the presence of vernacular music not only in public, Eucharistic processions, but also within the liturgy of the Mass.

A characteristic example of Haym's vernacular songwriting may be seen in Example 5.11, drawn from another of his publications, the *Passion, oder Das aller heyligist bitter leiden vnd sterben Jhesu Christi* (1581).[124] He offered this work, consisting of a simple setting of paraphrases of Christ's Passion drawn from the four Gospels, 'for the use and welfare of all Catholic pilgrims when they process with the cross';[125] an accompanying citation from the early Church Father Eusebius suggests that Haym intended his songs as much for public as for private devotions:

> In the year of our Lord 320 the Holy Doctor of the Church Eusebius Pamphilius was the Catholic Bishop of Caesarea, in Palestine. He writes in his church history in the ninth book, in the first chapter, the following about procession or pilgrimage songs: 'The Christians sing hymns, that is, songs of praise or psalms, for the entire route and

Example 5.11   Johann Haym, *In Gottes namen heben wir an*, from *Passion, oder Das aller heyligist bitter leiden vnd sterben Jhesu Christi* (1581)

In Got - tes   na - men   he - ben wir   an/   Das Ley - den
Chri - sti   sin - gen   schon.   O   Mensch lass   dirs   zu   Hert - zen   gahn.

---

[123] *Drey Gaystliche vnd Catholische Lobgesang/ Christo vnserm einigen Seligmacher/ vnd Mariæ allgemainer Christenhait fürbitten/ zuo lob vnd Ehrn/ auch der Lobwirdigen Brüderschafft zuom Hayligenberg/ Jn vnser lieben Frawen Thumbstifft zuo Augspurg/ vnd sonst allen from[m]en Catholischen Christen zu guettem inn Truck geben worden* (Augsburg: Johann Haym, 1584; RISM B/VIII, 1584[13]).

[124] 'In God's name we begin to sing of the suffering of Christ. O Man, let it speak to your heart.'

[125] *Passion/ oder Das aller heyligist bitter leiden vnd sterben Jhesu Christi/ vnsers einigen Erlösers vnd Seligmachers/ auß den vier Hey: Euangelisten genom[m]en/ vnd Reym[m]en weyß/ in ein Catholisch Creützgesang gemacht worden/ Zuuor inn Truck nye außgangen/ vnnd inn bey getruckter Melodey/ gar andechtig zusingen. Durch einen Catholischen Priestern/ Allein dem wahren einigen Sohn Gottes vnd Mariä/ zu ewiger dancksagung/ vnd frischer gedechtnuß/ seines aller Heyligsten Creutz verdienst/ für das gantz Menschlich geschlecht geschehen &c. Darnach auch der Christlobwürd: Brüderschafft (newlicher jaren in vnser lieben Frawen Thümb stifft Augspurg auffgericht) vnd sonst allen Catholischen Kirchfärttern/ wan[n] man mit dem Creutz geht/ zunutz vnnd wolfahrt inn denn Truck geben worden* (Augsburg: Josias Wörli [?], 1581; RISM B/VIII, 1581[11]). The only extant exemplar is D-Bds, 8° Eh 3512.

through the streets of the town', etc. *O Lord Jesus Christ, Your Passion is our salvation. And your death is our life.*[126]

Haym's historicist appeal to a Church authority from late antiquity was a characteristic move in the Counter-Reformation revival of traditional processions and pilgrimages, practices that in Augsburg would have encountered resistance from local Protestants.[127] This particular song is also not the only example of the singing of texts drawn from the four Gospels in processions in Augsburg: the official Rituals of the Augsburg diocese from both 1580 and 1612 call for the singing of the four gospels during the annual Corpus Christi procession, an activity that is confirmed in accounts of Corpus Christi processions beginning in the early seventeenth century (see Chapter 6).[128] Haym's Passion song is notable, however, in that it contains a vernacular text and was intended for use in non-liturgical contexts. Resembling a single voice extracted from Erbach's simple polyphonic Passion songs, it is easy to imagine both types of music being sung in similar settings.

Even though the Church hierarchy tended to de-emphasize the veneration of local saints (and was indeed resistant to the canonization of new local saints), these continued to have spiritual significance for the common people, and at times local church officials even promoted their cults.[129] St Ulrich (Bishop of Augsburg, 923–73) and St Afra (an early Christian martyr), were the traditional patron saints of Augsburg and the local Benedictine church and monastery was consecrated in their honour, while the cult of St Simpert, a late eighth-century bishop of Augsburg (778?–807?), experienced a revival around the turn of the sixteenth century and again around the turn of the seventeenth century.[130] The

---

[126] 'Anno Christj 320. lebt der Hey: Kirchenlehrer/ *Eusebius Pamphilius* Catholischer Bischoff zu *Cæsarien, in Palestina* gewesen. Der schreibt inn seiner Kirchen *Historien* im 9. Büch/ am ersten Capitel/ von den Creütz oder walfahrt gesängen also. Die Christen singen *Hymnos.* Das ist lobgesäng oder Psalm[m]en Den gantzen Weg/ vnd durch die Gassen der Statt &c. *O Domine Ihesu Christe Passio tua, salus nostra. Et mors tua, Vita nostra.*' From Haym's *Passion.*

[127] The venerability of allegedly 'ancient' devotions and associated songs was a guarantee of the authority of the Church's teachings. See Härting, 'Das deutsche Kirchenlied der Gegenreformation', p. 59.

[128] See *Ritus ecclesiastici Augustensis Episcopatus*, pp. 621 ff., and *Liber Ritualis, Episcopatus Augustensis*, vol. 3, pp. 177–206.

[129] As the Catholic reform movement gained momentum in the sixteenth century, the church made efforts to streamline and centralize the canonization process. Peter Burke, in 'How to Become a Counter-Reformation Saint', in Luebke, ed., *The Counter-Reformation: The Essential Readings*, pp. 129–42, has noted that newly canonized saints in the Counter-Reformation often embodied the church's emphasis on missionary work.

[130] St Simpert, whose remains also are housed at SS Ulrich and Afra, built the first church around the grave of St Afra, on the present site of SS Ulrich and Afra. Veneration of St Simpert seems to have increased in the fifteenth century under the influence of Bishop

continuing importance of saintly devotion among the laity is reflected in vernacular songsheets in honour of particular patron saints, or sections of Catholic songbooks that are devoted to the saints.[131] By contrast, little surviving polyphonic music from Augsburg honours particular saints, a

---

Petrus von Schaumburg (1424–69); in the early sixteenth century, Veit Bild (1481–1529), a Benedictine monk at SS Ulrich and Afra and a noted humanist and musical scholar, penned a hagiography of SS Ulrich, Afra and Simpert (1516). On his music treatise, *Stella musicae*, see Thomas Röder and Theodor Wohnhaas, 'Die Stella musicae des Benediktiners Veit Bild: Eine spätmittelalterliche Musiklehre aus Augsburg', *JVAB*, 32 (1998), pp. 305–25. An issue of the *Jahrbuch des Vereins für Augsburger Bistumsgeschichte* (vol. 12 (1978)) was devoted to the saint's veneration in the diocese; see especially Peter Rummel, 'Zur Verehrungsgeschichte des heiligen Simperts', pp. 22–49; Theodor Wohnhaas, 'Zur Frühgeschichte der Simpertliturgie', pp. 50–60; Wilhelm Liebhart, 'Zur St. Simpert-Bruderschaft der Augsburger Bortenmacher bei St. Ulrich', pp. 108–16; Karl Kosel, 'Der hl. Simpert in der bildenden Kunst', pp. 61–95; and Adolf Layer, 'Ein Wallfahrtsgesang zu Ehren St. Simperts (1611)', pp. 96–107, which concerns the song that I will discuss presently. The era of Catholic renewal saw another revival of the saint's cult, sponsored especially by Abbot Johann von Merk (1600–32) and promoted by the monk (and choir director) Karl Stengel, who had his Latin *Vita S. Simperti episcopi Augustani et confess[oris]* and the German *Das Leben vnnd Wunderwerck des H. Simperti* published in Augsburg in 1615 and 1616 respectively. Stengel also brought out his *Der weltberühmten Kayserlichen Freyen, vnd deß H. Rö: ReichsStatt Augspurg in Schwaben, kurtze Kirchen Chronik, sampt dem Leben vnd Wunderzeichen der Heyligen, welche daselbsten gelebt/ in fünff vnderschidliche Bücher abgetheilt* (Augsburg: Sara Mang) in 1620, which includes a lengthy description of miracles, some older and some recent, associated with Simpert and other saints (including SS Ulrich, Afra, Narcissus and Gualfardus) whose remains lay in SS Ulrich and Afra. Pötzl, in 'Volksfrömmigkeit' (in Brandmüller, ed., *Handbuch der bayerischen Kirchengeschichte*), pp. 906–7, has seen the revival of Simpert veneration during this period as one typical expression of saintly devotion in the Counter-Reformation, comparable to the cults of SS Benno, Cosmas and Damian, which were promoted by Duke Maximilian I of Bavaria. Soergel (*Wondrous in His Saints*, p. 25) has seen the revival of Simpert veneration as a part of a deliberate renewal of medieval grave cults. Bishop Heinrich V raised the feast of St Simpert to a duplex in 1624, thus crowning the saint's gradual rehabilitation.

[131] The well-known *Geistliche Lieder vnd Psalmen* by Leisentrit, for example, contains an entire section of songs in honour of various saints. Individual, contemporary songsheets devoted to particular saints in the south German region include *Ein Andächtiger Rueff für die Pilgram. Vom H. Bischoff Bennone: Darinn sein Leben geuten Theils, vnd etliche Wunderwerck begriffen* (Munich: Adam Berg, 1603; RISM B/VIII, 1603[13]); *SchutzEngel. Ein new anmütig vnd Geistlich Lied/ Von den H. Engeln Gottes/ vnd sonderlich vom lieben H. SchutzEngel. Gestelt/ Vnd erstlich zur Kinderlehr gesungen/ durch ein Geistliche Person* (Konstanz: Leonhard Straub, 1612; RISM B/VIII, 1612[15]); *Andächtiger Ruff von dem heiligen Leben vnd Marterkampff der glorwürdigen Jungfrau Sanct Barbara. Gezogen auß den namhafften Griechischen vnd Lateinischen Scribenten* (Ingolstadt: A. Angermayer, 1613; RISM B/VIII, 1613[12]); *Geistlicher Ruff, zu dem heiligen Martyrer S. Veit, darinn sein Leben vnd Leyden begriffen. Mehr ein schöner Ruff, von vnser lieben Frawen, zu alten Oettingen* (Ingolstadt: A. Angermayer, 1613; RISM B/VIII, 1613[13]); and *Andächtiger vnd Catholischer Ruff/ von dem H. Regenspurgischen Bischoff S. Wolffgango* (Ingolstadt: A. Angermayer, 1613; RISM B/VIII, 1613[17]).

reflection of the greater official sanction for and prestige of the Marian and Eucharistic cults.[132]

In 1611, a monk and member of the Brotherhood of SS Ulrich and Afra, Tobias Haldewanger, brought out a small German songsheet in honour of SS Ulrich, Afra and Simpert, and dedicated it to Abbot Johann von Merk, who had worked to promote the cults of these patron saints in his church.[133] Haldewanger's *Drey schöne Lobliche Creützgesang* resembles other hagiographical literature stemming from SS Ulrich and Afra in the early seventeenth century (see especially the works of Karl Stengel, who was the choir director at the church from 1602) in that it offered a lengthy explication of the miracles performed by these saints, serving as an aid to devotion as well as an apologia for their cults.[134] The song in honour of St Ulrich, *In deinem Nam[en], Herr Jesu Christ*, has no fewer than 326 stanzas describing Ulrich's life and miracles, a text that required a brief, easily memorizable melody like the one given by Haldewanger (see Example 5.12).[135] Haldewanger provides similar melodies for the 102 stanzas of the song for St Simpert and the

---

[132] One example is the four Litanies of the Saints included in Johann Haym's *Litaniae Textus triplex*: these are identical to the Tridentine Litany of the Saints except for the interpolation of an invocation to St Ulrich. The highly schematic style of the polyphony is illustrated in Example 7.1 below.

[133] *Drey schöne Lobliche Creützgesang/ Die ersten zwey von den H. Bischoff vnd Beuchtigern S. Vlrich vnd S. Simprecht/ Das dritt von der H. Märterin S. Affra/ Hilaria/ sampt jrer H. Gesellschafft/ vnd diser Loblichen Reichstatt Augspurg Patronen allhie/ darinn die Histori jres H. Lebens vnd Marter begriffen/ sehr andächtig zu singen vnd zulesen/ &c.* (Augsburg: David Franck, 1611; RISM B/VIII, 1611[15]). Layer has discussed the song at length in 'Ein Wallfahrtsgesang zu Ehren St. Simperts'. Haldewanger seems to have served as a *Vorsinger* in Catholic processions. An extant expense sheet from the Trinity and St Sebastian confraternities, concerning a procession on the feast of the Purification of the Virgin Mary in 1626, records a payment of 12 Kreutzer 'dem haldenwanger, so Vorgesung[en]'. From StAA, KWA L361, '1626 Conto die Procession zu den siben Kürchen alhie zu Augspurg betreffendt.'

[134] The following works of Karl Stengel offer a useful comparison: *Vita S. Wicterpi episcopi Augustani et confessoris* (Augsburg: Christophorus Mang, 1607); *Vindiciae S. Udalrico Augustae Vindelicae episcopo datae* (Augsburg, 1614); *Vita S. Simperti episcopi Augustani et confess.* (Augsburg, 1615); *Das Leben vnnd Wunderwerck des H. Simperti* (Augsburg, 1616); and *Der weltberühmten Kayserlichen Freyen, vnd deß H. Rö: ReichsStatt Augspurg in Schwaben, kurtze Kirchen Chronik, sampt dem Leben vnd Wunderzeichen der Heyligen, welche daselbsten gelebt/ in fünff vnderschidliche Bücher abgetheilt* (Augsburg: Sara Mang, 1620). Stengel (1581–1663) linked a strong interest in hagiography and Mariology with historical research and palaeography; like local Jesuits such as Jacobus Pontanus and Georg Mayr he may be considered as an exponent of Catholic humanism. See Bellot, 'Humanismus – Bildungswesen – Buchdruck und Verlagsgeschichte', p. 354. Stengel later became abbot of the Benedictine abbey of Anhausen an der Brenz (see Layer, *Musik und Musiker der Fuggerzeit*, p. 42).

[135] 'In your name, Lord Jesus Christ, you who are the beginning of all saints, Jesus, have mercy upon us.' It is possible, as Layer suggests, that a local composer such as Aichinger

Example 5.12   *In deinem Nam[en], Herr Jesu Christ*, from Haldewanger, *Drey schöne Lobliche Creützgesang* (1611)

In dei - nem   nam[en] Herr___ Je - su   Christ/   der du   al - ler Hei - li -

gen an - fang_____   bist/   Je - su er - barm dich___ vn - ser.

91 stanzas of the song for St Afra, although for Simpert's song he also suggests the traditional Catholic tune *Jesus ist ein süsser Nam*, which was allowed in the diocesan Ritual and would have been well known to most Augsburg Catholics. Simple songs like these represent a simplification and popularization of these saints' legends for the benefit of a common audience.[136]

There is little direct evidence to suggest that the Augsburg Jesuits produced such songs themselves, but a song in honour of St George, published in Augsburg in 1621, is extant and bears the Jesuit seal on its title page.[137] The *Rueff von dem heyligen Ritter S. Gergen* contains a mostly conjunct, syllabic melody (shown in Example 5.13) and 108 stanzas of text describing St George's confrontation with the anti-Christian Roman emperor Diocletian, at the hands of whom he was martyred.[138] Each line is followed by the refrain 'Kyrie eleison' or 'Alleluia', similar to contemporary pilgrimage songs, although no

Example 5.13   *Rueff Von dem heyligen Ritter S. Gergen* (1621)

Zu   Got - tes   Lob,   d[er]   geh - ret   würd/   Ky - ri - e   e -

le - i - son.   Vbr   al - le   ding wie   sich   ge - bürt/   Al -

le - lu - ia/   mit süs - sem   Ton/   ge - lobt sey   Gott   in   sei - nem   Thron.

or Erbach may have penned the melody; see Layer, 'Ein Wallfahrtsgesang zu Ehren St. Simperts', p. 99.

[136] Ibid., p. 105.

[137] *Rueff Von dem heyligen Ritter S. Gergen* (Augsburg: Sara Mang, 1621; RISM B/VIII, 1621[10]).

[138] The text begins 'In praise of God, who is to be honoured, Kyrie eleison. Of all things which are proper, Alleluia. With sweetest sound, praise be to God in his throne.'

particular pilgrimage is mentioned in the text. Curiously, the song makes virtually no mention of St George's slaying of the dragon, the most popular imagery associated with this saint; rather, it reports the historical circumstances of his martrydom and holds him up as an example of fortitude against the Church's enemies. Thus the song, according to Peter Burke, embodies a kind of purification of popular religious tradition summarized by his idea of the 'Triumph of Lent', the clerical suppression or modification of popular rituals and festivities.[139] The numerous references in the text to obscure church figures of the late Roman era (such as St Venantius Fortunatus), as well as the presence of the Jesuit seal, suggest that this *Rueff* was not an unalloyed expression of popular culture, but rather invented by clerical elites.

The only other extant, printed hagiographical songs from Augsburg are a small songsheet, the *Drey Schöne Geistliche Lieder* (1635), with songs for St Catherine, St Barbara and for the new year; and a litany for St Roch (*c*.1650), but melodies are not indicated in either case.[140] It is likely, however, that extant printed songs, whether from presses in Augsburg or in nearby cities, only represent a tiny fraction of what fundamentally must have been an orally transmitted repertory.

The rise of confessionalized Catholic music in Augsburg was not a unique phenomenon, but also may be observed in numerous towns, cities and courts in Catholic Germany by the turn of the seventeenth century. The traditional scholarly emphasis on musical developments in Protestant areas after 1600, however, has put this repertory at a significant disadvantage. The sacred music of early Baroque Munich may be the most compelling example of this neglect: the volume and quality of Orlando di Lasso's music, as well as the cutbacks imposed on the size of the Bavarian ducal chapel by Duke Maximilian I after Lasso's death, have tended to obscure the fact that polyphony continued to be composed, performed and printed there. Moreover, Lasso's successors (including his sons Rudolph and Ferdinand, as well as other composers like Anton Holzner and Bernardino Borlasca) adopted a distinctly

---

[139] Burke, *Popular Culture in Early Modern Europe*, pp. 207–43; on this song in particular, see p. 216. The dragon does in fact appear briefly in a short prose prayer appended to the song, but it may be taken to symbolize the fires of hell: 'Ich bitt dich demütigklich/ erwirb mir von Gott behütung vor dem Höllischen Trachen/ vnd vor allen meinen Feinden/ sie seyen sichtbar oder vnsichtbar/ auff daß ich Gott mit freyem Gemüht angeneme Dienst erzeigen/ vnd mit dir ewigklichen mich frewen möge/ Amen.'

[140] *Drey Schöne Geistliche Lieder. Das Erst Von Sant Catharina. Das Ander/ Von S. Barbara. Das Dritte/ Wie man das Newe Jahr ansinget* (Augsburg: Michael Stör, 1635; exemplar in D-As, 12° Th Lt K 322); and *Letaney von dem Leben deß H. Beichtigers Rochi* (Augsburg, [*c*.1650]; exemplar in D-As, 2° Aug 3865).

different approach in their music: even more decisively than Aichinger in Augsburg, they fully embraced the new *concertato* idiom from Italy, and tended to prefer texts celebrating the Virgin Mary, the official 'patroness of Bavaria' (*Patrona Boiariae*). With the help of the active Jesuit college there, Munich also became a centre for the production of Catholic vernacular songs in the early seventeenth century. These developments reproduced themselves in Catholic centres such as Innsbruck, Salzburg and Konstanz in the early decades of the seventeenth century. The devotional and musical renewal of Catholicism in Augsburg was not simply a local phenomenon, but also had its analogues in other places where the Counter-Reformation took hold. The main difference, perhaps, was that for Augsburg's Catholic minority the religious stakes were considerably higher.

In which aspects was this music unmistakably 'Catholic'? In Aichinger's *Lacrumae*, as in other polyphonic prints by Catholic composers in Augsburg around the turn of the seventeenth century, a 'Catholic' sensibility emerges not only from the choice of Marian and Christological themes, for example, but also from the texts' individualistic, subjective and often vividly imagistic character, contrasting with the more abstract and communal quality of Protestant psalms and chorales. One is naturally inclined to ask, however, whether this confessional differentiation extended itself also to compositional style. Composers in Augsburg were of course fascinated with Italian models, ranging from the madrigal to the canzonetta to the vocal concerto, but no sharp confessional lines can be drawn: Adam Gumpelzhaimer, the Protestant cantor of St Anna, wrote in the style of the canzonetta throughout his career (see Chapter 3), while Hans Leo Hassler, a Protestant composer once in the employ of the Fugger family, issued books of both madrigals and canzonettas.[141] Experimentation with thoroughbass technique seems to have been limited to Aichinger, Klingenstein and Zindelin, although Gumpelzhaimer did add a continuo part to his second book of *Sacrorum Concentuum* in 1614.[142] Given the active engagement of later Protestant composers such as Johann Hermann Schein, Heinrich Schütz and Samuel Scheidt with the vocal concerto, one can hardly argue that this genre had any definite confessional implications. Nor does any documentary evidence from

---

[141] See his *Canzonette a quatro voci ... libro primo* (Nuremberg: Catharina Gerlach, 1590; RISM A/I, H2335), *Madrigali a 5. 6. 7. & 8. voci* (Augsburg: Valentin Schönig, 1596; RISM A/I, H2339) and *Neüe Teütsche gesang nach art der welschen Madrigalien und Canzonetten, mit 4. 5. 6. unnd 8. Stimmen* (Augsburg: Valentin Schönig, 1596; RISM A/I, H2336).

[142] On the other hand, the continuo part in this polychoral collection assumes the character of a *basso seguente* rather than an independent part.

Augsburg survive that suggests the embrace or rejection of certain musical genres on confessional grounds, either by Catholics or Protestants. There is no reason, then, to doubt the assertion that there was no 'confessional music' with respect to style, since music inherently tends to lack the ability to make concrete statements in the absence of specific texts and specific performance circumstances.[143]

If one regards music as a cultural practice, however, one that embraces style but also the circumstances of the music's creation, the nature of its texts, the circumstances in which it was performed and its influence on performers and listeners, then the idea of 'confessional music' becomes not only possible but necessary. Although the creative abilities and personal prejudices of individual composers were essential conditions of this music's creation, much of this repertory can only be fully appreciated through an understanding of the institutional and patronage contexts in which it arose. As Leeman Perkins has recently written, the 'true historical significance and ... original esthetic sense' of Renaissance music 'become evident only when viewed – insofar as the present state of musical scholarship will allow – from the conceptual matrix that produced it'.[144] This matrix was constituted not only by the stylistic and technical resources of composers, but also by the networks of patronage, ideology, dissemination and performance that the music required.

The pervasive – yet understandable – tendency among music historians to equate the musical significance of the Counter-Reformation with its specific effects on the technique of polyphonic composition has tended to obscure the diversity and cultural significance of post-Tridentine Catholic music.[145] Despite discussions on various aspects of church music, the Council of Trent in the end only issued a vague canon that all things 'lascivious or impure' should be omitted from the divine service; the requirement of textual intelligibility, often seen as a central concern of the Council, was in fact never approved. The Council left the implementation of their decrees on music to local authorities, and it was in the hands of individual composers (like Vincenzo Ruffo, to use Lewis

---

[143] On this point see Danckwardt, 'Konfessionelle Musik?', p. 377.

[144] Perkins, *Music in the Age of the Renaissance*, p. 970.

[145] Robert Kendrick, noting this historiographical trend with respect to Italian repertories, has written (in *Celestial Sirens: Nuns and their Music in Early Modern Milan* (Oxford: Clarendon Press; New York: Oxford University Press, 1996), p. 8) that 'any considerations of possible polystilism have been lost in the teleological rush to separate "modern" monodic from "conservative" *stile antico* approaches, normally to the detriment of the latter, or to define "progressive" trends in the Seicento motet. Much work has relied on an explicitly evolutionist view, with "minor figures" important only in so far as they strove towards the formal syntheses and expressive devices of either Monteverdi or the "High Baroque".'

Lockwood's example) to imagine possible solutions, sometimes at the behest of specific prelates.[146] In the music of Catholic Augsburg, too, the content and intelligibility of texts seems to have been of paramount importance, but this point has been obscured by an overemphasis on the adoption of thoroughbass technique by Aichinger and Klingenstein.[147] From the standpoint of the Catholic renewal and its effect on musical culture, Aichinger's adoption of the thoroughbass is no more or less significant than the care with which he set texts, the strongly confessionalized content of his prints and the variety of devotional performance contexts for which he designed his music. For Aichinger genre and style were indeed important, not for their inherent value as 'progressive' or 'conservative' approaches, but rather for their suitability for contemporary musicians and audiences. Religious ideology, musical fashion and practicality were the main forces that shaped his music and that of his colleagues.

---

[146] For example, Carlo Borromeo and Vitellozo Vitelli, members of the commission of Cardinals charged with the implementation the Tridentine decrees, convened singers at Vitelli's residence in April 1565 'to sing some masses and test whether the words could be understood, as their Eminences desire'. The actual canon issued by the Council, however, makes no mention of this desire. The tendency towards syllabic homophony in Vincenzo Ruffo's church music, in particular, was a consequence of Borromeo's instruction to his vicar that 'I would like you to speak with the chapel master there [Ruffo] and tell him to reform the singing so that the words may be as intelligible as possible, as you know it is ordered by the Council.' Quoted in Monson, 'The Council of Trent Revisited', pp. 24–25.

[147] Bukofzer, for example, offered a severely distorted picture of their output, mentioning only the concertos of Aichinger's *Cantiones ecclesiasticae* (1607) and Klingenstein's *Liber primus s. Symphoniarum* (1607). Otherwise he asserted that Aichinger 'was indebted to the style of Palestrina rather than that of his teacher Gabrieli', a puzzling assertion given Aichinger's preference for fewer-voiced forms such as the sacred canzonetta. See Bukofzer, *Music in the Baroque Era* (New York: Norton, 1947), pp. 96–97. Bukofzer probably examined only the edition of Kroyer (see 'Gregor Aichingers Leben und Werke'), who included only Aichinger's works in a traditional, imitative style. Aichinger's use of thoroughbass has received close attention from Hettrick (see 'The Thorough-Bass in the Works of Gregor Aichinger' and his editions of the *Cantiones ecclesiasticae* and *The Vocal Concertos*) and Kirwan-Mott (*The Small-Scale Sacred Concertato*, pp. 48–52).

CHAPTER SIX

So vil Choros Musicorum: Music in Catholic Processions

No other phenomenon symbolized the consolidation of the Counter-Reformation in the city of Augsburg by 1600 more effectively than the elaborate Catholic processions that wound their way through city streets – and indeed, through Protestant residential areas. For local Catholic officials, processions involving images, quasi-theatrical displays of biblical stories, bloody self-flagellation, litanies and songs were an effective medium for sharpening the cultural boundaries between the city's Catholics and Protestants. Such displays of faith and solidarity served to bolster Catholic identity from within, while making a considerable impression – whether positive or negative – on Protestant observers. Particularly in the first decade of the seventeenth century, processions on Good Friday and on the feast of Corpus Christi were, in effect, multimedia spectacles involving the participation of hundreds of clergy, members of religious orders and confraternities and Catholic laypersons. Along with the revived pilgrimage to the 'Holy Mountain' of Andechs in Bavaria (discussed in Chapter 7), these public processions were tangible, public demonstrations of Catholic devotion and propaganda, and demanded appropriate music in the form of litanies and songs. Contemporary accounts demonstrate the types of music heard, as well as the integral role played by music in the conduct of these rituals.

The public processions that culminated in the yearly spectacles on Good Friday and Corpus Christi were in fact extensions of practices having a long tradition, at least within church walls.[1] Regular processions through the cathedral's cloister before Sunday Mass took place at least as early as the late fifteenth century; the diocesan *Obsequiale*, or Ritual, of 1487 mandated that the choir sing penitential antiphons (*Sancta Maria, succurre miseris*; *Iniquitates nostras aufer a nobis*), responsories (*Absolve Domine animas eorum*), and psalms (*Domine ne in furore tuo*) as the procession passed the graves of the

---

[1] A surviving early sixteenth-century processional from the cathedral, ABA, Hs 27, confirms the existence of musically accompanied processions well before the period under discussion. Processions were sometimes also called for in the yearly memorials for deceased persons (for example, Wolfgang de Zilnhart in 1514, in ABA, BO 8191).

departed.[2] In addition to these, processions with accompanying music (mostly responsories, antiphons, hymns and litanies) were mandated for first, second and sometimes both Vespers services for major feasts of the Sanctorale, although a few of these were eliminated with the introduction of the Roman Rite in 1597.[3] The only processions that seem regularly to have ventured beyond the properties of individual churches were the Rogation week processions held by the Benedictines of SS Ulrich and Afra. On the feast of St Mark the monks with their acolytes would process with banners and relics to the church of St Moritz; on the second day of Rogation week, they processed to the church of Heilig Kreuz; on the third day, to St Georg; and on the fourth day, to the cathedral. Several sixteenth-century manuscript processionals belonging to SS Ulrich and Afra, however, make no reference to any music sung in transit between the abbey and the other churches; the notated antiphons and responsories are to be sung upon entering the churches, leaving the churches, or during services within the churches.[4] Although one cannot exclude the possibility that the monks and acolytes sang along the public route, it is likely that (perceived or actual) Protestant opposition prevented excessive musical elaboration.

The late sixteenth- and early seventeenth-century bishops of Augsburg

---

[2] This procession survived into the nineteenth century, when it was often called a *visitatio sepulchri* or *sepulchrorum*; see Hoeynck, *Geschichte der kirchlichen Liturgie des Bisthums Augsburg*, pp. 177–78.

[3] An extant *Antiphonarium* from the cathedral sacristy, ABA, Hs 31, perhaps dating from the late sixteenth century, provides detailed instructions and chant notation for Vespers processions in both the Temporale and the Sanctorale. Comparing this possibly pre-1597 codex with a processional dating from around 1620 (ABA, Hs 31a), we find that few of the earlier processions were eliminated at the cathedral after the introduction of the Roman Rite: these were the processions for the feasts of the Purification of the BVM, St Gertrude, Annunciation of the BVM and the Beheading of John the Baptist. Those processions added were for the second, third and fourth Sundays of Advent, and the feasts of St Stephen, St John the Evangelist, Maundy Thursday, Holy Saturday, St Mark, Visitation of the BVM, St Augustine and Saints Simon and Jude. The particular feasts requiring Vespers processions, however, seem to have changed even before 1597. Hoeynck, in *Geschichte der kirchlichen Liturgie des Bisthums Augsburg*, pp. 194–96, provides a list of feasts from the Sanctorale requiring processions from a 1495 processional: between that time and the late sixteenth century, processions were added for the feasts of St Mary Magdalene, St Afra, the Beheading of John the Baptist, Guardian Angels, St Ursula and St Narcissus. Although the situation is clearly complex, we can say that the number of liturgical processions in the cathedral increased after the introduction of the Roman Rite.

[4] The processionals, housed in the Staats- und Stadtbibliothek Augsburg, include 4° Cod. 156 (dated 1572), 4° Cod. 157 (dated 1582), 8° Cod. 24 (dated 1554), 8° Cod. 60 (dated 1589), and 8° Cod. 63 (dated 1589). All of these agree in general terms as to the content of these processions. Only the first three of these refer to a procession to a church of St Margaret, a small chapel in the vicinity of SS Ulrich and Afra, on the feast of Corpus Christi.

promoted the gradual extension of Catholic processions beyond the churches and through the city, but they simultaneously sought to control their organization. Music, as an essential component of processions, was also mandated and regulated. The *Ritus ecclesiastici Augustensis Episcopatus* issued by Bishop Marquard von Berg in 1580 contains detailed instructions on the musical accompaniment for the liturgically sanctioned processions on the feast of St Mark (involving the *Litaniae maiores*, or Greater Litanies of the saints), on the three Rogation Days preceding the feast of Ascension (involving the *Litaniae minores*, or Lesser Litanies of the saints), on occasion of public supplications due to 'tyranny, the Turkish [threat] or a hostile invasion, for the aversion of calamity, plague, famine or war, or to pray for peace', and for the feast of Corpus Christi.[5] Marquard encouraged the use not only of litanies, but also of German vernacular songs on the feast of St Mark and Rogation Days:

> The use of old songs, which have been established to be Catholic and approved, is to be permitted to the populace. Moreover, let the voices of those singing in German be as pious, sweet and consonant as possible, especially when they come to this or that church in these processions, or otherwise, for the sake of religion.[6]

For processions on occasion of war, famine or other calamities, Marquard called for the singing of specific antiphons, responsories and hymns. For example, the responsory *Spiritus ubi vult spirat* was to be sung if the procession was against the 'infidels' [*infideles*], the responsory *Tua est potentia* was to be sung as a supplication for peace and the responsory *Exaudi* was to be sung as a supplication for rain or fair weather.[7] Although it is difficult to associate the symbolism of *Spiritus ubi vult spirat* with anti-Turkish sentiment,[8] the phrase 'da pacem, Domine' in *Tua est potentia* reflects the call for peace, while *Exaudi* is clearly a supplication to God that he hear the prayers of his people.

---

[5] *Ritus ecclesiastici Augustensis episcopatus*, pp. 604–13, 613–17 and 621–24. The litanies called for in the diocesan Rituals of the late sixteenth and early seventeenth centuries may have been only a fraction of those used in liturgical contexts in earlier centuries; the official sanction of the Litany of Loreto during this period may have led to the neglect of these alternatives. See Hoeynck, *Geschichte der kirchlichen Liturgie des Bisthums Augsburg*, pp. 187–89. On 'weather processions' as a form of supplication, see Scribner, *Popular Culture and Popular Movements in Reformation Germany*, pp. 34–35.

[6] 'Cantionum veterum vsus, cum eas catholicas & probatas esse constat, populo permittatur. Sint autem Germanicè canentium voces piæ, suaues & consonæ, quoad eius fieri potest, maximè quum in hisce Processionibus, aut aliàs, religionis ergô ad hance vel illam Ecclesiam peregrinantur.' See *Ritus ecclesiastici Augustensis episcopatus*, pp. 604–13.

[7] Ibid., pp. 613–17.

[8] A passage from John 3:8 in which Jesus assures the Pharisee Nicodemus that 'The wind blows where it wills; you hear the sound of it, but you do not know where it comes

Heinrich V's Ritual of 1612 also provided for such observances, although the musical accompaniment was now also to include litanies, a Mass and various psalms.[9]

In the 1580s Marquard von Berg also mandated a quarterly general procession (the so-called *Quatemberprozession*) throughout the diocese for the aversion of plague and war and for the defence of the church. He issued a detailed ordinance for this procession on 29 May 1587, which was to be held on Trinity Sunday, the Sunday following the feast of the Exaltation of the Cross, the Sunday following the feast of St Luke and the second Sunday of Lent. The first procession on Trinity Sunday was to have the following order:

> In this procession the following shall be sung or spoken while kneeling, according to the circumstances of the place: [the antiphon] *Veni sancte Spiritus* with versicle and collect, followed by the [antiphon] *Exaudi nos* with versicle and collect; then the [antiphon] *Exurge Domine*, with the antiphon *Oremus dilectissimi*. Following this [the procession] shall depart for the designated place, or proceed around the church, according to the circumstances of the place, with the responsory *Summæ Trinitati*. When [the procession] re-enters [the church], the antiphon *Iniquitates nostras* shall be sung; then, kneeling, [the people] shall pray Psalm 24, *Ad te Domine levavi*, with the usual prayers. After this begins the Office of the Holy Trinity, during which collects against plague, famine, ... and for whatsoever tribulations shall be heard, from the new Missal. After all of this is completed, [a] litany follows in all four [quarterly] processions, which is to be sung, or spoken with a distinct voice and prayed, according to the circumstances of the place and persons.[10]

The other three quarterly processions were to follow this basic order, except that the specific antiphons, responsories and collects were exchanged for others appropriate to the season. The wording of Marquard's ordinance, allowing the procession to proceed either to a designated destination or simply around the church [*an ein ort zu der Procession deputirt, oder vmb die Kirchen/ nach gelegenheit*], reflects the restricted range of public processions in the city of Augsburg.[11]

---

from, or where it is going. So with everyone who is born from spirit.' Trans. from *The New English Bible with the Apocrypha* (Oxford: Oxford University Press; Cambridge: Cambridge University Press, 1970).

[9] *Liber Ritualis, Episcopatus Augustensis*, pp. 145–62.

[10] From 'Ordnung der vier Quattemberlichen Processionen/ wie die/ nach laut des jüngst publicierten Mandats/ durch das gantz Bisthumb Augspurg sollen gehalten vnd angestellet werden', 29 May 1587, in ABA, BO 733.

[11] Hoeynck notes that Heinrich V reconfirmed the *Quatemberprozession* during his tenure, but I have as of yet been unable to find original documentation for this (*Geschichte der kirchlichen Liturgie des Bisthums Augsburg*, p. 181). By this time the procession surely

In the early seventeenth century, Bishop Heinrich V also called for processions with the Greater and Lesser Litanies on the feast of St Mark and Rogation Days, but Heinrich was more specific than Marquard about their organization and musical accompaniment. After providing a number of appropriate antiphons, the diocesan Ritual of 1612 gives the following order for the procession:

> Afterwards, all hitherto having knelt, two singers kneeling before the altar in back of the celebrant begin the ordained Greater Litanies ... each verse is to be completed gravely in its entirety; thus, *Pater de cælis DEVS, miserere nobis*, and likewise for the remaining verses, the chorus always responding similarly. And with the singing of *Sancta Maria, ora pro nobis*, the procession begins towards the destined church, and proceeds in this order: in the cathedral, as given in the Roman Ceremonial ...; in the remaining churches, the banners precede [the procession], along with the lay confraternities with their banners, if they are present. Then, if present, the religious [orders]; then the chorus of the singers. Then follows an acolyte carrying a cross, accompanied by two other acolytes carrying lanterns fixed onto poles, if they are available. Then follow two clerics or singers who sing the litany, immediately followed by the remaining clergy in order. In the last place comes the celebrant in a cope ... According to the custom of the place relics of the saints may be displayed, preceded immediately by a deacon and subdeacon clothed in a dalmatic and tunic of the same colour ...

> If the Litanies begun do not suffice, they may be repeated, and nothing else should be sung.

> If by chance the procession happens upon some church that is not the destination, the Litanies may be interrupted to sing a responsory or antiphon of the saint or saints in whose honour the church was consecrated, along with the appropriate versicle and collects; then the Litany may resume.
>
> Once the procession reaches the destined church, the following Psalm [*Deus in adiutorium*] is to be sung before the doors of the said church. Then, the cross being leaned against the wall, and the others (if present) arranged reverently at the altar, the priest, who is before the middle of the altar between two acolytes holding lamps, sings the following versicles and the chorus responds, everyone kneeling [there follows in the Ritual a series of short versicles and responses]. Then the celebrant rises alone, saying [a prayer] in the ferial tone [the prayer follows in the Ritual]. Then a Rogation Mass is celebrated as in the Missal ... When the Mass has ended an antiphon of the saint [or saints] who are the patron[s] of the church is to be sung with versicle and collect; and, the Litanies being resumed, the procession returns to the same church from which it had started. Upon entering the church, omitting the Psalm and prayers, the

would have been extended into Protestant neighbourhoods, as was customary for Good Friday and Corpus Christi (see below).

antiphon *Regina cœli lætare* is to be sung with versicle and collect as a conclusion, as below.[12]

Heinrich's ordinance confirms the centrality of music in this ritual, but it is noteworthy that he does not allow German vernacular song as had his predecessor Marquard von Berg. Marquard's Ritual of 1580 reflects the looser, more traditional practice of the Augsburg Rite, while Heinrich's Ritual of 1612 demonstrates his determination to adhere to the precise prescriptions of Roman, Tridentine practice, regardless of popular traditions. Heinrich's inflexibility may also have resulted from the difficulty of controlling the numbers and quality of the musicians who accompanied the processions. In June of 1609, for example, some musicians petitioned the cathedral chapter for compensation since Heinrich had dismissed them from a communal feast. It came out, however, that

> many musicians participate in the music, [who are] superfluous and are more of a hindrance than a help. The Herr *Kapellmeister* [i.e., Bernhard Klingenstein] should be spoken to and commanded, that when he wishes to have additional music in the future, he should submit a list of the musicians he wishes and needs to use.[13]

Apart from the regular quarterly processions and those falling on feast days such as St Mark, Rogation Days, Good Friday and Corpus Christi (see below), the bishop and/or the cathedral chapter ordered special processions in observance of political or ecclesiastical events (such as the election of a new bishop or emperor), or to invoke heavenly intercession (on occasion of war, pestilence or drought), with increasing frequency in the late sixteenth and early seventeenth centuries. Occasional processions fulfilled a spiritual function, in that they embodied the community's appeal to God, Christ, the Virgin Mary and the saints to come to their aid in times of great need. In this sense they played a role in a 'spiritual economy' not unlike that played by pilgrimage shrines, in which devotion could be exchanged for intercession.[14] On the other hand, occasional processions also fulfilled a political function, in that they represented a public projection of the Catholic Church's hierarchical authority – particularly when the procession observed the election of a new bishop or pope – while dramatizing the Catholic doctrine of an intercession that was tied to a particular supplication at a given time or place. The embellishment of these processions with music and images was, of course, not quite as elaborate as that called for in the great yearly processions, but much evidence suggests the

---

[12] *Liber Ritualis, Episcopatus Augustensis*, pp. 139–45.
[13] *DR*, 22 June 1609.
[14] See Soergel, *Wondrous in His Saints*, pp. 20–21.

participation of singers and instrumentalists, and the singing of litanies in particular.

One need not make a firm distinction between political processions and those invoking heavenly intercession. Although the latter type of procession arguably concerned itself less with political representation than with spiritual need, it nonetheless involved a public and quasi-theatrical demonstration of the Catholic Church's doctrine (as well as popular belief) that heavenly intervention could follow from the specific, public supplications at a given place and time (again, the relationship to pilgrimage is clear). The penitential antiphon *Media vita in morte sumus*, whose text brings out the need for heavenly intercession emphasized in Catholic doctrine (*amarae morti ne tradas nos* – 'do not give us over to bitter death'), was appropriate for processions called by the bishop to avert plague – a near constant threat in this period. In 1563, Bishop Otto Truchseß von Waldburg ordered one such procession with this antiphon, to take place after the completion of the Mass 'in order to placate the divine will'. Furthermore, he ordained that regular processions with litanies were to be held in the cathedral and other churches on every Tuesday.[15]

Litanies for the Virgin, Christ or the saints were a vital component of these penitential processions, having a cyclical form well suited to the rhythms of walking. Bishop Johann Otto von Gemmingen called for litanies and the *Media vita* in a public procession in 1592 to avert the plague as well as the Turkish threat:

> On 19 August 1592 the first procession against the plague and the Turks was established, with the celebrant and two levites dressed in purple robes. In this procession, which was led on the high road (but not beyond this) to the church of St Johannes, two crosses, four banners, the sacred robes of St Ulrich (his chasuble and cope), a vessel of holy water, and a censer were carried; after the litanies had been sung [the procession] arrived again at the new [east] choir, where, after the Office had been completed, the antiphon *Media vita* with its collect was sung.[16]

Litanies were also called for in the so-called *actio gratiarum*, or

---

[15] 'Augustæ uerò Clerus communicatis consilijs statuit, ad placandum Numen Diuinum, ut omnibus parochijs post absolutio Mißæ officium, antiphona, Media in uita sumus ~ canatur ... Singulis itidem diebus Lunæ in ecclesia B.V. Mariè proceßio cum litanijs ... et imitati cæteri religiosi et capitula in suis etiam ecclesijs instituunt.' From the 'Annales Augustani' of Reginbald Möhner, ABA, Hs 52, vol. 2, p. 1054.

[16] From 'Geschichtliche Darstellungen in Latein', ABA, BO 2296, p. 8. Other accounts of processions specifically to avert the plague, but without musical references, may be found in ABA, BO 733 (a mandate, dated 7 September 1580, by Marquard von Berg) and in *DR*, 9 August 1627 (which discusses plans to participate in a procession organized by the St Sebastian confraternity).

thanksgiving, when plague had passed. Eight months after the aforementioned procession, on 19 March 1593, the chapter ordered a procession that likewise was to make its way to the nearby church of St Johannes. The services included an Office of the Holy Trinity and the singing of litanies.[17]

Litanies also formed the core of the musical accompaniment to late sixteenth-century processions to avert the Turkish threat or to celebrate military victories over the Turks. In a procession against the Turks in January 1595, for example, the chapter instructed that litanies were to be sung on the streets each time the procession entered or left the cathedral.[18] A much more detailed account survives for a procession celebrating the imperial victory over the Turks at Raab in Hungary a few years later, which was one of the first Catholic processions to travel the length of the city (see also below). Held on 12 April 1598, the procession went from the cathedral to SS Ulrich and Afra, and included the bishop, the cathedral clergy, members of religious orders, confraternities and other laypersons, all accompanied by over a hundred soldiers, which were ordered by the city government for the occasion. Within the procession itself, the Marian Congregation from St Salvator 'sang a fine litany of Our Blessed Lady', while other singers from the cathedral 'sang figurally a litany of the Name of Jesus all of the way to St Ulrich [and Afra]'.[19] Following this manuscript's listing of the order of the procession is a narrative of the events of the day. Before the procession departed from the cathedral, a polyphonic setting of the *Veni sancte Spiritus* was

---

[17] 'Anno 1593 die 19 Martij ex mandato Reverendissimi Capitulis propter Contagionem cessantem pro gratiarum actione Processio fuit instituta hoc modo: finità missà matutinà, habitisque vigiliis, Prima, et Tertia /: sub quibus officiator sacris vestibus induebatur:/ decantatæ sunt. tum Processio in chorum ac mox sine statione, per stratum altum vulgò *über den hochen weeg* ad ecclesiam S. Joannis ducta fuit, ubi officio de SS. Trinitate cantato, cum litaniis iterum in novum chorum reversa fuit ~'. From 'Geschichtliche Darstellungen in Latein', ABA, BO 2296, p. 8.

[18] 'herr Sigmundt Hueber, soll vom wogen schierister gemainer *processionum, Contra Turcam*, beschaiden werden. Meine gnedige herrn, lassen Innen gefallen, Erstmalls dz *officium de S: Cruce*, vnd dz anndermall dz *officium de Beata Maria Virgine*, durch meinen gnedigen herrn *Suffraganeum* zuhaltten, vnnd dz jedesmalls ann hinauß vnd herein geen, ein letanei vff den gassen gesungen werde, Wie aber vnnd durch was ortt, Mann gehen, Er Minister, Sich schiersten afftermontags zuuor, bei wolermelten meinen gnedigen herrn, nach gelegenhaitt wetters, entlichen beschaidts erhallen solle.' DR, 20 January 1595. Bishop Johann Otto von Gemmingen's mandate for the procession had come on 6 January; see Zoepfl, *Das Bistum Augsburg*, p. 718.

[19] 'die *Congregation* daselbst, welche ein schöne Letaneÿ gesungen von vnser Frawenn' ... 'die Leser von vnser Frawen, Welche die Letanei *de n[omine] JESV* biß geen S. Vlrich *figuraliter* gesungen'. From ABA, Hs 34, 'Anweisungen über die Abhaltung verschiedener Feierlichkeiten in der Augsburger Domkirche 1582–1603', fols. 14r–16r.

sung,[20] and upon arrival at SS Ulrich and Afra a Te Deum was performed while all the church bells of the city were rung for 15 minutes.[21] After this the consecrating bishop sang a Mass of the Holy Trinity, and then the litany of the saints was begun as the procession left the church; the litany continued to be sung all of the way back to the cathedral.[22]

Since this procession celebrated a military action against the Turks, it may not have given rise to Protestant objections such as those against the Good Friday procession (see below); indeed, Augsburg's Catholics may well have chosen this celebration of Imperial (as opposed to Catholic) arms as a suitable opportunity to extend their procession over the length of the entire city. This lack of a strong confessional orientation may also explain its elaborateness, and the city's approval of a military escort for it. On the other hand, the near constant presence along the route of monophonic and polyphonic litanies for the Virgin, the Name of Jesus, and the saints gave this procession a specifically Catholic aural profile, not unlike other Catholic processions for Good Friday or Corpus Christi, or the pilgrimages to nearby Andechs discussed in Chapter 7.

Occasional processions with litanies embodied the Catholic ideal of public supplication, but they also helped to promote the authority of Catholic tradition in the eyes of participants and observers. The custom of holding public processions on important political occasions was observed at least as early as 1548, when Bishop Otto Truchseß celebrated the Imperial promulgation of the Interim (ensuring the religious rights of Catholics in Imperial cities and leading to the installation of a patrician oligarchy in the city government, guaranteeing a share of civic authority to Catholics) with a procession including Emperor Charles V and his musical chapel, which 'dolefully sang the hymn *Pange lingua*'.[23] After roughly 1590, processions were mandated in observance of Jubilee years, which were intermittently declared by the

---

[20] 'Nach solchem hat man vf dem fruemeß altaar ein meß gelesen, vnd darzwischen die *Sextum* vnd *Nonam* in dem Chor gesungen, darnach hatt man dz *Veni S. Spiritus &c.* *figuraliter* gar herrlich gesungen, mit volgend[er] *collecta*.' Ibid.

[21] 'Nach den *precib.* hat man dz *Te DEVM laudamus &c.* gar *solemniter* gesungen, Intzwischen ist in d[er] gantzen statt in allen Kirchen vnd Capelln ein gantze Viertl stund mit alen glokhen zusamben gelitten worden.' Ibid.

[22] 'Nach dem *Te DEVM laudamus &c.* hat der herr Weihbischoff dz ambt vf S. Vlrichs altar von der allerheyligisten dreyfaltigkheit gesungen. Nach dem ambt hat man die gewondlche Letaneÿ von den lieben heyligen angefangen zuesingen vnd ist wid[er]vmb herab gangen, wie man hinauf gangen, vnd hat die Letanei alle weil gesungen'. Ibid.

[23] 'Othone Episcopo cum cathedrali Capitulo et choro occidentalj pœnitentibus obviam eunte, et Cæsarenis Musicis Hymnum: *Pange Lingua* ~ lugubrè Concinentibus.' This event is described in ABA, BO 2296, 'Geschichtliche Darstellungen in Latein', pp. 5–6, as well as in ABA, BO 7257, 'Domkapitelische Chronologie'. The latter refers to the participation of the 'Imperial singers, trumpeters, and pipers' [*cantores, tubicines et tibicines Imperatoris*].

papacy; evidence survives for such processions in 1592, 1606, 1620, 1628, 1630 and 1632.[24] Unfortunately we know little about the musical accompaniment for these processions, but at the very least the cathedral cantorate would have been involved: for example, during the preparations for the 1592 procession, the cathedral dean sought to determine whether polyphonic music would be required. The chapter resolved that 'such polyphonic music shall be allowed, as it was also used similarly last year during Lent'.[25]

The bishop also mandated processions on the accessions or deaths of important political or church leaders. Bishop Otto Truchseß von Waldburg mandated prayers and processions for the accession of Ferdinand I in 1558;[26] and on 28 May 1572 he ordered that the recent death of Pope Paul V should be commemorated throughout the diocese with an Office or Mass for the Dead, 'after which a public, communal procession shall be held with the highest possible devotion and humility, with a sung or prayed litany, and Holy Mass'.[27] Similarly elaborate processions were held for the election of new bishops in the diocese of Augsburg. The election of Johann Otto von Gemmingen in 1591, for example, occasioned 'a solemn procession to the chapel of St John, where the Office of the Holy Trinity was sung by the suffragan bishop; afterwards the procession, accompanied by the singing of litanies, proceeded from the nave into the choir, where the silver high altar was opened'.[28] In this case litanies called for celestial intercession on behalf of the newly elected bishop. The mere presence of the emperor in Augsburg inevitably triggered a procession with musical embellishment. An extant processional from the cathedral (c.1620) records that in 1619,

> on the Feast of the Dedication of Augsburg Cathedral, the Roman Emperor Ferdinand II was received around 11.00 by Heinrich V,

---

While the former source speaks of the procession extending to various public squares in the city [De urbis Plateis pro Candandis Euangeliis quatuor erigebantur altaria], the latter source states that the procession merely went 'around the cathedral' [circa Ecclesiam Cathedralem].

[24] Most of these references are culled from the DR; see 14 and 16 March 1592, 6 March 1620, 3 June 1628, 29 December 1629 and 21 January 1632. For the Jubilee procession of 1606, see ABA, BO 2296, p. 11.

[25] 'Vff meines gnedigen herrn Thumbdechandts proposition, ob beÿ schierister publica proceßione deß Jubilei halber, cantus figuratus zugebrauchen seye, oder nicht, Isst befolhen, sollichen cantum figuratum fürgehen zulassen, wo es in gleichem vor einem Jhar In der Fassten, auch allso gehalten worden sein, zubefinden.' DR, 16 March 1592.

[26] StAA, KWA B17³.

[27] 'Nach solchem aber ein offentliche gemaine Proceßion mit gesungner ober gebetteter Letania vnd ampt der heyligen Meß/ mit höchster möglichster andacht vnd demut halten'. StAA, KWA B10⁵.

[28] ABA, BO 2296, 'Geschichtliche Darstellungen in Latein' (1457–1741), p. 7.

Bishop of Augsburg, with the entire clergy; [the bishop] processed out of the church to meet [the emperor] at [his] lodging with a canopy carried by six canons ... The order of ceremony followed that prescribed in the Pontifical, except that following the prayers of absolution and the collects, the Te Deum laudamus was intoned by [the bishop] and sung in polyphony by the musicians with the organ; to this were added the versicle and collects of the Holy Trinity. The versicle was *Benedicamus Patrem et Filium cum Sancto spiritu*. The responsory was *Laudemus et superexaltemus eum in sæcula*.[29]

The Te Deum carried a great symbolic weight and was sung particularly on the occasion of military victories or other important political events, not only in processions but also in other paraliturgical contexts. Although liturgical books fixed the order of such ceremonies, there was some flexibility in the musical accompaniment; for example, as the emperor approached the church, the antiphon *Ecce mitto Angelum meum* (again, the antiphon makes explicit the theme of heavenly intervention) could be followed by whatever 'hymns or other devotional songs might be desired' [*Hymni vel alia cantica devota, prout magis placebit*].[30]

Military conflicts, from those between Imperial and Turkish armies, to the battles of the Thirty Years War, also occasioned processions on behalf of Christian – or Catholic – victory. The above-mentioned *Quatemberprozessionen* mandated by Bishop Marquard von Berg in 1587, in fact, were occasioned in part by the ongoing military conflict in the Netherlands between the Spanish and the Dutch.[31] Furthermore, the cathedral chapter minutes record processions that were mandated at the outset of the Thirty Years War in 1618, as well as in 1620.[32] Perhaps the most elaborate of these 'political' processions, and the one about which we are best informed, accompanied the return of the holy host of Heilig Kreuz, the *Wunderbares Gut*, to Augsburg after the Swedish army abandoned the city in March 1635. In Chapter 8 I shall return to the written accounts of the music and engravings depicting this event, which provide a suitable ending point for our narrative.

Music, Spectacle and Propaganda in Early Seventeenth-Century Processions

With the exception of the 1635 procession honouring the return of the

---

[29] ABA, Hs 31a, 'Processionale pro Cathedrali Choro Augustanum renovatum Anno 1620', p. 296.

[30] Ibid., p. 291.

[31] See his mandate dated 27 April 1587, in StAA, KWA B10[11].

[32] *DR*, 3 August 1618 and 6 March 1620.

Wunderbares Gut, the processions described so far – including regular liturgical processions in and around Catholic churches and occasional processions to invoke heavenly intercession or to celebrate political events – remained limited in scope. Beginning roughly with the accession of the militant Bishop Heinrich V von Knöringen in 1598, however, certain public processions in Augsburg took on a spectacular, propagandistic and at times even militaristic profile. Deliberately routed through or near Protestant areas of the city, processions on the feasts of Good Friday and Corpus Christi, especially, developed into elaborate spectacles involving visual displays such as banners, crosses and theatrical representations of biblical scenes, as well as music, including polyphonic motets, vernacular songs and litanies in honour of the Virgin Mary, the Eucharist or patron saints. Through these media, participants expressed a peculiarly Catholic mode of devotion based on an ideal of emotionally laden display, and there is evidence to suggest that organizers hoped to influence Protestant spectators as well as bolster the confessional identity of Catholics.[33]

A published dispute from the first decade of the seventeenth century dramatizes the controversial nature of some Catholic processions. Melchior Volcius, pastor of the Protestant church of St Anna, published two sermons in 1607 roundly attacking Catholic processions in Augsburg. His critique of the yearly Good Friday procession is useful for its description of the procession, even if somewhat overdrawn. Taking into account Volcius's obvious prejudice against such spectacle, he provides us a glimpse of the strong element of public display:

> But our adversaries in the Papacy hold a special, great nightly procession with great pomp and apparatus yearly on this very day with many lights and torches, in which there are presented to the people not only histories of Christ's passion, with painted and pasted pictures and idols thereof, but also persons hired and assigned to play as in a comedy. In this procession there are also a good number who, supposedly in honour of and following the example of Christ's pains, flagellate and strike themselves until their blood flows profusely off of their haunches; many of the flagellants' clothes, backs and hips become so bloody and tattered that they stagger in their own blood; some carry and drag large wooden crosses, others walk with outstretched arms, wanting to believe these things to be a divine service pleasing and agreeable to God.[34]

---

[33] Robert Scribner (see *Popular Culture and Popular Movements in Reformation Germany*, p. 14) has emphasized the sensuous relationship with sacred objects, such as the Eucharist, in the ritual life of the late medieval church.

[34] Volcius, *Zwo Christliche Predigten von der abscheulichen Geisselungsprocession, welche jährlich im Papsthumb am Charfreytag gehalten würdt* (Tübingen: in der Cellischen Truckerey, 1607), pp. 2–3.

Volcius also notes that this gory display was deliberately routed through Protestant areas:

> Afterwards [they] began not only to flagellate themselves privately and in secret, but also to hold public processions, just like those old heretical flagellants condemned by the Pope; [they held them] particularly in those places where proper, true Lutheran Christians lived, not keeping them in those places and streets where they had always held them; rather [they] crawled out of the alleys and came into the public, most prominent streets, where others joined the spectacle with their naked, cut, lashed and bloody backs and haunches, not without particular horror and revulsion of honest, knowledgeable persons; and they whipped themselves in great numbers longer and harder, all for the purpose of gaining followers and making a special demonstration of their zeal for their religion, and for deceitfully catching and taking unto themselves pious, simple and innocent hearts under the pretence of great holiness.[35]

Surely many Protestants observed these spectacles, since Volcius felt the need to admonish his flock to stay away from them:

> And what do [these Catholics] do? They forbid their people to visit our church, hear our sermons and attend our services, in which they would hear nothing but God's pure, unsullied word, along with pure Psalms and sacred songs; they would see nothing but the holy Sacrament as it was given to us by Christ himself. But you run to this blasphemous, abominable event in night and fog, where you see nothing but sheer atrociousness and idolatry; you hear nothing by which you can better yourself.[36]

Volcius saw the 'Pure Psalms and sacred songs' [*reinen Psalmen vnnd Geistlichen Liedern*] of Protestant tradition as a worthy alternative to this 'idolatry' [*Abgötterey*], but he made the alarming admission that many in his flock willingly attended the procession. 'When these flagellants' processions are held', he writes, 'for our part many Lutherans go there in great numbers, and fill all of the alleys and streets so full that it seems as if there are often more of our people there than those marching in the procession.'[37]

Catholic organizers – the Jesuits, confraternities or the church establishment – would have felt some vindication at Volcius's disclosure that a large Protestant audience attended these processions. The Ingolstadt Jesuit Conrad Vetter (1547–1622), a prominent Catholic polemicist, mocked Volcius openly in his 1608 pamphlet *Flagellifer* [A flagellant's zeal]. Volcius's warning to his flock was so effective, Vetter wrote, that on the previous Good Friday 'not a single Lutheran (except

---

[35] Ibid., pp. 23–24.
[36] Ibid., p. 52.
[37] Ibid., p. 51.

women and men, young and old) would allow himself to be seen on the streets or in the windows' during the procession.[38] Furthermore, Vetter claimed that Volcius himself would be unable to resist their power:

> This procession [on the day after the Feast of the Ascension], I say, should not displease our Herr Volcius at all, because it is held in the full light of day. I also have no doubt that his own heart would leap in his breast if he heard the singing of so many choirs of musicians, and the magnificent ringing of the great bell of St Ulrich in his ears, and saw the whole procession pass by St Ulrich's church before his own eyes.[39]

Although Vetter did not further specify the types of music heard in the procession, he was hardly unfamiliar with Catholic song: in 1605 he himself had issued his *Rittersporn*, a collection of devotional songs, reissued in 1613 and again in 1624 as the *Paradeißvogel*. In his note to the reader in the 1613 edition of *Paradeißvogel* Vetter claimed that his songs were intended to counter the offensive songs sung by the young in streets and taverns,[40] but it is not inconceivable that they may also have been suitable for a procession like that decried by Volcius.

Volcius's reference to 'pure Psalms and sacred songs' and the 'many choirs of musicians' (*so vil choros musicorum*) praised by Vetter point to

---

[38] 'Welche so scharff- vnd strenge Ermanung ohne Frucht nicht abgangen/ welches sich daher genugsam bescheint/ das verganges Jar am H. Carfreytag/ als man nach deinen deiden Predigten vnd Predicantischem Geschrey/ dise Proceßion offe[n]lich angestelt vnnd gehalten/ sich nicht ein eintziger Lutheraner (außgenommon was Weiber vnd Männer/ junge vnd Alte seyn möchten) weder auff der Gassen noch in dem Fenster hate blicken noch sehen lasst …'. Vetter, M. *Conradi Andreæ &c. Volcius Flagellifer. Das ist: Beschützung vnd Handhabung fürtreflicher vnd herlicher zweyer Predigten von der vnleydenlichen vnd Abschewlichen Geysel Proceßion, erstlich gehalten, hernach auch in Truck gegeben durch den Kehrwürdigen, vnnd Wolgekerten Herrn M. Melchior Voltz Lutherischen Predicanten zu Augspurg bey Sant Anna* (Ingolstadt: In der Ederischen Truckerey, durch Andream Angermayer, 1608), pp. 28–29. Vetter took the pseudonym 'Andreae' in some of his writings.

[39] Ibid., p. 12.

[40] Vetter issued his collection 'weil meniglichen bewüßt/ was bißweilen/ vnd schier gemeinlich für unschambare/ unzüchtige/ ärgerliche/ vnd der Jugend hochschädliche Reimen vnd Rayen Lieder/ den gantzen Som[m]er auff der Gassen/ vnd den Winter in den Stuben gesungen werden/ da man doch bedencken soll/ wie vil den Eltern selber daran gelegen/ ob die zarten junge Hertzen irer Söhnen vnd Töchtern/ als noch newe Geschirlein/ mit Hönig oder Gifft/ mit gutem oder bösem Safft.' From Vetter, 'An den Leser', in *Paradeißvogel/ Das ist/ Himmelische Lobgesang/ vnd solche Betrachtungen/ dadurch das Menschliche Hertz mit Macht erlustiget/ von der Erden zum Paradeiß/ vnd Himmelischen Frewden gelockt/ erquickt/ entzündt/ vnd verzuckt wirdt* (Ingolstadt: A. Angermayer, 1613; RISM B/VIII, 1613[19]). It is worth noting that Vetter's songbook emphasizes the poetry of Bernard, so highly praised by Catholic writers, including the Augsburg composer Gregor Aichinger; see above, Ch. 5. For discussion of Vetter's songbooks, see Ruth Hofmann, 'Notendruck', in Hofmann, ed., *Musik in Ingolstadt*, pp. 137–38.

a fundamental way in which music helped to constitute religious and cultural differences between the Protestant and Catholic communities in this confessionally divided city: while Volcius alludes to the decades-old Protestant tradition of vernacular Psalms and chorales, Vetter's text suggests the role of music as part of a dramatic spectacle meant to overwhelm the senses. Catholics increasingly turned to explicit, public demonstrations of their faith that were designed not only to promote unity within their own ranks, but also to impress the city's Protestant majority. Although Volcius and Vetter do not describe the musical element of these processions in great detail, their tracts, in general terms, suggest that music was a vital part of a richly layered spectacle involving different media.

Catholic officials knew that such processions could also become the focus of Protestant resistance and, sometimes, violence. The most ready example was the nearby Imperial city of Donauwörth, where a Protestant attack on a Catholic procession (the so-called *Fahnenschlacht*, which included sung litanies and the carrying of flags)[41] led to the occupation and forcible recatholicization of the city in 1607 by Maximilian I of Bavaria. Before the late sixteenth century Catholic officials in Augsburg seem to have feared the consequences of leading processions through Protestant neighbourhoods. The consecration of St Salvator in 1584 occasioned a proposal from the Jesuits to expand the usual procession, which previously had been restricted to the churches of St Salvator, Heilig Kreuz and St Stephan in the northern end of the city, to encompass the churches of St Peter, SS Ulrich and Afra and St Moritz as well. This was rejected by the city council, which argued that it would neither advise such a procession nor aid it due to the 'current difficult times and the hatred of the Jesuits'.[42]

When the Catholics finally expanded their public processions in the late 1590s, they were conscious that Protestant resistance had prevented them from doing so in the past. The Catholic chronicler Reginbald

---

[41] An Augsburg chronicle by Reginbald Moehner tells of the presence of litanies during the *Fahnenschlacht*: 'Donawertenses quoque, qui Euangelici uideri uolebunt, contrà expressam Religionis pacem notebant pati, ut Catholici in eo urbe constituti dieb[us] Rogationum, iuxtà antiquißimum Ecclesiæ ueræ ritum cum Crucib[us] et vexillis Litanias decantantes publicè procederent …'. From 'Annales Augustani Reginbaldi Moehneri', ABA, Hs 52, vol. 2, p. 1268.

[42] '*Sindici Relation* nach, das herr StattPfleger Relinger vff mit herrn Marx Fugger vnnd zwayen gehaimen gehabte vnnderrödt, Sich erclert, dz Sÿ beÿ jetzigen alhieigen zerriten weßen, vnnd *odio Jesuitarum*, die *proceßiones* inn der herrn Jesuiten Kirchen zuextendiern Ires thaills nit Ratten noch darzue helffen kinden.' *DR*, 4 May 1584. The cathedral chapter seems to have served as an intermediary between the Jesuits and the city council in this matter. The Jesuits' original proposal was discussed by the chapter in *DR*, 30 April 1584.

Moehner, writing around 1640, recalled the re-establishment of processions in the city just before the turn of the century:

In the year 1595 public processions in the city began to be held according to ecclesiastical rites, [processions] that previously were not held except within the churches and their environs owing to fear of the Lutheran masses. The first public supplication of the entire clergy was instituted on the third Sunday of Easter, [going] out of the cathedral to the church of Ulrich and Afra, when, after the solemn hymn Te Deum laudamus had been sung, and an Office had been sung by the suffragan bishop, the church bells of the entire city sounded, and most of the cannons on the fortifications were fired in thanksgiving for the conquest of Raab.[43]

Another document from the cathedral, probably describing the same procession (12 April 1598), notes that 'for 70 years the entire clergy feared to hold such a procession owing to the Lutherans'.[44] The next year, emboldened by the success of the previous year's procession, the Catholics dared to hold a similar procession on the feast of Corpus Christi:

After Luther's heresy arose in Germany, and the city council of Augsburg also adopted it, the clergy was driven from the city in 1537; before [that time], and just as after 1548, when Emperor Charles V restored the clergy, public Catholic ceremonies, where they were not neglected entirely, could not be celebrated with the solemnity demanded by the Catholic Church. Likewise the glorious procession on the feast of Corpus Christi had to be held in narrow [streets] ... until 1599 when at the behest of godly persons, since the procession in the previous year on the occasion of the fall of Raab was successful, [we] dared to extend the procession.[45]

At this stage, however, the Corpus Christi procession in particular seems to have been confined to the northern, ecclesiastical quarter of the city (even though it now ventured on to the so-called 'hohen Weg', the main north-south axis through this part of the city), and did not proceed to

---

[43] From 'Annales Augustani Reginbaldi Moehneri', ABA, Hs 52, vol. 2, pp. 1437–48. Moehner seems to have remembered the date of the Christian military victory over the Turks at Raab in Hungary incorrectly, which was in spring of 1598.

[44] 'Beschreibung | Der statlichen *Procession* od[er] Creuzgang, so zu dankhsagung | wegen d[er] eroberten herrlichen vöstung Rhaab in Hungern, | vnd vmb fernern seegen werenden Hung[er]ischen Kriegs | von dem Allmechtigen Gott zuerpitten A° 1598. den 12. | Aprilis zu Augspurg von dem Tombstifft auß in S. | *Vdalrici et Afræ* Kürchen gehalten word[en], Nach | dem inner .70. Jarn die samentliche Clerisey | wegen d[er] Lutherei dergleichen *Procession* | anzustöllen sich gefürcht.' From 'Anweisungen über die Abhaltung verschiedener Feierlichkeiten in der Augsburger Domkirche 1582–1603', ABA, Hs 34, fols 14r–16r.

[45] 'Anweisungen über die Abhaltung verschiedener Feierlichkeiten in der Augsburger Domkirche 1582–1603', ABA, Hs 34, fols 21v–22r.

SS Ulrich and Afra at the southern end of the city, as the other two above-mentioned processions did. Catholic officials may have felt in 1599 that a large procession in honour of the Eucharist would simply have been too provocative.

If Catholic leaders feared Protestant resistance to their processions before 1600, there is much evidence to suggest that they welcomed their potential as propaganda in the subsequent period. A 1621 tract recording the origins, statutes and activities of the Marian Congregation in Augsburg, for example, gives the following account of an Easter procession in Augsburg in 1605:

> There went out from Augsburg an Easter procession with such religious pomp that a tailor, from the Lutheran flock, was a spectator. He saw in long order a great crowd carrying statues of Christ depicting his diverse torments, followed by a troop of horses most splendidly decorated and laden with [an image] of the crucified Christ, boys under the embellished standards of the Angels singing songs, [a representation] of the earth shaking made from beams, [he heard] the striking of scourges, [he saw] the heavens burning with fire, and all of the Catholics inflamed with piety; he was wracked, seething, envious and indignant on account of these wondrous ways, and everything was burdensome and sorrowful to him. What more is there to say? He went immediately home and shut his wretched soul away from this snare. It is uncertain whether he did so out of his own desperation or out of envy of us. Afterwards the Catholics joked cheerfully that the Lutherans would not want to be willing spectators. While the Catholics would represent the sufferings of Christ, the [Lutherans] would represent Judas.[46]

Catholic processions like this one involved music as one part of a larger event designed to engage the senses of the spectators, whether positive or negative. The author writes that 'but in those places where heretics live, holding their affairs [the Congregation's] in contempt, there the fervour and strength of the Sodality shows forth the greatest'.[47]

Catholic confraternities, too, organized public processions with confessional propaganda in mind. A request for papal indulgences in 1586 from the Trinity (Andechs) Confraternity of Augsburg Cathedral cited its many activities in the service of the Catholic religion, including processions with sung litanies of the saints that, reportedly, made a great impression on Protestant bystanders:

---

[46] *Sodalis Parthenius. Siue libri tres quibus mores sodalium exemplis informantur. Operâ maiorum sodalium academicorum B. Mariæ Virginis Annunciatæ in lucem dati* (Ingolstadt, 1621), pp. 108–11.

[47] 'Sed q[ui]bus locis hæretici earum rerum contempores degunt, ibi Sodalium se maximè feruor virtusque effert.' Ibid., p. 108.

> Here in Augsburg, and in the countryside, this praiseworthy
> brotherhood has carried out many devotions and divine services
> (and still does); thus pious, Catholic, and ardent Christians have
> held public processions with banners into and out of all of the [city]
> gates, and organized several choirs in great numbers which sang
> German and Latin Litanies of All Saints, and many Protestants
> walking by saw this and stood there with terrified hearts, and many
> of them showed reverence to the clergy.[48]

Litanies were a vital part of a ritual that was designed, in part, to
challenge the consciences of local Protestants. Pope Sixtus V explicitly
granted 50 days' indulgence to any member of the confraternity who
'prays devoutly to God, and calls on him for the extermination of heresy,
and the growth of the Catholic Church'.[49] The litanies heard in
processions like the one cited above had a distinctly Catholic nature (as
a genre it was rare among Lutherans), and served a political as well as a
religious function.

   More detailed accounts survive for the annual procession on Good
Friday evening, attacked explicitly by Melchior Volcius in his sermons
(see above). The Marian Congregation was responsible for instituting
regular processions on Good Friday beginning in 1594, although these
were probably limited in scope.[50] The eighteenth-century chronicler Paul
von Stetten reported that beginning in 1603, the Jesuits held a Good
Friday procession from St Salvator to the nearby Capuchin cloister of
SS Francis and Gualfardus, thus remaining entirely in the northern
quarter of the city.[51] Regular and elaborate Good Friday processions
probably began in 1604 (the confusion about the date stems from
the fact that at least four manuscript accounts of the first Good
Friday procession survive, accounts that are identically worded yet
give different dates)[52] and were organized by the Corpus Christi

---

[48] 'Concept der Bruderschafftt zum Heÿ: Berg Andex Suplication an die Bäbst: hey: zu
Rom vmb zuerlanngen ettliche Indulgentias Anno Christi 1586.' StAA, KWA E45[8].

[49] 'Item welcher zu Gott andechttig rueffen, vnnd betten wurdt, vmb hinnemung unf
außtilckhung der Ketzereÿen, vnd erweÿtterung der Catholischen Kirchen, der sol seiner
Seelen zu guetten gewinnen vertzeÿhung der sunnden fuenfftzig tag.' From 'Concept der
Bruderschafftt zum Heÿ: Berg Andex Suplication', StAA, KWA E45[8].

[50] See Singer, 'Leben und Werke des Augsburger Domkapellmeisters Bernhardus
Klingenstein', pp. 37–38.

[51] Stetten, *Geschichte der Heil. Röm. Reichs Freyen Stadt Augspurg*, vol. 1, p. 872.

[52] This Latin account, a part of which is quoted below, appears identically in: (1) the 'De
initijs ac progressu omnium Fraternitatum', fol. 22r–v, giving the date of 1604; (2) *HCA*,
vol. 1, pp. 424–46, giving the date of 1605; (3) the 'Domkapitelsche Chronologie', ABA,
BO 7257, giving the date of 1605; and (4) the 'Historia episcoporum Augustanorum usque
ad annum 1611', ABA, Hs 64, fol. 209r–v, giving the date of 1605. One of these four
manuscripts, or a missing exemplar, must have served as the model for the remaining
copies, suggesting that Catholic chroniclers in Augsburg shared texts with one another in

Confraternity, which was founded early in that year. Less than a month after their foundation, the members of this brotherhood held a procession on 31 March (the Wednesday following Laetare Sunday) from Heilig Kreuz to St Salvator wearing red sackcloth with the brotherhood's insignia.[53] The confraternity then organized a procession on Good Friday (16 April), involving some 150 participants (including members of other brotherhoods), beginning between 6 and 7 in the evening and winding its way from Heilig Kreuz to SS Ulrich and Afra, with stations at the cathedral and at St Salvator.[54] This procession is described in some detail in several sources, and involved images of and actors representing the events of Christ's Passion from the Mount of Olives to the tomb. Accompanying this were several groups of singers, including 'a chorus of four boys singing a tearful dirge to Christ', a 'mournful symphony' [Sÿmphonia mœsta], a 'doleful funeral song sung by a choir of angels' [næniam rursus angelorum chorus lugubrem meditabatur], and another group of musicians at the very end of the procession [Postremum agmen togata et linteata Musicarum harmonija claudebat supplicationem totam].[55]

The Corpus Christi Confraternity would probably not have been able to produce such a spectacle with their resources alone, and indeed there is evidence to suggest that the bishop and/or the cathedral chapter approved the participation of the cathedral musicians. The use of the

---

the creation of their histories. The discrepancy in the date for this procession is difficult to explain. The German chronicle of the foundation of the Corpus Christi Confraternity (ABA, BO 2480, fol. 3r–v) gives the date of 16 April 1604, and a Good Friday procession organized by the Corpus Christi brotherhood in Augsburg with images and penitential acts was described by an anonymous (probably Jesuit) author in the 1604 tract Gratulation An die andächtige deß Heiligen Fronleichnams JEsu CHristi, vnd andere Brüderschafften zu Augspurg, pp. 3–4. Based on this last evidence, I believe that this first Good Friday procession must have taken place in 1604, not in 1605.

[53] ABA, BO 2480, fol. 3r.

[54] See ABA, BO 2480, fol. 3r–v. The female members of the confraternity (who otherwise participated in all the group's activities) were not permitted to participate in this Good Friday procession, presumably because it was held after nightfall. Instead, they could obtain 200 days' indulgence for praying during the procession (see ABA, BO 2480, fol. 10r). However, the Protestant preacher Melchior Volcius, who criticized Catholic processions sharply in his Zwo Christliche Predigten, charged that the Good Friday procession involved a measure of dubious interaction between men and women: 'Zugeschweigen/ was sonst bey solcher Nächtlichen Procession für groß Sünd vnnd ärgerlichs Wesen in der finster von Mann vnd WeibsPersonen fürgehn mag/ beyderen vil/ offt schlechte Andacht gesehen vnd gespürt würdt/ vnd wol zusorgen/ mehr Sünden begangen/ dann gebüßt werden'. See Volcius, Zwo Christliche Predigten, p. 19. He may not necessarily have been referring to female members of the Corpus Christi brotherhood, however.

[55] From 'De initijs ac progressu omnium Fraternitatum', fol. 22r–v.

term 'Sÿmphonia' in the chronicle 'De initijs' to describe the choral laments accompanying these images suggests polyphony, and the use of boys as singers points to the probable participation of the cathedral's choirboys in the procession, who would have obtained their music for this occasion from Bernhard Klingenstein, the cathedral *Kapellmeister*. An entry from the cathedral chapter's minutes some two decades later confirms that the cathedral was still providing music in the form of instruments and sheet music.[56]

The Augsburg Good Friday procession, then, involved the services of multiple institutions in the creation of a visual and aural spectacle. The goal was stated by the anonymous (probably Jesuit) author of a tract in praise of the newly formed Corpus Christi brotherhood in Augsburg, referring specifically to this Good Friday procession:

> The praiseworthy zeal for a Christian, godly and spiritual life [was seen] particularly in the edifying example of the devout, magnificent, well-considered and orderly procession through the whole city of Augsburg last Good Friday, in which various images of the bitter sufferings of Jesus Christ, our sole redeemer and saviour, [were carried,] along with other severe acts of penitence [i.e., flagellation] done to yourselves, through which not only the hearts of Catholics, but also those of Christians deceived in religion, were moved and softened, so that [their hearts] must have burst at the same time from inner sighs and hot tears.[57]

The tract concludes with an admonishment that the brotherhood not be dissuaded from their tasks by the mockery of the Protestants, who, as Melchior Volcius had admitted, observed the proceedings in large numbers.

The Corpus Christi Procession

Another Jesuit tract published in Ingolstadt three years later and dedicated to the Corpus Christi Confraternity presents a fictional 'debate' between a Catholic and a Protestant about whether worship of the Eucharist was a form of idolatry. In the course of the debate – in which the Lutheran is predictably enlightened and renounces his former opposition – the antagonists mention music performed in processions several times, suggesting that music played an important role in these

---

[56] 'der vncossten so über außgebutzt Posaunen vnd etliche abgeschribne gesänger auf den Charfreÿtag aufgangen, soll bezalt werden'. *DR*, 24 March 1627.

[57] *Gratulation An die andächtige deß Heiligen Fronleichnams JEsu CHristi, vnd andere Brüderschafften zu Augspurg* (Ingolstadt: in der Ederischen Truckerey, durch Andream Angermayr, 1604) pp. 3–4.

'spectacles' designed for edification and propaganda.[58] At first the Lutheran criticizes the lack of biblical foundation for such elaborate processions in honour of the Sacrament:

[Catholic:] Mein guter Freund glaubstus aber was sie sage[n]?	My good friend, do you really believe what they are saying?
[Lutheran:] Warumb das nicht?	Why not?
[C:] Was für Prob bringens auff die Bahn?	What proof can they offer?
[L:] Christus hat nicht befohlen daß Sacrament anzubetten: nienderst stehet geschriben/ daß mans mit Creutzen/ Fahnen/ Stangen/ Fackeln/ herumb trage/ wo ist einiges gebott vom singen/ blerren/ pfeiffen/ orglen/ vnd dergleichen Münch vnd Pfaffen wercken?	Christ did not command that the Sacrament should be prayed to: nowhere is it written that one should carry around crosses, banners, staves or torches; where is there a single command for singing, bawling, piping, organ [playing] and similar works of monks and priests?

The Catholic responds by arguing the real presence of Christ in the Eucharist, thus making the latter a suitable object of veneration. Furthermore, the Lutheran is forced to admit that King David and his armies revered the Ark of the Covenant 'with all kinds of strings made out of all kinds of wood, with citharas and lyres and drums and cymbals, and songs and harps, psalteries [and] trombones'.[59] The Catholic goes on to criticize the hypocrisy of the Lutherans, who will tolerate all kinds of music for secular occasions but recoil when the same music is employed to honour Christ. 'It is a wonder', the Catholic says, 'that the [Lutheran] preachers accept drums, pipes, violins, lyres, lutes and other instruments, garlands, dancing [and] rejoicing in their wedding processions, but they wish to eliminate the same that honours Jesus Christ?'[60] Although the author of this tract does not refer to the Corpus Christi processions in Augsburg specifically, his argument implies that music, and instrumental music in particular, was a prominent feature during these events. This

[58] *Fronleichnams Frag, Eines Lutheraners, Ob es Abgötterey sey vmbtragen, verehren, anbetten das allerheiligste Sacrament deß Altars. Verantwort von einem Catholischen Anno 1607. den 28. Aprill, Mündlich vnd geschrifftlich, jetzund auch in offenen Truck verfertigt, Zu nutz vnd wolgefallen der hochlöblichen Brüderschafft Corporis Christi, bey dem H. Creutz in Augspurg* (Ingolstadt: in der Ederischen Truckerey, durch Andream Angermayr, 1607).

[59] 'Das gantze Hauß Jsrael spileten vor dem HERRN her auß gantzer macht mit allerley Seytenspil von allerley Holtz/ mit Cytharn vnd Leyren vnd Trummen vnd Schöllen vnnd Cymbaln/ vnnd Liedern vnnd Harpffen/ Psalern/ Posaunen.' Ibid., pp. 11–13.

[60] 'Ein wunder ist es/ daß die Predicanten gedulden auff die Hochzeitliche Kirchengäng Trummel/ Pfeiffen/ Geigen/ Leyren/ Lauten vnd andere Jnstrument/ Kräntz/ Täntz/ Frewdenspiel/ Vnd Christo Jesu zu ehren/ wolten sie abschlagen.' Ibid., pp. 19–21.

'debate' and the congratulory tract of 1604 previously cited also demonstrate that the processions held by the confraternity not only were designed for the spiritual edification of its members but also courted a reaction – whether positive or negative – from Lutheran bystanders.[61]

The yearly procession on the feast of Corpus Christi was the most elaborate Catholic public spectacle in early seventeenth-century Augsburg. It was not only the largest and most varied procession, involving the contributions of hundreds of clergy and laypersons with images, banners, theatrical displays, self-flagellation and musical performances, but also the most potent symbolic expression of the church militant. Bishop Heinrich V made this explicit in the section of his 1612 Ritual devoted to the celebration of Corpus Christi when he wrote that

> Among all of the celebrations of the Catholic church there is not one that is more exclusive to Catholics, and offends the eyes of the heretics more acutely, than [that of] the most holy body of CHRIST alone. Thus it is fitting that this [feast] be celebrated most solemnly both in the Divine Office as well as in processions, according to the abilities of the place. Therefore, let the priest take care that all things are well prepared, and that all persons are brought together in order, who proclaim and confirm their true Catholic faith in an outward manner.[62]

---

[61] At least one other printed apologia for the Corpus Christi brotherhood appeared from an Ingolstadt press in 1607, the *Encyclica, Das ist, ein Gemein Craißschreiben. Zu dienst vnd gefallen den hochlöblichen Bruderschafften deß allerheiligisten Fronleichnams Christi, vnd andern mahren in vnd ausser der weitberhümbten Reichsstadt Augspurg. Gestellet wider den newen Gaisselfeind Jacob Heilbrunner. Durch einen sondern Freundt vnd Patron deß Bußfertigen Lebens* (Ingolstadt: Andreas Angermayer, 1607). Music, however, is not mentioned in this tract, which is concerned mainly with a theological defence of sacramental worship.

[62] 'INTER omnes Catholicæ Ecclesiæ festiuitates non est, que Catholicorum magis propria sit, Hæreticorumque oculos offendat acriùs, quàm sola sacratissimi Corporis CHRISTI. Vndè decet eam pro cuiusque loci facultatibus solemnissimè tàm in diuinis Officijs, quàm Processionibus celebrari. Det igitur operam Parochus, vt omnia tempestiuè parentur, omnesque hominum ordines congregætur, qui veram & Catholicam fidem suam externo etiam ritu declarent & comprobent.' *Liber Ritualis, Episcopatus Augustensis*, vol. 3, pp. 177–78. Compare this wording with that of Marquard von Berg in his Augsburg Ritual of 1580, who does not emphasize the propagandistic aspect of the procession to the same degree: 'QVONIAM venerandum & adorandum Christi Domini nostri Corpus hoc sacro die publicè circumgestatur, & honorificentissime colitur: sollemnis etiam processio, qualis vix toto anno cernitur, institui solet ac debet in Ecclesijs: proinde det operam Parochus, vt ad eandem Processionem hominum ordines congregentur, qui veram & Catholicam fidem suam externo etiam ritu declarent & comprobent.' *Ritus ecclesiastici Augustensis episcopatus*, pp. 621–24. Heinrich's change of wording may well reflect his own experience of the effect of the Corpus Christi procession on Augsburg's Protestant community.

Although the celebration of Corpus Christi and sacramental devotion in general had experienced an upswing in late medieval Europe (and especially in France and England),[63] the doctrine of Eucharistic transubstantiation appealed to Counter-Reformation ideologues like Heinrich von Knöringen, who saw them as a militant symbol of Catholic truth in the face of heretical opposition. Nowhere was this more true than in nearby Munich, where the dukes actively promoted the yearly Corpus Christi procession, an event that by the late sixteenth century reportedly involved the annual participation of several *thousand* individuals (indeed, a substantial percentage of the entire city's population!).[64] Although such processions certainly were of a popular origin, in Bavaria they were quickly appropriated by the Church establishment, which saw the processions as an opportunity to reinforce clerical authority and more firmly to inscribe the hierarchical lines between clergy and laity. At the same time, the Corpus Christi procession served as a particularly dramatic and sensible form of Catholic propaganda, one that stressed the centrality of *seeing* the host and its accompanying procession as a tangible symbol of Catholic truth and authority.[65] Participants and observers also heard music, ranging from plainchant to polyphony to instrumental music, provided by the city *Stadtpfeifer* as well as by the ducal choir under the direction of Orlando di Lasso.[66]

Although most of these processions took place well removed from Protestant regions (and thus served more directly to strengthen Catholic identity than to impress Protestant populations),[67] Augsburg in the early seventeenth century forms a prominent exception. Unlike Munich (where Marian propaganda, if anything, tended to dominate), Augsburg

---

[63] Soergel, *Wondrous in His Saints*, p. 81.

[64] The order of the Munich Corpus Christi in 1574 included standard bearers from the local guilds, the confraternity of St George on horseback, no fewer than 55 theatrical scenes from the Old and New Testaments produced by local guilds and confraternities (involving over 1400 persons alone), clerics and students from Catholic schools, ducal trumpeters, 12 children of noblemen dressed as the Apostles and carrying instruments of Christ's torture, two pairs of priests escorting the host, and finally members of the ducal court and Duke Albrecht V himself. In total some 2000 persons participated, out of a total population of about 15000. Later years would only see an *increase* in the numbers of participants. See ibid., pp. 87–88 and Alois Mitterwieser, *Geschichte der Fronleichnamsprozession in Bayern*, pp. 34–35.

[65] Soergel, *Wondrous in His Saints*, pp. 85–90.

[66] Lasso appears in a (perhaps apocryphal) account of the Munich Corpus Christi procession in 1584, when a performance of his motet *Gustate et videte, quam suavis sit Dominus* occasioned the end of a rainstorm so that the procession could continue. See Boetticher, *Orlando di Lasso und seine Zeit*, p. 127, and Mitterwieser, *Geschichte der Fronleichnamsprozession in Bayern*, pp. 42–43.

[67] Mitterwieser, *Geschichte der Fronleichnamsprozession in Bayern*, p. 33.

in fact had housed a Eucharistic shrine of regional importance for several centuries, an allegedly miraculous host known as the *Wunderbares Gut* at the church of Heilig Kreuz. The founding of the Corpus Christi confraternity at Heilig Kreuz in 1604 reinforced the church's role as the focus of sacramental devotion in the city. In addition to the many miracle books concerning this host and Eucharistic devotion in general that appeared from local presses in the early seventeenth century,[68] Eucharistic polyphony was composed and published by Gregor Aichinger, a member of the Corpus Christi brotherhood. His *Solennia augustissimi Corporis Christi* (1606) consists exclusively of liturgical and processional music for the feast Corpus Christi, and is dedicated to the leadership and members of his brotherhood (see p. 144); furthermore his *Corolla eucharistica* (1621) and his *Flores musici ad Mensam SS. Convivii* (1626) both have a strong Eucharistic orientation (with the exception of the processional hymns in his *Solennia*, however, most of this music, was probably not intended specifically for these processions, but rather for liturgical and non-liturgical Eucharistic services).

Not coincidentally, it was around the same time as the founding of Aichinger's brotherhood that the Corpus Christi procession expanded in size and range. Before this time, it is unclear whether large-scale Corpus Christi processions were held regularly in Augsburg. Bishop Marquard

---

[68] According to the legend, in the year 1194 a local woman visited the church of Heilig Kreuz, where instead of swallowing the host she took it home secretly and encapsulated it in wax. Having revered the host for five years in her home, she was plagued by guilt and returned it to the head of the church's chapter, who noticed that it had physically changed to resemble flesh and blood. After consulting with the bishop, the host was exposed for veneration on the cathedral's altar, where it grew dramatically in size, bursting out of its wax capsule. The bishop had the miraculous host and its wax container placed in a crystal monstrance and delivered in a festal procession to Heilig Kreuz, where it was to remain. Early modern literature on this miracle includes Gilbert Bremens, *Historia Sacramenti Miraculosi in monasterio Sanctæ Crucis Augustæ Vindelicor.* (Augsburg: Christophorus Mang, 1604); the *Gratulation An die andächtige deß Heiligen Fronleichnams JEsu CHristi, vnd andere Brüderschafften zu Augspurg*; the *Fronleichnams Frag*; the *Encyclica, Das ist, ein Gemein Craißschreiben*; Kaspar Scioppius, *Emmanuel Thaumaturgus Augustae Vindel. hoc est relatio de miraculoso corporis Christi sacramento, quod Augustae in S. Crucis ecclesia servatum est* (Augsburg, 1612); *Maximiliani deß ersten, Caroli deß fünfften, vnd Ferdinandi, aller dreyen Römischen Kayser. Recht Catholische andächtige Verehrung deß hochwürdigsten Sacraments deß Altars* (Augsburg: Christoph Mang, 1614); Georg Mayr, *Officium Corporis Christi, De Festo et per octauam latinè et græcè editum, ac Fraternitati Eucharisticæ Augustanæ dedicatum* (Augsburg, 1618); Octavian Lader, *Historia dess Sacraments, so beym H. Creutz in Augspurg verehrt wirdt* (Augsburg: Andreas Aperger, 1625); Anastasius Vochetius, *Thaumaturgus Eucharisticus sive de Sacramento ad s. crucem historia* (Augsburg, 1637); and Peter Thyraeus, *Tractatus de apparitionibus sacramentalibus ad gloriam miraculosi sacramenti, quod Augustae in ecclesia S. Crucis colitur illustrandam* (Dillingen, 1640). These probably represent only a fraction of the Eucharistic literature concerning the *Wunderbares Gut* published during this period.

von Berg allowed for significant musical elaboration of the procession in his Ritual for the Augsburg diocese in 1580. At the beginning of the procession,

> The chorus in the procession sings the responsory *Homo quidam fecit cænam magnam*, and the hymns *Pange lingua gloriosi* and *Sacris solemnijs*, as well as more pieces of the same kind. At times trumpets, pipes, organs and other musical instruments may be used in the same procession for the glory of Christ, and for the devotion of the faithful, just as David used them in front of the ark of the Lord, which was carried in the procession. 2 Kings 6.[69]

There seems to be no evidence, however, that an elaborate Corpus Christi procession was held in Augsburg until 1599. As mentioned above (see p. 241), in this year the procession was extended to include the churches of Heilig Kreuz and St Salvator in the northern quarter of the city. Two sets of singers were employed, both apparently drawn from the cathedral choirboys: 'students, with the singers of the school' [*scholares, cum cantorib. scholæ*], probably referring to the cathedral school, and another group of 'two or four singers' [*duo vel .4. chorales*] several positions back.[70]

Between 1599 and 1603 this procession was probably continued, although only the cathedral chapter minutes make reference to it in 1601.[71] We are much better informed about the Corpus Christi processions beginning in 1603, when Bishop Heinrich V instructed the cathedral chapter to make all the necessary arrangements. The cathedral's notary recorded that the chapter agreed to Heinrich's request on 14 May (about two weeks before Corpus Christi), and his wording of the minutes suggests that the procession was to be institutionalized to a degree it had not been before: 'It pleases my lords', the notary writes, 'to hold [the procession] on Corpus Christi, with the participation of the entire clergy, foundations and monasteries of Augsburg, just as it has become customary in Italy and in certain notable cities in Germany.'[72]

Two documents, both originating at the cathedral, describe an elaborate sacramental procession held in Augsburg in 1603, but it is not

---

[69] *Ritus ecclesiastici Augustensis episcopatus*, pp. 621–64.

[70] From ABA, Hs 34, 'Anweisungen über die Abhaltung verschiedener Feierlichkeiten in der Augsburger Domkirche 1582–1603'.

[71] *DR*, 20 June 1601.

[72] 'Vff meines gnedigen Fürsten vnd herrn schreiben, vnd darinnen verleibte vrsachen, lassen meine gnedige herrn, inen gefallen, dz die vorsteende *processio* am Tag Corporis Christi, durch beÿwonung ganntzer Clerisei, der Stifft, vnd Clöster zu Augspurg, inmassen inn Ittalia, allß auch am öttlichen fürnemen Stätten unn Teutschlandt gebreichig, angestöllt werde.' *DR*, 14 May 1603. The bishop and chapter may have been encouraged by a successful procession from the cathedral to SS Ulrich and Afra.

clear whether it took place on the feast of Corpus Christi. 'In 1603', both documents read (one in Latin, the other in German), 'a general procession out of the cathedral with the Venerable Sacrament and all of the clergy of the entire city has been ordained, and the other parish churches are to join their processions in that week [with this one].'[73] Both sources then describe the order for the procession, which included not only the clergy from Augsburg's Catholic churches and religious orders, but also children from Augsburg's Catholic schools, confraternities, Catholic members of the city council, and lay men and women. Music may have been performed by the Catholic students, who were dressed in choir robes, but no explicit mention is made of their singing. On the other hand, the Marian Congregation from the Jesuit church of St Salvator performed music, or at least hired musicians for the occasion.[74] A group of choirboys and boys on scholarship from the cathedral, wearing their surplices, followed in a group,[75] although the cathedral cantorate as such is listed separately; the latter, under the direction of Klingenstein, may well have included the cathedral's lay instrumentalists, although it is impossible to determine this from the sources.[76] Like the above-mentioned Corpus Christi procession of 1599, this procession remained in the northern quarter of the city (stations were held at the churches of Heilig Kreuz and St Salvator), and did not venture into the more heavily Protestant residential areas to the south.

One week before the feast of Corpus Christi in 1604, the city's Catholics finally resolved to extend the Corpus Christi procession to SS Ulrich and Afra at the southern end of the city. The moment of the decision was recorded by the cathedral chapter's notary, who cited the Corpus Christi Confraternity's prominent role, as well as the liturgical requirement of the singing of the four Gospels:

---

[73] 'Volgents Aᵒ. 1603. ist verordnet worden järlich ein General *Procession* mit aller Clerisei d[er] gantzen Statt ain samentliche *procession cum Venerabili Sacramento* auß der Thumbkürchen zuhalten, vnd die and[er]e Pfarrkürchen ire *Processiones* in d[er] wochen hinumb bey ihnen anstöllen sollen.' From ABA, Hs 34, 'Anweisungen über die Abhaltung verschiedener Feierlichkeiten in der Augsburger Domkirche 1582–1603.' The Latin version is found in ABA, BO 1860, fols. 1r–2v.

[74] '*Congrega[tio] B. Virginis*, welche ein *Music* halten khönden', ABA, Hs 34, 'Anweisungen über die Abhaltung verschiedener Feierlichkeiten in der Augsburger Domkirche 1582–1603'; 'Studiosi Congregationis B: V. Mariæ cum Musica', ABA, BO 1860, fol. 1v.

[75] 'Die Chorschueler vndt Stipendiaten in Chorrökhen', ABA, Hs 34, 'Anweisungen über die Abhaltung verschiedener Feierlichkeiten in der Augsburger Domkirche 1582–1603'; 'Chorales et stipendiati in cottis', ABA, BO 1860, fol. 2r.

[76] 'Die *Cantar*ei in einem hauffen', ABA, Hs 34, 'Anweisungen über die Abhaltung verschiedener Feierlichkeiten in der Augsburger Domkirche 1582–1603'; 'Chorus musicus', ABA, BO 1860, fol. 2r.

As my gracious lord, the cathedral dean, has reported, as well as Herr Cleophas Distelmayr [the cathedral preacher], that certain zealous Catholics, and particularly Herr *Stadtpfleger* Welser, have wished to further promote the Corpus Christi procession, and indeed to extend it to St Ulrich [and Afra], to sing the four Gospels and to have the canons carry torches; also, as my gracious lord, the cathedral dean, has reported that Herr Marcus Fugger wishes that he and his company, the Corpus Christi Confraternity, would like to carry the canopy [over the Eucharist], and that his Grace [Bishop Heinrich V] has told him that he would approve, and that Herr Fugger said that he would appear in formal dress; so it is resolved, for sake of Catholic zeal, that this procession, since it should make a circuit and not travel on the same street twice, should proceed over the Perlach, and through the Steingasse towards the Heilig Kreuz gate; then it should proceed down the Kreuzgasse to the gate of Our Lady, and then return back into the cathedral. The four Gospels are to be sung at four different places, where they may be the most appropriate.[77]

It is unclear what the notary intended as the 'most appropriate' places for the singing of Gospels, but the wording does not necessarily justify the conclusion that they were to be sung particularly in Protestant areas.[78] In any case, the extension of the Corpus Christi procession over the major north–south axis of the city may have been sufficiently provocative in itself. The advocacy of Marcus Welser, one of the two *Stadpfleger* in the highest reaches of the city government, also represents a notable departure from the confessionally neutral politics typical of Augsburg's patrician council.

The singing of the four Gospels at four different stations during the procession had been prescribed in Marquard von Berg's Ritual of 1580, and was continued in Heinrich V's Ritual of 1612. As in most other areas of liturgical ceremony, Heinrich brought the Corpus Christi procession into line with the Roman Rite, which meant, among other things, the omission of any mention of instruments.[79] After the Mass, the priest was to take the monstrance containing the Eucharist and turn towards the people while the versicle *Procedamus in pace* was sung. As the procession began, the choir was to sing the hymn *Pange lingua gloriosi* with all six of its verses. The procession was to be led by the confraternities, followed by the religious orders, a choir [*chorus musicus*], the clergy, boys dressed as angels, the Eucharist carried by the priest under a canopy, and finally the laity. In addition to the hymns, the choir could sing psalms from Matins [*psalmi Matutinales*] or the

---

[77] *DR*, 11 June 1604.

[78] As Kroyer implies in 'Gregor Aichingers Leben und Werke', pp. lxxiii–lxxiv.

[79] The following is taken from *Liber Ritualis, Episcopatus Augustensis*, vol. 3, pp. 183–206.

sequence *Lauda Sion salvatorem*. The procession was to pause at four stations along the route, at which makeshift altars were erected; once it arrived at each altar, the choir could sing a polyphonic motet [*aliquod Motettum figuraliter*] or the responsory *Homo quidam fecit*. The focal point of each station was the singing of passages from the four Gospels in sequence, sung monophonically by a deacon. The order was similar for each of the other three altars, and the choir was directed to sing hymns as the procession returned to the church from which it originated. An extant seventeenth-century book of Gospel readings for the Corpus Christi procession, originally created for the cathedral sacristy, confirms this basic order.[80]

Although the Augsburg Corpus Christi procession adhered to this framework, contemporary documents show that the musical embellishment at times went far beyond the bishop's prescriptions. The year 1606 seems to have witnessed a particularly elaborate procession involving the participation of numerous musicians, described in impressive detail in an Augsburg Jesuit chronicle.[81] Bishop Heinrich V personally carried the host through the streets. The first station of the procession was held before the residence of the patrician Ilsung family, which seems to have been in the vicinity of St Peter's church in the city centre next to the Rathaus.[82] Either before or after the Gospel was sung,

> A chorus of angels from our [Jesuit] schools who were present [entreated] Christ, singing a song most sweetly and with gestures. In the same way, in the vicinity of the city hall and towers, the city trumpeters, at the command of the magistrates, received the coming [body of] Christ with the sweet harmony of instruments, and followed it as it departed. In the meantime, the festal, ringing harmony of military drums and trumpets along the route and at the same altars made the entire city joyful, as did the choirs of musicians, of which there were many.[83]

Conrad Vetter, in his defence of Catholic processions, also noted the participation of the city *Stadtpfeifer*, most of whom were in fact Lutherans in this period. He described the yearly holding of the Corpus Christi procession where 'the Lutheran tower [musicians], trumpeters, trombonists and military drummers all refuse to withhold their

---

[80] ABA, Hs 26, 'Evangelienbuch für die Fronleichnamsprozession', fols 2r–22r.

[81] *HCA*, vol. 1, pp. 433–50.

[82] The Jesuit chronicle records that 'et ad Ilsungi patricij ædes, peristromatis elegantissimè uestitis, excitato altari primum Euangelium decantatum' (*HCA*, vol. 1, p. 433), while the 'Historia episcoporum Augustanorum usque ad annum 1611', ABA, Hs 64, fol. 208v, notes that the procession went 'ad diuum [*sic*] Diui Petri ubi fuit cantatum Euangelium', referring to the first Gospel.

[83] *HCA*, vol. 1, pp. 433–44. Note the pagination error at this point in the Jesuit chronicle.

services'.[84] Apart from the effect of the sheer numbers of musicians present (if the Jesuit chronicler can be taken at his word), the militaristic aspect of the musical accompaniment would not have been lost on the onlookers or the participants. One Protestant chronicler, Georg Kölderer, lamented the presence of many Protestant bystanders, who heard trumpets and drums 'as used in warfare' [alls wie mann inn krieg pflegt zue thuen].[85] The participation of trumpets and drums underscored for the city's populace the symbolism of Corpus Christi as an occasion to celebrate the triumph of the Catholic Church over its antagonists.

From the first altar the procession proceeded south through the wine market [Weinmarkt], past the church of St Moritz, and to the business quarters of the Fugger family, where a second ornate altar had been erected. After the second Gospel had been sung, the procession went towards the Göggingen gate, where a group of armed soldiers from the city militia 'magnified the triumph with the beating of four drums'.[86] From there the procession went past the Protestant church of St Anna to the courtyard of the patrician Bernhard Rehlinger, where the third altar and a 'most sweet symphony of the musicians' awaited the arrival of the host.[87] The final station was held at St Salvator before the procession returned to the cathedral. According to the chronicler, the procession lasted four hours and involved the participation of 2724 persons (how this number was determined, however, is unknown).[88]

---

[84] He refers to the procession 'welche järlich zu Augspurg an dem Tag deß heiligen FRONLEICHNAMS CHRISTI gantz herrliche mit zierlichem Pracht/ Pomp/ vnnd Apparat/ durch die fürnembsten Gassen der Stadt/ angestelt vnnd gehalten würd/ allda auch die Lutherische Turner/ Trommeter/ Posauner/ vnnd Herbaucker ihren Dienst vnuersagt erzeigen.' Conrad Vetter, Conradi Andreæ &c. Volcius Flagellifer, p. 11. Of course, for these musicians the procession was an opportunity to be paid and probably had little confessional significance. An extant expense sheet for a procession held on the feast of the Purification of the BVM in 1626 (18 October), organized by the Trinity and St Sebastian confraternities and proceeding to seven major Catholic churches in the city, records a payment of 40 Kreutzer to the musicians from the Perlach tower, along with other payments to a Vorsinger, several Marianer from the cathedral, and other singers. StAA, KWA L361, '1626 Conto die Procession zu den siben Kürchen alhie zu Augspurg betreffendt'.

[85] From D-As, 2° Cod. S. 44, fol. 51, quoted in Roeck, Eine Stadt im Krieg und Frieden, pp. 184–85.

[86] 'ad portam ciuitatis Gögginganam, ubi cohors ex pr[æ]sidio militum in ordines digesta, armis tormentisque instructa, quaternis tympanis concrepantibus triumphum auxit'. HCA, vol. 1, p. 444.

[87] 'Descensum indè uia regia per S. Annæ uicum usque ad Bernardi Rehlingeri uestibulum, in quo extructa ara, nobilique pictura uisenda, cum suauissima Musicorum Symphonia Christus expectabatur.' HCA, vol. 1, p. 444.

[88] 'Durauit horas ab egressu quatuor. Incedentium fueræ quatuor et uiginti supra bis mille septingentos.' HCA, vol. 1, p. 444.

The chronicler goes on to describe the constitution and the order of the procession in greater detail, and from his remarks we can get a fuller picture of the musical complement. Amid the Marian Congregation, for example, was a choir of 27 Jesuit students.[89] The clerical confraternity of St Sebastian was followed by 'seven trumpets, all draped in silk, and a military drum carried by two persons and crowned with the insignia of the Corpus Christi sodality; alternating with these was the chapel master of the musicians [i.e., Bernhard Klingenstein] from the cathedral, of which there were thirty-three, all clothed in white'. Shortly after the cathedral cantorate followed 'twenty boys dressed as angels, of which eight … were singing at the altars'.[90] Two levites shared the singing of the Gospels at the four stations along the route.[91] A document from the Corpus Christi brotherhood also mentions their hiring of trumpeters and drummers, though in greater numbers than were described in the Jesuit chronicle:

> for the first time, among other embellishments introduced by this brotherhood, sixteen trumpeters and two military drummers were engaged to walk in front of the musicians of the cathedral, and who performed their service before and after the sung Gospels and benedictions, as well as at other places, and gave the procession a fine character.[92]

Trumpets continued to lend a military aura to the Corpus Christi procession at least into the 1620s; in 1625, for example, the chapter was presented with an invoice from the trumpeters, and the cathedral paid them 'the usual remuneration, just as in other years'.[93]

There is little doubt that the Corpus Christi brotherhood, more than the cathedral, episcopate or the Jesuits, played a central role in organizing and embellishing this procession. The cost of arranging it, which must have been considerable, may have led its members to petition the cathedral chapter on 2 May 1609 to grant them a permanent subsidy for this purpose, and to finance their processions with the sacrament to the sick.[94] On 12 June, about one week before Corpus

---

[89] 'Hic interposit[us] est chor[us] n[ostri] music[us] togat[us] et linteatus, qui XXVII. symphoniacos continebat.' *HCA*, vol. 1, p. 446.

[90] 'uiceni pueri cælitum habitu, ex quib[us] octo ad altaria, ut dixi, cantauere'. *HCA*, vol. 1, p. 446.

[91] 'Hinc Leuitæ bini, qui Euangelia ad aros canebant.' *HCA*, vol. 1, pp. 446–47.

[92] ABA, BO 2480, no. 2, 'Kurtze beschreibung, wie die andächtige bruederschafft des allerheiligsten Fronleichnambs *Jesu Christi* … wider vfgericht, und was weither darinn geordnet, vnd fürgenom[m]en worden', fol. 7v.

[93] 'Die heut dato einkhomne vncossten zettel, was über die Procession in festo *SS. Corporis Christi* gang[en], sollen außbezalt; auch den Trometeren wie andere Jahr die gebreüchige *remuneration* gegeben [werden].' *DR*, 10 June 1625.

[94] See *DR*, 2 May 1609.

Christi, the cathedral's notary recorded the chapter's favourable response to the confraternity's request, a response that also included elaborate praise for the group's efforts. The chapter offered, from that time forward, 'to support at its own cost the canopy [over the Sacrament] (which otherwise would have had to have been paid for by a brotherhood), along with its apparatus, as well as the students from the cathedral who accompany the Sacrament to the sick; and [the chapter] shall also request musicians for the processions and lend as many as might be spared, at no cost to the honorable brotherhood'.[95] A decade later, however, as the city was sliding into economic crisis, the chapter concluded that these expenses were too great. In 1620, the Corpus Christi procession, which was to be held on Thursday, 18 June, was postponed until the following Sunday due to rain. On Friday the chapter met and discussed payments for the musicians:

> Regarding the report by the cathedral schoolmaster, the musicians shall be paid next Sunday, as the Corpus Christi procession will be held [then] instead of last Thursday due to the weather; at the next meeting it shall be deliberated how certain expenses from the purser and elsewhere might occasionally be done away with, or at least moderated and reduced, in these difficult times.[96]

At least until this time, then, the Corpus Christi procession received substantial musical support from the cathedral. Whether or not the pomp of the 1606 procession continued to be cultivated in later years is difficult to say, since detailed descriptions of these processions are lacking; however, it is likely that the procession continued to enjoy a martial musical accompaniment at least into the 1620s, as noted above. None of these processions, however, would be as militaristic as that which accompanied the return of the *Wunderbares Gut* to Augsburg in 1635 after three years of Protestant occupation (see Chapter 8): trumpets and drums, indeed, but also the ringing of church bells throughout the city and the deafening roar of musket and cannon fire.

---

[95] 'auch mitt dißem sonderbaren erbieten, den himel (wöllichen sonnsten ain Bruederschafften selbst zuevnderhalten hette) sambt seiner zugehör, vnd die schueller, zue der beglaittung döß hochwirdigen Sacraments, auß dem Thumbstufft zue den Kranckhen, forthin vf iren Cossten zue vnderhalten, vnd dann ir *Music* zue den *Processionibus* vf ersuechen, souill Manns jederweill entraten mag, ohne mitgelt ehrngedachter Bruederschafft, darzugöben'. *DR*, 12 June 1609.

[96] *DR*, 19 June 1620.

CHAPTER SEVEN

The Holy Mountain: Music
in Catholic Pilgrimage

The nature of pilgrimage, and the dynamics of individual and collective consciousness within it, have been hotly debated in anthropological as well as in historical circles. Victor and Edith Turner offered a model of pilgrimage in which participants left their usual social roles to enter a 'liminal' state, leading to a temporary feeling of group consciousness or solidarity (*communitas*).[1] Other scholars have criticized this view from a number of angles. Ian Reader, summarizing recent scholarship, has noted that pilgrimage may be a site of social conflict instead of *communitas*; also, it may arise out of individual motivations rather than group dynamics.[2] These perspectives are important, since the relationship of individual to community is of profound importance in the study of pilgrimage in the Counter-Reformation. Pilgrimage, of course, was at least in part a popular phenomenon that survived the Reformation and, to some degree, existed independently of the church hierarchy.[3] On the other hand, Catholic apologists such as Robert Bellarmin, Peter Canisius and Jakob Gretser sought to appropriate pilgrimage as a means of bolstering Catholic confessionalization and as a potent symbol of specifically Catholic devotion. Surviving accounts of pilgrimages from Augsburg in the early seventeenth century, mostly to the nearby shrine of Andechs in Bavaria, provide evidence to support both cases: these pilgrimages were attended by a wide cross-section of Augsburg's Catholic populace, but they were also carefully regulated by the Church.

---

[1] Turner and Turner, *Image and Pilgrimage in Christian Culture*.

[2] See Reader and Walter, eds, *Pilgrimage in Popular Culture*, pp. 10–15.

[3] Unlike the Protestant church, Catholicism enjoyed the advantage of tapping into a pre-existing reservoir of popular beliefs among the rural laity, especially, about saintly intercession and the magical nature of pilgrimage shrines (see R. Po-Chia Hsia, 'The Structure of Belief: Confessionalism and Society, 1500–1600', in Robert W. Scribner, ed., *Germany: A New Social and Economic History*, Vol. 1: *1450–1630* (London and New York: Arnold, 1996), pp. 369–70). While both the Protestant and Catholic churches militated against what they identified as 'superstitious' practices, the Catholic doctrine of justification through works, as well as the idea of intercession tied to supplications at specific places and times, were more consistent with late medieval traditions of popular religion. Like their medieval predecessors, 'Bavaria's shrines were marketplaces in a sacred economy, exchanging healing, intercession, and indulgences in return for a pilgrim's visits, prayers, and gifts' (Soergel, *Wondrous in His Saints*, p. 28).

Whether the Andechs pilgrimage is seen as a devotional practice that was developed and practised from below, or imposed from above, it played a part in the crystallization of Catholic identity in a crucial period in Augsburg's history and deserves close attention.

As in the Catholic processions described above, litanies in German or Latin formed the core of the musical content and gave a specifically Catholic aural imprint to these events. At its root the litany represented a communal plea for the intercession of a heavenly being – most often the Virgin Mary or one or more saints – who would look out for the fortunes of the marchers during and after the pilgrimage. Through the medium of the litany, pilgrims appealed for spiritual sustenance as well as temporal protection, since pilgrimages could last for many days, traverse difficult terrain and be subject to inclement weather. The litany, then, served a useful cultural function, but its inherent properties also suited it well for pilgrimage: on the one hand, its repetitive structure – varied invocations by the celebrant or leader, alternating with standard short responses of 'ora pro nobis' or 'Bitt für uns' by the populace – facilitated the memorization of short passages of text and music, obviating the need for written aids; on the other, the steady rhythm and lack of contrapuntal elaboration suited the pace of walking.

Among the various popular litanies the Litany of Loreto in particular held a special place, partly as a result of its connection with the famous Marian shrine, but also through the advocacy of Peter Canisius.[4] According to Martin Eisengrein, whose *Unser liebe Fraw zu alten Oetting* (1571) promoted the Marian shrine of Altötting and helped to fuel an upsurge in Bavarian pilgrimage in general, Canisius led one Anna von Bernhausen, who was allegedly possessed by a demon, to Altötting in 1570 along with her Fugger employers in order to perform an exorcism. To magnify their chances of success, the group recited the Litany of Loreto before entering the chapel.[5] Canisius had probably been responsible for the first German printing of the Litany of Loreto in 1558, the *Ordnung der Letaney von unser lieben Frawen, wie sy zu Loreto alle Samstag gehalten wird*;[6] he also promoted its use at the Jesuit college in Prague in 1560, and included it in a Latin prayer book, his *Manuale*

---

[4] On the miraculous background of the Loreto chapel itself, as well as its many copies in Catholic Germany by the early seventeenth century, see esp. Pötzl, 'Volksfrömmigkeit', pp. 895–902.

[5] See Soergel, *Wondrous in His Saints*, pp. 119–26. Eisengrein's book is one of the most prominent examples of the propagandistic literature of the Bavarian Counter-Reformation. Naturally, books like Eisengrein's and Jakob Gretser's *De sacris et religiosis peregrinationibus* (Ingolstadt, 1606) were directed towards Catholic elites who would act as instruments of the Catholic confessionalization.

[6] Printed in Dillingen by Sebald Mayer.

Catholicorum, in 1587.[7] In the same year pope Clement VIII made it the official Marian litany, without banning the usage of other types of litanies, of which there were many.[8] David Crook has described the enthusiasm with which the Litany of Loreto was adopted in the Bavarian ducal household following Canisius's exorcism, a reaction that surely accounted for the remarkable number of polyphonic settings of the text by Orlando di Lasso.[9] The sources that describe the Augsburg pilgrimages to Andechs do not specify what type of litany was habitually sung; however, the official imprimatur granted to the Litany of Loreto in particular by the Church hierarchy, as well as the strict regulation of these pilgimages by the Church, suggest that the Litany of Loreto would very likely have been heard.[10]

Although common pilgrims presumably sang (or spoke) the short responses of litanies monophonically, at least one surviving print suggests that members of confraternities were also apt to sing polyphonic litanies. In 1582 Johann Haym of the Trinity (Andechs) Confraternity in Augsburg brought out his *Litaniae textus triplex*, a collection of 12 polyphonic Latin litanies for four voices, with four litanies each for Christ, the Virgin Mary and the saints; to these he added a four-voice setting of the *Regina caeli*.[11] Although the collection lacks a dedication, Haym's title page confirms that he intended these pieces for brotherhoods like his own: the litanies are 'for the use of sodalities and fraternities going here and there to holy places: and indeed first [for the use] of the Fraternity of the Holy Mountain (known commonly as Andechs) in Bavaria, at the Cathedral of the Blessed Virgin Mary in Augsburg'.[12] An excerpt from the second litany in the collection, a

---

[7] See Crook, *Orlando di Lasso's Imitation Magnificats*, pp. 73–74.

[8] Peter Bergquist, introduction to *Litaneien, Falsibordoni und Offiziumssätze*, Neue Reihe, vol. 25 of Orlando di Lasso, *Sämtliche Werke* (Kassel: Bärenreiter, 1993), p. vii.

[9] See Crook, *Orlando di Lasso's Imitation Magnificats*, esp. pp. 74–75.

[10] Note that members of the Munich Corpus Christi Confraternity were instructed to sing the Litany of Loreto, along with the *Salve Regina*, on their pilgrimage to the church of Heilig Kreuz in Augsburg; see Ch. 5.

[11] *LITANIÆ Textus triplex. I. De dulcissimo nomine Iesu. II. De Beata Maria semper virgine. III. De omnibus Sanctis. Quibus singulis præfixa est quadruplex Harmonia quatuor vocibus composita. DEO TER OPT. MAX. FILIOQVE EIVS Iesu Christo Domino nostro: nec non B. Mariæ semper virgini, Sanctisque Cœlitibus. IN VSVM SODALITATVM AC FRATERnitatum, ad loca sancta hinc inde peregrinantium: In primis verò Fraternitatis montis Sancti (vulgo Andechs appellati) in Bauaria, apud Cathedralem Ecclesiam Beatæ Mariæ virginis Augustæ Vindelicorum, &c. ... Addita est in fine pulchra quædam Compositio, supra antiphonam, Regina cœli lætare, &c.* (Augsburg: Josias Wörli, 1582; RISM A/I, H4905). The only extant exemplar is D-Mbs, 4 Mus. pr. 53.

[12] David Crook suggests that the function of litanies like Haym's may also apply to the many litanies composed by Orlando di Lasso at the Bavarian ducal court; see Crook, *Orlando di Lasso's Imitation Magnificats*, pp. 76–77.

setting of the Litany of Loreto, is shown in Example 7.1, and may be taken as representative for the book as a whole:

Kyrie eleyson.	Lord, have mercy.
Christe eleyson.	Christ, have mercy.
Kyrie eleyson.	Lord, have mercy.
Christe audi nos.	Christ, hear us.
Christe exaudi nos.	Christ, graciously hear us.
Pater de coelis Deus,	God, father in heaven,
miserere nobis.	have mercy upon us.
Fili redemptor mundi Deus,	Christ, God the redeemer of the world,
miserere nobis.	have mercy upon us.

The style suits the intended function well. The repetitive structure of the text is mirrored by the highly formulaic and schematic nature of the polyphonic fabric: each voice is simply constructed and moves within a narrow range, while the regular homophony is broken up only at cadences by a brief decoration in the discantus. Singers of a litany such as this would only have had to memorize a brief phrase of music, which

Example 7.1   Johann Haym, opening of the Litany of Loreto from *Litaniae textus triplex* (1582)

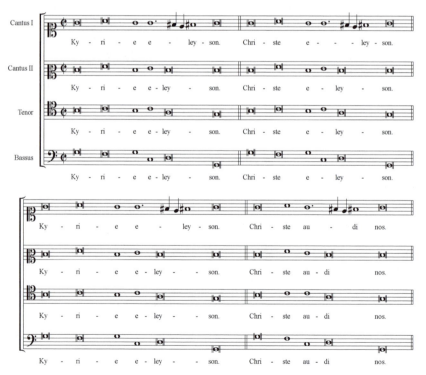

Example 7.1 *concluded*

could be endlessly repeated for the dozens of invocations. The regular rhythms of breves and semibreves match the steady pace of the marchers, while the clear, syllabic declamation foregrounds the words themselves; the style, indeed, is not far removed from that of *falsobordone* and reflects the need for a versatile medium for a varied range of participants.[13]

Room was made, of course, for vernacular songs that described the miracles attributed to specific shrines, or venerated the Virgin or local patron saints; doubtless these had been sung in pilgrimage contexts for many centuries.[14] With the revival or establishment of numerous

---

[13] A Catholic songbook published in Munich decades later, in 1631, also contains simple polyphonic litanies that are quite similar stylistically to Haym's, suggesting that this type of formulaic setting for litany texts persevered: see Valentin Schlindel, *Catholisches Gesangbuch/ in Kirchen/ zu Hauß/ in Processionibus vnnd Kirchfahrten/ gar hailsam: nutzlich/ löblich/ vnd andächtigklich zugebrauchen* (Munich: Nikolaus Heinrich, 1631; RISM B/VIII, 1631⁰⁶), which contains polyphonic litanies for God, the Virgin, the Eucharist and All Saints.

[14] Soergel notes that in late medieval Germany, itinerant singers often performed at pilgrimage sites in exchange for money, sometimes in front of banners or panels depicting

pilgrimage shrines in late sixteenth-century Catholic Germany, printed editions of vernacular pilgrimage songs, many of them compiled by Jesuits, appeared in ever increasing numbers. While some of these songs, such as *In Gottes namen wallen wir* and *Gegrüßt seyst du Maria*, were traditional and of pre-Reformation origin, others were newly composed and reflected the more militant spirit of the Counter-Reformation Church. One such song, connected with the shrine of Altötting, emerged from the Jesuit-controlled press in Ingolstadt in 1599, the *Schöner Catholischer Ruff Von vnser lieben Frawen/ vnd vralten Capellen zu alten Oettingen.*[15] In effect, this song provided musical settings for the miracles described in Eisengrein's *Unser liebe Fraw zu alten Oetting*, and it did not spare the opportunity to attack Lutheran 'falsehoods'. The melody appears in Example 7.2. Stanzas 1 and 40–44 are given here:

Example 7.2   *Nun laßt uns frölich heben an*, from *Schöner Catholischer Ruff Von vnser lieben Frawen/ vnd vralten Capellen zu alten Oettingen* (1599)

1. Nun laßt vns frölich heben an/
Kyrieeleison/
Zu singen alls was singen kan/
Alleluia/ Alleluia/ Gelobt sey
Gott vnd Maria.
...

Now let us happily begin,

Kyrie eleison,
To sing what we can,
Alleluia, Alleluia, praise be
to God and Mary.
...

---

the miracles associated with the particular shrine. It is not unlikely that such practices persisted into the early modern era. See Soergel, *Wondrous in His Saints*, p. 36.

[15] *Schöner Catholischer Ruff Von vnser lieben Frawen/ vnd vralten Capellen zu alten Oettingen / Auch Außzug deß außerlesenen Büchleins D. Martini Eysengreins. Allen Walfartern zu Gefallen vnd geistlicher Ergetzung auff nachgesetzten Thon/ von newen Reimen gestellet* (Ingolstadt: Andreas Angermeyer in der Ederischen Truckerey; RISM B/VIII, 1599[07]). Philip Soergel sees the revival of the Altötting shrine in the late sixteenth century as a signal event in the promotion of pilgrimage in Counter-Reformation Bavaria. The dukes placed special emphasis on *local* shrines (rather than the famous but more distant shrines of Loreto and Rome) as a means of consolidating state power through the patronage of religious cults. See Soergel, *Wondrous in His Saints*, pp. 4, 10–11 and 161–62. On the Bavarian dukes' personal patronage of Altötting, see also Crook, *Orlando di Lasso's Imitation Magnificats*, pp. 65–68, and Pötzl, 'Volksfrömmigkeit', p. 889.

40. Vnd durch das gantze Bayerland/	And through all of Bavaria,
Kyrieeleison/	Kyrie eleison,
Der Glaub ist aller Welt bekand/	its faith is known to the whole world,
Alleluia/ Alleluia/ Gelobt sey Gott vnd Maria.	Alleluia, Alleluia, praise be to God and Mary.
41. Der bleibt vnd steht noch heut fürwahr/	[The faith] remains true to this day,
Kyrieeleison/	Kyrie eleison,
Wie er vor tausend Jaren war/	As it was a thousand years ago,
Alleluia/ Alleluia/ Gelobt sey Gott vnd Maria.	Alleluia, Alleluia, praise be to God and Mary.
42. Der Luther vnd der Lucifer/	Luther and Lucifer,
Kyrieeleison/	Kyrie eleison,
Die kommen mit eim newen Plerr/	They come with a new howling,
Alleluia/ Alleluia/ Gelobt sey Gott vnd Maria.	Alleluia, Alleluia, praise be to God and Mary.
43. Gott lob sie kommen vil zuspatt/	Thank God they have come too late,
Kyrieeleison/	Kyrie eleison,
Mit ihrem Klitterwerck vnd Kaht/	With their grime and excrement,
Alleluia/ Alleluia/ Gelobt sey Gott vnd Maria.	Alleluia, Alleluia, praise be to God and Mary.
44. Auß auß mit ihrem Ketzermist/	Out, out, with their heretic-dung,
Kyrieeleison/	Kyrie eleison,
Wers mit ihm hält/ der ist kein Christ	He who stands by [them] is no Christian,
Alleluia/ Alleluia/ Gelobt sey Gott vnd Maria.	Alleluia, Alleluia, praise be to God and Mary.

A subtle link to the genre of the litany may be seen in the continuous responses of 'Kyrieeleison' and 'Alleluia/ Alleluia/ Gelobt sey Gott und Maria', paralleling the series of responses (usually 'ora pro nobis' or 'Bitt für uns, Maria') found in litanies. This practice, which suggests alternation between a *Vorsinger* and the marchers, may be a peculiar characteristic of pilgrimage songs.[16]

---

[16] For example, in the *Catholisch Gesangbüchlein/ Auff die fürnembste Fest durchs gantze Jahr/ in der Kirchen: Auch bey den Processionen/ Creutzgängen/ Kirch- vnd Walfahrten/ nutzlich zugebrauchen* (Munich: Anna Berg Witwe, 1613; facs. ed. by Otto Holzapfel as *'Catholisch Gesangbüchlein'. München 1613. Photomechanischer Nachdruck, mit Kommentar und Nachwort von Otto Holzapfel* (Amsterdam: Holland University Press, 1979)), the five songs intended for processions and pilgrimages all contain short refrains such as 'Kyrieeleison', 'O Vatter mein' and 'Maria rein'. This songbook does not appear in RISM B/VIII, since no melodies are included.

Like the phenomenon of Counter-Reformation pilgrimage itself, songs like the *Schöner Catholischer Ruff* were designed with propagandistic as well as devotional intent, promoting the efficacy of Catholic shrines while sharpening the confessional distinctions between believing Catholics and the falsehoods [*Klitterwerck*] of heretics.[17] While the song itself is new, a significant aspect of this propaganda consists in the assertion of the agelessness of the Church's truth: 'The belief', the text reads, 'remains and stays true today / just as it was a thousand years ago', while 'Luther and Lucifer' come with 'a new howling'. Furthermore, the designation of the song itself as a *Ruff* also links it with pre-Reformation tradition, even if in spirit it is quite new.[18] On the one hand, this repertory of Catholic song was unprecedented in its militancy and in its vigorous promotion of shrines favoured by the Church hierarchy. On the other hand, by favouring the designation of *Ruf* over the more generic *Gesang*, and by bringing out the historical continuity of shrines' efficacy through narrative means (many songs parallel contemporary miracle books in their chronological accounts of recorded miracles), this repertory had a strong element of historicism.

The Andechs Pilgrimage in the Counter-Reformation

The single most important pilgrimage from the city of Augsburg by the early seventeenth century was that to the 'Holy Mountain' of Andechs, roughly three days removed to the south-east by foot. Some

---

[17] Klaus Guth, in his article on Marian pilgrimage in Germany, describes Luther's objections to the institution of pilgrimage. While images as such were unobjectionable on the grounds that they served to remind people of holy things, Luther vigorously opposed pilgrimage: 'solten alle wallefart nydergelegt werden, den es ist kein guttis nit drynnen, kein gepot, kein gehorsam, sondern untzehlich der sunden unnd gottis gebot zu vorachtung. Daher kummen szo viel betler, die durch solch wallen untzehlich buberey treyben, die betteln on not heren und gewonnenn' (quoted in Guth, 'Geschichtlicher Abriß der marianischen Wallfahrtsbewegung im deutschsprachigen Raum', in Wolfgang Beinert and Heinrich Petri, eds, *Handbuch der Marienkunde* (Regensburg: Pustet, 1984), p. 370). Nevertheless, pilgrimage persisted even in some Lutheran areas well into the sixteenth century, contributing to what might be called a 'confessionally mixed' culture; see ibid., pp. 372–74.

[18] A similar strategy may be seen, for example, in the *new Rueff-Büchlein/ Von Etlichen sonderbaren Catholischen/ Wahlfahrten-Gesängen* (Straubing: Andre Sommer, 1607; RISM B/VIII, 1607[13]): in addition to *Rufe* devoted to Christ's Passion, the cross, the Virgin Mary, the Eucharist and the angels, we find *Rufe* concerning particular shrines of more recent interest, such as that of St Benno in Munich (Benno, canonized in 1524 and whose relics were deposited in the Frauenkirche in Munich, became a notable object of veneration in the early seventeenth century), and the two Eucharistic shrines of Deggendorf and Andechs.

of the credit for the shrine's revival (it had existed from the twelfth century) may be attributed to Bishop Otto Truchseß von Waldburg of Augsburg, who in 1543 helped to establish the Trinity Confraternity, which was obliged to make the journey to Andechs twice yearly (by the late sixteenth century this group was commonly known as the Confraternity of the Holy Mountain of Andechs). Interest in Andechs was probably further stoked by the appearance of chronicles of the shrine and miracle books published in the late sixteenth and early seventeenth centuries.[19] Although detailed accounts of pilgrimages from Augsburg do not appear until after 1600, Andechs seems to have enjoyed considerable traffic by the early 1570s. By the early seventeenth century a half million pilgrims per year were making their way to the shrine.[20]

A manuscript from 1572 describing the procedures for displaying the holy relics at Andechs survives, giving useful information not only about the variety of holy objects present there, but also about the appropriate music to be performed while the relics were displayed for veneration.[21] Preceding the display of the relics were a series of prayers and Gospel readings. 'Then the antiphon *Salvator mundi* shall be sung by the clergy. And for the greater stirring of devotion and attention in the hearts of the people, instrumental music shall be heard, and afterwards it shall begin [again] after the presentation of the relics.'[22] The relics were divided into several groups: first relics of holy widows and female martyrs were displayed, followed successively by those of confessors, martyrs, the Apostles, the Virgin Mary, and the Passion; then followed thorns from the crown of Christ, pieces of the true cross, and a fragment of the shroud. After each of these relics was shown, instrumental music was played.[23] The ceremony culminated in the display of the three holy hosts; this was accompanied by the singing of an unnamed text (perhaps the Sanctus?) 'three times, each time beginning higher'.[24] Musically as well

---

[19] Pötzl cites two books, the *Cronica von dem hoch Würdigen vnd löblichen Heilthumb auff dem heiligen Berg Andechs* (1572 and 1575) and the *Außzug der Wunderzaichen vnd Gnaden so der Allmechtig Gott auff dem Hailigen Berg Andechs an den rechtglaubigen durch das Hochwürdigst daselbst rastende Haylthumb etlich jar her gewürcket vnnd erzaiget hat* (1595). See Pötzl, 'Volksfrömmigkeit', p. 890.

[20] See Hüttl, *Marianische Wallfahrten im süddeutschen-österreichischen Raum: Analysen von der Reformations- bis zur Aufkärungsepoche* (Köln: Bohlau, 1985), p. 46.

[21] BHSM, Klosterliteralien, Andechs 33, 'Ordo demonstrandi reliquias monasterii in monte sancto Andecensi'.

[22] 'Hic cantetur â Clero Antiphona Saluator mundi. Et ad maiorem in cordibus hominum attentionem et deuotionem excitandam, sone[n]t instrumenta Musices, et postea incipiatur ab ostensione Reliquiarum.' Ibid., fol. 13v.

[23] After each entry appears the phrase 'Hic sonent rursum Instrumenta Musices.' Ibid.

[24] 'Cantetur tribus uicibus semper altius incipiendo.' Ibid., fol. 28v.

as otherwise, the ceremonies at Andechs seem to have been quite elaborate at a relatively early stage.

Evidence from another manuscript, a chronicle of Andechs penned by the abbot Johann Chrysostomus in 1609 (and continued in a different hand thereafter), suggests an active musical life at the monastery in the following decades.[25] In 1581, for example, a woman identified as 'Maria Hirschpergerin Regitzern' established a foundation for the singing of a litany every Wednesday in four-voice polyphony, and the abbot Joachim instructed that the usual litany sung at Saturday Vespers also be used for that purpose.[26] Between 1588 and 1604 the monastery purchased music by Orlando di Lasso at least six times, including the *Lagrime di San Pietro* in 1595 and, most likely, the *Magnum opus musicum* in 1604.[27] Other references appear to purchases of music by the Augsburg composers Hans Leo Hassler, Adam Gumpelzhaimer and Gregor Aichinger.[28] Especially after 1600 and before the privations of the war in the 1630s, the scribe of the chronicle recorded numerous indications of polyphonic music of various kinds, the singing of litanies and the presence of at least an organ and clavichord.[29] Unfortunately, it is not clear how many of these musical resources were brought to bear on the ceremonies attended by Augsburg pilgrims, but the chronicle, together with the 'Ordo demonstrandi' of 1572, does at least suggest that the pilgrims heard fairly elaborate music at their destination as well as on the route thereto.

By the early seventeenth century, if not earlier, the Trinity Confraternity at Augsburg Cathedral was joined in its biannual

---

[25] 'Origo comitum Andecensium et florentissimi Monasterii Andecensis. Autore Joanne Chrysostomo Abbate'. ABA, Hs 104.

[26] 'den 3 Maÿ stifftet alhie ein wochentliche *Letanei*, all mitwochen mit vierstim[m]en zue singen, Maria Hirschpergerin Regitzern genant. Darfür sie hergeben 100R. vnnd damit, dise stifftung ohn felbar volzogen werdt, soll der Abbt seinem *Conuent* Järlich daruon 5R zinßgeben; *si dijs placet, dignum patella operculum*.

Alhie ist auch zuemerckhen, daß diser Abbt Joachim geordnet hat, zusingen die Litanei, die man alle sambstag pflegt zue singen. Wie nit weniger daß *placebo* daß man auch ieden sambstag nach d[er] *Vesper* beten thuet.' From 'Origo comitum Andecensium', ABA, Hs 104, p. 375.

[27] The manuscript records the purchase of 'Bicinia, Tricinia et Lachrymæ D. Petri per Orlandum p 1R 8K' in 1595 (ABA, Hs 104, p. 421); they also paid 'pro Cantionib. Orlandi 17R 30K' in 1604 (ibid., p. 519), a very large sum, which would imply the purchase of the monumental *Magnum opus musicum*. Other references to purchases of Lasso's music may be found on pp. 392–93, 394–95, 447 and 519.

[28] Ibid., pp. 490–91 and 603.

[29] In addition to the citations given above, see ibid., pp. 402–3, 406–7, 411–12, 417–18, 453, 457, 481, 499, 521–23, 529–30, 556–57, 565, 571, 584, 586, 587–88, 598, 622, 626, 627, 629, 634, 641, 655, 660, 662, 664–65, 684 and 695–96, all falling within the time period 1581–1640.

procession to Andechs (held around the feasts of Ascension in the spring and St Michael in the autumn) by other groups. On 20 May 1604, only two months after its inception, the Corpus Christi brotherhood met at Heilig Kreuz and 18 members volunteered to join the pilgrimage wearing red coats. The group financed a large candle decorated with their insignia that was to be carried to the chapel at Andechs containing the holy hosts, and which the brotherhood committed itself to maintaining in perpetuity. Once the pilgrims arrived at Andechs on the feast of Ascension one week later, the abbot allowed six members of the brotherhood to carry the canopy over the holy hosts in a procession, and also designated a special chamber at the monastery for the confraternity's housing.[30] The Corpus Christi confraternity may also have had a hand in raising funds to encourage the participation of poorer laypersons.[31]

It is not until the end of the 1610s that we have more detailed accounts of the Andechs pilgrimage and its musical accompaniment. Surviving ordinances, account books and descriptions allow us to paint a relatively vivid picture of these pilgrimages, including their order, route, itinerary and music, between roughly 1618 and 1630. These records testify not only to the broad-based participation of Catholics from various social strata, but also to the scope and variety of music, ranging from performances of polyphonic motets to litanies and vernacular songs. Perhaps the most fascinating collection of documents relating to the Andechs pilgrimage dates from around 1621 and is housed in the Katholisches Wesensarchiv at the Stadtarchiv Augsburg.[32] Contained here are, all in manuscript, an ordinance describing the order of the procession to Andechs, two ordinances for the final procession from the church of St Afra (just outside Augsburg) to the cathedral, and a small duodecimo itinerary of the pilgrimage. All these documents provide valuable musical information, and will be quoted at length.

The first ordinance, describing the order of the procession, begins by stating that a Mass will be held at SS Ulrich and Afra, and that the

---

[30] See the detailed account in the 'Kurtze beschreibung, wie die andächtige brueterschafft des allerheiligsten Fronleichnambs *Jesu Christi* … wider vfgericht', ABA, BO 2480, no. 2, fol. 4r. See also the shorter Latin account in the 'De initijs ac progressu omnium Fraternitatum, quae in alma hac urbe Augustana fuerunt diversis temporibus erectae', D-As, 2° Aug 346, fol. 22v.

[31] *DR*, 25 May 1612.

[32] StAA, KWA E45[11]. The wrapper is labelled 'Augsburg. | Domcapitel. | Capital, und Zinßzahlungen für verschiedenen | Bruderschaften, besonders für die Bru- | derschaft der allerheiligsten Drefal- | tigkeit, dan[n] Beschreibung der Ord- | nung be heil. Berg-Einzug | vom 17ten Jahrhundert'. My suggestion of 1621 as the date for this collection is based on the writing on the back page of the first document (an ordinance describing the order of the procession), which reads '6 Ordnung. 21 | Wie die Processiones der | grossen Kürchfahrt zum | haÿl Berg anzustöllen'.

procession will begin after the singing of the *Veni sancte Spiritus*. The order of the procession is given as follows:

1. First a member of the Brotherhood of the Most Holy Trinity with a staff.
2. The banner of the clerical Confraternity [of the Trinity], along with the banner of the Corpus Christi Brotherhood.
3. A cross, flanked by two boys with burning torches.
4. The priest of the clerical Brotherhood of the Most Holy Trinity.
5. The Franciscans from the Barfüßerkirche as directors [of the procession].
6. The musicians with their instruments.
7. The pilgrims in black cloaks from the Brotherhood of the Holy Trinity.
8. The priest of the Corpus Christi Brotherhood.
9. The pilgrims in red cloaks from the same brotherhood.
10. All male pilgrims, as well as other brotherhoods with their banners.
11. The lay brotherhood's banner from the Brotherhood of the Holy Trinity.
12. Distinguished [i.e., patrician] women.
13. [Singers singing] a German song with a *Vorsinger*.
14. All [other] women.

Another list immediately follows describing the order as it approaches Andechs; it is similar to one given above, except that explicit mention is made of members of the Marian Congregation (who walk after the red-cloaked members of the Corpus Christi Confraternity), as well as of other pilgrims from the neighbouring towns of Dillingen, Neresheim and Wallerstein, who march with the other lay men and women and presumably would have joined the procession in Augsburg. This order is somewhat schematic but reflects the typical arrangement of the order of these pilgrimages: first, the prominent position given to the main confraternities; second, the position of laypersons at the end, divided by gender; and third, the presence of distinct musical groups (here, instrumental musicians and, at least, a *Vorsinger* leading the performance of vernacular song) dispersed throughout the length of the procession. The order given here is confirmed by another extant ordinance for the spring 1622 pilgrimage, stemming from the Franciscan order and largely identical to the one quoted above.[33]

---

[33] See 'Ordnung, so Anno 1622 .23.24. | 25. 26. 27. 28. 29. auff den H. Berg ge- | halten worden, vnd noch soll gehalten werd[en]', in StAA, KWA E47⁶, fol. 1r.

The small itinerary mentioned above provides invaluable information on the conduct of such a procession to Andechs and back, and illustrates the variety and ubiquitousness of music. This document is worth quoting in its entirety:

Instruction concerning the Holy Mountain.

In the morning at 4 o'clock the pilgrims should assemble at St Ulrich [and Afra], where a Mass is celebrated. After the *Agnus Dei* the *In viam pacis* is intoned, then the *Benedictus*, then a hymn verse or another. After this *In viam pacis* is finished, the priest sings the *Kyrie* with its verses, which are responded to in polyphony. The benediction follows, and then the litany [is sung] in the church and through the city [as the procession] reaches the Red Gate.

2.

At the church of St Francis near Mering the musicians come together, and the litany is sung through [the streets] of Mering.

3.

The litany is sung again for a half-hour in *Mering*, through the town and into the church. There shall be a mass, and *three or four pieces* will be sung. The midday meal follows until 12 o'clock.

4.

Midday

Around 12 o'clock the pilgrims again assemble in the church at *Mering*, and there will be singing through the streets of the town. The cloaks and staves may be left there.

5.

Evening

The pilgrims assemble again at *Grafrath*, and go continuously over the Ammer bridge; then the litany is sung until we reach the church; the *Regina cœli* is sung back and forth; there we stay overnight.

6.

Morning

Around 4 o'clock or 4.30 the Mass is sung contrapuntally and short throughout. From there [the procession] goes to *Inningen*, where there is also continuous singing, then no more. By midday we are [to arrive] at *Herrsching, or Steindorf* by the lake. Around midday at 12 o'clock [the procession] leaves for the Holy Mountain, and the pilgrims assemble themselves on the Holy Mountain in a field where the benediction is given. When the procession emerges [from the church], the musicians sing the *Regina cœli* in four voices from the altar in the choir. After this there is nothing else to do.

7.

The next day, on the feast of the Ascension, there is a Mass at 5 o'clock. Afterwards [the pilgrims] come to show their reverence [to the relics] and to have breakfast. There is nothing else at all to do until [the procession] reaches Türkenfeld, where there is singing and a sermon. From there we go to *Mohrenweiß*, where there is also singing, and finally the singing of the *Regina cœli*.

8.

Morning
At 4 o'clock or 4.30 there is a Mass during which they sing *two or three motets*; after this we immediately depart with a sung litany, towards *Merching* and *Mering*, but finally during the Mass *several motets* are heard, and the final midday meal is taken. There is a break at Mering, in the church dedicated to St Michael.

9.

At 12 o'clock we go out of the church with a sung litany to the castle chapel, where, after the litany is finished, the *Regina cœli* is sung; then we continue with the litany to the tavern, and the procession continues to St Afra.

10.

We are met in the field [by people coming from Augsburg]; there are responses to each verse [versicle] [sung] by the fathers of St Ulrich [and Afra]. Outside St Afra the litany begins and [is sung] through the church. [There] is a sermon.

11.

First we come together at Augsburg by the brook at 5 o'clock. [There] is a procession; when [the church bells] of St Ulrich [and Afra] are rung, we must begin the litany, and continue it all of the way to the cathedral.

The itinerary is concluded by a short series of Latin versicles and responses, probably spoken or sung upon returning to Augsburg (see point 9). This account vividly demonstrates the role played by music in the course of the entire ritual. Litanies were sung continuously while the procession was under way, while polyphonic masses and motets (and especially settings of the Marian antiphon *Regina cœli*) were frequently heard at stations along the route. The previously cited ordinance's references to instrumental musicians and a *Vorsinger* indicates that the musical offerings may have even been more elaborate than this itinerary suggests; furthermore, instrumental and polyphonic vocal music would have awaited the pilgrims upon their arrival at the Holy Mountain.

The author of the itinerary mentions what was a common practice in the Andechs pilgrimage, namely, that the returning pilgrims were welcomed outside Augsburg at the church of St Afra by another procession emerging from the city. The other two documents in this fascicle describe the combined procession of these groups between St Afra and the cathedral, a procession that surely must have been one of the most spectacular events of the year (with some 40 different groups) and involved a considerable amount of music-making. Musicians were placed at eight different locations within this procession. After the first group of clergy and monks came 'the musicians who were on the Holy Mountain'.[34] Separate groups of musicians (the complements are unknown) accompanied the Corpus Christi brotherhood,[35] the Jesuit Marian Congregation,[36] the clergy of the cathedral and St Moritz[37] and the Benedictines of SS Ulrich and Afra.[38] German songs were sung in two places towards the end of the procession, where most of the women (both pilgrims and non-pilgrims) marched.[39] The final document in the fascicle, indicating the order of the procession as it entered the cathedral, shows that the pilgrims went first as a group, followed by the cathedral clergy headed by banners, torches and the cathedral cantorate;[40] other confraternities, religious orders and laypersons (again, divided by gender) followed. From the beginning of the pilgrimage to the end, monophonic, polyphonic and instrumental music complemented the emphatic visual display of banners, crosses and torches.

While the Franciscans apparently kept order during the procession, it was the Trinity Confraternity, the originators of this pilgrimage, who paid for priests, banner-carriers, musicians, food and drink. A series of balance sheets from the confraternity survives, dated between autumn 1618 and autumn 1629, which indicates these expenses specifically, and allows us to track which musicians were paid and what amounts.[41] The brotherhood typically paid the most money to the *Vorsinger*, whose earnings grew from 36 Kreutzer to 2 Reichstaler (an increase of over 300 per cent) by 1627; this suggests that he was kept quite busy during the pilgrimage. Lesser amounts were paid to a cantorate (*kanthereÿ*) and to some girls who met the procession along the route and sang songs. The

---

[34] 'Die Musicanten welche vf dem h. berg gewest'.

[35] 'Die bilger von der bruederschafft deß hayligen fronleichnambs Christi mit ihrem fahnen vnd *Music*'.

[36] 'Die *Sodales* von den herrn Jesuitern, welche vf dem h. berg gewest seindt sambt ihren *Music* &c.'

[37] 'Alle Gaistliche Prælaten der Statt, vnd zufordst der herr dombprobst, dechant, vnd dombherrn darauf die von vnser L. frawen, vnd St: Mauriz mit einer *Music*'.

[38] 'Die herren von S. Vlrich mit iren fahnen vnd *Music*'.

[39] In both cases, 'Ain Teütsch gesang'. The ordinance from the Franciscans confirms that a *Vorsinger* was involved here: 'Ein teütsch gesang mit einem vorsinger'. See StAA, KWA E47[6], fol. 2r.

[40] 'Hierauf volgen die so nit auf dem H: Berg gewest. &c. 5. Die 4 Chorfahnen des Thombstiffts, wie auch ein Crucifix neben 2. Windtliechten. 6. Darauf die Music des dombstiffts volgen soll.'

[41] The account sheets for the pilgrimages in autumn 1618, autumn 1619 and spring 1629 are located in 'Rechnungen über Ausgaben zur Wallfahrt zum Berg Andechs (1618–1750) – Jahrtags-Stiftungen und Vermächtnisse (1625–1761) – Jahres Rechnungen und Belege (1626–1764)', StAA, KWA L361; those for autumn 1621, autumn 1627, spring 1628 and autumn 1629 may be found in 'Legate und Jahrtagsstiftungen zur Dreifaltigkeitsbruderschaft (1590–1714)', StAA, KWA L404.

total expenses for music would typically amount to a little less than 10 per cent of the total.

Table 7.1 shows the expenses for musicians as given in the extant balance sheets, arranged chronologically. The table shows the dramatic increase in resources devoted to the Andechs pilgrimage between 1621 and 1627, as well as the gradual expansion of payments for musicians. Apart from the dramatic increase in payments for the *Vorsinger*, the brotherhood paid another *Vorsinger* from 1628 to accompany the procession between the church of St Afra outside the city and SS Ulrich and Afra within the city walls (by the time the procession reached St Afra, its numbers were swelled considerably by the rendezvous with the procession coming from Augsburg).[42] Also in 1628 and 1629, 30 Kreutzer were paid for the services of an organist at Andechs. The 'duren blaßer' identified in these two years may have been a member (or members) of the Augsburg *Stadtpfeifer*, but there are no further details in the account books themselves. Finally, the musicians are identified in some years as 'Musicanten' and in other years as the 'kantereÿ'; they were probably not attached to the cathedral (in fact, the account given in StAA, KWA E45[11] states that the cathedral cantorate accompanied the procession only as it returned from Andechs), but rather to the church of St Moritz. The autumn 1627 account book records a payment of 20 Kreutzer to 'the schoolmaster of St Moritz and his choirboys, who sang on the way out and on the way in [to the city]'.[43] The autumn 1629 balance sheet gives more specific confirmation that this group of musicians sang primarily on the way out of Augsburg and during the final procession from the church of St Afra.[44] The singing of this choir and the engagement of a second *Vorsinger* as the procession entered Augsburg suggests a motivation to enhance the aural impact of the pilgrimage as it approached the mixed confessional area of the city.[45]

---

[42] The wording of the balance sheet from spring 1628 reads: 'vorsinger der von St: Affra herein gsungen', while that from one year later reads: 'Mehr dem vorsing[er] von St: Affra herrin'. It is unclear whether this *Vorsinger* was associated with the church of St Afra itself. StAA, KWA L404.

[43] 'Mehr dem hrn schuel maister bei St: Moritzen, vnd seinen kantttoreibuben die hinauß vnd widerumb hrein haben gsungen'. StAA, KWA L404.

[44] 'Mehr dem hern schuelmaister bei St Moritz[en] vnnd seinen canthoribus die hinauß vnd widerumb von St: Affra herein hab[en] gsungen'. StAA, KWA L404.

[45] The Protestant chronicler Georg Kölderer may well have been thinking of such spectacles when he revelled in a thunderstorm that soaked members of the Corpus Christi confraternity as they held their procession to or from Andechs: 'Da füell so starckhes regenwetter ein, dz sie es wie die katzen, so man durch die bäch zeucht, aller trieff nass verrichten muessen.' From D-As, 2° Cod. S. 43, fol. 237, quoted in Roeck, *Eine Stadt im Krieg und Frieden*, p. 185 n.

Table 7.1 Music expenses for the Andechs pilgrimage, 1618–1629

Date	Expenses for music		Total expenses	% for music
Autumn 1618	*Vorsinger*	36K		
	Cantorate	<u>15K</u>		
		51K	9R 51K 1H	8.6
Autumn 1619	*Vorsinger*	36K		
	Girls	3K		
	Cantorate	<u>15K</u>		
		54K	10R 18K	8.7
Autumn 1621	*Vorsinger*	36K		
	Girls	3K		
	Cantorate	<u>15K</u>		
		54K	12R 28K	7.2
Autumn 1627	*Vorsinger*	2R		
	Girls	8K		
	Cantorate	<u>20K</u>		
		2R 28K	25R 10½K	9.8
Spring 1628	*Vorsinger*	2R		
	Girls	6K		
	Organist	30K		
	Piper	30K		
	Musicians	20K		
	Vorsinger from			
	St Afra	<u>15K</u>		
		3R 41K	26R 33K	13.9
Spring 1629	*Vorsinger*	2R		
	Girls	10K		
	Organist	30K		
	Musicians	20K		
	Vorsinger from			
	St Afra	15K		
	Piper	<u>30K</u>		
		3R 45K	27R 28K	13.6
Autumn 1629	*Vorsinger*	2R		
	Girls	10K		
	Cantorate	<u>1R</u>		
		3R 10K	26R 24K	12.0

Other Local Pilgrimages

The Andechs pilgrimage was surely the most significant pilgrimage for Augsburg's Catholics in this period, but it was not an isolated phenomenon. Traditional pilgrimage sites like the Marian shrines of Einsiedeln in Switzerland and Loreto remained prominent destinations, especially for pilgrims with the means for longer journeys.[46] Copies of the Holy House of Loreto or Roman pilgrimage churches constructed in various places in Catholic Germany offered a suitable substitute for pilgrims of lesser means.[47] One of these 'Maria Hilf' chapels, built to resemble the church of S Maria Rotonda (i.e., the Pantheon) in Rome and built not far from Augsburg on the so-called Lechfeld (the site of Emperor Otto I's decisive victory over the Hungarians in 955), was visited regularly by the Corpus Christi brotherhood by the second decade of the seventeenth century.[48] Pilgrims en route to more distant shrines like Loreto and Rome could hope for a financial contribution (called a *Steur* or *Viaticum*) from the Augsburg Cathedral chapter; the chapter's minutes record numerous such contributions, especially after 1600.[49] Another traditional pilgrimage destination lay within Augsburg itself: the *Wunderbares Gut* at the church of Heilig Kreuz. Contemporary records indicate that the Corpus Christi brotherhood from Munich travelled to Heilig Kreuz on at least two occasions, in 1615 and again in

[46] The Corpus Christi Confraternity was able to make a pilgrimage at least twice to Einsiedeln, in 1607 and 1614; see 'De initijs', fols 27r and 29v.

[47] Many copies of the *santa casa* were constructed by the Fugger family in the wake of their successful pilgrimage to Loreto in 1570; see Soergel, *Wondrous in His Saints*, p. 223.

[48] 'De initijs', D-As, 2° Aug. 346, fol. 29v. On the background of this chapel, see Pötzl, 'Volksfrömmigkeit', p. 902, and Ludwig Dorn, 'Das Mirakelbuch der Wallfahrt Maria Hilf in Speiden', *JVAB*, 20 (1986), pp. 143–44. In 1641 a collection of brief, homophonic songs for cantus and bass in honour of 'Maria Hilf' chapels in Augsburg, Munich and Passau was published in Munich, the *Maria hilff/ Das ist: Fünff schöne newe Geistliche Lieder/ Von der Allerglorwürdigsten milt- vnd hilffreichisten Jungkfrawen vnd Mutter Gottes MARIA. Welche vnder dem trostreichen Tittul MARIA hillf Bey Augspurg auff dem Lechfeld in Schwaben. Bey München auff der Aw/ in Bayern. Bey Passau auff dem Capuccinerberg in Oesterreich* (Munich: n.p., 1641; RISM B/VIII, 1641[14]).

[49] Augsburg was a popular way station for northern European pilgrims on their way to Rome. See Walter Pötzl, 'Die Sorge des Augsburger Domkapitels um die Pilger (1600–1620)', *Bayerisches Jahrbuch für Volkskunde* (1982), pp. 2–5, 10–15. Loreto was a particularly popular destination for members of the Jesuit Marian Congregation such as Johannes Rid, who recorded his pilgrimage there in 1602; see Rolle, *Heiligkeitsstreben und Apostolat*, pp. 22–23. Many Augsburg Catholics chose to go on a pilgrimage to Rome during the Holy Years of 1575 and 1600. These were encouraged by Bishops Johann Egolph von Knöringen and Heinrich V von Knöringen respectively, in letters to their flock: see StAA, KWA B10[6] and the *Summarischer bericht von würckung vnd geniessung deß Jubeljars. Dem Christlichen Pfarrvölcklein im Bistumb Augspurg, von den Predigstülen offentlich zuuerlesen* (Dillingen: Johann Mayer, [c.1600]). On 27 July 1602 the Augsburg

July 1642; a surviving ordinance attests that on the latter occasion the brotherhood sang the *Salve Regina* and litanies of the Virgin Mary along the route.[50]

While traditional shrines like Loreto and Einsiedeln remained popular with Augsburg pilgrims, they did not neglect shrines of more recent vintage whose establishment coincided with the rise of Counter-Reformation ideology and propaganda. One of the most prominent of these was the shrine of St Benno at the Frauenkirche in Munich. Benno, bishop of Meissen in the late eleventh century, had been canonized in 1524, but the exigencies of the Reformation led Bishop Johann of Meissen to give Benno's relics to Duke Albrecht V of Bavaria in 1576.[51] Albrecht and his successor Wilhelm V, eager to bolster the case for moving the seat of the bishopric to Munich from Freising, vigorously promoted the cult of Benno by enshrining his relics at the Frauenkirche and by constructing a massive arch inside the church in Benno's honour, known as the *Bennobogen*. Although Wilhelm failed to bring the Bishop of Freising to Munich, the promotion of the Benno cult resulted in a Jesuit drama in 1598,[52] the establishment of a Benno Confraternity in 1603, and a rising tide of pilgrims from Bavaria and Swabia. On 10 September 1605 a 600-strong procession arrived from Augsburg, consisting of clergy and various confraternities.[53] We have no information about the particular music the Augsburgers used in this pilgrimage, but a song concerning St Benno had been available since 1603, published as *Ein Andächtiger Rueff für die Pilgram. Vom H.*

Cathedral chapter announced that extra indulgences were granted by Pope Clement VIII for those who attended church on the feast of the Assumption of the Virgin, since so many were not able to make the long trek to Rome two years previously (see *DR*, 27 July 1602). The cathedral's support for pilgrimage is further reflected in a book for pilgrims to Marian shrines penned by Cleophas Distelmayr, the preacher at the cathedral. His *Wall- und Bilgerfahrth. Der aller seeligsten Jungkfrawen vnnd Mutter Gottes Marie: Das ist/ andächtige Betrachtungen/ von dem allerheiligsten Leben/ Wandel/ auch Leyden vnd Sterben/ vnsers Seligmachers JESV Christi/ vnd seiner gebenedeyte Mutter Maria* (Augsburg: Johann Schultes, 1596) consists of a lengthy explication of the Virgin Mary's virtues for the pilgrim.

[50] 'Ordnung/ Der *Procession* oder Wallfahrt/ welche deß zarten Fronleichnam[m]s ErtzBruderschafft zu München/ nacher Augspurg zu dem Wunderbarlichen Hochheiligsten Sacrament auff den 2. 3. 4. 5. vnd 6. Julij 1642. Jahr angestellet', StAA, KWA A42[13]. The 1615 pilgrimage is mentioned in the 'De initijs', fol. 29v.

[51] Rebecca Wagner Oettinger has treated Benno's canonization and Luther's reaction to it extensively in *Music as Propaganda*, pp. 69–88.

[52] Published in Munich by Adam Berg in 1603. On the cult of St Benno in general, see Pötzl, 'Volksfrömmigkeit', pp. 906–7, and especially Soergel, *Wondrous in His Saints*, pp. 181–91, who notes the significance of the Benno cult as having largely been created out of a vacuum.

[53] See Pötzl, 'Volksfrömmigkeit', pp. 906–7, and the manuscript 'De initijs', fol. 23r.

Bischoff Bennone: Darinn sein Leben geuten Theils, vnd etliche Wunderwerck begriffen.[54] This lengthy song of 89 stanzas, with the incipit *Ihr lieben Christen singen her* and a repeated refrain of 'Alleluia/ Bitt GOTT für vns S. Benno', was reprinted by Berg's widow Anna in 1613 along with two other songs about St Benno, one to be sung while kneeling before his reliquary, and another to be sung at the beginning of the route home.[55] The texts of these songs consist largely of a catalogue of miracles imputed to St Benno.

Somewhat closer to Augsburg, a shrine dedicated to the Holy Trinity was erected in Burgau in 1612 with the approval of Bishop Heinrich V von Knöringen. Although there are few references to the shrine in contemporary Augsburg documents, it did occasion the printing of the *Ter tria cœlestia cantica* (1636), a set of pilgrimage songs by a former priest there, Gallus Thomae.[56] The title and the contents, consisting of three sets of three songs each for the Trinity, Christ and the Virgin Mary respectively (interspersed with numerous other individual songs and prayer texts), allude to the threefold nature of the Trinity honoured at the shrine. Characteristic of songbooks published in the early seventeenth century (Thomae claims in his preface that this book had twice been printed earlier), Thomae's songbook calls for traditional, well-known melodies (the tune *Gelobet seyst du Jesu Christ* appears in seven of the 25 songs) to which both old and new texts have been affixed. Among the more traditional items are the German version of the *Salve Regina*, *Frew dich du Himmelkönigin*, and the song *Reich vnd Arm sollen frölich seyn*; newer texts include *Maria O betrübtes Hertz*, sung to the old tune *Da Jesus an dem Creutze stund* (thus linking the sorrows of the Virgin with the Passion of Christ), and *O Jesu mein höchstes Guet*, sung to the tune *Gelobet seyst du Jesu Christ*. It is curious that Thomae provides notation for two songs only, which are among the oldest in the repertory: *Maria zart von edler Art* and *Patris Sapientia*.

Despite the bewildering variety in pilgrimage songs and texts by the early seventeenth century, involving both traditional and newer elements,

---

[54] RISM B/VIII, 1603[13]. The only extant copy, previously housed at D-Bds, has been lost.

[55] These two songs' incipits are *Wir grüssen dich von hertzen sehr* and *Wir kommen wider zu dir her*. See the *Catholisch Gesangbüchlein/ Auff die fürnembste Fest durchs gantze Jahr in der Kirchen: Auch bey den Processionen/ Creutzgängen/ Kirch- vnd Walfahrten/ nutzlich zugebrauchen.* All three songs are intended to be sung to the same melody.

[56] *TER TRIA COELESTIA CANTICA, Das ist: Neun Himmelische Lobgesäng/ vnd andächtige Gebett/ auß heyliger Schrifft genommen/ zu der aller hochheyligsten Dreyfaltigkeit. Der Himmelkönigin Maria/ vnd andern heyligen Patronen deß newgeweichten Capellins zu Burggau im Allgew/ wider Krieg/ Thewrung vnnd Pestilentz* (Augsburg: Andreas Aperger, author, 1636; RISM B/VIII, 1636[10]).

it is worth remembering that church authorities continued to exert a strong influence over which songs were sung and disseminated. Thomae's *Ter tria cœlestia cantica* is a fine example of this influence. On the reverse of the title page we find the official sanction of vicar-general Caspar Zeiller, who states that 'Since these songs oppose neither the Catholic faith, nor good morals, we permit them to be published.'[57] Several pages later, Thomae himself provides the following epigram:[58]

WIlt deinem Leyd vnd Schmertzen wehren.	If you wish to guard against pain and suffering,
So liß diß Gsang gar offt vnd gern.	Then read these songs often and well.
Deinen Ohren/ diß Saitenspil/	To your ears this sounding of strings
Bringt Christlich Frewd vnd Wollust vil.	Brings Christian joy and desire.
Vnkeusch Gesang/ dir nicht gefall/	Let unchaste songs not please you,
Auß rainem Hertz/ lob Gott mit schall.	Praise God loudly with a pure heart.
Darinnen nichts mit Ketzerey/	In [here] is nothing to do with heresy,
Beschuldet ist/ noch Triegerey.	Nor with deception.
Dise Gesang gar schaden nicht/	These songs indeed harm no one,
Nach heyliger Schrifft seynd sie gericht/	They are made according to Holy Scripture,
Zu Lob vnd Ehr/ Gottes gar wol/	For the praise and honour of God,
Den man allzeit recht loben soll.	Whom one should always praise rightly.

Thomae's epigram reminds us that pilgrimage song (and Catholic song in general) in this period must not only be seen as an expression of devotion, but also as a means of Catholic propaganda. The descriptions of pilgrimages to Andechs and elsewhere cited above testify to the broad-based participation of different social groups, and thus may well have provided an opportunity for the kind of short-term *communitas* emphasized in the Turners' influential study. On the other hand, attempts by Catholic authorities to control pilgrimages, not only with respect to their overall organization but also their symbolic content, lends support to the Turners' critics, who have tended to frame these events more as

---

[57] 'CVm ista cantica nec fidei Catholicæ, nec bonis moribus aduersentur, ea publicari permittimus. | Gaspar Zeillerus SS. | Theologiæ D. Vica- | rius Augustanus.' From *Ter tria coelestia cantica*.

[58] Ibid., p. 7.

sites of contestation.[59] The crystallization of Catholic identity in Augsburg proceeded more rapidly in the upper echelons of society than among the masses. While processions, pilgrimages and their associated music certainly played a propagandistic role, serving to bolster Catholic identity from within while making an impression upon Protestant spectators, we must assume that the meaning of these spectacles could be construed variously among participants and observers alike.

---

[59] John Eade writes that 'it is necessary to develop a view of pilgrimage not merely as a field of social relations but also as a *realm of competing discourses*.... Accordingly, the analytical emphasis shifts from positivist, generic accounts of the features and functions of pilgrimage, and of the extrinsic characteristics of its focal shrines, towards an investigation of how the practice of pilgrimage and the sacred powers of a shrine are constructed as varied and possibly conflicting representations by the different sectors of the cultic constituency, and indeed by those outside it as well.' See Eade and Sallnow, eds, *Contesting the Sacred*, p. 5. Many German prelates of the fifteenth and sixteenth centuries, as Soergel argues (*Wondrous in His Saints*, pp. 49–52), linked popular pilgrimage with the threat of rural revolts and often sought (sometimes unsuccessfully) to subject them to church control.

CHAPTER EIGHT

Music, Confession and the Disaster of the Thirty Years War

Until the early 1630s Augsburg had been spared from any direct depredation from the periodic military conflicts that ravaged areas of Bohemia and northern and western Germany. While Imperial Catholic forces subdued Protestant armies – most decisively at the Battles of White Mountain (1620), Dessau (1626) and Lutter (1626) – most citizens of Augsburg could only hope that the relative religious peace and confessional balance enshrined in the city's constitution in 1555 would hold. Yet indications of confessional consciousness among the citizenry had been proliferating for several decades. The *Kalenderstreit* of 1584 and the resulting expulsion of Protestant superintendent Georg Müller was a dramatic sign that local Protestants would not easily accept perceived infringements of their religious rights. Vernacular song, which for many decades had served Protestants well as a means of collective religious expression and confessional propaganda, once again became an effective vehicle of Protestant resistance against the seeming bias of the patrician-dominated city council. For the most part the biconfessional council – trapped, as it were, between a potentially restive Protestant population and the military power of the neighbouring Catholic state of Bavaria – steered a religiously neutral course, but by 1600 key councillors from the Catholic Fugger and Welser families were embracing the Counter-Reformation cause more explicitly. The Jesuits, whose church and Gymnasium of St Salvator had been established with Fugger money in the 1580s, promoted confessionalization through education, sermonizing and the organization of public religious spectacles. As confraternities multiplied, processions wound their way through Protestant neighbourhoods, and pilgrims made regular journeys to Andechs, composers like Gregor Aichinger and Christian Erbach responded with music celebrating the Virgin Mary, the Eucharist and other Catholic devotional symbols.

Direct confessional confrontation, however, was rare. Cooperation, not conflict, characterized the day-to-day conduct of business and governmental affairs. Worsening economic conditions and periodic outbreaks of plague (the city suffered from a period of massive hyperinflation in 1622–23 and an epidemic in 1627–28) affected both sides of the confessional divide equally. Musically, no identifiable 'confessional style' emerged on the part of Protestants or Catholics. The strict religious beliefs of the Fugger had not prevented one of their members from employing a Protestant, Hans Leo Hassler, as a chamber musician, while the Protestant cantor Adam Gumpelzhaimer did not hesitate to add Catholic sacred music to his choir's repertory. Clearly, the increasing awareness and expression of confessional differences through music and other media did not necessarily lead to overt conflict. The provocative songs by hot-headed Protestants denouncing the patriciate, emperor and pope in the wake of the *Kalenderstreit* were a serious matter demanding investigation and, in some cases, prosecution, but by and large the council succeeded in maintaining the confessional peace.

This changed dramatically on 6 March 1629, when Emperor Ferdinand II, emboldened by the success of Catholic arms, promulgated the Edict of Restitution. Signs had been ominous since June of the previous year, when the emperor unilaterally elevated 11 Catholic families to the Augsburg patriciate and called for their election to the city council. With the Edict the following March he demanded the return to Catholic control of all ecclesiastical properties that had been secularized or lost to the Protestants since the Treaty of Passau in 1552; more directly relevant to the case of Augsburg was his insistence on Catholic jurisdiction in the Imperial cities. Initially the council refused to enforce the Edict, but direct pressure from the emperor's commissar led the Catholic *Stadtpfleger* to dismiss the 14 Protestant preachers on 8 August. Subsequently Protestant members of the city council were dismissed, and churches were either closed or turned over to Catholic control. In February 1630 the authorities gained control over St Anna, the nerve-centre of Augsburg Protestantism; by the following October the Jesuits began teaching in the St Anna Gymnasium. All Protestant services within city walls were strictly banned, whether in public or private.

The Edict did not eliminate the performance of Protestant song, but channelled it in new directions. In the public sphere, the city council outlawed all distribution of unapproved songs and banned all singing apart from the regular street-singing of Catholic choirs on Sundays, further mandating that only songs with Latin, Catholic texts [*Lateinische Cantiones et textus Catholicos*] were to be allowed.[1] The reading or singing of psalms, too, was forbidden in the schools. An anonymous chronicler reported that the council summoned all Protestant Latin and German schoolmasters to the city hall on 30 September 1629, demanding that they cease all reading or singing of the Lutheran catechism and psalter. Refusing to do this on grounds of religious conscience, all were dismissed from their posts early the next

---

[1] D-As, 2° Cod. Aug. 123, 'Singularia Augustana', no. 14, fol. 3r.

month.[2] The council's action here would be entirely consistent with demands made the following spring by Bishop Heinrich von Knöringen, who according to the terms of the Edict enjoyed spiritual jurisdiction over all the city's residents. On 4 April 1630 Heinrich would submit 29 points for the council's consideration, among which were the outright banning of all 'heretical' [*ketzerisch*] books and pictures, the forbidding of Lutheran students' singing in Latin and mandatory Catholic catechism and Mass attendance for all city orphans. The council would confirm the demands by the end of the month.[3]

As in the period of the *Kalenderstreit*, some Protestants resorted to music as a means of resistance. Already in October 1629, a chronicler reported that three nights in a row 'three angels' (children, perhaps?) sang *Ein feste Burg ist unser Gott* and *Erhalt uns Herr bei deinem Wort*, two of the most confessionally inflammatory Protestant chorales, in front of a city gate. By the time city guards arrived, the perpetrators had disappeared.[4] About a year later, as I discussed in Chapter 2, the weaver Martin Haller was prosecuted for owning (but not necessarily for singing) several songs decrying the Edict, including *Die Zeit die Ist So Trawrigkleich* (an ironic contrafactum of the Christmas song *Der Tag der ist so freudenreich*), *Ach Gott, mein Seel ist sehr betriebt* (model unknown) and *Wo es Gott nit mit Augspurg helt* (a contrafactum of *Wo Gott der Herr nicht bei uns hält*); the latter song in particular had troubled the authorities considerably in the era of the *Kalenderstreit*. During his third interrogation on 4 November 1630, Haller also admitted to the authorities that around the time of the Edict's promulgation his wife's friend Barbara Magenbuch had given him yet another song lamenting the position of Augsburg's Protestants:

> 2. How could he say that the aforementioned Magenbuch only gave him one song, namely, *Die Zeit die ist so traurigelich*? For she herself has admitted that there were three, including the above-mentioned song, *Wo es Gott nit mit Augspurg hällt*, and *Ach Gott mein Seel ist sehr betriebt*.

> Upon hearing this he did not deny that right at the beginning of the Reformation [i.e., Restitution] he received from Magenbuch

---

[2] StAA, Reichsstadt-Chroniken 28, 'Gründtliche Beschreibung Dessen was sich von A:° 1629. biß A°~1648. Jn Gaist: vnd Welttlichen Händlen Zwischen beeden *Religionen* Inn Augsburg begeben vnd zugetragen. Durch Eine Wahrhaffte, vnd der sachen selbst erfahrne Persohn aufgezaichnet', fols. 1v–2r.

[3] See Joseph Spindler, *Heinrich V. von Knöringen, Fürstbischof von Augsburg (1598–1646): Seine kirchenpolitische Tätigkeit* (Dillingen: Verlagsanstalt von J. Keller & Co., 1915), p. 34.

[4] D-As, 4° Cod. S. 8, fols. 66v–67r. Also cited in Roeck, *Eine Stadt im Krieg und Frieden*, p. 674.

a little song in the tune of *An Wasserflüssen Babylon*. This was the song that the fisherman Glatz had altered, but he cannot remember the beginning or the end of it. Otherwise he stands by his previous answer.[5]

Christoph Glatz himself had already proved troublesome to the Restitution government on account of this song, which clearly linked the fate of Augsburg's dismissed Protestant clergy with the Israelites' Babylonian exile. The previous March Glatz had met several friends at a local tavern, 'Bey der Gretha', where he allegedly sang this song. A weaver by the name of Christoph Obermayr listened to the song and insisted that he already owned a copy of it himself, which Glatz could not believe. Glatz wagered one Reichsthaler (or Gulden, a not inconsiderable sum of money for someone with modest means) that Obermayr did not actually have the song, and demanded to see it. A few days later Obermayr met Glatz again in the tavern, and produced his copy of the song. Although Glatz claimed that it was a different song, those around the table agreed with Obermayr and insisted that Glatz make good on the bet; otherwise they would report him to the authorities. In the documents concerning the case it was alleged not only that Glatz had sung the song in the tavern, but also that he had at least recited several stanzas of it in a public place.[6]

Having increased its surveillance of forbidden music in public places such as taverns, the council also moved against private prayer meetings, which often involved praying, reading of devotional tracts and psalm-singing. The council instructed the city bailiff, Hans Voth von Berg, to have his deputies patrol the city and report the existence of any of these meetings:

> The Imperial bailiff shall order two, three, four or more [of his deputies] to patrol the city on Sundays and feast days during church services, as well as from time to time on work days, and especially on Saturday evenings. The first time they hear any blasphemy, preaching or singing of Lutheran psalms, they should stop it and inform [the perpetrators] about the punishment described below. The second time [their houses] shall be entered, and if they are in the company of lesser persons, [the deputies] should list the names of those assembled for singing and praying, and especially those of neighbours or people in the adjoining rooms; they should warn the facilitators alone, and these people should be forbidden from such

---

[5] StAA, Urgichtensammlung, 4 November 1630, Martin Haller.

[6] See StAA, Strafamt, Urgichten, 7 March 1630. For his misdeeds, Glatz was pilloried and exiled on 14 March 1630; he was readmitted to the city in July. See StAA, Strafbücher, 1615–32, 14 March 1630. Glatz was frequently in trouble with the authorities: he was convicted of striking a woman and committing incest in 1632 (see ibid., 5 August 1632) and of stirring up rebellion in 1633 (see StAA, Strafbücher, 1633–53, 31 March 1633).

singing and preaching in the name of the Imperial Executors. Afterwards they should inform the city bailiff about these houses or warned persons, and the bailiff should hold the heads of the households responsible for such open blasphemy, preaching and singing in their houses in violation of the previous warning, and hold them to the punishment described below. If these persons deny [their crimes], or other circumstances do not intervene, the aforementioned Imperial city bailiff shall refer these persons to the *Stadtpfleger*.[7]

Those heads of households who were caught holding such meetings for the second time were to be fined anywhere from 4 to 12 Gulden, depending on their income; other persons [*frembde*] or neighbours also present at such meetings were also to be fined.[8] Jakob Wagner, a Protestant merchant, bitterly described this espionage by the Catholic authorities in a manuscript chronicle:

> Throughout the city scouts, agents and spies were hired, who would go through all of the streets, particularly on Sundays and feast days, listening at houses for praying, singing or the reading of sermons. If they heard anything, they would enter the house and order [the participants] to stop, demanding that they go to church and cease this reading and bawling; many of these persons were taken in and punished. That was the greater and more serious sin, which we committed, that we honoured the Holy Trinity, God Father, Son and Holy Ghost, with praying, reading and a Christian psalm, and called on him in our need.[9]

Official suspicion of private religious meetings, in fact, pre-dated the Catholic takeover and reflects the council's distrust of the practice of religion outside sanctioned gatherings.[10] Although, as is well known, secular authorities in many cities and territories of both confessions expanded their oversight of popular religion during the sixteenth century, the Augsburg city council was particularly concerned to control any religious practice not falling directly under the auspices of the Lutheran or Catholic churches.[11] After the Edict of Restitution, when the

---

[7] D-As, 2° Cod. Aug. 123, 'Singularia Augustana', no. 25, fol. 2r. The deputies were also authorized, even when off duty, to drive away people singing in the streets who did not belong to the approved Catholic street choirs [*herumbsingenden Catholischen Cantoreÿen*] (fols. 2v–3r).

[8] D-As, 2° Cod. Aug. 123, 'Singularia Augustana', no. 25, fol. 3v.

[9] StAA, Reichsstadt-Chroniken 27ª, Chronik von Jakob Wagner (1613–47), 104 (11 March 1631).

[10] Nor was the use of informants a new practice. Paid by the city Baumeister, spies or *Kundschafter* joined the city watch in ensuring internal security in the city (see Roeck, *Eine Stadt im Krieg und Frieden*, pp. 253–54). However, it is likely that the Restitution saw an expansion of this practice.

[11] In 1590, for example, a certain Barbara Nestele had been arrested for having held regular meetings in her home, including around 20 neighbours and members of her own

city council endeavoured not only to maintain the religious peace but also simultaneously to eliminate all possible vestiges of Protestant practice, surveillance of such gatherings was heightened. Mere acts of praying, reading or singing outside the approved contexts were subtle forms of resistance against the regime, regardless of the content of the prayers, writings or songs in question.[12] Not surprisingly, those caught and tried for holding secret meetings usually denied the political significance of their actions; Wilhelm Pfaudler, a weaver who was arrested in 1629, insisted that 'he wanted to do nothing more than read the weekly Gospel of Martin Luther and its interpretation. He has never given a sermon, nor could he, since he is only a lay person and a weaver, and is neither qualified nor called for such a function.'[13] Yet the council recognized the political implications of such gatherings and punished offenders accordingly. A Protestant chronicler reported that 'on 6 April [1631] David Harscher, a cloth-cutter and citizen here, was laid in irons for having read, prayed and sung with his children in his house. Thus he was laid in irons for eight days, and given only bread and water for four days.'[14] Even if there was no sermon, the council believed prayers, songs and readings in themselves to be sufficiently dangerous to merit

---

household, at which the participants read aloud (from the histories of the Apostles, the Old Testament, devotional tracts and Luther's writings), prayed and sang. She told the council that she no longer attended sermons in the church because 'she wanted to hear the word of God with a freely willing heart, which she could never do at today's sermons' (wöll dz wort gottes ein frey willig herz haben. Dz hab sy gegen den yezigen predigen bey ir nie finden können). StAA, Strafamt, Urgichten, 28 September 1590, Barbara Nestele, quoted in Roeck, *Eine Stadt im Krieg und Frieden*, p. 175.

[12] Ibid., pp. 671–72. Psalm-singing in particular, in Augsburg and elsewhere, was construed as an act of resistance. In the towns of Neuburg and Höchstädt in the territory of Pfalz-Neuburg, for example, the recatholicization process begun by Duke Wolfgang Wilhelm was met by continued avoidance of Catholic services and singing of Lutheran psalms and chorales; see Zeeden, *Die Entstehung der Konfessionen*, p. 133; Spindler, *Heinrich V. von Knöringen*, pp. 131–32, and Merkl, 'Kunst und Konfessionalisierung', pp. 206–7.

[13] 'Zugleich hab er nichts anderes, weder [als] das sontägliche evangelium d. Martini Lutheri sambt der auslegung darübert abgelesen: Khein predig habe er nie gethon, auch nit thuen khönden, dieweil er nur ein lay und weber, zu solcher function weder gstudiert noch berueffen seye.' StAA, Strafamt, Urgichten, 18 September 1629, Wilhelm Pfaudler, quoted in Roeck, *Eine Stadt im Krieg und Frieden*, pp. 671–72. Roeck also cites a case against one Thomas Schuler, who hosted a handful of men and women in his home on occasional Sundays in the autumn of 1630 for reading the Gospels and singing. Likewise, Schuler claimed that his meetings were merely 'for the arousal of devotion and the spirit of God'. Quoted ibid., p. 672.

[14] 'Adj 6 Aprill hat man M. Dauid Harscher, tuechscherer vnd burger alhie in die Eyßen gelegt, von wegen dz er in seinem Haus mitt seinen kindern, gelesen, gebettet, vnnd gesungen hat, ist also 8 tag in der Eyßen gelegen, vnd 4 tag mit Wasser vnd brott gespeiset.' StAA, Reichstadt-Chroniken 28, fol. 6r–v.

prohibition. On the other hand, council members knew that psalm-singing in private homes would be nearly impossible to eradicate:

> At the same time it is to be desired that such private psalm-singing could be eliminated, but it cannot be done without being too precipitate. Then, if one or another accommodates himself to hearing the [Catholic] sermon, he will presumably stop this singing *per se*, but when he goes out [of the church], he will again have his way.[15]

As the authorities increased the surveillance of Protestants within city walls, by autumn 1629 many began to meet regularly in the Protestant graveyard, just outside the city, for the kind of praying and singing that was explicitly forbidden in the city itself. On 25 November Bernhard Bohm, a gravedigger, witnessed such a gathering and reported it the next day to the city council:[16]

> On every feast day and Sunday for the last six weeks, people have been coming to this graveyard in the afternoon, at first around 2 o'clock, but lately around 12 o'clock, and they stay until about 4 o'clock. At first only 10, or at the most 20, people came, but every week there were more and more, until yesterday, the 25th of November, there were over a thousand people assembled, mostly women and single men, and indeed also highly placed women, but he does not know them. There must be few from the surrounding neighbourhood, because otherwise he would recognize them. He thinks that they must be mainly from the upper city.[17] ... Yesterday they were standing around and sitting on the gravestones, and a boy, the son of the goldsmith N. Pontier, read to them out of a book, and afterwards the women and the rest of the people sang. Yesterday between 2 and 3 o'clock ... two city guards came to break up the crowd, and they seized one or two of them, after which there was such a commotion that the guards could not carry out their orders, and one of them had to abandon his weapon to save himself. The people did not allow themselves to be dispersed, and they continued with their singing and stayed until 4 o'clock; they also said that they would gather again, and not allow themselves to be stopped.

Such gatherings, then, had begun modestly with only 10 or 20 persons, but rapidly expanded to the point that Bohm could report the presence of some 1000 persons, including many women, in his graveyard on 25 November. Two days later, two cloth-cutters, Matthäus Weiss and Balthasar Hain, were arrested and interrogated separately about their roles in the event. Both men belonged to the local guild of Protestant *Meistersinger*, and were accustomed to leading the singing of

---

[15] D-As, 2° Cod. Aug. 123, 'Singularia Augustana', no. 14, fol. 3r.
[16] Laid in with StAA, Strafamt, Urgichten, 27 November 1629, Matthäus Weiss and Balthasar Hain.
[17] The *Oberstadt*, i.e., the southern end of the city, well removed from this graveyard.

participants in burial services in the graveyard.[18] These may have been the men, in fact, that the city guards attempted to apprehend, only to be thwarted by the crowd. During their interrogation they claimed to have been on their way to a tavern when they heard the singing coming from the graveyard, and decided to investigate themselves. The judges questioned both men sharply on their actions and motives:

> 7. What was he doing there? Was not someone sermonizing? And what was the sermon about? And who engaged him? Were there not one or more persons preaching or reading every Sunday and feast day?
>
> > Weiss: For his part he knows of no sermon, except for what other people had said.
> > Hain: He knows absolutely nothing about it, and insists on his oath that except for this time, he has never gone there, nor to any other gathering. On the other hand, since he is a Meistersinger, he was engaged twice to sing at burials; he did not know that this was forbidden.
>
> 8. Did he not lead the singing himself in the graveyard? And did he not persuade others to go there?
>
> > Weiss: He has never led the singing, but sang with [the crowd], nor has he ever spoken to or directed anyone [to go there].
> > Hain: He meant no harm; when he was given the book, he also helped to lead the singing, but faithfully and without evil intent.
>
> 9. Last Sunday, did not the Burgermeister's guards, following orders, demand that they all go home? Why, then, did they remain there so disloyally, and continue in their singing in defiance of the authorities?
>
> > Weiss: Mayer and Bauer, the two guards, came there and ordered everyone in the name of the Devil [ins Teüfls namen] to go to church, and not to make the graveyard into a sermon-house. Then Bauer drew his sword and and struck at a man with the flat side, so that the man fell down. He does not know what they had between them. For his part, he left directly after this.
> > Hain: Since, as he said, he was standing far away from the crowd and the guards, neither hearing nor seeing anything, and departed immediately, he does not know what happened there.
>
> 10. Did he not resist the aforementioned guards, push them and attack them, so that one had to abandon his weapon in order to help the other?
>
> > Weiss: In truth no one can say that he insulted anyone, rather, he was standing far away from the guards, and resisted them neither with word nor deed.

---

[18] On the Augsburg *Meistersinger* as a product of the city's Protestant guild tradition, see Bellot, 'Humanismus – Bildungswesen – Buchdruck und Verlagsgeschichte', p. 350.

> Hain: He claims his innocence, and knows that the guards would neither complain nor say anything against him.

11. Did he not defiantly answer the guards that it is better that one sings than whore around, and that he would not allow anyone to stop him? Did he not say that it would be better to stay home on weekdays and stay away from work, rather than to sit in the tavern, where one could have sought and found him yesterday?

> Weiss: He admits to saying that it is better to sing than to whore around. However, he denies that he would not allow anyone to keep him from singing. He had finished his work in the shop, and since he had nothing else to do, he went with the other masters to have a drink.
> Hain: He said nothing to anyone, nor would he have had reason to. Otherwise he is also innocent, and was separated [from the others] in the tavern, to where he had come solely to have a drink.

The council released them only two days later, perhaps lacking concrete evidence that Weiss and Hain had been major actors in the events at the graveyard. On the other hand, the huge number of people who participated in this gathering may have encouraged the city council not to punish the two men severely, which might have provoked further defiance of the authorities. The city's response to this episode was to ban all meetings, praying and singing in the graveyard so as to prevent similar gatherings in the future.[19] In a time of great tension between the city government and the majority of the populace, rituals such as burial services did not lose their religious significance, but they added a political dimension.

Such were the difficult conditions under which Augsburg's Protestant majority lived, but their fortunes would change quickly in 1632 as the Swedish Protestant army of Gustavus Adolphus swept into southern Germany following their rout of the Catholic general Tilly at Breitenfeld the previous September. Having defeated Tilly again (and mortally wounding him) at Rain am Lech on 15 April, the Swedish general stood before the gates of Augsburg three days later and demanded a peaceful surrender of the city. On the 24th Gustavus entered the city in a triumphal procession, and enjoyed a celebratory service at St Anna including a performance of the Te Deum;[20] he immediately took up residence in the palaces of the Fugger family, which had dispersed. Gustavus demanded loyalty oaths from the citizenry to the Swedish crown, and placed his deputy Count Benedikt Oxenstierna in charge of

---

[19] See reports of the decree in StAA, EWA 146, 1629, no. 91; also StAA, Reichsstadt-Chroniken 28, fol. 2v.

[20] StAA, Reichsstadt-Chroniken 28, fol. 9r.

the city before leaving. Under Oxenstierna's administration the city council was to be reconstituted as an entirely Protestant body, over the objections of some local Protestants who wished to preserve a semblance of confessional balance. Catholics could continue their observances only with difficulty, but after the death of Gustavus at the battle of Lützen in November 1632 persecution of Catholics was heightened. All Catholics refusing to swear oaths to the Swedish authorities were expelled the following May, and much of the clergy fled south to Füssen (Bishop Heinrich von Knöringen, for his part, had fled to Tyrol before the Swedish takeover). Only the Benedictines of SS Ulrich and Afra, an Imperial monastery, were allowed to retain control of their church. Meanwhile Protestant services resumed throughout the city.[21]

At least two extant songs celebrating the Swedish 'liberation' of Augsburg may have been printed in or found their way into the city in the wake of Gustavus's entry. The image of Job's patience in suffering, highly relevant for Augsburg Protestants under the Restitution, was exploited in an anonymous set of three songs entitled 'The Patient Job' [Der geduldige Hiob] and containing a 'song of comfort', a 'song of thanks', and a 'song of victory'. Although an acrostic within the song gives the date as 1632, there is no indication of place, publisher or tune(s).[22] The source for a second song celebrating the city's liberation, however, is explicit: in 1633 Erasmus Widmann, the Protestant cantor of the Jakobskirche in Rothenburg ob der Tauber, published a set of five simple polyphonic songs with the partisan title 'Augsburg Thanksgiving: Song of Thanks and Praise for the Deliverance of the Most Worthy City of Augsburg from the Papist Affliction.'[23] Widmann had published

---

[21] For an overview of Augsburg's religious-political history in this period, see Immenkötter, 'Kirche zwischen Reformation und Parität', pp. 408 ff.

[22] Der Geduldige Hiob/ Das ist: Augspurgisches Trost-Liedlein. Vn gebührendes Danck-Liedlein. Auff erfolgte/ von GOtt dem Allerhöchsten/ erbettne/ auch erlangete Victori- vnd Sieges-Liedlein/ der Augspurgischen Confession vnd deren Freyheit betreffendt/ &c. Was ein Vogel bloß nur sang/ Jst geziert mit Staden-Klang. Gedruckt im Jahr/ Der LöWen MVth LLebt eWigs GVt. Extant in D-As, 4° Aug 628. The date acrostic in the title yields the numerals 'DLWMVLIWV', which may be arranged as MDLLVVVVVVI, or 1631 [!]; however, within the song also appears the acrostic 'Jm Jahr/ AVgspVrg Lehrt nVn WIDer frey/ GOTT hIerVMb geLobet sey', yielding MDLLVVVVVVII, or 1632.

[23] AUGUSTÆ VINDELICORUM GRATIÆ: Danckh- und Lobgesang für die Erlösung auß der Päpstischen Trangsal der Hochlöblichen Stadt Augspurg: Jn der Melodey: O HErre Gott dein Göttlich Wort/ &c. Sampt andern Gebeten vmb Abwendung allerley Noth der Christenheit: Gestellt vnd mit 4. Stimmen componiert Durch Erasmum Widmannum Halensem P. L. bestellten Cantoren vnd Organisten zu Rotenburg ob der Tauber: ANNO GVstaVVs Magnos hostes ReX orDIne VICIt. König GVstaV ADoLph slegte ob | AVß Gottes TrIeb/ zV EVVIgM Lob (Rothenburg ob der Tauber: Jacob Mollyn, 1633 [RISM B/VIII, 1633[08]]).

timely compositions of this nature before: a dialogue composition between 'Concordia' and 'Discordia' had appeared in 1620, shortly after the outbreak of hostilities; and in 1629 he had brought out his *Piorum suspiria* [Sighs of the Pious], which included several cantional movements setting lengthy texts decrying the tribulations of wartime.[24] The turn in Protestant military fortunes in 1631–32, however, compelled him to issue two collections, the *Helden-Gesäng dem ... Gustav Adolpho von Schweden* (1633) and the aforementioned 'Augsburg Thanksgiving'. In the five four-voice songs of the latter Widmann turned to highly partisan texts and models, including a setting of *Gott ist unser Zuversicht* based on the melody of *Ein feste Burg ist unser Gott*, and a dialogue between Man and Christ to the tune of *Erhalt uns Herr bei deinem Wort*. It is unclear, however, whether any of these songs reached the troubled city.

Augsburg's Protestant community had little time to reconsolidate their institutions before the threat of violence returned. On 6 September 1634 the Swedish army was routed at Nördlingen, and within four weeks Imperial and Bavarian troops had surrounded Augsburg. The Swedish garrison refused to surrender and a disastrous siege ensued through the winter of 1634–35, during which thousands died of hunger and disease. The remaining Swedish soldiers having abandoned Augsburg at the end of March, the Catholic clergy returned on 28 March 1635 and was welcomed by a performance of a Te Deum at SS Ulrich and Afra.[25] A little over a week later, on 6 April, the Good Friday procession was restored, which began symbolically by marching through the formerly Protestant church of St Ulrich (which was and is attached to the Catholic SS Ulrich and Afra), and continuing to the churches of St Moritz, St Anna, Heilig Kreuz, St Salvator and the cathedral.[26] At each Protestant church the keys were ceremonially delivered to the vicar-general Caspar Zeiller, and an antiphon concerning the Holy Trinity, with versicle and collect, was

---

[24] See his *Ein Schöner Neuer Ritterlicher Auffzug vom Kampff und Streyt zwischen Concordia und Discordia* (Rothenburg ob der Tauber: the author [Hieronymus Körnlein], 1620; RISM A/I, W1039); and his *Piorum suspiria. Andechtige Seufftzen unnd Gebet umb den lieben Frieden und abwendung aller Hauptplagen und Straffen: Gesangsweiß gestellt: Darbey auch egliche nach der newen Viadanischen Art gesetzten Moteten unnd Gesäng auff die hohen Fest bey der Communion und Copulationen zu musiciren* (Nuremburg: Simon Halbmayer, 1629; RISM A/I, W1044).

[25] See Spindler, *Heinrich V. von Knöringen*, p. 59.

[26] Ibid., p. 60; this was also recorded by Stetten in *Geschichte der Heil. Röm. Reichs Freyen Stadt Augspurg*, vol. 2, p. 1191. On 20 April the cathedral chapter also ordered the restoration of the regular liturgical procession on the feast of St Mark (*DR*, 20 April 1635); on 30 June it also ordered the continuation of the procession to SS Ulrich and Afra on the feast of St Ulrich (14 July; see *DR*, 30 June 1635).

sung.[27] In June the cathedral chapter also restored the Corpus Christi procession, but the poor financial situation forced them to keep expenses to a minimum.[28]

The largest celebration, however, took place on 10 May, when the *Wunderbares Gut* arrived back from its wartime hiding-place at Chiemsee and was carried in a triumphant procession to its original home at Heilig Kreuz. Several accounts of this procession survive, but surely the most vivid is found in a letter to Bishop Heinrich V from his vicar-general, Caspar Zeiller, written the day after the event unfolded. The procession, and its associated music, had an undeniably militaristic quality. It began with a service held outside the city in the village of Lechhausen:

> The suffragan bishop in pontifical dress arrived, took the most worthy Sacrament, and placed it, with the usual ceremonies, upon an altar erected in a field for that purpose, while several pieces were played by the trumpeters, military drummers and musicians. Then a short exhortation was given by the preacher from Heilig Kreuz, the Capuchin Father Chrysostomus, accompanied by a threefold [fanfare] with military drums and trumpets in honour and thanksgiving. Finally, the suffragan bishop gave the benediction, and all the people present shouted 'JESUS, JESUS, JESUS' three times, not without some tears.
>
> Then the musketeers who were present, of which there were several companies, fired all their weapons, as did those who were standing atop the fortifications. At this, the procession made its way in good order towards the city. The clergy, which remains quite small, went with crosses and banners, just as is customary on Corpus Christi, each one in his respective place; then the beautiful cavalry, then the pilgrims from Munich, then, following the clergy, the musicians. After this came the prelate of Heilig Kreuz in pontifical dress; then St Ulrich's Cross [an important relic from the

---

[27] 'placuit ut in ipso Parasceues die Supplicatio uniuersalis instituerentur cum Musicâ, quâ omnes Ecclesiæ, quarum Poßeßores adorant, obirentur et cuilibet per Vicarium Generalem suæ claues redderentur ...'. Furthermore, 'die *Procession* gienge durch vnser lutherisch predigthauß, nachdem in vnserm *Choro* vorhero ein *Antiphon cum versiculo et Collecta de SS. Trinitate*, welche herr *Vicari[us] æquali modo* in allen nachbenenten Kürchen verrichtet ...'. See 'Triennium Sueco-Augustanum' by Father Reginbald Moehner of Ulrich and Afra, ABA: Hs 53, fols 25v and 385 respectively. Stetten also described this event in *Geschichte der Heil. Röm. Reichs Freyen Stadt Augspurg*, vol. 2, p. 1191.

[28] The provision of a meal was one expense that had to be trimmed: 'Herren *Vicario* anzuezaigen, Ein Ehrw: domCapitul lasse Ihme gefallen, daß die gewonliche *procession* an *Festo Corporis Christi* (da es anderst ein wettertag sein solte) angestölt werde. dieweilen aber de[r] maiste vncossten wegen haltung der Mahlzeit Ihren Frl: Gnl: obgelegen seÿe, alß werden sein Ehrw: dißfahls den sachen recht zuethuen wissen, vnd etwan die Mahlzeit als einene der Zeit vnnöttigen cossten abzustöllen wissen. Sovil vnd aber die vncössten, welche Einem Domcapitul obligen anbelanget, soll Herr Anthoni Maÿr deroselben firderlich ein verzaichnuß übergeben.' *DR*, 1 June 1635.

church of Ulrich and Afra] was carried, which was also missed [during the Swedish occupation]; then the suffragan bishop with the Venerable Miraculous [Sacrament], and his attendants under a canopy; then followed the city magistrate in fine garb, then the other imperial Commissars also finely dressed, with lighted candles, escorted on both sides by many companies of musketeers. Finally came the city council, citizens and women, with their banners before them. As [the procession] approached the Red Gate, the muskets were fired again, and at Ulrich and Afra the holy Cross [of St Ulrich] was left, and the people rested for some time during the music. From there [the procession] went through the Weinmarkt and by the Perlach. In the finest squares [of the city] the regiments lined themselves up in good order, and where the Holy Sacrament was carried, all of the soldiers fell to their knees, placing their axes, pikes, muskets and guns underneath them, which was beautiful and fine to see. Under the great door of the city hall an altar had been erected, decorated like that in the cathedral, and the people sang for some time. Then the procession made its way to Heilig Kreuz with a magnificent *Te Deum laudamus* and Vespers; during the *Te Deum laudamus* a salute was again fired by all of the musketeers and guns around the city. On the streets, where the Catholics were standing or walking, there was a general weeping for joy, that finally, after having endured so much misery and sadness, the city could be blessed with this great treasure and Catholic ceremonies. Today the feast of the Most Wonderful Sacrament was magnificently held with great solemnity and devotion in the above-mentioned church of Heilig Kreuz, in the presence of the city magistrate and other members of the city authorities.[29]

Another, shorter account of this triumphal procession notes that in front of the altar at the city hall 'one collect was sung for the emperor, and other motets' before the procession continued to the cathedral.[30]

Although we might expect that Zeiller's account was embellished to please his superior, his description of the musical accompaniment – trumpets and military drums in addition to a choir, and a performance of the Te Deum – agrees with a series of engravings by Wolfgang Kilian illustrating the reception of the *Wunderbares Gut* outside of the city walls, the procession into the city and the ceremonies in front of the *Rathaus*.[31] The first of these images, showing the veneration of the

---

[29] Letter from Caspar Zeiller to Bishop Heinrich V, 11 May 1635, ABA, BO 2308. About a week earlier Zeiller had been involved in planning the procession with the cathedral chapter; see *DR*, 5 May 1635.

[30] 'von darauf d[en] berlach (alla vnd[er] dem Stathaus ein Altar auf gemacht word[en], vnnden 1 Collect für den Kaiser gesung[en] vnnd andre *muteten*), vnnd forth ins thumb zue vnser l: frauen.' From 'Diarium Augustanum' (*c.*1652) by Johann Georg Mayr, priest from Oberhausen, D-Mbs, Cod. germ. 3313, 10 May 1635.

[31] D-As, Graphiken, 28/44.

sacrament on a makeshift altar erected outside the city walls, surrounded by clergy, musicians, confraternities, cavalry and soldiers firing their guns, is shown in Figure 8.1, and gives a sense of the scope of the event. Figure 8.2, a detail of the altar, shows the sacrament flanked at the left by a pair of kettledrums and at least seven trumpeters, and at the right by a choir of at least 14 singers, led by a conductor with a baton and accompanied by one musician on what appears to be a slide trumpet or trombone.

In the second engraving, depicting the procession into the southern gate (the *Rotes Tor*) of the city, the trumpeters, drummer and choir are located just behind the confraternities with their banners, and immediately preceding the higher clergy accompanying the sacrament under a canopy (see Figures 8.3 and 8.4) (a final engraving, not shown here, depicts the veneration of the *Wunderbares Gut* at the *Rathaus*, but no musicians are shown). That trumpets and drums accompany this procession is entirely consistent with the militancy of the event, and echoes earlier processions on the feast of Corpus Christi (see Chapter 5)

8.1   Engraving by Wolfgang Kilian showing the return of the *Wunderbares Gut*, 1635. No. 1: 'Das H. Wunderbarliche Sacrament wirt vor der Statt von der gantzen Clerisei und Catholischen Gemeind empfangen.' D-As, Graphiken 28/44

8.2 Detail of Figure 8.1, showing the *Wunderbares Gut*, clergy and two groups of musicians

8.3 Wolfgang Kilian, No. 2: 'Das H. Wunderbarliche Sacrament wirdt In vnd durch die Statt mit großer Andacht begleittet.' D-As, Graphiken 28/44

8.4 Detail of Figure 8.3, showing trumpeters, drummer and choir, followed
immediately by the higher clergy

in which the public display of the host became an act of political
assertion as much as religious devotion.

The pomp surrounding the return of the *Wunderbares Gut* only
lightly concealed the demographic disaster that had struck Augsburg
during the previous three years. By the time that Catholic troops took
over the city in March 1635, the city's population had dwindled to just
over 16 000, about two-thirds of its prewar size.[32] A second siege by
French and Swedish soldiers in 1646 would ensure that Augsburg would
not again reach its former cultural and economic prominence during the
seventeenth century. The city's considerable, though dwindling,
prosperity of the pre-war years had supported numerous musical
institutions in which the gradually widening cultural divide between
Catholicism and Protestantism could be expressed. In the decades after
1635, however, those same institutions lay in ruin and would only
gradually recover a basic competency. For Augsburg's survivors of the
religious wars, the time for confessional propagandizing, in music or
otherwise, was over. The damage done to the city's musical institutions
by the war is expressed no better than in a short entry in the cathedral
chapter's minutes, dated 9 June 1635: 'The organist Christian Erbach is
to be told that the honourable cathedral chapter, which as he knows has

---

[32] Immenkötter, 'Kirche zwischen Reformation und Parität', p. 410.

fallen into deep decline in the past three years, is at the time no longer able to support an organist.'[33] Erbach, who had served the city so loyally as a composer, organist, leader of the *Stadtpfeifer* and most recently as a member of the Catholic city council, died a short time later.

[33] 'Christian Erbachen organisten anzuezaigen, dieweilen Ein Ehrw: DomCapitul dise .3. Jahr herumb in großen abgang vnd ohn vermögenheit gerathen alß wisse er der zeit keinen organisten mehr zue vnderhalten.' *DR*, 9 June 1635.

Transcripts of Trial Records

1. Abraham Schädlin, 5 April 1585

Source: StAA, Ad Kalenderstreit-Criminalia, 1583–89

Abraham Schedel in fronuest soll angesproch[en] werd[en].

1. Wie er haiss vnnd von wannen er seÿ.
   Er haisse Abraham Schädlin, seÿ von Augspurg.
2. Was sein thuen seÿ dauon er sich erhalte.
   er seÿe ein Weber, vnd könne auch schreib[en].
3. Ob er nit aussgewesen vnd fluchtig fues gesetzt hab, auch warumb.
   Ja er seÿ [ein weil] gen Vlm gezog[en], von weg[en] eines Lieds, dz er gemacht
   hab, den Hn doctor Müller betreffendt, welches [one letter, scratched out] er
   gleichwol nit außgeben, sonder ‡ dem daniel weiß habs [margin: ‡ habs deß
   daniel weißen hausfrauen dediciren wöll[en], so habs aber einer, Georg Braun
   genannt,] beÿ Im gefund[en], vnd Ine gebett[en], er soll Ims lassen widerfaren,
   dz ers sein weib lesen laßß[en], darnach habs [one letter, scratched out] der
   Weiss [above: 'Braun'] abschreib[en] vnd weitten kom[m]en lassen, dardurch
   es von Ime offenbar, vnd er darüber gewarnet worden, der vrsach hab er sich
   gen Vlm begeb[en], biss er vertröstung bekom[m]en, weil ers von er diß Lied
   von eines E. Rhats berueff gemacht hab, darinn alle sach[en], so sich daruor
   v[er]loffen, vffgehabt vnd verzig[en] seÿ[en], dz es desshalb[en] mit Ime keine
   not hab[en] werde. Doch hab er diß Lied gemacht, allein vff anderer leuth
   anzeig[en], vnd habe erst hernacher erfaren, dz er vnrecht bericht word[en]
   seÿ. [about eight illegible words, scratched out]
4. Wo er sich mitler zeit enthalt[en] vnd wess er sich beholffen hab.
   er hab sich in Vlm, beÿm Roten Lowen vffgehalt[en], vnd sich mit schreib[en]
   beholff[en], seÿ auch zu Nördling[en] 14. tag gewesen.
5. Man wiss dz er verschiner zeit vil schmachlieder vnd reimen gemacht hab,
   darumb sol er dieselben alle vnd[er]schidlich antzaig[en].
   die Bauern Klag hab er gemacht, vnd sonst weitter nichts, als dz Lied, wie
   obsteet.
6. Ob er nit auch ein lied gem vom doctor Müller vnd der oberkait alhie
   gemacht hab.
   er hab dz obgemeldt Lied von 49. gesetzen gemacht, welches den ganntzen
   handel, so sich mit d. Müllern v[er]loff[en] begreiff[en] soll, wie er von andern
   bericht word[en].
7. wer in hierzue angewisen hab.
   niemand.
8. warumb er die oberkait darinn mit vngrund so hessig angezog[en] hab.
   er seÿ hierinnen vff der gemein sag gang[en].
9. was er vermaint hab hierdurch anzurichten.
   hab nichts darmit begert anzuricht[en].

10. Was er sonst für schmach zetln gemacht vnd angeschlag[en] hab.
hab sonst durchauß nichts gemacht. Bitt vmb gnad.

2. Jonas Losch and Leonhard Deisenhoffer, September 1584
Source: StAA, Strafamt, *Urgichten*, 3–10 September 1584

A. *First interrogation of Jonas Losch, 3 September 1584*

Actum Montags den .3. *Septembris Anno* ~ 84. hat Jonas Losch auf beiligende
fragstuckh vnnd ernstlich betroet ansprechen güetlich geantwort wie volgt.
1. Wie er haiss vnd von wannen er seÿ.
    Er haiß Jonas Losch sei Burg[er] alhie.
2. Was sein thuen seÿ dauon er sich erhalte.
    Er sei ein Weber, behelf sich seines handwerckhs, vnnd dann so pfleg er auch
    bei gemainen hochzeiten zwischen dem dantz vnd der nachtmalzeit den
    hochzeit leuten lieder zu sing[en], damit er auch etwas gewinne, als er nun bei
    disem fragstuck gefragt worden ob er auch schreib[en] kündt, vnnd Ja darauf
    geantwort, hat man begert etwas zuschreib[en], darauf er dann hiebej
    verwarte schrifft gemacht.
3. Die weil er lange zeit her nicht gearbaitet hab, soll er anzaigen woher er gelt
zu seiner vnd[er]haltung genummen.
    antwort er hab seinem handwerck fleissig abgewartet, sich desselben, vnnd
    dann deß singens vf hochzeiten, welches er gemaingelich nach .5. Vhrn
    angefang[en], vnd biß zu nachtess[en] getrib[en], beholffen.
4. Ob er nit verschiner zeit ausgetrett[en] vnd fluchtig fues gesetzt hab,
auch warumb, soll er vnd[er]schidlich anzaig[en] vnd and[er]n ernst nit
verursachen.
    Es hab sich gleich des nechsten tags nach dem auflauf begeben, das er mit
    einem der Michael haiß vnnd beim Reischlen Metzger das gelt einneme nach
    mittag aufstossig worden, vnnd In auf Barfüesser brucke ein Pfaffen Knecht
    gescholt[en], aber hernacher diser [one illegible word, scratched out] Michael
    von Ime außgeb[en], er hab Ine ein Redlefüerer des Doctor Müllers auspürens
    halben gehaissen, dess[en] er aber sich nit wiß zuerinnern, daher er dann
    durch disen Michael vor den Strafhern verclagt, vnd Ime fürgebott[en]
    worden. Weil er nun gefürcht, er möcht etwan solcher reden vnnd dann auch
    deßhalb[en], das vngefärlich .14. tag vorm auflauf herr Christof Ilsung als er
    In Burgermaisterambt gewest Ine etlich lieder nemen lassen φ [margin: 'φ
    darunder er sechs mit aigner hand geschrib[en] dann die andern getruckt
    gewesst, auch vnder disen .6. lidern die fünf selbst gemacht, des sechst aber
    von ein truck abgeschrib[en] hab.'] In gefar khommen, sei er ~~bei~~ hinweg
    gezog[en], vnnd sich zu Stuckgart [above: 'ein tag'] vnnd zu Vlm drei
    wuch[en] lang aufgehalt[en] da er dann bei Samuel Faulhabern sich vf seinen
    handwerck hab gebrauch[en] lassen, sei volgents von Vlm widerumb hieher
    khommen nach dem er von seinem weib verstanden, das die sach alhie
    allenthalb[en] richtig sein.
5. Wo er sich dise zeit herumb enthalt[en] vnd wess er sich beholff[en] hab.
    Er hab sich zu Vlm aufgehalt[en] wie ob.

6. Wo er im iungsten auflauf gewesen, vnd ob er nit auch mit einer wehr auf den platz geloff[en] seÿ.

Er sei alhie gewesen, vnnd weil andere In seine nachbaurschafft bei der Kalchhüeten, mit Irem haubtman dem Megges Lobwebern gang[en], sei er auch mit einer seitenwher vnd einem knebelspieß, welcher Im auß des Lempels Metzg[er]s hauß durch ein schueler sei gelieh[en] worden, mit obernant[en] sein[en] gassen haubtman gezog[en], als sie aber zu der klaine Sachsengassen khomen sei Inen anzaigt worden es sei alles gestilt, darauf sie zuruck vnd Jeder widerumb haim zog[en].

7. Ob er nit Peter Farenschons tochter leng[er] als vor einem jar die ehe versproch[en], vnd warumb er sie bisher nit zu kirch[en] gefuert hab.

Er hab deß Farenschons tochter vor einem Jar alhie zu kirchen gefürt, vnd hauß noch mit Ir.

8. Wann er wid[er] hieher kummen seÿ vnd bei wem er sich aufgehalt[en] hab.

Antwort vor dreien wuchen, vnnd hab sich erst .5. Wuch[en] nach dem auflauf weg begeb[en].

9. Was er ietz neulich in seines schwechers gessle bei nechtlich[er] weil fur einen rumor angefangen hab.

Es sei verschienen sontag acht tag gewesen das Michael Schön Weber vor seinem Weib Ine mit beschaidenhait zu melden ein schelmen vnd dieb gescholt[en] von deßweg[en], das er zuuor ein zeitlang außgetrett vnd hinweg gezog[en] sei, darauf gleich wol sein Weib Ine vorm h[er]n Christof Ilsung solcher Schmachwort halb[en] verclagt, welcher sie aber für die Strafhern gewisse, bald hernach hab sichs begeb[en], das diser Michael Schön ein Weber den man den Meüßle haist Γ [margin: 'Γ vnd In seines Schwehers hauß wone'] zu Ine geschickt, vnd Ime bitt[en] lass[en] Ime solche reden die er geg[en] Ime außgestoss[en] zuuerzeihen, vnd er wöl etwan ein maß wein mit Ime trincken, darauf ers seinstails gescheh[en] lassen, aber hernacher hab er erfarn vnd inner worden, das diser Schön In vor dem Strafh[er]n verklagt, wie er dann auch fürgeferdet worden sei.

10. Dieweil er mit grossem gotslestern geschrien, sein schwecher muess zur stat hinaus, vnd die in verrat[en] haben als die schelmen, bleiben hinnen, soll er anzaig[en] wen er gemaint hab.

Er hab solch Gotslestern vnd reden nit gethon, sonder als ~~Ime der Schön~~ [above: 'er'] entzwischen ~~vf der gassen~~ vor des Schönen hauß † [margin: '† vbergangn[en] vnd deß Schonen ansichtig worden'] ~~bekhomme~~, hab er Ine gefragt, ob er In noch also ausschrei wie er vor seinem weib gethon, ~~vnd~~ darauf ~~disen Schön~~ der Schön Ime ein lumpen gehaissen, den er entgeg[en] diser gestalt widerumb gescholt[en] vnd dabei vermeld hab, er werd Ine darumb nit zur statt hinaußbring[en], wie seinen Schweher.

11. Man befind vnd wiss dz er ein lange zeit her vil schand vnd schmach lieder gemacht hat, darumb soll er dies[elben] alle anzaig[en].

Er hab wol allerlaÿ lieder vnnd derselb[en] biß in 30. gemacht, welche man zum tantz vnd sing[en] gebraucht, von disen hab der h[er] Ilsung bei 5. [margin: 'darunder eins vom Babst'] vnnd dann so hab er die andern in ein buech zusamen geschrib[en], welches buech in seinem hauß in der stuben auf einem bret ob der thüt lige, seien aber nur von bulereien, vnnd kaine schendlied[er].

12. Wann er dz schmachlied von den maistern des weberhandwerckhs zu vlm, vnd von einer köchin dasselbst gemacht hab, vnd warumb.

Diß lied hab er nit, sonder Abraham Schedle das lied von d[er] Köchin gemacht, wer das ander gemacht sei Ime vnwissend, hab Ims zu Vlm ein Ringmacher so In der Fraw[en] gassen vnfer von der Nusshartin Wirtin hauß daselbst was geb[en].

13. Wo inn die schmachlied vom Babst vnd den Jesuitern, herkum[m]en, welliche man in seinen buechern finde, vnd ob ers nit selbst gemacht hab.

Er hab diß lied selbst gemacht, vnnd auß einem gerrümbt ~~getru~~ truck den er vom Aaron buechkeüfel – so vnder den Gieg[er] feil hat, kaufft, gezog[en] vnd also in ein ~~gezo~~ geseng gebracht, vnnd hab der h[er] Ilsung diß lied.

14. wer damalen bei ime gwesen als er [margin: 'v[er]schiner zeit'] dises lied bei nacht auf d[er] gassen gesung[en] hab, soll er gleich so mer guetlich als gemartet anzaig[en].

Er hab diß lied auf ofnen gassen nie gesung[en], wiß auch nit das es von and[er]n gesung[en] worden sei, aber nit ohn sei es das er vngefärlich vor $^3/_4$ Jarn mit .n. Brimmel vnnd .n. Hardern, auch des Würts vf der Kaufleüt stuben jungen, Wölfle genant, bei nächtlicher weil durch vnser fraw[en] grab[en] gang[en], dazu[mal] hab[en] sie gleichwol gesung[en], aber solch lied gar nit.

15. Wellicher damaln vn[der] inen den Jesuitern die fenster eingeworff[en] hab soll er laut anzaig[en], dann man im wol leut fürstellen keine die guet wissen darmit haben.

Er hab den Jesuitern die fenster nit eingeworff[en] wiß auch nit welcher es gethon, vnnd sei [margin: 'seines wissens'] von Irer kainem bescheh[en]. Vnnd sei [above: 'auch'] vngefärlich .4. wuch[en] nach dem sie an vnser frawen graben gesungen, dz hanns Schmotz Weber zu Ime khomen, vnnd Ime anzaigt, was massen er losch in verdacht sei es also hab er s[am]bt oberzelten den Jesuitern dazu mal wie sie gesung[en], die fenster eingeworfen hab[en], vnnd geb solches Martin Schmid von Inen auß. darauf er geantwort er helt den Martin Schmid den für kain ehrlich man er mach dann mehr das sie den Jesuitern die fenster eingeworff[en] hab[en].

16. Wo er dz lied vom iungst auflauf vnd D. Müllern wid[er] die oberkait gemacht hat, soll er guetlich anzaigen od[er] man werds doch durch den nachrichter aus im bring[en].

Es sei verschinen Sontag ein Knap mit namen Michael Karg, so bei Memming[en] gebürtig, zu Ime khommen, vnnd solch lied getruckht gebracht, welches er abgeschrib[en], vnnd darauf geschrib[en] hab: dieses Lied hab Ich ~~gemacht~~ Jonas Losch gemacht, aber [one illegible word, scratched out] er habs doch nit gar sonder etwas daran gemacht, vnnd etlich gesetzlen geendert, vnnd sonderlich das letst gesetzlen gar gemacht, vnnd wiß nit wohin der Karg gezog[en]. hab sich gleichwol vernemen lassen er wöl ghen Vlm. Vnnd soll ein Predicant zu Vlm mit namen herr Peter auch ein Lied, vom hiegen auflauf gemacht, welches er zu Vlm hab horen sing[en].

17. Wer ime hierzue geholffen hab.

Obberüerter Karg hab Ime erstlich ein getruckt lied gelieh[en], darnach er oberermelt sein lied gemacht vnd gebessert hab wie obsteet.

18. Was er sonst mer für schand zeteln vnd schrifften gemacht, wo er dieselben angeschlag[en] vnd sonst hab posten lassen.

Er hab solche schrifft weder gemacht angeschlag[en] noch fallen.

19. Ob er nit wiss dz sollche schmachschrifften bei leibs vnd lebens straff verbot[en] seien.

Das hab er nit gewust das so hoch verbotten sei.

20. Wie er dann vermaint hab sollisches an straff hinaus zu bring[en].

Er bitt vmb Gottes willen vmb gnad.

B. *Second interrogation of Jonas Losch, 5 September 1584*

Jonas Losch soll peinlich angesproch[en] vnd die warhait mit ernst aus im gebracht werd[en].

1. Man befind aus seiner vrgicht dz er den grund guetliche nit anzaig[en] well, derohalben hab man beuelch ine durch den nachricht[er] vnd peinliche frag zu bekantnus d[er] warhait zu bring[en], darnach soll er sich richt[en] vnd ime selbst vor marter sein.

Nach fürhaltung des ersten.

2. Wann vnd wo er dz lied vom doctor Müller wid[er] die oberkait gemacht, vnd was in darzue verursacht, od[er] wer es von im begert hab.

Sagt er vfs ander fragstuckh, das am nechst uerschienen Sontag acht tag gewesen, als einer mit namen Michael Karg vnfer vom Memming[en] gebürtig so ein Knap sei alhie vf dem Perlach zu Ine khommen, vnnd angezaigt, das er ein schöns lied von D. Müllern vnd dem hiesigen auflauf vnnd ob er dasselbig nit auch hab, nach dem es aber nit gehabt vnd disem Kargen mit sich in sein hauß gefürt, hab er diß lied auß einem truck abgeschrib[en], doch im abschreib[en] als bald etlich wörter geendert, vnnd das letst gesetzlein zu beschluß auch für sich selbst darzu gesetzt, vnnd weil das lied kain Melodei gehabt, hab er vd sein lied so er geendert geschrib[en], das es in dem thon gesungen werd: Ich stund an einem morg[en] haimlich an einem orth. vnnd sei diß lied nit wider die oberkait, das ers dann abgeschrib[en], vnd geendert sei auß seinem vnuerstand gescheh[en], hab die sach nit so weit bedacht, oder vermaint das ine ein nachtail daraus entsten soll. Sonst[en] hab er von dem obernanten Michael Karg verstanden das diß getruckht lied zu Vlm sol gemacht sein worden, mit vermelden das er vor einem monat auch ein ander lied zu Vlm auf ofnem blatz auch vom hiesig[en] auflauf vnd dem D. Müller hab hören sing[en], vnnd daselbst gehört das dasselb lied von einem Predicanten mit namen herr Peter zu Vlm soll gemacht worden sein. Zaigt auch neben dem an das niemand an ine begert ~~obernant~~ hab, das er obernant lied abschreib vnd endere, sonder habs für sich selbst gethon. Volgents ist ime ein ander lied so geschrib[en] ~~fürg~~ vnnd auch vom D. Müller vnnd dem hieig[en] auflauf in der Melodei Wo Gott der herr nit bei vns helt ~ gesungen würdt fürgehabt, vnnd er darauf gefragt worden, wer dasselb lied gemacht, hat er geantwort, es hab Abraham Schädle so ein Weber vnnd von Augspurg aber auch außgetret[en] ist, gemacht.

3. Warumb er die oberkhait darinn mit erdicht[en] vngrund so hessig anziech, vnd es dahin deute als wan sie hierinn vnrecht gethan hett, da er doch wol wiss vnd offentlich vernem[m]en hab, was massen ein E. Rhat hierzue also hoch verursacht word[en], dz die wurtemberigsche vnd Vlmische gesante, auch sonst menikhlich so d[er] sach[en] berichtet word[en], damit ersettigt vnd zufriden bliben seÿ.

Er sagt es sei in disem seinem geendertem lied nichts wider die hieig oberkait angezog[en], als allein dz die selb beschlossen hab man soll den D. Müller hinaußfüren vnnd sei darauf der Statt Vogt khomen, vnd dem D. Müller anzaigt dz er vrlaub hab. ferner sagt er das solch lied wie er es anfänglich geendert von niemand abgeschrib[en], er auch solches nach dem er ins gewelblen gelegt [above: 'werden'] darin zerrissen hab, also das durchauß kain Copej mehr dauon vorhanden sej, allein hab er diß lied Leonhard Deisenhouern Webern vf dem Genßbüel lesen lassen.

4. Ob er nit einem E. Rhat gelobt vnd gschworn seÿ.

Antwort Ja, wie er dann neülich neben andern Burg[er] widerumb gelobet vnd geschworen hab.

5. Warumb er dann sein aigne oberkait mit seinem vnwarhafften schmehlichen gedicht[en] vnd schrifften dermassen felschlich vnd schmehlich antaste.

Sagt sein vnschuld, hab die hieig Oberkait nit geschmeht.

6. Wer in hierzue angewisen vnd was man in desshalben gethan hab.

Es hab in niemand hierzu angewisen.

7. Wie offt vnd wem er dises lied abgeschriben vnd geten hab.

Er habs anderer gestalt nit abgeschrib[en], als wie er es auß des obbesagt[en] Karg getruckht lied geendert, habs auch niemand andern abschreiben lassen sonder das seinig lied so nur einmal geschrib[en] gewesen in gewelb wie obalut zerrissen, damit mans nit bei ine find[en].

8. Ob ers nit selbst hab truckhen lassen vnd wo.

Er habs nit truckhen lassen.

9. Was er sonst weiter für schmachlied[er] vnd schrifften gemacht hab, auch wid[er] wen.

Hab sonst kaine schmachlied[er] oder schrifft[en] gemacht, als das lied vom Babst, so Ime der h[er] Ilsung genommen.

10. Wer im hierzue geholffen hab vnd was gstalt.

Hab kain gehülffe darzu gehabt.

11. Was er sond[er]lich wid[er] die oberkait für schmach zettl vnd schrifften gemacht hab, soll er gleich so mer guetlich als gemartet anzaig[en].

Sagt sein vnschuld, hab solches nie in sein gehaltt.

12. Wo vnd durch wen er solliche zettl angeschlag[en] od[er] die sonst ausgebraitet hab.

Sagt sein vnschuld.

13. Ob er nit selbst dz schmachlied vom Babst vnd Jesuitern offentlich auch auf der gassen gesung[en] vnd [above: 'wer'] inen die fenster eingeworffen hab.

Er hab ein lied von Babst gemacht welches h[err] Christoph Ilsung hab, aber dasselb vf der gassen nit gesung[en], auch den Jesuitern die fenster nit eingeworff[en], noch darzu geholffen.

14. Wer sonst mer alhie solliche schmachlied[er] vnd schrifften mache.

der Abraham Schädle mach auch lieder, doch weiß er nit was dersselb für lieder sein.

Jonas Losch soll ferner befragt werd[en].

15. Ob er sich nit ein Zeitlang bei Leonhard Deisenhofern Webern haimlich enthalt[en] hab.

Er hab wol zu disem Deisen Deisenhofer [*sic*] als der in seiner nachbarschafft wone kundtschafft, aber nie bei ine gewont, sonder hab sich ein zeitlang [margin: 'nemblich 14 tag'] in seinem hauß nach dem er widerumb herein khomen haimlich aufgehalt[en].

16. Was er von disem Deisenhofer für bese aufruerische red[er] gehert hab wid[er] die oberkait.

Diser Deisenhouer sei vnderweilen zu ine in sein hauß khomen, aber er hab solche aufrüerische reden von ime nit gehört.

17. Ob nit d[er] Deisenhofer etlich wol gesagt es thue kain guet bis man die bäpstschen in d[er] oberkait zum rhathaus herab werff, vnd man solte es im iungst[en] auflauf than haben, es mecht inen jetz nit so guet mer werd[en].

Er habe solche red nit gethon, aber er Deisenhouer hab wol doch bald nach dem auflauf auf ofner gassen zu ine gesagt, es neme in wunder das die Oberkait nit D Müllern also vmbgeen, vnd das die gemain also zusehen mag.

18. Was in verursach dz er [above: 'vnd sein weib'] vom herrn Ilsung so bese schmachliche red[en] ausgiessen.

Er hab von hörn Ilsung nichts schmeliches außgestossen, wiß auch nit das es sein weib gethon hab.

19. Man wiss dz er sich ob seines schwehers tisch beruembt, er hab den Jesuitern dz schmachlied bei nacht vor dem haus gesung[en], warumb er dann jetz darfür laugne.

Es habs nit gethon.

Nachdem [above: 'er'] nun vber vilfeltig zu sprech[en] vnd vermanen weiter nichts bekhennen wöllen, ist er erstlich mit leeren scheiben aufgezog[en], vnnd als [above: 'er'] an der tortur gehang[en] gesagt, der Deisenhouer hab vngefärlich vier tag nach dem auflauf auf der gassen zu ine gesagt, man solt die herrn welche also mit dem doctor Müllern gehandlet zum rathhauß herauß hencken, item so hab er dem Lutzen Maler das lied welches er geendert vnd zerrissen [margin: 'selbst abgeschrib[en] vnnd geb[en].'] ~~abzuschreib[en] geb[en],~~ vnd wone diser Lutz bei der Brüelprug, darauf als er gar lang an der tortur gehang[en] doch ferner nichts bekhennen wöllen ist er herunder gelassen worden, vnnd nach dem ine solches was er an den tortur außgesagt blössig fürgelesen vnd er dasselb bestettet ist er in ein vergicht gefallen also das man mit ine genug zuthun gehabt. Derweg[en] vnd weil er ohne das gar vbel sicht, auch der züchtig wider rath[en] das man ferner tortur geg[en] ine fürneme, er dißmals weiterer marter erlassen worden. Bitt vmb Gottswillen vmb gnad.

C. Confession of Jonas Losch, 6 September 1584 (excerpt)

... will ich E. W. anzaigen, Es ist also gangen das verschinen acht tagen Ein [margin: 'Er haist Michill Karg ~'] Knap ist zu mir auf den Pirlin kommen vnd micht angesprochen ob ich daß liedt nit hab von dem doctor miller vnd dem aufflauff da ich gsagt hab nain hat Er gsagt er habs, vnd ist mit mir in mein hauß gangen, vnd da hab Ichs ab geschriben, doch Ettlichen wörter darin ver Endert aber wider die hochen Oberkeit gar nichts drein gemacht, vnd hab dis lied, meinem gefatter dem Lutzen geben doch in gehaim, des Er mit versprochen hat gar stil zu verhalten, doch hab Ich lassen zuuor den Lenhart diessenhoffer lassen lessen, da hat er mich gefragt wers gmacht hab. Ich zu im gsagt Ich habs gemacht. Des mir dan der laidig seitan Ein geben hat, ob Er mich mecht in Ein vnglimpffen bring[en] gegen meiner hohe Oberkeÿtt: aber von wegen deß gsangs auff der gassen wider die Jesuiter oder Ein werffen der glesser in irer Kirchen, noch der Zedell halben an zuschlagen oder abzunemen, noch zu verzetten das hab Ich so war wider mein Oberkeÿt noch wider andern nie in meinen sin genommen, So war gott lebt, wie von wegen deß lieds des ich bin gefragt worden des auch vom aufflauff des mir der Ein gnedig her vor gelessen hat so hat Es firwar der Abraham Schödlin alhie gemacht, vnd ist zu Vlm schon im truckh außgangen vnd alhie darum flichtig worden, vnd von wegen, des Lenhart Deissenhoffer reden halben, so hat er nachdem aufflauff zu mir gesagt, man sollt drauff griffen, haben an dem montag, vnd die herrn so also mit dem her Miller hendlen, sÿ zuem rathauss rab geworff[en] haben. weiter waiß ich ich [sic] nichts von im, darum bit Ich Euch vmb deß hern Jesu willen vmb gnad vnd barmhertzig hilffe zue meinem betruebtem weib, will Ich erwart[en] wie Es Einem Jungen medlichen man gebirt vnd wil Ein brieff vber mich selbs geben, vnd mein leib vnd leben verfalen haben, wan ich mer Ein liedt machen thue, das will Ich auch meinem Gott im himell geloben, daß Ich solcher sachen will miessig....

D. Third interrogation of Jonas Losch, 10 September 1584

Jonas Losch inn Fronuest soll ferner angesprochen werden.

1. Weil er Jüngstlich bekhänt, er hab das lied von doctor Müller wider die Oberkait mit etlichen Wörtern geendert, vnd das letst gesetzlin für sich selbs darzu gemacht, wöll man von Im wissen, wie solliche geenderte Wort, vnd das letst gesetzlin lauten.

Auf fürhaltung dessen sagt er er künds nit außwendig, habs auch nur zweimal abgeschrib[en], wolts sonst g[er]n anzaig[en].

2. Ob nit eben diß Lied, so Ime fürgehalten werden soll, das Jenige seÿ, wellichs er von Michel Kargen bekhomen, vnd wer dasselb geschriben oder gemacht hab.

Er habs [above: 'nit gar'] gemacht, sonder etwas darinnen geendert, vnd sonderlich das letste gesetzt daran gehenckht, auch gleicher gestalt das .25. gesetzlin vons D. Müllers weib gemacht

3. Was er [one word, struck through] an disem lied gemacht, oder geendert hab, soll er lauter vnd vnderschidlich anzaigen.

Er hab nur die zwaÿ obermelte gesetz daran gemacht, vnnd sonst nichts darin verendert.

4. Weil diß lied ein andere Melodeÿ hab, dan das Jenig dauon er Jüngst außgesagt, ob er dan nit dasselb von neüem gedicht vnd gemacht hab.

Er hab sich am nechst[en] gmaint in dem er den Ton angezaigt: Ich stund an einem morg[en], vnnd hab disen Ton so vf dem lied vornen geschrib[en] hinzugesetzt: als nemblich lobt Gott Ir frommen Christ[en]. sonst hab Ime der Michael Karg dises lied an allererst getruckt gezaigt, dauon ers auch abgeschrib[en] vnd wie obsteet gemert hab.

5. Wem er dasselb abgeschriben, oder mitgethailt hab.

Er habs zwaÿmal geschrib[en], das ein in der gefengnus zerrissen, vnd das ander dem Lutz[en] zugestelt, welches eben dises so im fürgehalten sein.

Bitt vmb Gotteswillen vmb gnad mit vermelden das er sein lebtag solch[er] sach[en] müssig geen wöll.

E. *Interrogation of Leonhard Deisenhoffer, 10 September 1584*

Leonhart Deissenhofer Inn fronuest soll ernstlich bedroht angesprochen werden.

1. Wie er haiß vnd von wannen er seÿ.

Er haiß Leonhard Deissenhofer sei Burg[er] alhie.

2. Was sein thun seÿ dauon er sich erhelt.

Er sei ein Weber behelf sich seines handwerck, vnnd als er vf beschehene frag anzeigt er künd gat schlechtlich schreib[en], ist an in begert word[en] etwas zuschreib[en], darauf er dann beiuerwarte schrifft gemacht.

3. Wo er In Jüngstem auflauf gewesen, vnd ob er nit auch mit einer wehr auf den platz geloffen seÿ.

Er sei alhie gewesen, vnnd mit N Meges so gassen haubtman auf den Genßbüel sei, aus andern seiner nachbarn mehr, mit einer seiten wher vnnd feüstling welchen Ime hanns Megeles weib gelieh[en], biß zum Prügeln Im Sächsengäßlen khommen, alda sie vernommen das alles widerumb abgestilt sei, derweg[en] sie widerumb zuruck gezog[en] vnd sich ghen hauß verfüegt hab[en].

4. Man wiß das er ein Zeit her vil schand vnd schmach lieder vnd schriften gemacht, vnd in seinem haus behlaten hab, darumb soll er dieselb alle anzaigen.

Er hab gar kain lied sein lebtag nie gemacht, auch kains abgeschrib[en], dann er so vil als nichts schreib[en] künd, wie er sich dann auf beiligend sein schrifft deßhalb[en] wil gezog[en] hab[en], item so hab er gar kaine lieder als nur .4. welche ime Jonas Losch an S. Bartholmei tag iungst hingeben dageg[en] er Ime ein Haspel in einem glaß geschenckt habe, vnnd sei das ein lied wider D. Müller, das ander wider den jenig[en] so erstermelt lied außgeen lassen, vnd hab solch ander lied der Jonas Losch gemacht, das drit lied sei von Christo vnnd dem Babst, welches der Losch auch gemacht, das viert sei vom Naßen, wiß nit wer dises gemacht, vnnd doch vom Loschen verstendt das er dasselb nit gemacht hab, vnd seien dise vier lieder nur geschrib[en]. sonst aber wol allerleÿ getruckte lieder, ~~welche aber zu diser sach nit gehörig~~, darunder [one word, struck through] nur ains von dem D. Müller vnd der hieig[en] auflauf gemacht ist welches er bei Aaron Stier khaufft, wiß aber nit wer desselb lied gemacht hab.

5. Ob er nit das lied von Jüngstem auflauf vnd D. Müllern wider die Oberkhait gelesen vnd abgeschriben hab.

Antwurt wie ob hab es getruckt kaufft, vnnd demnach gelesen, welches in seiner behausung in einer thruen ligt, im klainen thütlin.

6. Wer Im dasselb gegeben, vnd was er für sich selbst daran geendert, oder gemacht hab.

Er habs bei Stier kaufft, vnnd nichts daran geendert.

7. Ob er nit den Zettel von D. Müller, so Ime fürgehalten werden soll, selbs geschriben, vnd von wem er denselben bekhomen hab.

Er hab disen brief weder gedicht noch geschrib[en], sonder sei seines bruders hannsen Deisenhofers schrifft, welche er [two illegible words, struck through] ermelten sei brueder von einem andern abgeschrib[en], wiß aber nit wer derselb sei, vermaint sein brueder werds wol wissen anzuzaig[en], vnnd wone sein brueder bei seiner mueter in der Klesatlen gassen.

8. Es seÿ gut zudenckhen, er hab disen brief selbs gedicht, darumb soll er anzaigen, was er damit gemaint, vnd wo er denselben ausgestrengt hab, oder man werds durch andern ernst aus Im bringen.

Er künd mit solchen gedicht nit vmbgeen, welches er vfs höchst nimbt, vnnd werd sein brueder wissen anzuzaig[en] [one illegible word, struck through] wer Ine disen brief abzuschreib[en] gegeben, vnnd hab er disen brief nie in seiner gewalt gehabt, sonder in nur blösig von seinem brueder hören lassen, auch den gar niemand mitgetailt.

9. Was er sonst mehr für schandlieder, zettel vnd schrifften gemacht, geendert, oder sonst angeschlagen, vnd fallen hab lassen.

Er hab dergleich[en] nit in sin genommen, vil wenig[er] ins werck gebraucht.

10. Wer Im darzu jedesmals geholfen hab.

Sagt sein vnschuld vnd hab Ime niemand darzu geholff[en].

11. Wem vnd wie oft er dergleichen lieder vnd schrifften, abgeschriben vnd mitgetailt hab.

Er künd nit schreib[en], vnd wendet sein vnschuld für.

12. Ob er nit wiß das solliche schmachschrifften beÿ leibs vnd lebens straf verpoten seien.

Er halt darfür, solche schrifft werden hoch verbott sein, doch hab er dergleich[en] nie gemacht, oder außgespraitet.

13. Ob er nit eim E. Rhat alhie gelobet vnd geschworen seÿ.

Sagt Ja, wie er dann solches neülicher Zeit verrichtet hab.

14. Warumb er [one word, struck through] dan sovil böser aufrüerischen reden wider ein E. Rhat außgossen, vnd offenlich gesagt hab, Er thüe kain guet biß man die Bäpstischen In der Oberkait zum rhathaus herab werf, vnd man solt es Im Jüngsten auflauf thun haben, es möcht Inen Jetz nit so gut mehr werden.

Er hab solch red, oder dergleich[en] sein lebtag nie gethon, welches er vfs höchst beteurt auch nie in sinn genommen.

15. Wie er vermaint hab, solliche sein aufrüerisch fürhaben inn das werckh zurichten, vnd was er derowegen, auch mit wem, für rhat vnd anschlag gehalten vnd gemacht hab.

Entschuldiget sich vfs höchst das er solch red nit gethon.

16. Weil Ime vnd meniglich von eim E. Rhat gleich recht vnd gerechtigkait mitgethailt, auch schutz vnd schirm gehalten worden, was Ihn dan zu sollichem seinem bösen fürnemen verursacht hab.

hab solche sach[en] nie in sin genommen, auch nit geredt.

17. Ob er dan nit gewust, das sie verloffne sach[en] durch die Hn. Wirtembergische vnd Vlmische gesanten verglichen worden seien.

Er wiß dises wol.

18. Warumb er sich dan seines thails vnderstandt ein neüe aufruhr zuerweckhen.

dessen hab er sich im wenigist weder mit wort noch wercken vnderstanden, sonder sei fro gewesst, das die sach widerumb zu einer rue khommen.

19. Wie er vermaint hab solliches alles ohne straf hinaus zubringen, vnd waß er sich hierinn getröst hab.

Nimbt vfs hochst das er sich solchen sach[en] nie vnderfang[en], oder in sin gehabt hab.

Bitt vmb gnad.

3. Anna Borst and Sabina Preiss, January 1588

Source: StAA, Strafamt, *Urgichten*, 13 January 1588 (Borst/Preiss)

A. *Interrogation of Anna Borst, 13 January 1588*

1. Wie sie haiss vnd von wannen sie seÿ.

Sÿ haisse Anna Müllerin, seÿ von Augspurg, weilund Hannß Borsten Schneiders s: wittib.

2. Wie lang sie jetz im Spital, bnd ob sie nit stubenmuetter darinn seÿ.

im 6.ᵗ Jar, vnd seÿ auch Stubenmueter darinn.

3. Ob nit die Sabina Preissin verschiner tagen in Irem beisein ein lied von doctor Müllern im spital offentlich gesungen hab.

Ja.

4. Warumb sie sollichs zuegesech[en] vnd Ihr nit gewehrt hab, da sie dich wol wiss, das dergleich[en] wid[er] vnd schrifft[en] alhie verbot[en] seien.

Sÿ habs warhafftig nit gewüsst, hett es Ir sonst nit gestattet. Sÿ hab auch v[er]maint, weil der Ziechvatter solchs selb gehört, vnd dem singen aufgeleset, er werd es wol selbst andern, wann es Im zuwider weer.

5. Ob nit an d[er] verschine Martinsnacht Ir Sun bei Ir im Spital gewesen seÿ.

Ja.

6. Wer Ir erlaubt hat Iren Sun in dem Spital zu laden

der Ziechvatter hab Ir vnd andern erlaubt, mit den Irischen die martinsnecht zuhalt[en]. wie dann d[en] gantz Spital voll gäst gewesen seÿ

7. Man wiss dz Ir Sun [two words illegible] dises lied auch gesung[en] hat, daher sech man wol dz durch sie vnd die jenigen sollich lied in den spital keinen seÿ, darumb soll sie die warhait guetlich anzaig[en] vnd and[er]e ernst nit verursach[en]

Ja, er habs gesungen, aber dz solches lied eben durch in oder sÿ in den spital kom[m]en seÿ, dz künd sÿ nit sagen, dann sÿ daran vnschuldig. Ir sun hab auch solches lied nit für sich selbst gesungen, sond[er] habe ine die Sabina Preissin, auch 2. alte weuben, eine, die appel Schützin vnd die ander die Fridlin genant, gar hoch vnd vil darumb gebetten, welches so lang nit gern gethon hab, vnd seÿen Ir 21. beÿ einander gewesen, die habens alle gern gehört, sÿ weiss aber vom wort dauon, so gar ein blöde gedächtnus hab sÿ. Vnd müess die warhait sagen, dz von disem lied nichts were gesungen noch

geredt worden, wann die Sabina Preissin nit gewesen war, dann dieselb
habs aller anfangs auf die Pan gebracht, als welche vor disem beÿ Doctor
Müllern, ein Neerin gewesen, vnd haben sie inn Irer stuben sonst nie vil
gesung[en], seÿen lautter alte weiber beÿeinander, die such deß singens nicht
achten, haben mit Irem Och vnd wer zuschaffenn, seÿ der aber die Sabina
Preissin, zu Inen kom[m]en, sing dieselb, als noch en Jungs mensch, bißweiln
ein lied. wie sÿ dann dißmals auch ein lied gesung[en], der Närrisch vesper
genant, darumb sÿs gestrafft, vnd gesagt, sÿ soll darfür die Dorothee sing[en],
So hat sÿ darnach dz lied vom Doctor Müller angefang[en], vnd angezeigt, sÿ
habs Inn Ires bruders hauss bekom[m]en, vnd seÿ Ir bruder ein Weber. Zeigt
auch daneben an, ob sÿ wol wiss, dz doctor Müllers bildtnus im Spital
v[er]botten seÿ, so hab sÿ doch sÿ dieselb nie gehabt, auch von den schrifften
oder liedern, Iresteils nichts gehört, oder da sÿ es je gehört hab[en] solte, Ir
doch solches wurklich auss gedächtnus kom[m]en seÿ, vnd künd der
Ziechvatter, Ires gantzlich[en] [ver]sehens, sonst ob Ir dzwenigist nit clag[en].

8. wer Ihr vnd Irem Sun dises Lied geben hat.
Ir Son hat dz lied allein ausswendig gesungen, sÿ abs auch nit gehabt, künd
weder schreiben noch lesen.

9. Wo vnd durch wen es gewurckt worden seÿ.
sÿ weiß es nitt.

10. Was sie vermaint hat hierdurch an zu richten.
Nichts überal, hat sÿ durch obsteendes vnrecht gethan, so seÿ es Ir auss
vnbedachtem mit widerfaren.
Bitt vmb gnad, seÿ üb[er] 60. Jar.
Nachdem nun die Sabina Preissin mit Ir nit über ain stim[m]et, ist Ir dieselb
vnder augen gefürt, vnd Ir zugesprochen word[en], dz sÿ der Börstin
nochmaln vnder aug[en] sagen soll, wie sich die sach [ver]lauff[en] hat
welches sÿ gethon. Darauff bekennt sÿ Börstin, doch habs die Preissin begert,
antwortt die Preissin, wann die Preissin, wann die Börstin nit selbst vom lied
gesaget, so hett sÿ nit gewüsst, dz Ir son ein solches lied hett, zu dem, so hab
sÿ anfangs nit gewüsst, sÿ der Preissin dz lied erstmals gebracht hat, doch habs
die Preissin dz wz sÿ für ein lied maine, daher dann sÿ gefragt, ob sÿ das lied
main, Wir Müssen alle sterben? hat sÿ gesaget, Nain, es seÿ vom doctor
Müller, wie man In hinauss geschafft hat. Da seÿ wol nit on, dz sÿ gesagt, Ja,
so soll sÿ Irs bringen, darauff abennt die Börstin, solches also, wie obsteet,
wenn sein, der Martins nacht halben, stim[m]en sie letzlich, über vil vnd lang
erinnern, in dem über ain, dz die Sabina nit die anfängerin gewesen, doctor
Müllers lied zubegern, vnd dz die Börstin Irem son zugesproch[en] hat, daselb
zusing[en]. Sÿ Börstin henckt aber daran, dz solches von Ir besche[en] seÿ,
vff der alten Fridlin begern, dz sÿ Ir nemlich Irn son gemeltes lied sing[en]
lassen wölle, damit sÿ es nicht ein mal vor Irem tod hören mög, Welches der
Fridlinbegern die Sabina Preissin (Irem anzaig[en] nach) anfangs nit gehört,
aber wol so vil, dz [margin: 'die Appel Schützin'] Ine den Borst[en] ain
halb[en] batz[en] zu lohn [ver]sproch[en] hat, darauff hat sÿ Sabina Preissin
Ime auch ein mass bier zuzalen zugesagt. Vnd hat der Borst dz lied nit gern
gesung[en].
Darauff hat man sie beede frid[en] abgeschafft, Bitten fürsatz für gang[en].

B. Interrogation of Sabina Preiss, 13 January 1588

Sabina Preiss in fronuest soll ernstlich bethroet angesproch[en] werd[en].

1. Wie sie haiss vnd von wannen [above: 'auch wie alt'] sie seÿ.
   Sÿ haisse Sabina Preissin, seÿ von Augspurg, weiss ir alter nitt, ist dem anseh[en] nach vmb 24. Jar.
2. Wie lang sie jetz in dem Spital gewesen seÿ.
   Werd ÿetzt ein Jar, dz sÿ darein kom[m]en.
3. dieweil sie noch ~~starck~~ jung vnd starckhs leibs seÿ, warumb sie den Spital beschwer, vnd sich nit vil mer mit dienen vnd hand arbait ernahre.
   sÿ seÿ irer glider halben ein ellends armselig mensch, seÿ zuuor im Pilgram hauss vnnd Platterhauss gelegen, vnd seÿ den ziechvatter im Spital ir anlig[en] vnd ellend wol bekannt.
4. Ob sie nit verschiner tag im Spital ein lied von doctor Müller gesung[en] hab.
   Ja, dz hab sÿ gethon.
5. Ob ~~sie~~ Ir nit d[er] ziechvater dises lied genum[m]en hab.
   sagt Ja.
6. Wer Ir dises lied geben hab, soll sie lauter anzaig[en].
   Ir bruder hanss Georg Preiss Web[er] vnd burger alhie habs gehabt, so hab sÿ in darumb gebetten, der hab irs auff ir bitt geben.
7. Wo dises lied getruckht worden seÿ.
   sÿ künd es nit sag[en], dann es stee nit darinn, wo es auch ir bruder genom[m]en, dz künd sÿ nit wissen.
8. Ob sie nit wiss das solliche schrifft[en] alhie verbot[en], vnd hieuor etlich dessweg[en] gestrafft word[en] seien.
   Nain, habs nie gehört, vnd nichts darumb gewüsst, seÿ es beschehen, so müess es nur besceh[en] sein, ehe sÿ hinein kom[m]en.
9. warumb sie dann dessen vngeachtet dises lied nit allain vmbgenngen, sondern auch offentlich gesung[en] hab.
   Sÿ habs auß keinem argen gesung[en], sond[er] hab sich die sach also v[er]loffen, nemlich, als sÿ ernstlich inn den Spital kom[m]en, hab Ir Stubenmueter Ir angezaigt, sÿ müeß auch beten, wie andere, darauff sÿ geantwortt, wann sie die gebet künd, die man im Spital bete, so wöll sÿ gern beten, darnach habs die Stubenmueter gefragt, ob sÿ lesen künd, sÿ gesaget, den truckh künd, sÿ ein wenig lesen, So hab die Stubenmueter gemeldt, Batz, mein son hat ein lied vom Doctor Müller, Ich will dirs bring[en], du must mirs lesen, wie sÿ auch gethon, vnd seÿ solches gescheh[en], als sÿ noch kaum 4: woch[en] im Spital gewesenn. Die Stubenmueter hab v[er]maint, sÿ soll dz Lied außwendig lernen, vnd Ir deroweg[en] dasselb gelassen, ~~biß~~ vngewonlich 8. oder 9. woch[en] lang, da hab sÿs wider von Ir gefordert, vnd Irem son wider geben. vnd hab sÿs nit lernen künden, dann es seÿen gar schwere wort darinn, vnd seÿ sÿ inmittelst kranckh gewesen. als nun die Stubenmuetter v[er]meint, sÿ soll dz Lied außwendig künden, sÿ es doch nitt gekündt, seÿ die Stubenmuetter schier nit wol zufriden gewesen, dz sÿ es so lang gehabt, vnd noch nit gelehrnet haben soll, darnach an der Martinsnacht hab der Stubenmuetter son ‡ [margin: 'Hannß Borst web[er]'] mit seiner mutter geessen [sic], vnd ~~solches lied anfahen singen.~~ nachdem sonst noch einer, der

Beürle gut, so ein Weber, vnd ein mal in der Wacht alhie gewesen, beÿ seiner dochter, die im Spital, damaln auch gewesen, vnd beede, der Beürle vnd der Stubenmuetter son miteinander angefang[en], vom alt[en] vnd neuen Calender zustudiern, [one word illegible] hab sÿ ~~ge~~ Sabina Preissin vermeldt, sie sollen Ir studiern bleiben lassen, vnd darfür einer ein schöns lied singen, da hab die Stubenmutter zu Irem son gesagt, Sing vns den doctor Müller, So hab Ir son solches gethon, anderst seÿ es nitt gang[en]. Auß solchem singen hab sÿ erst v[er]merckt, dz es dz lied seÿ, welches sÿ auf ein zeit beÿ Irem brüder geseh[en] hab, Seÿ derowegen hingang[en], vnd dasselb beÿ Irem bruder außgebetten, wie obsteet, hab es aber erst 8. tag vor Weihenacht[en] bekom[m]en. sÿ habs auch ~~aber~~ niendert vmbgetrag[en], ~~auch~~ vnd keinem andern mensch[en] geben, sonder alle weil beÿ Ir selbst behalt[en]. Wz die herren miteinander gestudieret haben, dz künd sÿ warlich nitt wissen, anderst, als dz der alt, welcher an die ÿetziger Prædigten ~~gieng~~ gang, angefangen hab, vom Newen Calender, man soll es halten, wie mans gemacht hab, wz der ander dageg[en] gesetzet, dz künd sÿ nit wissenn, sÿ hab gleich darfür gebetten, wie obsteet.

10. wie sie vermaint hab dz on straff hinaus zu bring[en].

Sÿ habs nit v[er]stand[en]. hab daruor nie dauon gehört, seÿ wol ein mal ~~in seinem~~ in doctor Müllers hauß ein Neerin gewesen, hab aber von disem Lied nie gehört, dessen vngeachtett hab sÿ die Stubenmuetter gefragt, ob man dz lied sing[en] dörff, hab sÿ gesaget, es seÿ Im Spital nit verbotten.

Bitt vmb gnad, vnd erzeigt sich ainfaltig vnd vnuerdächtig.

4. Martin Haller and Barbara Magenbuech, October/November 1630

Source: StAA, Strafamt, *Urgichten*, 21 October 1630 (Haller)

A. *First interrogation of Martin Haller, 21 October 1630*

Martin Haller soll ernstlich bedrohet angesprochen werden.

1. Wie Er haisse? von wannen? vnnd wie alt Er seÿe?

Er haisse Martin Haller, Seÿe alhie Burger, in .53. Jahr altt.

2. Was sein thun seÿe davon Er sich erhalte?

Am Weberhandtwerckh erhaltte er sich vnd sein Ehewürtin.

3. Wie offt Er zueuor mehr inngelegen vnnd warumben? auch was gestallt Er iedesmahls entlassen worden?

Seÿe, ausser ÿetz, nie nirgentz inngelegen.

4. Ob Er nit bald nach einander ettliche kinder als ein Gevatter aus der heÿligen Tauff gehabt? wie Er darzue komme? vnnd ob mann Ihme nit dessentwegen verehrungen thuen muessen?

Seither deß abgestölten *Exercitij* habe er seinen beden Haußwhüertten, aus Christlicherr schuldigkheit, ohne ohn allen gewiess, zwaÿ Khinder aus d[er] heiligen Tauff gehöbt: vnnd nit mehrer, darzue er allemhal erbetten worden, vnd sich gar nit eingetrungen habe.

5. Ob Er nit zue zwaÿen vnderschidlichen mahlen in St. Johannes Pfarkirchen beÿ dem heÿligen Tauff [above: 'als ein gevatter'] sich gantz vngebührlich verhalten, von dem heÿligen Chrisom vnnd anderen alten Christlichen

Ceremonien gar spöttlich geredt, vnnd dieselb vor menigkhlich verlacht, auch solliche vnbeschaidenheit verüebt, das Er den hern helffer, so das kind getaufft, [one word, struck through] *perturbiert*, vnd schier Irr gemacht?

Im vorigen Windter, alß er auch ein Khindt außm Heiligen Tauff gehäbt, Seÿe seins thails khein andere vngebür fürgangen, alß dz er sich nach dem Tauff gegen dem Mößner deß handtweschens vmb so vil verwaigert, Biß er ihn hette berichten mögen, Warumben es zuthuen, vnd ob daßselbige Wasser geweicht, od[er] nit? Ÿezt letstmhals, habe er dem Priester [one word, struck through] wegen deß Hl. Chrisombs eingeredt, dz selbiger (wie ihm aus Gottes wortt wol bewusst) von Gott nit zum Tauff gehörig seÿe, noch beuolch[en] worden: darübert ihm der Priester ettwas vom Pranger zu verstehn gegeben, vnd v[er]meldt habe, v[er]haffter möge wol ein boser Mann sein, welches er mit seinem guetten gewissen bezeugen, dz er wheitters nichts dabeÿ gespöttlet, noch ains vnnd anders v[er]lacht habe.

6. Ob Er nit wisse, das schon von alters hero beÿ schweren straffen verbotten gewesen, den Catholischen an Irem Gottsdienst, *Ceremonien*, vnd Kirchengebrauchen ainige hinderung zuethuen? warumben Er dann diss ordts so vermessen sein derffen?

Er seines allerwenigsten thails seÿe niemhals bedacht gewest, den Catholischen an ihrem *Exercitio* hindterung zuthun, Wann nur ihnen Euangelischen das ihrig gelassen wurdte; vnnd also hab er auch diss ortts anderst nichts mouiert, noch gesuecht, als was er aus rechtem eÿfer gegen Christi wortt gleichsamb nit v[er]schweigen könd[en]: Gantz nit der mainung, sich dardurch einer vngebühr zu vermössten, sonder die wharheit zu v[er]theidig[en], vnd das ohnschuldige Khindlein dabeÿ, vnd ob seinem glauben, zu erhalt[en].

7. Wer das beÿ Ihme gefundene schmachlied, darinn der Römische Kaÿser für einen Tÿrannen, wellicher noch an sein aigen schwerdt fallen miess, Ir Frl Gdl der herr Bischoff zue Augspurg für Gottloß, die gaistlichen für beschouens bueben vnd Nattergezücht, ausgeschrien werden, *componiert?* vonn weme Ers bekommen? vnd was für Personen Ers weitter *communiciert* habe?

Nach vilem, langem, vnd gnuegsamben zuesprechen, vnnd aller treuhertziger vermhanung, Erclert Er sich, Er wölle lieber selbs die Straff ausstehn, weder andere mit sich anzugeben, vnnd in gefahr zubringen, Woher er nemblich solches Schmachliedt bekhomben, vnd wer es componiert? dann, ob er wol vndter disß gesagt, Es hab ihms ein Weib geben, vnnd er habe es selbß nit gemacht; So bittet er doch, man wölle ihne der Specialanzaig nit anmuetten, sonder Seiner vnd anderer darmit v[er]schonen: betheürt dabeÿ, dz er solches Liedt durchaus niemande com[m]unicirt

8. dessgleichen woher Er die den Catholischen fälschlich aufgedichten, vnd allein dahin, die Catholische Religion dardurch verhafft zuemachen, angesehene *confession* oder beicht bekhommen habe? vnd weme Ers mitgethailt?

Mit erstv[er]standener wid[er]holung seiner andtwortt vnnd entschuldigung, Will er darfür haltten, als wie dergleichen ausgesprengte beichten vil alhie vmbgangen, mögs ihme auch zu hauß khomben sein, dern er sich nichtzit sonderlichs geachtet, vnnd gar nit gedacht habe, dz dise sach[en] aus seinem hauß ÿemand anderm offenbar werden sollen, dann ers auch kheinem Menschen mitgethailt.

9. Wie Er Ihme sein schwere misshandlung zueverantwordten getrawe?

Dieweil sein Intent vnd gedanckhen nit dahin gewest, Sich wider die gebott der obrigkheit zu vergreiffen, Sonder allain ratione deß Gewissens ainig vnd allain in allem guetten sich an Gottes wortt zuhaltten, vnd dasselbe zu seiner ewigen v[er]sicherung nottwendig beÿ der Tauf zuandten: So dann, weil er das Liedt, vnnd die Beicht, beÿ sich in seinem hauß ob seinem whertt vnnd vnwhertt habe sein lassen, vnd dasselbe weitters nit ausgebracht; Als hofft vnnd bittet er, Ihme es zum üblisten nit aus zurechnen, Sonder, in ansehung der Eÿfer d[er] religion nit vnbillich ÿe groß vnd starckh, demselben ettwas nachzugeben, vnnd seiner desto mehr zu v[er]schonen: Da er aber hierübert hie zeittlich ÿe vnrecht gethon soltte haben, welches er doch vor Gottes angesicht ihme zu verandtwortten wol getraue? So müesse vnnd wölle er sein straff gedultigelich darumb ausstehn. [one word illegible] sich aber der lobl obrigkheit zu milder v[er]söhnung, vnd beruhembten gnad[en]: Mit erbietten sich fürtters wolgfellig vnd ohne weittere klag zu v[er]halten. ~

B. *Second interrogation of Martin Haller, 25 October 1630*

Martin Haller soll ferner ernstlich bedroht angesprochen werden.

1. Weilen Er iungst in seiner vrgicht die warheit, vnd woher Er das Schmachlied sambt der erdichten Beicht bekhommen, nit anzaigen wollen, so solle Ers nach thuen, oder anders erwartten, dann mann von Ihme nit lassen werde, biß Er den rechten grund bekhennt haben wirdt.

Demnach mans abermhal lang vnd vil mit güete vnd ernst an ihm getriben, damit er die begertte specialanzaig güettlich von sich lassen möchte? Hat er sich doch lediglich nichtzit erklert, Sonder ist ob deme beharrt, daß mans ihne nit anmuetten solte, Seithemal er niemande in gfahr vnnd vngelegenheit zubringen gedenckhe.

2. demnach Er neülich gezaigt, Er habe dz lied von einem Weib bekhommen, so wölle mann wissen wer dasselbe weÿb seÿe? vnnd wann Sÿe Ihms geben habe?

Mit erstv[er]standener Andtwortt vnd welerung, Sagt er, Ihme seÿe auch nitmehr wissendt, wann er das Liedt vom Weib empfangen habe. ÿedoch bekhendt er nunmehr, dz seiner Ehewürtin Befreundte [one word illegible] deß Magenbuechs, Wohlkhembers Eheweib, an einem Sontag abents vngefähr vor ainem vierttl Jahr in sein hauß khomben seÿe, vnd selbiges Liedt mit sich gebracht, das hab er zwar gelesen, doch sich gleich selbß drübert entsetzt, vnnd es, ohne weitters hinderdenckhen vnd vorhaben, zue ain [above: 'den'] Buech gelegt, ferners niemandt mitgethailt, Noch vil weniger gedacht, dz es and[er]orthz auskhomben, oder d[er]gestalt gfunden w[er]den solle.

3. Weilen Er ohne zweifel wol wisse, wer dises Schmachlied gemacht habe, so solle Er anzaigen wer derselbe seÿe, vnd wird mann sonsten Ihne so lang für den *authorem* hallten, bis Er einen andern mit grund benemen wirdt.

Der *author* deß Liedts seÿe er selbß nit, vnd wisse auch nit, wer es gemacht, villeicht aber möchte es obbemelts Weib wissen: darfür er doch allerhöchstens bitten thüe, Ihrer nach möglicheit zu v[er]schonen.

4. Ob Er das beÿ Ihme gefundene lied selbsten, oder wers sonsten, geschriben habe? wenn Ers zuelesen geben oder abschreiben lassen? vnd ob Er nit solliches in seiner dunckh vnd in den wirtshaüsern vilfälltig gesungen habe?

v[er]andtworttets ebenmessig mit seiner vnwissenheit, vnd vnschuldt: Schändt wol mit der wharheit betheüren, dz ers, seither ers gleich nach v[er]lesung von sich gelegt, gar niemher angesehen, vilwenig[er] es ÿemandt zulesen gegeben, od[er] an ainzigem ortt gesungen habe.

5. Obwolen Er fürgeben, die ausgesprengte glaubens bekhonndtnuss seÿe Ihme vngefahr in das haus kommen, so künde mann doch mit diser antwordt nit vergnüegt sein, sonder wölle wissen, woher Er Sÿe aigentlich bekhommen?

Dieweil es mit denen *Confessionen* vasst ein gemaines ausspargiern gewest, So khönde er ÿs nit aigentlich sagen, wie selbige zu ihm khomben, Sonder vermaine, dz es ohngefahr dahin gebracht worden sein mag, dabeÿ er abermhals betheürt, dz ers gar nit gelesen, oder gewüsst habe.

6. Ob er nit noch mehr dergleichen Schmachschrifften habe? wo Sÿe zuefinden? vnd von weme Ers habe?

Sagt von Nain, wölle sich beÿ seiner vnschuldt frid[en] lassen: vnnd bittet hierauf waÿnendt, Ihme gnadt zuerzaigen; vnd vmb dz er die P[er]sohn nit ehender benant, Ihne Gl. für entschuldigt zuhaltten, dieweil er seines beengstigten hertzens halber sicherlich nit gewüsst habe, was er sagen solle, Damit er ihme ohne aigentliche vrsach, beÿ seinem Nechsten kheinen nachteil vßladen thette, vnd dieweil er in seinem v[er]standt nit erkhennen mögen, darb so groß vnrechts zusein, Seithemaln wed[er] das Lied noch die Beicht nirgentz auskhomben, Noch auch böser mainung beÿ ihe v[er]bleib[en]. Will daneben auch scheinen lass[en], dz er sond[er]lich hierundter nit allerdings *sanæ mentis* sein möchte, d[er]ohalben desto eÿfriger vmb Gn. erlassung anrueffendt. ~

C. Third interrogation of Martin Haller, 4 November 1630

Martin Haller soll ferner ernstlich bedrohet angesprochen werden.

1. Demnach Er der Obrigkheit den grund, sonderlich wegen der Schmachlieder hinder halten, so werde mann Ihne mit ander[en] mittlen aus Ihme bringen, Er bekhenne dann guetwillig, wie vil derogleichen Schmah Sekartekhen Er von der Barbara Magenbuechin oder andern empfangen?

Er habe alberaitt den rechten grundt vnd die wharheit angezaigt, dabeÿ wölle er sich finden lassen, vnnd darob leben vnd sterben; Betheurt auch mit seiner Seelen Seligkheit, dz ihme auf sein letsts Endt nit bewüsst seÿe, Was ihme die Magenbuechin anders, vnd mehrers gegeben haben solle, als was in dem befundenen Liedt beÿsamben geschriben, Welche er sogar wenig in obacht vnd gedechtnus genomben, dz er auch nitmher wisse, wie ains oder das ander anfange: Ja er bezeugt mit Gott, dz solches sein fürgeben whar seie, vnnd er wheitter sich nit erind[er]n könde, Etwas mehrers von ÿemande empfangen zuhab[en].

2. Wie Er sagen künde, das erstgedachte Magenbuechin Ihme nuhr Ein Lied nemblich, die Zeit die ist so traurigelich ~ gegeben habe? da Sÿe doch selbst bekhendt, es seÿen dreÿ gewesen, als, vorgedachtes, so dann, Wo es Gott nit mit

Augspurg hällt ~, vnd, Ach Gott mein Seel ist sehr betriebt. ~

Zu obiger anzaig thuet er erinderlich nit wid[er]sprechen, dz er von der Magenbuechin gleich von anfang des Reformationwesens ein Liedlein empfangen, In d[er] Melodeÿ An Wasserflüessung Babÿlon ~, das seie des Liedts gewest, wie es hernach der Glatz Vischer v[er]end[er]t hatt, dessen anfang, Trumb, noch endt, er nit wisse. Beruefft such im übrigen vf sein erst v[er]standene an v[er]andtwort.

3. Wo Er die andere hingethon? vnnd weme Ers zue lesen, oder abzuschreiben gegeben habe?

Woferr es d[er] Stattknecht nit miteinand[er] genomben, So werde es sich noch in seinem hauß beÿ den büechern finden: Sagt sonnst, Er habe es kheinem Mensch[en] mitgethailt, vnnd betheürt nochmals, dz weder Er, noch sein Weib, sich derlaÿ gantz nichts geachtet haben, vnd ihnen selbs nit wol dabeÿ gewest. Bittet demnach flehentlich, die lobl. obrigkheit wölle an seiner nunmehr langwürigen v[er]hafftung, ein g[nad] bewegen haben, vnnd in ansehung er kheinen bösen willen vnd vorsatz mit den Lied[er]n gehabt, noch selbige and[er]n mitgethailtt, Ihme die Straff nit zum schärpfisten anzustöllen, Sonder ihme gnadt wid[er]faren zulass[en].

D. *Interrogation of Barbara Magenbuech, 31 October 1630*

Barbara Magenbuechin in fronuest soll ernstlich bedrohet angesprochen werden.

1. ~~Barb~~ Wie Sie haisse? von wannen? vnnd wie alt sie seÿe?

Sie haisse Barbara Praklin nach ihrem Vatter, Seÿe deß Hansen Magenbuechs, Growgrienwebers vnd Bürgers alhie Ehewürttin, Vngeuhärlich ob ihren .49. Jahrn altt.

2. Was Ir thuen seÿe, dauon Sÿe sich erhalte?

Ernöhre sich hörttigelich mit Würklen.

3. Wie offt Sÿe zuevor mehr inngelegen? vnd warumben?

Seÿe gar nie inngelegen.

4. Ob Sÿe nit wisse das nit allein allhie wegen der beschehenen vnderschidlichen ernstlichen anschläg, sondern auch ins gemain beÿ schweren straffen verbotten, schmachbrief vnd lieder zuemachen, zuehaben vnd andern mitzuethailen?

Ihr seÿe nit sogar vnwissendt, dz d[er]gleichen dings verbotten, vnd nit recht.

5. warumb sÿe dann dem Martin Haller vnderschidliche solliche schmachlieder zuekommen lassen? wie vil? vnd wie Sÿ haissen? auch ob Sÿ noch mehr abschrifften davon zue haus? ~~habe~~ vnnd was Haller Ir darfür gegeben habe?

Ehe dann das v[er]bott ergangen, v[er]maine Sie gentzlich, habs ihr Sohn, Hans Magenbuech, welcher darsider [sic] in Krieg zogen, ihr zu hauß gebracht, wie ers etwha von den Pierlamppen überkhomben: Was sie dem Haller geben, seÿe gar nit aus argem, sond[er], wie ein ~~Nachbar~~ [margin: 'freundt'] zum andern khombt, der vrsach[en] vnd mit denen Röden and[er]seitz bescheh[en], dz sie darübert gleichsamb selbs wund[er] genomben, Wer doch solche böse Sachen machen habe dürffen? and[er]st es khains geachtet. Ihres erind[er]ns seÿen der Lieder .3. gewest, ains: Die Zeit ist so traurigelich: das Ander, who es Gott nit mit Augsp[ur]g hältt: vnd das dritte: Ach Gott mein Seel ist sehr betrüebt: Ÿedoch, wöll sie diser anzaig

khein gfahr haben, Weil sie daran gar nitmehr gedacht, Vnnd habe Sie gar
kaine Abschrüfften daruon behaten, darfür ihe d[er] Haller, alß ihr Vötter, gar
nichts gegeb[en].

6. Von weme Sÿe dise lieder bekommen? sollen den rechten grund anzaigen,
sonnsten Sÿe dessen nit zuegeniessen haben solle.

7. Weilen Sÿe vor dem herrn Bürgermaister fürgegeben, Ir Sohn Hans so der Zeit
in dem Krieg seÿe, haben dise lieder zuehaus gebracht, so werde Sÿe zweifels
ohne von Ihme auch verfremden haben, von weme Ers bekommen, soll dissfalls
die warheit bekhennen, vnnd Ir selbsten vor mehrerer vngelegeneit sein.

   [Answer to nos. 6 and 7:] Sÿe erst v[er]standen, dz es ihr Sohn zu hauß
   gebracht, Von dem sie gar nit ~~v[er]standen~~ [margin: 'v[er]nomben'] vnd noch
   nit wiss, wie ers bekhomben.

8. Wer die lieder, so Sie dem Martin Haller geben, abgeschriben habe? Vnd ob
Sÿe Ihme nit auch ein erdichte beicht oder bekhandtnuss habe zuelassen
kommen? von weme Sÿes [one word illegible]?

   Ihr Jungers Söhnle, Elias, so ob seinen .14. Jahrn altt sein möchte, habs
   abgeschriben, So sie ~~dar~~ von deß fürwitz wegen, weils~~s~~ ied[er]man
   d[er]gleichen dings gern gehört, vnd glesen, geschehen lassen, zuemhaln
   selbiger Zeit noch khein v[er]bott gewest; Wisse gentz vmb khein Beicht.

9. Wie Sÿe Ir vnrecht Ir zueverantwortten getrawe?

   Sie erkhenne ihr vnrecht, welches Sie, als ein schlechts weibsbildt, so wheit nit
   gerechnet, Sonder beÿ ihr allzeit gedacht habe, der, so es gemacht, werde es
   müessen v[er]andtwortten; Bittet derohalben Vmb gnadt, vnd grl erlassung:
   Ihrer auch von ihrer Sechs armen Khinder wegen zuv[er]schonen.

Bibliography

Aichinger, Gregor, *Thymiama sacerdotale, hoc est, Meditationes piae, a Sacerdotibus ante Celebrationem Missae per singulos Hebdomadae Dies devotè exercendae* (Augsburg: Sara Mang, 1618). Exemplar: D-As, Th Pr 2631.

Bremens, Gilbert, *Historia Sacramenti miraculosi in Monasterio Sanctæ Crucis Augustæ Vindelicorum* (Augsburg: Christophorus Mang, 1604). Exemplar: D-As, 8° Aug 1004.

Bruderschaft Vnser L. Frauen Him[m]elfart zu Augsburg 1631 ([Augsburg], 1631). Exemplar: D-As, 8° Aug. 313.

Copey oder Verzaychnuß, der Gnedigsten vnnd Vätterlichen, auch Hayligen Indulgentien oder Ablaß, welche Babst Sixtus Quintus Pontifex Maximus, Anno domini 1587. Der aller hayligsten Tryfaltigkayt, Christenlichen Lobwürdigen Bruderschafft deß Hayligenbergs Andex, inn Bayren vor wenig Jaren, inn vnser lieben Frawen Thumbstifft zu Augspurg, von etlichen Gottseligen Catholischen Christen, Gaystlichs vnnd Weltlichs Standts, angestelt vnnd auffgericht worden, Vätterlich verlichen hatt, &c. Sampt einem kurtzen Begriff, was einem jeden Bruder oder Schwester, so sich inn solche Bruderschafft Einzuschreyben begehrt schuldig, vnnd zuwissen von nötten ist (Augsburg: Josias Wörly, 1588). Exemplar: D-As, 4° Aug. 163 -2-.

Encyclica, Das ist, ein Gemein Craißschreiben. Zu dienst vnd gefallen den hochlöblichen Bruderschafften deß allerheiligisten Fronleichnams Christi, vnd andern mahren in vnd ausser der weitberhümbten Reichsstadt Augspurg. Gestellet wider den newen Gaisselfeind Jacob Heilbrunner. Durch einen sondern Freundt vnd Patron deß Bußfertigen Lebens (Ingolstadt: Andreas Angermayer, 1607). Exemplar: D-As, 4° Aug 306 a, b.

Erscheinung vnd Offenbarung der allerheiligsten vnd glorwürdigsten Mutter Gottes/ so die heylig Königin Elisabeth (wie gottselig geglaubt wirdt) gehabt hat. Aus den Opusculis deß H. Kirchen Lehrers Bonauenturæ ins Teutsch gebracht. Sampt einem Geistlichen Gesang/ zu höchstgemeldter Mutter Gottes (Augsburg: Chrysostomus Dabertzhofer, 1611). Exemplar: D-As, 8° Th Pr 4882 -Beibd. 5.

Fronleichnams Frag, Eines Lutheraners, Ob es Abgötterey sey vmbtragen, verehren, anbetten das allerheiligste Sacrament deß Altars. Verantwort von einem Catholischen Anno 1607. den 28. Aprill, Mündlich vnd geschrifftlich, jetzund auch in offenen Truck verfertigt, Zu nutz vnd wolgefallen der hochlöblichen Brüderschafft Corporis

Christi, bey dem H. Creutz in Augspurg (Ingolstadt: in der Ederischen Truckerey, durch Andream Angermayr, 1607). Exemplar: D-As, 4° Aug 421.

Gratulation An die andächtige deß Heiligen Fronleichnams JEsu CHristi, vnd andere Brüderschafften zu Augspurg. Prouerb. 18. Ein Bruder der Hülffe hat vom Bruder, ist wie eine feste Stadt (Ingolstadt: in der Ederischen Truckerey, durch Andream Angermayr, 1604). Exemplar: D-As, 4° Aug. 421.

Holder, M. Wilhelm, *Bericht welchermassen Papst Sixt, der fünffte dises Namens, die newe Augspurgische Bruderschafft, des H. Bergs Andex, mit Gnad vnd Ablaß bedacht, auch was von solchem Ablaßkrom zuhalten. Gestellet Durch M. Wilhelm Holdern/ Stifftspredigern zu Stutgarten* (Tübingen: Georg Gruppenbach, 1588). Exemplar: D-As, 4° Aug. 163 -1-.

Kurtzer Bericht, Von der Gnadenreichen Bruderschafft deß H. Rosenkrantzs, oder Psalter vnser lieben Frawen. Erstlich, Vom Anfang vnd Vrsprung diser Bruderschafft, auch wie man sich darinn verhalten soll. Fürs ander, Von vilfältigen Ablassen, von vnderschiedlichen Bäpsten (wie auch von jetzigem Bapst PAVLO V.) gegeben vnd zum öfftern bestettigt worden. Zum dritten, Von Monatlicher Procession, bey den Ehrwürdigen Vättern Prediger Ordens in jhren Kirchen, vnnd an andern Orten, dahin sie die Gnad ertheilen, Procession zuhalten. Zum vierdten, Von Miraclen deß H. Rosenkrantzs (Augsburg: Christoph Mang, 1616). Exemplar: D-As, 12° Th Pr 215.

Lader, Octavian, *Historia dess Sacraments, so beym H. Creutz in Augspurg verehrt wirdt* (Augsburg: Andreas Aperger, 1625). Exemplar: D-As, 8° Aug 800.

Letaney von dem Leben deß H. Beichtigers Rochi (Augsburg, [c.1650]). Exemplar: D-As, 2° Aug 3865.

Liber Ritualis, Episcopatus Augustensis, distinctus in tres Partes, et ad usum Romanum accommodatus. Continens Canones et Ritus sacros, qui in Administratione Sacramentorum, & cæteris Munijs Ecclesiasticis, præsertim pastoralibus ritè obeundis, obseruari debent (Dillingen: Johann Mayer, 1612). Exemplar: D-As, 4° Aug 1281.

Lobwasser, Ambrosius, ed., *Psalmen Dauids In Teutsche Reymen verständtlich vnd deutlich gebracht* (Düsseldorf: Bey Bernhardt Buyß, 1612).

Maximiliani deß ersten, Caroli deß fünfften, vnd Ferdinandi, aller dreyen Römischen Kayser. Recht Catholische andächtige Verehrung deß hochwürdigsten Sacraments deß Altars (Augsburg: Christoph Mang, 1614). Exemplar: D-As, 4° Aug. 163 -3-.

Mayr, Georg, ed., *Fasciculus sacrarum Litaniarum ex sanctis Scripturis & Patribus, Romæ approbatus. Nunc primùm in pium Usum*

Studiosæ Iuuentutis Græcè redditus (Augsburg: Christophorus Mang, 1614). Exemplar: D-As, 12° H 543, Beibd. 1.

——, *Officium Angeli Custodis Pauli V. Pont. Max. Authoritate publicatum* (Antwerp: Apud Heredes Martini Nutij, & Ioannem Meursium, 1617). Exemplar: D-As, 8° Th Lt K 670.

——, *Officium Beatæ Mariæ Virginis Latino-Græcum* (Augsburg: Ad insigne pinus, inprimebat David Francus, 1612). Exemplar: D-As, 12° Th Lt K 412.

——, *Officium Corporis Christi, De Festo et per Octauam Latinè et Græcè editum, ac Fraternitati Eucharisticæ Augustanæ dedicatum* (Augsburg, 1618). Exemplar: D-As, 12° Th Lt K 413.

Psalterium Mariæ, Der heyligsten Junckfraw vnd Gottes gebererin ... (Augsburg: Christoph Mang [Chrysostomus Dabertzhofer?], 1611). Exemplar: D-As, 8° Th Pr 4882 -Beibd. 4.

Scioppius, Kaspar, *Emmanuel Thaumaturgus Augustae Vindel. hoc est Relatio de miraculoso Corporis Christi Sacramento, quod Augustae in S. Crucis Ecclesia servatum est* (Augsburg, 1612). Exemplar: D-As, 4° Aug 1404.

Sodalis Parthenius. Siue Libri tres quibus mores Sodalium Exemplis informantur. Operâ maiorum Sodalium Academicorum B. Mariæ Virginis Annunciatæ in Lucem dati (Ingolstadt, 1621). Exemplar: D-As, 12° Th Pr 2460.

Stengel, Karl, *Das Leben vnnd Wunderwerck des H. Simperti* (Augsburg, 1616). Exemplar: D-As, 8° Aug 2324, a.

——, *Vindiciae S. Udalrico Augustae Vindelicae episcopo datae* (Augsburg, 1614). Exemplar: D-As, 8° Aug 2322.

——, *Vita S. Wicterpi Episcopi Augustani et Confessoris* (Augsburg: Christophorus Mang, 1607). Exemplar: D-As, 8° Aug 2321, a.

——, *Der weltberühmten Kayserlichen Freyen, vnd deß H. Rö: ReichsStatt Augspurg in Schwaben, kurtze Kirchen Chronik, sampt dem Leben vnd Wunderzeichen der Heyligen, welche daselbsten gelebt/ in fünff vnderschidliche Bücher abgetheilt* (Augsburg: Sara Mang, 1620). Exemplar: D-As, 2° Aug 328.

Stetten, Paul von, *Geschichte der Heil. Röm. Reichs Freyen Stadt Augspurg, Aus Bewährten Jahr-Büchern und Tüchtigen Urkunden gezogen*, 2 vols. (Frankfurt am Main and Leipzig: In der Merz- und Mayerischen Buch-Handlung, 1743). Exemplar: D-As, 4° Aug 1463.

——, *Kunst-, Gewerb- und Handwerks-Geschichte der Reichs-Stadt Augsburg*, 2 vols (Augsburg: Conrad Heinrich Stage, 1779).

Summarischer Bericht von Würckung vnd Geniessung deß Jubeljars. Dem Christlichen Pfarrvölcklein im Bistumb Augspurg, von den Predigstülen offentlich zuuerlesen (Dillingen: Johann Mayer, [c.1600]). Exemplar: D-As, 8° Aug 174.

Thyraeus, Peter, *Tractatus de Apparitionibus sacramentalibus ad Gloriam miraculosi Sacramenti, quod Augustae in Ecclesia S. Crucis colitur illustrandam* (Dillingen, 1640). Exemplar: D-As, 8° Aug 1404 -1-.

Vetter [Andreae], Conrad, M. *Conradi Andreæ &c. Volcius Flagellifer. Das ist: Beschützung vnd Handhabung fürtreflicher vnd herlicher zweyer Predigten von der vnleydenlichen vnd Abschewlichen Geysel Proceßion, erstlich gehalten, hernach auch in Truck gegeben durch den Kehrwürdigen, vnnd Wolgekerten Herrn M. Melchior Voltz Lutherischen Predicanten zu Augspurg bey Sant Anna* (Ingolstadt: In der Ederischen Truckerey, durch Andream Angermayer, 1608). Exemplar: D-As, 4° Aug. 1586.

Vochetius, Anastasius, *Thaumaturgus Eucharisticus sive de Sacramento ad s. Crucem Historia* (Augsburg, 1637). Exemplar: D-As, 8° Aug 2534.

Volcius, Melchior, *Zwo Christliche Predigten, von der abscheulichen Geisselungsprocession, welche jährlich im Papsthumb am Charfreytag gehalten würdt* (Tübingen: in der Cellischen Truckerey, 1607). Exemplar: D-As, 4° Aug 1576.

Secondary Sources

Adrio, Adam, *Die Anfänge des geistlichen Konzerts* (Berlin: Junker und Dünnhaupt, 1935).

Aichinger, Gregor, *Ausgewählte Werke von Gregor Aichinger (1564–1628)*, ed. Theodor Kroyer, Denkmäler der Tonkunst in Bayern, 10. Jahrgang, vol. 1 (Leipzig: Breitkopf & Härtel, 1909).

——, *Cantiones ecclesiasticae*, ed. William E. Hettrick, Recent Researches in the Music of the Baroque Era, vol. 13 (Madison, Wis.: A-R Editions, 1972).

——, *The Vocal Concertos*, ed. William E. Hettrick, Recent Researches in the Music of the Baroque Era, vols. 54–55 (Madison, Wis.: A-R Editions, 1986).

Altmann, Lothar, 'Michaelskirchen im Bistum Augsburg', in Mai, ed., *Sankt Michael in Bayern*, pp. 76–87.

Anderson, Gary L., 'The Canzonetta Publications of Simone Verovio' (DMA diss., University of Illinois, 1976).

Arnold, Denis, 'Music at a Venetian Confraternity in the Renaissance', *Acta musicologica*, 37 (1965), pp. 62–72.

Atlas, Allan W., *Renaissance Music: Music in Western Europe, 1400–1600* (New York: Norton, 1998).

Baer, Wolfram, 'Michaelsgruppe am Zeughaus (vollendet 1607)', in Mai, ed., *Sankt Michael in Bayern*, p. 88.

——, and Hans Joachim Hecker, eds, *Die Jesuiten und ihre Schule St. Salvator in Augsburg 1582* (Augsburg: Stadtarchiv Augsburg; Munich: Karl M. Lipp, 1982).

Barth, Fredrik, ed., *Ethnic Groups and Boundaries: The Social Organization of Cultural Difference* (Bergen and Oslo: Universitets Forlaget; London: George Allen & Unwin, 1969).

Batz, Karl, 'Universität und Musik', in Hofmann, ed., *Musik in Ingolstadt*, pp. 111–24.

Bäumker, Wilhelm, *Das katholische deutsche Kirchenlied in seinen Singweisen von den frühesten Zeiten bis gegen Ende des siebzehnten Jahrhunderts*, 4 vols (Freiburg im Breisgau and St. Louis, Mo.: Herder, 1883–1911).

Becker, Carl Ferdinand, *Die Tonwerke des XVI. und XVII. Jahrhunderts oder systematisch-chronologische Zusammenstellung der in diesen zwei Jahrhunderten gedruckten Musikalien* (2nd edn, Leipzig: Ernst Fleischer, 1855; repr. Hildesheim: Georg Olms, 1969).

Beer, Axel, *Die Annahme des 'stile nuovo' in der katholischen Kirchenmusik Süddeutschlands*, Frankfurter Beiträge zur Musikwissenschaft, vol. 22 (Tutzing: Hans Schneider, 1989).

Bellingham, Bruce A., 'The Bicinium in the Lutheran Latin Schools during the Reformation Period' (Ph.D. diss., University of Toronto, 1971).

Bellot, Josef, 'Augsburg – Porträt einer Druckerstadt', *Zeitschrift für Bibliothekswesen und Bibliographie*, 17 (1970), pp. 247–64.

——, 'Humanismus – Bildungswesen – Buchdruck und Verlagsgeschichte', in Gottlieb et al., eds, *Geschichte der Stadt Augsburg*, pp. 343–57.

Bergquist, Peter, 'Vorwort', in *Litaneien, Falsibordoni und Offiziumssätze*, vol. 25 of Orlando di Lasso, *Sämtliche Werke, Neue Reihe* (Kassel: Bärenreiter, 1993), pp. vii–xii.

Bernstein, Jane A., 'Buyers and Collections of Music Publications: Two Sixteenth-Century Music Libraries Recovered', in Jessie Ann Owens and Anthony M. Cummings, eds, *Music in Renaissance Cities and Courts: Studies in Honor of Lewis Lockwood* (Warren, Mich.: Harmonie Park Press, 1997), pp. 21–33.

Beyschlag, Daniel Eberhardt, *Kurze Nachrichten von dem Gymnasium zu St. Anna in Augsburg nebst einem Verzeichniß gesammter ordentlicher und besonders aufgestellter Lehrer desselben vom Jahre 1531 bis zum Jahre 1831* (Augsburg: Albrecht Volkhart, 1831).

Bidermann, Jakob, *Cenodoxus*, ed. Rolf Tarot (Tübingen: N. Niemeyer, 1963).

Blaufuß, Dietrich, 'Das Verhältnis der Konfessionen in Augsburg 1555 bis 1648: Versuch eines Überblicks', *JVAB*, **10** (1976), pp. 27–56.

Boetticher, Wolfgang, *Orlando di Lasso und seine Zeit, 1532–1594* (Kassel: Bärenreiter, 1958).

Böhme, Franz Magnus, *Altdeutsches Liederbuch: Volkslieder der Deutschen nach Wort und Weise aus dem 12. bis zum 17. Jahrhundert* (Leipzig: Breitkopf & Härtel, 1877; repr. Hildesheim: Georg Olms, 1966).

Braun, Placidus, *Geschichte der Bischöfe von Augsburg*, 4 vols (Augsburg: In der Moy'schen Buchhandlung, 1815).

——, *Geschichte des Kollegiums der Jesuiten in Augsburg* (Munich: Jakob Giel, 1822).

Braun, Werner, 'Kompositionen von Adam Gumpelzhaimer im Florilegium Portense', *Die Musikforschung*, **33** (1980), pp. 131–35.

Bredero, Adriaan Hendrik, *Bernard of Clairvaux: Between Cult and History* (Grand Rapids, Mich.: William B. Eerdmans, 1996).

Brennecke, Wilfried, 'Kerle, Jacobus de', in *MGG*, vol. 7, cols 846–50.

Brusniak, Friedhelm, and Horst Leuchtmann, eds, *Quaestiones in musica: Festschrift für Franz Krautwurst zum 65. Geburtstag* (Tutzing: Hans Schneider, 1989).

Bucher, Otto, 'Adam Meltzer (1603–1610) und Gregor Hänlin (1610–1617) als Musikaliendrucker in Dillingen/Donau', *Gutenberg-Jahrbuch*, **31** (1956), pp. 216–26.

——, 'Bibliographie der Druckwerke Johann Mayers und seiner Witwe Barbara zu Dillingen 1601–1619', *Archiv für Geschichte des Buchwesens*, **10** (1970), pp. 899–944.

Büchler, Volker, 'Die Zensur im frühneuzeitliche Augsburg 1515–1806', *Zeitschrift des Historischen Vereins für Schwaben*, **84** (1991), pp. 69–128.

Bukofzer, Manfred F., *Music in the Baroque Era from Monteverdi to Bach* (New York: Norton, 1947).

Burke, Peter, 'How to Become a Counter-Reformation Saint', in Luebke, ed., *The Counter-Reformation: The Essential Readings*, pp. 129–42. Originally published in Kaspar von Greyerz, ed., *Religion and Society in Early Modern Europe, 1500–1800* (London: German Historical Institute, 1984), pp. 45–55.

——, *Popular Culture in Early Modern Europe* (rev. repr. Aldershot: Scolar Press; Brookfield, Vt.: Ashgate, 1994).

Bushart, Bruno, 'Die Hochaltarblätter des Barock in Augsburg', *JVAB*, **25** (1991), pp. 190–225.

——, 'Kunst und Stadtbild', in Gottlieb et al., eds, *Geschichte der Stadt Augsburg*, pp. 363–85.

Carter, Tim, *Music in Late Renaissance and Early Baroque Italy* (Portland, Ore.: Amadeus Press, 1992).

Carver, Anthony F., 'Stuber [Stuberus, Stueber], Conrad', in *New Grove II*, vol. 24, pp. 618–19.

Casimiri, Raffaele, 'Simone Verovio da Hertogenbosch', *Note d'archivio per la storia musicale*, **10** (1933), p. 189; **11** (1934), p. 66.

Charteris, Richard, *Adam Gumpelzhaimer's Little-Known Score Books in Berlin and Kraków*, Musicological Studies and Documents, vol. 48 (Neuhausen: Hänssler-Verlag–American Institute of Musicology, 1996).

——, 'An Early Seventeenth-Century Manuscript Discovery in Augsburg', *Musica disciplina*, **47** (1993), pp. 35–70.

——, 'Two Little-Known Manuscripts in Augsburg with Works by Giovanni Gabrieli and his Contemporaries', *R. M. A. Research Chronicle*, **23** (1990), pp. 125–36.

Chartier, Roger, *The Cultural Uses of Print in Early Modern France*, trans. Lydia G. Cochrane (Princeton: Princeton University Press, 1987).

Chevalley, Denis A., *Der Dom zu Augsburg*, Die Kunstdenkmäler von Bayern, neue Folge, vol. 1 (Munich: B. Oldenbourg Verlag, 1995).

Clasen, Claus Peter, 'Arm und Reich in Augsburg vor dem Dreißigjährigen Krieg', in Gottlieb et al., eds, *Geschichte der Stadt Augsburg*, pp. 312–36.

——, *Die Augsburger Steuerbücher um 1600* (Augsburg: Mühlberger, 1976).

——, *Die Augsburger Weber: Leistungen und Krisen des Textilgewerbes um 1600*, Abhandlungen zur Geschichte der Stadt Augsburg: Schriftenreihe des Stadtarchivs Augsburg, vol. 27 (Augsburg: H. Muhlberger, 1981).

Corpis, Duane J., 'The Geography of Religious Conversion: Crossing the Boundaries of Belief in Southern Germany, 1648–1800' (Ph.D. diss., New York University, 2001).

Crawford, David, 'Liturgischer Buchdruck in Augsburg, 1470–1600', in Gier and Janota, eds, *Augsburger Buchdruck und Verlagswesen*, pp. 323–35.

Creasman, Allyson F., 'Policing the Word: The Control of Print and Public Expression in Early Modern Augsburg, 1520–1648' (Ph.D. diss., University of Virginia, 2002).

Crook, David, *Orlando di Lasso's Imitation Magnificats for Counter-Reformation Munich* (Princeton: Princeton University Press, 1994).

Culley, Thomas D., S.J., *Jesuits and Music*, vol. 1: *A Study of the Musicians Connected with the German College in Rome during the 17th Century and of their Activities in Northern Europe*, Sources and

Studies for the History of the Jesuits, vol. 2 (Rome: Jesuit Historical Institute; St. Louis: St. Louis University, 1970).

Cusick, Suzanne G., and Noel O'Regan, 'Madrigale spirituale', in *New Grove II*, vol. 15, pp. 572–73.

Cuyler, Louise, 'Musical Activity in Augsburg and its Annakirche, ca. 1470–1630', in Johannes Riedel, ed., *Cantors at the Crossroads: Essays on Church Music in Honor of Walter E. Buszin* (St. Louis, Mo.: Concordia Publishing House, 1967), pp. 33–43.

Danckwardt, Marianne, 'Konfessionelle Musik?', in Reinhard and Schilling, eds, *Die katholische Konfessionalisierung*, pp. 371–83.

Dorn, Ludwig, 'Das Mirakelbuch der Wallfahrt Maria Hilf in Speiden', *JVAB*, **20** (1986), pp. 141–45.

——, *Die Wallfahrten des Bistums Augsburg* (Augsburg: Verlag Winfried-Werk, 1961).

Duhr, Bernhard, *Geschichte der Jesuiten in den Ländern deutscher Zunge in der ersten Hälfte des XVII. Jahrhunderts*, 5 vols (Freiburg im Breisgau and St. Louis, Mo.: Herder, 1913).

Duke, Alastair, *Reformation and Revolt in the Low Countries* (London and Ronceverte: The Hambledon Press, 1990).

Dülmen, Richard van, *Theatre of Horror: Crime and Punishment in Early Modern Germany*, trans. Elisabeth Neu (Cambridge: Polity Press; Cambridge, Mass.: Blackwell, 1990).

Eade, John, and Michael J. Sallnow, eds, *Contesting the Sacred: The Anthropology of Christian Pilgrimage* (London and New York: Routledge, 1991).

Eikelmann, Renate, ed., *Die Fugger und die Musik: Lautenschlagen lernen und ieben. Anton Fugger zum 500. Geburtstag: Ausstellung in den historischen Badstuben im Fuggerhaus Augsburg, 10. Juni bis 8. August 1993* (Augsburg: Hofmann Verlag, 1993).

Erbach, Christian, Hans Leo Hassler, and Jakob Hassler, *Ausgewählte Werke von Christian Erbach (um 1570–1635). Erster Teil. Werke für Orgel und Klavier. Werke Hans Leo Hasslers (1564–1612). Erster Teil. Werke für Orgel und Klavier. Mit beigefügten Stücken von Jacob Hassler (geb. 1565)*, ed. Ernst von Werra, Denkmäler der Tonkunst in Bayern, 4. Jahrg., 2. Bd.; 5. Jahrg., 1. Bd. (Leipzig: Breitkopf & Härtel, 1903).

Evennett, H. Outram, 'Counter-Reformation Spirituality', in Luebke, ed., *The Counter-Reformation: The Essential Readings*, pp. 47–63. Originally published in his *The Spirit of the Counter-Reformation*, ed. John Bossy (Notre Dame: University of Notre Dame Press, 1970), pp. 23–42.

Fellerer, Karl Gustav, ed., *Geschichte der katholischen Kirchenmusik*, 2 vols (Kassel: Bärenreiter, 1976).

Fielitz, Sonja, *Jakob Gretser Timon. Comoedia Imitata (1584).* *Erstausgabe von Gretsers Timon-Drama mit Übersetzung und einer Erörterung von dessen Stellung zu Shakespeares Timon of Athens* (Munich: Wilhelm Fink Verlag, 1994).

Fischer, Hermann, and Theodor Wohnhaas, *Die Augsburger Domorgeln* (Sigmaringen: Thorbecke, 1992).

—— 'Miscellanea zur Augsburger Dommusik', in Brusniak and Leuchtmann, eds, *Quaestiones in musica*, pp. 123–45.

Fisher, Alexander J., 'Fugger', in *MGG*², Personenteil, vol. 7, pp. 246–52.

——, 'Music in Counter-Reformation Augsburg: Musicians, Rituals, and Repertories in a Religiously Divided City' (Ph.D. diss., Harvard University, 2001).

——, 'Song, Confession, and Criminality: Trial Records as Sources for Popular Musical Culture in Early Modern Europe', *Journal of Musicology*, **18** (2001), pp. 616–57.

Fleckenstein, Franz, 'Marienverehrung in der Musik', in Wolfgang Beinert and Heinrich Petri, eds, *Handbuch der Marienkunde* (Regensburg: Pustet, 1984), pp. 173–214.

Flotzinger, Rudolf, 'Die kirchliche Monodie um die Wende des 16./17. Jahrhunderts', in Fellerer, ed., *Geschichte der katholischen Kirchenmusik*, vol. 2, pp. 78–87.

Forster, Marc, *The Counter-Reformation in the Villages: Religion and Reform in the Bishopric of Speyer, 1560–1720* (Ithaca, NY: Cornell University Press, 1992).

——, 'The Thirty Years' War and the Failure of Catholicization', in Luebke, ed., *The Counter-Reformation: The Essential Readings*, pp. 163–97.

François, Étienne, *Die unsichtbare Grenze: Protestanten und Katholiken in Augsburg 1648–1806* (Sigmaringen: Jan Thorbecke Verlag, 1991).

Franz, G., 'Johannes Frosch, Theologe und Musiker in einer Person?', *Die Musikforschung*, **28** (1975), pp. 71–75.

Fritz, D.F., *Ulmische Kirchengeschichte vom Interim bis zum dreißigjährigen Krieg (1548–1612)* (Stuttgart: Chr. Scheufele, [1934]).

Gamber, Klaus, *Cantiones Germanicae im Regensburger Obsequiale von 1570: Erstes offizielles katholisches Gesangbuch Deutschlands* (Regensburg: Pustet, 1983).

Gier, Helmut, and Reinhard Schwartz, eds, *Reformation und Reichsstadt: Luther in Augsburg* (Augsburg: Verlag Dr. Wissner, 1996).

Gier, Helmut, and Johannes Janota, eds, *Augsburger Buchdruck und Verlagswesen: Von den Anfängen bis zur Gegenwart* (Wiesbaden: Harrassowitz, 1997).

Glixon, Jonathan, *Honoring God and the City: Music at the Venetian Confraternities, 1260–1806* (New York: Oxford University Press, 2003).

Gmeinwieser, Siegfried, 'Kirchenmusik', in Brandmüller, ed., *Handbuch der bayerischen Kirchengeschichte*, pp. 981–96.

Goovaerts, Leon, *Écrivains, artistes et savants … de l'orde de Prémontré: Dictionnaire bio-bibliographique*, 4 vols (Brussels: Société belge de librairie, 1899–[1920]).

Göthel, Forkel, 'Das reichstädtische Musikleben Augsburgs im 17. und 18. Jahrhundert', in *Musik in Bayern. II. Ausstellungskatalog. Augsburg, Juli bis Oktober 1972*, ed. Forkel Göthel (Tutzing: Hans Schneider, 1972), pp. 221–42.

Gottlieb, Günther, et al., eds, *Geschichte der Stadt Augsburg: 2000 Jahre von der Römerzeit bis zur Gegenwart* (2d edn, Stuttgart: Konrad Theiss Verlag, 1985).

Gumpelzhaimer, Adam, *Ausgewählte Werke*, ed. Otto Mayr, Denkmäler der Tonkunst in Bayern, 10. Jahrgang, vol. 2 (Leipzig: Breitkopf & Härtel, 1909).

Guth, Klaus, 'Geschichtlicher Abriß der marianischen Wallfahrtsbewegung im deutschsprachigen Raum', in Wolfgang Beinert and Heinrich Petri, eds, *Handbuch der Marienkunde* (Regensburg: Pustet, 1984), pp. 721–848.

Häberlein, Mark, 'Weber und Kaufleute im 16. Jahrhundert: Zur Problematik des Verlagswesens in der Reichsstadt Augsburg', *Zeitschrift des Historischen Vereins für Schwaben*, 91 (1998), pp. 43–56.

Haggenmüller, Martina, *Als Pilger nach Rom: Studien zur Romwallfahrt aus der Diözese Augsburg von den Anfängen bis 1900* (Augsburg: AV-Verlag, 1993).

Hamacher, Theo, *Beiträge zur Geschichte des katholischen deutschen Kirchenliedes* (Paderborn: im Selbstverlag, 1985).

Härting, Michael, 'Das deutsche Kirchenlied der Gegenreformation', ibid., pp. 59–63.

Hettrick, William E., 'Aichinger, Gregor,' in *New Grove II*, vol. 1, pp. 249–50.

——, 'The Thorough-Bass in the Works of Gregor Aichinger' (Ph.D. diss., University of Michigan, 1968).

Hoeynck, F. A., *Geschichte der kirchlichen Liturgie des Bisthums Augsburg. Mit Beilagen: Monumentae liturgiae Augustanae* (Augsburg: Litterar. Institut von M. Huttler [Michael Seitz], 1889).

Hofmann, Ruth, 'Jesuitentheater in Ingolstadt', in Hofmann, ed., *Musik in Ingolstadt*, pp. 168–86.

——, 'Notendruck', ibid., pp. 125–42.

Hofmann, Siegfried, ed., *Musik in Ingolstadt. Zur Geschichte der Musikkultur in Ingolstadt. Ausstellung des Stadtarchivs und Stadtmuseums Ingolstadt vom 19.10. bis 18.11.1984* (Ingolstadt: Historischer Verein Ingolstadt, 1984).

Holl, Konstantin, *Fürstbischof Jakob Fugger von Konstanz (1604–1626) und die katholische Reform der Diözese im ersten Viertel des 17. Jahrhunderts* (Freiburg im Breisgau: im Commission der Gesellschaftsstelle des 'Caritasverbandes für das katholische Deutschland', 1898).

Hsia, R. Po-Chia, *Social Discipline in the Reformation, Central Europe 1550–1750*, Christianity and Society in the Modern World (London and New York: Routledge, 1989).

——, 'The Structure of Belief: Confessionalism and Society, 1500–1600', in Robert W. Scribner, ed., *Germany: A New Social and Economic History*, Vol. 1: *1450–1630* (London and New York: Arnold, 1996), pp. 355–77.

——, *The World of Catholic Renewal, 1540–1770,* New Approaches to European History, vol. 12 (Cambridge and New York: Cambridge University Press, 1998).

Hüttl, Ludwig, *Marianische Wallfahrten im süddeutschen-österreichischen Raum: Analysen von der Reformations- bis zur Aufkärungsepoche* (Köln: Bohlau, 1985).

Immenkötter, Herbert, 'Kirche zwischen Reformation und Parität', in Gottlieb et al., eds, *Geschichte der Stadt Augsburg*, pp. 391–412.

——, and Wolfgang Wüst, 'Augsburg: Freie Reichsstadt und Hochstift', in Anton Schindling and Walter Ziegler, eds, *Die Territorien des Reichs im Zeitalter der Reformation und Konfessionalisierung* (Münster: Aschendorff, 1993), vol. 5, pp. 9–35.

—— ——, 'Reichsstadt und Hochstift Augsburg', *Zeitschrift des Historischen Vereins für Schwaben*, 86 (1993), pp. 197–210.

Iserloh, Erwin, Joseph Galzik, and Hubert Jedin, *Reformation and Counter Reformation*, trans. Anselm Biggs and Peter W. Becker, ed. Hubert Jedin and John Dolan, History of the Church, vol. 5 (New York: Seabury Press, 1980).

Jedin, Hubert, *Katholische Reformation oder Gegenreformation? Ein Versuch zur Klärung der Begriffe nebst einer Jubiläumsbetrachtung über das Trienter Konzil* (Luzern: Verlag Josef Stocker, 1946); repr. as 'Catholic Reformation or Counter-Reformation?', in Luebke, ed., *The Counter-Reformation: The Essential Readings*, pp. 19–45.

Johandl, Robert, 'David Gregor Corner und sein Gesangbuch', *Archiv für Musikwissenschaft*, 2 (1920), pp. 447–64.

Karg, Franz, 'Die Fugger im 16. und 17. Jahrhundert', in Eikelmann, ed., *Die Fugger und die Musik*, pp. 99–110.

Kellenbenz, Hermann, 'Wirtschaftsleben der Blütezeit', in Gottlieb et al., eds, *Geschichte der Stadt Augsburg*, pp. 258–301.

Kemper, Hans-Georg, 'Das lutherische Kirchenlied in der Krisen-Zeit des frühen 17. Jahrhunderts', in Alfred Dürr and Walther Killy, eds, *Das protestantische Kirchenlied im 16. und 17. Jahrhundert: Text-, musik- und theologiegeschichtliche Probleme* (Wiesbaden: in Kommission bei O. Harrassowitz, 1986), pp. 87–108.

Kendrick, Robert L., *Celestial Sirens: Nuns and their Music in Early Modern Milan* (Oxford: Clarendon Press; New York: Oxford University Press, 1996).

Kerman, Joseph, 'On William Byrd's *Emendemus in melius*', in Dolores Pesce, ed., *Hearing the Motet: Essays on the Motet of the Middle Ages and Renaissance* (New York and Oxford: Oxford University Press, 1997), pp. 329–47. Originally published in *Musical Quarterly*, **49** (1963), pp. 431–49.

Kießling, Rolf, 'Augsburg zwischen Mittelalter und Neuzeit', in Gottlieb et al., eds, *Geschichte der Stadt Augsburg*, pp. 241–51.

Kirwan, A. Lindsey, and Stephan Hörner, 'Keifferer, Christian', in *New Grove II*, vol. 9, pp. 842–43.

——, 'Zindelin, Philipp', in *New Grove II*, vol. 27, pp. 843–44.

Kirwan-Mott, Anne, *The Small-Scale Sacred Concertato in the Early Seventeenth Century*, 2 vols (Ann Arbor: UMI Research Press, 1981).

Klingenstein, Bernhard, *Rosetum Marianum*, ed. William E. Hettrick, Recent Researches in the Music of the Renaissance, vols 24–25 (Madison, Wis.: A-R Editions, 1977).

Körndle, Franz, '"Ad te perenne gaudium": Lassos Musik zum "Vltimum Judicium"', *Die Musikforschung*, 53 (2000), pp. 68–71.

Kosel, Karl, 'Der hl. Simpert in der bildenden Kunst', *JVAB*, **12** (1978), pp. 61–95.

Koutná-Karg, Dana, 'Feste und Feiern der Fugger im 16. Jahrhundert', in Eikelmann, ed., *Die Fugger und die Musik*, pp. 89–98.

Krammer, Otto, *Bildungswesen und Gegenreformation: Die Hohen Schulen der Jesuiten im katholischen Teil Deutschlands vom 16. bis zum 18. Jahrhundert*, Veröffentlichungen des Archivvereins der Markomannia, vol. 31 (Würzburg: Gesellschaft für deutsche Studentengeschichte; Archivverein der Markomannia, 1988).

Krautwurst, Franz, 'Die Fugger und die Musik', in Eikelmann, ed., *Die Fugger und die Musik*, pp. 41–48.

——, 'Musik der Blütezeit', in Gottlieb et al., eds, *Geschichte der Stadt Augsburg*, pp. 386–91.

——, 'Musik in Reichsstadt und Stift', in Volker Dotterweich et al., eds, *Geschichte der Stadt Kempten* (Kempten: Verlag Tobias Dannheimer, 1989), pp. 303–21.

——, and Werner Zorn, *Bibliographie des Schrifttums zur Musikgeschichte der Stadt Augsburg* (Tutzing: Hans Schneider, 1989).

Kroyer, Theodor, 'Gregor Aichinger als Politiker', in Karl Weinmann, ed., *Festschrift Peter Wagner zum 60. Geburtstag* (Leipzig: Breitkopf & Härtel, 1926), pp. 128–32.

——, 'Gregor Aichingers Leben und Werke: Mit neuen Beiträgen zur Musikgeschichte Ingolstadts und Augsburgs', in Aichinger, *Ausgewählte Werke*, pp. ix ff.

Künast, Hans-Jörg, 'Entwicklungslinien des Augsburger Buchdrucks von den Anfängen bis zum Ende des Dreißigjährigen Krieges', in Gier and Janota, eds, *Augsburger Buchdruck und Verlagswesen*, pp. 3–21.

——, '"Getruckt zu Augspurg". Buchdruck und Buchhandel zwischen 1468 und 1555' (Ph.D. diss., Tübingen, 1997).

Lais, H., 'Petrus de Soto, Mitbegründer der Universität Dillingen', *Jahrbuch des Historischen Vereins Dillingen an der Donau*, 52 (1950), pp. 145–58.

Lane, Anthony N.S., *Calvin and Bernard of Clairvaux* (Princeton: Princeton Theological Seminary, 1996).

Langbein, John H., *Torture and the Law of Proof: Europe and England in the Ancien Régime* (Chicago: University of Chicago Press, 1977).

Lasso, Orlando di, *Cantiones sacrae sex vocum (Graz, 1594)*, ed. David Crook, The Complete Motets, 16 (Madison, Wis.: A-R Editions, 2002).

Lasso, Rudolph di, *Virginalia Eucharistica*, ed. Alexander J. Fisher (Madison, Wis.: A-R Editions, 2002).

Layer, Adolf, 'Augsburger Musikdrucker der frühen Renaissancezeit', *Gutenberg-Jahrbuch*, 40 (1965), pp. 124–29.

——, 'Augsburger Musikkultur der Renaissance', in Wegele, ed., *Musik in der Reichsstadt Augsburg*, pp. 43–102.

——, 'Augsburger Notendrucker und Musikverleger der Barockzeit', *Gutenberg-Jahrbuch*, 44 (1969), pp. 150–53.

——, 'Musik und Theater in St. Salvator', in Baer and Hecker, eds, *Die Jesuiten und ihre Schule St. Salvator in Augsburg 1582*, pp. 67–75.

——, *Musikgeschichte der Fürstabtei Kempten*, Allgäuer Heimatbücher, vol. 76 (Kempten: Verlag für Heimatpflege, 1975).

——, 'Musikpflege am Hofe der Fürstbischöfe von Augsburg in der Barockzeit', *JVAB*, 11 (1977), pp. 123–47.

Layer, Adolf, 'Musikpflege am Hofe der Fürstbischöfe von Augsburg in der Renaissancezeit', *JVAB*, **10** (1976), pp. 199–211.

——, 'Die Residenz- und Universitätsstadt Dillingen in der Musikgeschichte', *Jahrbuch des Historischen Vereins Dillingen an der Donau*, **80** (1978), pp. 197–204.

——, 'Ein Wallfahrtsgesang zu Ehren St. Simperts (1611)', *JVAB*, **12** (1978), pp. 96–107.

——, 'Zindelin, Philipp', in *MGG*, vol. 14, cols 1301–2.

——, ed., *Musik und Musiker der Fuggerzeit: Begleitheft zur Ausstellung der Stadt Augsburg 1959* (Augsburg, 1959).

Leitmeir, Christian Thomas, 'Catholic Music in the Diocese of Augsburg c. 1600: A Reconstructed Tricinium Anthology and its Confessional Implications', *Early Music History*, 21 (2002), pp. 117–73.

Lewis, Mary S., *Antonio Gardano, Venetian Music Printer, 1538–1569: A Descriptive Bibliography and Historical Study*, 2 vols (New York: Garland, 1988).

Lieb, Norbert, *Die Fugger und die Kunst*, 2 vols (Munich: Schnell & Steiner, 1952–58).

——, *Octavian Secundus Fugger (1549–1600) und die Kunst*, Studien zur Fuggergeschichte, vol. 27 (Tübingen: Mohr, 1980).

Liebhart, Wilhelm, *Die Reichsabtei St. Ulrich und Afra zu Augsburg 1006–1803: Studien zu Besitz und Herrschaft* (Munich: Kommission für Bayerische Landesgeschichte, 1982).

——, 'Zur St. Simpert-Bruderschaft der Augsburger Bortenmacher bei St. Ulrich', *JVAB*, **12** (1978), pp. 108–16.

Lipowsky, Felix Joseph, *Geschichte der Jesuiten in Schwaben* (Munich: I. U. Lentner et al., 1819).

Lipphardt, Walther, and Dorothea Schröder, 'Corner, David Gregor', in *New Grove II*, vol. 6, pp. 479–80.

Lockwood, Lewis, *The Counter-Reformation and the Masses of Vincenzo Ruffo*, Studi di musica veneta, vol. 2 (Vienna: Universal Edition, 1970).

——, 'Vincenzo Ruffo and Musical Reform after the Council of Trent', *Musical Quarterly*, **43** (1957), pp. 342–71.

Loesch, Heinz von, *Das Werkbegriff in der protestantischen Musiktheorie des 16. und 17. Jahrhunderts: Ein Mißverständnis* (Hildesheim and New York: Olms, 2001).

Luebke, David M., ed., *The Counter-Reformation: The Essential Readings* (Oxford and Malden, Mass.: Blackwell Publishers, 1999).

Mai, Paul, 'Die Michaelsverehrung an der Schwelle zur Neuzeit', in *idem*, ed., *Sankt Michael in Bayern*, pp. 31–35.

——, ed., *Sankt Michael in Bayern* (2nd edn, Munich and Zurich: Schnell und Steiner, 1979).

Mauer, Benedikt, 'Zur Organisation städtischen Bauens zwischen Elias Holl, Marcus Welser und Bernhard Rehlinger', *Zeitschrift des Historischen Vereins für Schwaben*, **89** (1996), pp. 75–94.

Mayr, Otto, 'Adam Gumpelzhaimer: Ein Beitrag zur Musikgeschichte der Stadt Augsburg im 16. und 17. Jahrhundert' (Phil. Diss., Munich, 1908).

Merkl, Franz Josef, 'Kunst und Konfessionalisierung – das Herzogtum Pfalz-Neuburg 1542–1650', *JVAB*, **32** (1998), pp. 188–211.

Mitterwieser, Alois, *Geschichte der Fronleichnamsprozession in Bayern* (Munich: Knorr & Hirth, 1930).

Moeller, Bernd, *Reichsstadt und Reformation* (Gütersloh: Gütersloher Verlagshaus, G. Mohn, 1962).

Monson, Craig A., 'The Council of Trent Revisited', *Journal of the American Musicological Society*, **55** (2002), pp. 1–37.

Moser, Dietz-Rudiger, *Verkündigung durch Volksgesang: Studien zur Liedpropaganda und -katechese der Gegenreformation* (Berlin: Erich Schmidt Verlag, 1981).

Naujoks, Eberhard, 'Vorstufen der Parität in der Verfassungsgeschichte der schwäbischen Reichsstädte (1555–1648): Das Beispiel Augsburg', in Jürgen Sydow, ed., *Bürgerschaft und Kirche* (Sigmaringen: Thorbecke, 1980), pp. 38–66.

Oestreich, Gerhard, 'Strukturprobleme des europäischen Absolutismus', in *Geist und Gestalt des frühmodernen Staates* (Berlin: Duncker und Humblot, 1969), pp. 179–97.

Oettinger, Rebecca Wagner, *Music as Propaganda in the German Reformation* (Aldershot: Ashgate, 2001).

O'Malley, John, 'Was Ignatius Loyola a Church Reformer? How to Look at Early Modern Catholicism', *Catholic Historical Review*, 77 (1991), pp. 177–93.

O'Regan, Noel, *Institutional Patronage in Post-Tridentine Rome: Music at Santissima Trinità dei Pellegrini, 1550–1650*, Royal Musical Association Monographs, vol. 7 (London: Royal Musical Association, 1995).

Osthoff, Helmuth, 'Einwirkung der Gegenreformation auf die Musik des 16. Jahrhunderts', *Jahrbuch der Musikbibliothek Peters*, **41** (1934), pp. 32–50.

Paumgartner, Bernhard, 'Zur Musikkultur Augsburgs in der Fuggerzeit', in Götz Freiherr von Pölnitz et al., eds, *Jakob Fugger, Kaiser Maximilian und Augsburg 1459–1959* (Augsburg: Stadt Augsburg, 1959), pp. 77–89.

Perkins, Leeman L., *Music in the Age of the Renaissance* (New York: Norton, 1999).

Pittroff, Karl, 'Aus vier Jahrhunderten evangelischer Kirchenmusik in Augsburg', *Zeitschrift für evangelische Kirchenmusik*, **9** (1931), pp. 31–36, 59–61, 115–20, 39–44, 70–75, 87–94.

Posset, Franz, *Pater Bernhardus: Martin Luther and Bernard of Clairvaux* (Kalamazoo, Mich. and Spencer, Mass.: Cistercian Publications, 1999).

Pötzl, Walter, 'Santa-Casa-Nachbildungen und Loreto-Patrozinien im Bistum Augsburg', *JVAB*, **13** (1979), pp. 7–33.

——, 'Die Sorge des Augsburger Domkapitels um die Pilger (1600–1620)', *Bayerisches Jahrbuch für Volkskunde* (1982), pp. 1–15.

——, 'Volksfrömmigkeit', in Brandmüller, ed., *Handbuch der bayerischen Kirchengeschichte*, pp. 871–963.

Reader, Ian, and Tony Walter, eds, *Pilgrimage in Popular Culture* (London: Macmillan, 1993).

Reese, Gustave, *Music in the Renaissance* (rev. edn, New York: Norton, 1959).

Reichert, Georg, 'Keifferer, Christian', in *MGG*, vol. 7, cols 779–80.

Reinhard, Wolfgang, 'Gegenreformation als Modernisierung?', *Archiv für Reformationsgeschichte*, **68** (1977), pp. 284–301.

——, 'Konfession und Konfessionalisierung in Europa', in Wolfgang Reinhard, ed., *Bekenntnis und Geschichte: Die Confessio Augustana im historischen Zusammenhang* (Munich: Verlag Ernst Vögel, 1981), pp. 165–89.

——, 'Reformation, Counter-Reformation, and the Early Modern State: A Reassessment', in Luebke, ed., *The Counter-Reformation: The Essential Readings*, pp. 105–28. Originally published in the *Catholic Historical Review*, **75** (1989), pp. 383–405.

——, 'Was ist katholische Konfessionalisierung?', in Reinhard and Schilling, eds, *Die katholische Konfessionalisierung*, pp. 419–52.

——, 'Zwang zur Konfessionalisierung? Prologemena zu einer Theorie des konfessionellen Zeitalters', *Zeitschrift für historische Forschung*, **10** (1983), pp. 257–77.

——, and Heinz Schilling, eds, *Die katholische Konfessionalisierung: Wissenschaftliches Symposion der Gesellschaft zur Herausgabe des Corpus Catholicorum und des Vereins für Reformationsgeschichte 1993* (Gütersloh: Gütersloher Verlagshaus, 1995).

Röder, Thomas, 'Innovation and Misfortune: Augsburg Music Printing in the First Half of the Sixteenth Century', in Eugeen Schreurs and Henri Vanhulst, eds, *Music Fragments and Manuscripts in the Low Countries – Alta Capella – Music Printing in Antwerp and Europe in the 16th Century. Colloquium Proceedings Alden Biezen 23.06.1995, Alden Biezen 24.06.1995, Antwerpen 23–25.08.1995* (Peer: Alamire, 1997), pp. 465–77.

——, and Theodor Wohnhaas, 'Die Stella musicae des Benediktiners Veit Bild: Eine spätmittelalterliche Musiklehre aus Augsburg', *JVAB*, **32** (1998), pp. 305–25.

Roeck, Bernd, 'Kunstpatronage in der Frühen Neuzeit', in Bernd Roeck, ed., *Kunstpatronage in der Frühen Neuzeit: Kunst, Künstler und ihre Auftraggeber in Italien und Deutschland vom 15.–17. Jahrhundert* (Göttingen: Vandenhoeck & Ruprecht, 1998), pp. 11–34.

——, *Eine Stadt im Krieg und Frieden: Studien zur Geschichte der Reichsstadt Augsburg zwischen Kalenderstreit und Parität*, 2 vols (Göttingen: Vandenhoeck & Ruprecht, 1989).

Rolle, Theodor, 'Die Anfänge der Marianischen Kongregation in Augsburg', *JVAB*, **23** (1989), pp. 27–68.

——, *Heiligkeitsstreben und Apostolat: Geschichte der Marianischen Kongregation am Jesuitenkolleg St. Salvator und am Gymnasium der Benediktiner bei St. Stephan in Augsburg 1589–1989* (Augsburg: im Eigenverlag St. Stephan, 1989).

Roper, Lyndal, *The Holy Household: Women and Morals in Reformation Augsburg* (Oxford: Clarendon Press; New York: Oxford University Press, 1989).

Rummel, Peter, 'Die Augsburger Diözesansynoden: Historischer Überblick', *JVAB*, **20** (1986), pp. 9–69.

——, 'Das Bistum Augsburg im Zeitalter der Reformation und Gegenreformation', *JVAB*, **14** (1980), pp. 114–32.

——, 'Petrus Canisius und Otto Kardinal Truchseß von Waldburg', in Oswald and Rummel, eds, *Petrus Canisius – Reformer der Kirche*, pp. 41–66.

——, 'Zur 400-Jahr-Feier der St. Annabruderschaft in Augsburg', *JVAB*, **32** (1998), pp. 57–65.

——, 'Zur Verehrungsgeschichte des heiligen Simperts', *JVAB*, **12** (1978), pp. 22–49.

Rupp, Paul B., 'Aufbau und Ämter des Jesuitenkollegs Augsburg', in Baer and Hecker, eds, *Die Jesuiten und ihre Schule St. Salvator in Augsburg 1582*, pp. 23–34.

——, ed., *Fünfhundert Jahre Buchdruck in Lauingen und Dillingen: Ausstellung anläßlich des 100jährigen Bestehens des Historischen Vereins Dillingen* (Dillingen: Studienbibliothek, 1988). Ch. 5

Sabean, David Warren, *Power in the Blood: Popular Culture and Village Discourse in Early Modern Germany* (Cambridge and New York: Cambridge University Press, 1984).

Safley, Thomas Max, *Charity and Economy in the Orphanages of Early Modern Augsburg* (Atlantic Highlands, NJ: Humanities Press, 1997).

Sandberger, Adolf, *Beiträge zur Geschichte der bayerischen Hofkapelle unter Orlando di Lasso. Drittes Buch: Dokumente. Erster Theil* (Leipzig: Breitkopf & Härtel, 1895).

——, 'Bemerkungen zur Biographie Hans Leo Hasslers und seiner Brüder, sowie zur Musikgeschichte der Städte Nürnberg und Augsburg im 16. und zu Anfang des 17. Jahrhunderts', in *Werke Hans Leo Hasslers*, Denkmäler der Tonkunst in Bayern (Leipzig: Breitkopf & Härtel, 1904).

Schaal, Richard, 'Georg Willers Augsburger Musikalien-Lagerkatalog von 1622', *Die Musikforschung*, **16** (1963), pp. 127–39.

——, *Das Inventar der Kantorei Sankt Anna in Augsburg: Ein Beitrag zur protestantischen Musikpflege im 16. und beginnenden 17. Jahrhundert*, Catalogus musicus, vol. 3 (Kassel: Internationale Vereinigung der Musikbibliotheken, Internationale Gesellschaft für Musikwissenschaft, 1965).

——, *Die Kataloge des Augsburger Musikalien-Händlers Kaspar Flurschütz, 1613–1628*, Quellenkataloge zur Musikgeschichte, vol. 7 (Wilhelmshaven: Heinrichshofen, 1974).

——, 'Die Musikbibliothek von Raimund Fugger d.J.: Ein Beitrag zur Musiküberlieferung des 16. Jahrhunderts', *Acta musicologica*, 29 (1957), pp. 126–37.

——, 'Die Musikinstrumenten-Sammlung von Raimund Fugger d. J.', *Archiv für Musikwissenschaft*, **21** (1964), pp. 212–16.

——, 'Neues zur Kantorei St. Anna in Augsburg', *Archiv für Musikwissenschaft*, **22** (1965), pp. 43–51.

——, 'Zur Musikpflege im Kollegiatstift St. Moritz zu Augsburg', *Die Musikforschung*, 7 (1954), pp. 1–24.

Schilling, Heinz, 'Die Konfessionalisierung im Reich. Religiöser und gesellschaftlicher Wandel in Deutschland zwischen 1555 und 1620', *Historische Zeitschrift*, **246** (1988), pp. 1–45.

——, 'Die Konfessionalisierung von Kirche, Staat und Gesellschaft – Profil, Leistung, Defizite und Perspektiven eines geschichtswissenschaftlichen Paradigmas', in Reinhard and Schilling, eds, *Die katholische Konfessionalisierung*, pp. 1–49.

Schindling, Anton, 'Konfessionalisierung und Grenzen von Konfessionalisierbarkeit', in *idem* and Walter Ziegler, eds, *Die Territorien des Reichs im Zeitalter der Reformation und Konfessionalisierung* (Münster: Aschendorff, 1997), vol. 7, pp. 9–44.

Schletterer, Hans Michael, 'Aktenmaterial aus dem städtischen Archiv zu Augsburg', *Monatshefte für Musikgeschichte*, 25 (1893), pp. 1–14, 9–34, 72–78, 81–84.

——, ed., *Katalog der in der Kreis- und Stadt-Bibliothek, dem Staedtischen Archive und der Bibliothek des historischen Vereins zu*

Augsburg befindlichen Musikwerke (Berlin: T. Trautwein'sche kgl. Hof- Buch- und Musikalienhandlung, 1878).

Schmalzriedt, Siegfried, *Heinrich Schütz und andere zeitgenössische Musiker in der Lehre Giovanni Gabrielis: Studien zu ihren Madrigalen*, Tübinger Beiträge zur Musikwissenschaft, vol. 1 (Stuttgart: Hänssler, 1972).

Schmid, Ernst Fritz, 'Hans Leo Haßler und seine Brüder', *Zeitschrift des Historischen Vereins für Schwaben*, 54 (1941), pp. 60–212.

Schmidmüller, Martina, *Die Reihe der Augsburger Domkapellmeister seit dem Tridentinum bis heute* (Augsburg, 1989).

Schwemer, Bettina, 'Aichinger, Gregor', in *MGG*[2], vol. 1, cols 265–68.

Scribner, Robert W., *For the Sake of Simple Folk: Popular Propaganda for the German Reformation* (Oxford: Clarendon Press; New York: Oxford University Press, 1994).

——, *Popular Culture and Popular Movements in Reformation Germany* (London and Ronceverte: Hambledon Press, 1987).

Senn, Walter, *Musik und Theater am Hof zu Innsbruck: Geschichte der Hofkapelle vom 15. Jahrhundert bis zu deren Auflösung im Jahre 1748* (Innsbruck: Österreichische Verlagsanstalt, 1954).

Sieh-Burens, Katarina, *Oligarchie, Konfession und Politik im 16. Jahrhundert: Zur sozialen Verflechtung der Augsburger Bürgermeister und Stadtpfleger, 1518–1618* (Munich: E. Vogel, 1986).

Singer, Alfons, 'Leben und Werke des Augsburger Domkapellmeisters Bernhardus Klingenstein 1545–1645' (Inaug. Diss., Munich, 1921).

Smith, Helmut Walser, *German Nationalism and Religious Conflict: Culture, Ideology, Politics 1870–1914* (Princeton: Princeton University Press, 1995).

Soergel, Philip M., *Wondrous in His Saints: Counter-Reformation Propaganda in Bavaria*, Studies in the History of Society and Culture, vol. 17 (Berkeley: University of California Press, 1993).

Specht, Thomas, 'Zur Geschichte der Dillinger Buchdruckerei im 17. und 18. Jahrhundert', *Jahrbuch des Historischen Vereins Dillingen*, 21 (1908), pp. 36–45.

Spindler, Joseph, 'Heinrich V. von Knöringen, Fürstbischof von Augsburg (1598–1646): Seine inner-kirchliche Restaurationstätigkeit in der Diözese Augsburg', *Jahrbuch des Historischen Vereins Dillingen*, 24 (1911), pp. 1–138.

——, *Heinrich V. von Knöringen, Fürstbischof von Augsburg (1598–1646): Seine kirchenpolitische Tätigkeit* (Dillingen: Verlagsanstalt von J. Keller & Co., 1915).

Stalla, Gerhard, *Bibliographie der Ingolstadter Drucker des 16. Jahrhunderts* (Baden-Baden: Koerner, 1977).

Stalla, Gerhard, *Der Ingolstadter Buchdruck von 1601 bis 1620: Die Offizinen Adam Sartorius, Andreas Angermaier und Elisabeth Angermaier*, Bibliotheca bibliographica Aureliana, vol. 77 (Baden-Baden: Koerner, 1980).

Steuer, Peter, *Die Außenverflechtung der Ausgburger Oligarchie von 1500–1620: Studien zur sozialen Verflechtung der politischen Führungsschicht der Reichsstadt Augsburg* (Augsburg: AV-Verlag, 1988).

Stuart, Kathy, *Defiled Trades and Social Outcasts: Honor and Ritual Pollution in Early Modern Germany* (Cambridge and New York: Cambridge University Press, 1999).

Tawney, R.H., *Religion and the Rise of Capitalism: A Historical Study* (London: J. Murray, 1926).

Tlusty, B. Ann, *Bacchus and Civic Order: The Culture of Drink in Early Modern Germany* (Charlottesville: University Press of Virginia, 2001).

Turner, Victor and Edith, *Image and Pilgrimage in Christian Culture: Anthropological Perspectives* (New York: Columbia University Press, 1978).

Ursprung, Otto, 'Die Chorordnung von 1616 am Dom zu Augsburg: Ein Beitrag zur Frage der Aufführungspraxis', in *Studien zur Musikgeschichte: Festschrift für Guido Adler zum 75. Geburtstag* (Vienna: Universal-Edition, 1930), pp. 137–42.

——, *Jacobus de Kerle (1531/32–1591): Sein Leben und seine Werke* (Munich: Hans Beck, 1913).

——, *Münchens musikalische Vergangenheit: Von der Frühzeit bis zu Richard Wagner* (Munich: Bayerland-Verlag, 1927).

Veit, Patrice, *Das Kirchenlied in der Reformation Martin Luthers: Eine thematische und semantische Untersuchung*, Veröffentlichungen des Instituts für Europäische Geschichte Mainz, vol. 120 (Wiesbaden: Steiner, 1986).

——, 'Kirchenlied und konfessionelle Identität im deutschen 16. Jahrhundert', in Ursula Brunhold-Bigler and Hermann Bausinger, eds., *Hören, Sagen, Lesen, Lernen: Bausteine zu einer Geschichte der kommunikativen Kultur. Festschrift für Rudolf Schenda zum 65. Geburtstag* (Bern and New York: Peter Lang, 1995), pp. 741–54.

Wackernagel, Philipp, *Bibliographie zur Geschichte des deutschen Kirchenliedes im XVI. Jahrhundert* (Frankfurt am Main: Heyder & Zimmer, 1855).

——, *Das deutsche Kirchenlied von der ältesten Zeit bis zum Anfang des XVII. Jahrhunderts*, 5 vols (Leipzig: B.G. Teubner, 1864–77; repr. Hildesheim: Georg Olms, 1964).

Warmbrunn, Paul, *Zwei Konfessionen in einer Stadt: Das Zusammenleben von Katholiken und Protestanten in den paritätischen Reichsstädten Augsburg, Biberach, Ravensburg und Dinkelsbühl von 1548 bis 1648* (Wiesbaden: Franz Steiner, 1983).

Weber, Max, *The Protestant Ethic and the Spirit of Capitalism*, trans. Talcott Parsons (New York: C. Scribner, 1958).

Wegele, Ludwig, ed., *Musik in der Reichsstadt Augsburg* (Augsburg: Verlag Die Brigg, 1965).

Wilczek, Gerhard, *Die Jesuiten in Ingolstadt von ihrer Ankunft im Jahre 1549 bis zum Jahre 1671* (Ingolstadt: G. Wilczek, 1993).

Wohnhaas, Theodor, 'Der Augsburger Musikdruck von den Anfängen bis zum Ende des Dreißigjährigen Krieges', in Gier and Janota, eds, *Augsburger Buchdruck und Verlagswesen*, pp. 291–331.

——, 'Notizen zu Druck und Verlag katholischer Kirchenmusik in Augsburg', *JVAB*, **31** (1997), pp. 152–63.

——, 'Die Schönig, eine Augsburger Druckerfamilie', *Archiv für Geschichte des Buchwesens*, 5 (1964), pp. 1473–84.

——, 'Zur Frühgeschichte der Simpertliturgie', *JVAB*, **12** (1978), pp. 50–60.

——, 'Zur Geschichte des Gesangbuchs in der Diözese Augsburg', *JVAB*, **10** (1976), pp. 212–20.

Wüst, Wolfgang, 'Censur und Censurkollegien im frühmodernen Konfessionsstaat', in Gier and Janota, eds, *Augsburger Buchdruck und Verlagswesen*, pp. 569–86.

——, *Das Fürstbistum Augsburg: Ein geistlicher Staat im Heiligen Römischen Reich Deutscher Nation* (Augsburg: Sankt Ulrich Verlag, 1997).

——, 'Konfession, Kanzel und Kontroverse in einer paritätischen Reichsstadt: Augsburg 1555–1805', *Zeitschrift des Historischen Vereins für Schwaben*, **91** (1998), pp. 115–42.

Zager, Daniel, 'Liturgical Rite and Musical Repertory: The Polyphonic Latin Hymn Cycle of Lasso in Munich and Augsburg', in Ignace Bossuyt, Eugeen Schreurs and Annelies Wouters, eds, *Orlandus Lassus and his Time: Colloquium Proceedings, Antwerpen 24–26.08.1994* (Peer: Alamire, 1995), pp. 215–31.

Zeeden, Ernst Walter, *Die Entstehung der Konfessionen: Grundlagen und Formen der Konfessionsbildung im Zeitalter der Glaubenskämpfe* (Munich: R. Oldenbourg, 1965).

——, 'Grundlagen und Wege der Konfessionsbildung in Deutschland im Zeitalter der Glaubenskämpfe', *Historische Zeitschrift*, **185** (1958), pp. 249–99.

——, *Konfessionsbildung: Studien zur Reformation, Gegenreformation und katholischen Reform*, Spätmittelalter und Frühe Neuzeit, vol. 15 (Stuttgart: Klett-Cotta, 1985).

Zeeden, Ernst Walter, *Das Zeitalter der Glaubenskämpfe, 1555–1648*, Handbuch der deutschen Geschichte, vol. 9 (Munich: Deutscher Taschenbuch Verlag, 1973).

Ziegler, Adolf Wilhelm, ed., *Eucharistische Frömmigkeit in Bayern* (Munich: Seitz, 1963).

Zoepfl, Friedrich, *Das Bistum Augsburg und seine Bischöfe im Reformationsjahrhundert*, Geschichte des Bistums Augsburg und seiner Bischöfe, vol. 2 (Munich: Schnell & Steiner, 1969).

Zorn, Wolfgang, *Augsburg: Geschichte einer europaischen Stadt* (3rd edn, Augsburg: D. Wissner, 1994).

Index